The Digital Agricultural Revolution

Scrivener Publishing
100 Cummings Center, Suite 541J
Beverly, MA 01915-6106

Publishers at Scrivener
Martin Scrivener (martin@scrivenerpublishing.com)
Phillip Carmical (pcarmical@scrivenerpublishing.com)

The Digital Agricultural Revolution

Innovations and Challenges in Agriculture through Technology Disruptions

Edited by
Roheet Bhatnagar
Nitin Kumar Tripathi
Nitu Bhatnagar
and
Chandan Kumar Panda

WILEY

This edition first published 2022 by John Wiley & Sons, Inc., 111 River Street, Hoboken, NJ 07030, USA and Scrivener Publishing LLC, 100 Cummings Center, Suite 541J, Beverly, MA 01915, USA
© 2022 Scrivener Publishing LLC
For more information about Scrivener publications please visit www.scrivenerpublishing.com.

Wiley Global Headquarters
111 River Street, Hoboken, NJ 07030, USA

For details of our global editorial offices, customer services, and more information about Wiley products visit us at www.wiley.com.

Library of Congress Cataloging-in-Publication Data

ISBN 978-1-119-82333-9

Cover image: Pixabay.Com
Cover design by Russell Richardson

Set in size of 11pt and Minion Pro by Manila Typesetting Company, Makati, Philippines

Printed in the USA

10 9 8 7 6 5 4 3 2 1

Contents

Preface

The practice of agriculture began in ancient civilizations and farmers have always contributed to nation-building by growing produce to feed an ever-growing population. Moreover, agriculture is the foundation of an economy, providing livelihoods for millions of farmers. Therefore, there is a need for synergy between application of modern scientific innovation in the area of artificial intelligence (AI) and agriculture, while taking into consideration the major challenge brought on by climate change, viz., rising temperatures, erratic rainfall patterns, emergence of new crop pests, droughts, floods, etc. The intent of this edited volume is to report high-quality research (practical theory, including prototype and conceptualization of ideas, frameworks, real-world applications, policies, standards, psychological concerns, case studies and critical surveys) on recent advances toward the realization of a digital agricultural revolution resulting from the convergence of different disruptive technologies.

This book highlights the latest achievements in the field of modern agriculture, which is highly driven by technology and aimed at sustainable agriculture. In it is a collection of original contributions by researchers/academicians from across the globe regarding state-of-the-art solutions using newer methods to enhance and improve crops for smart agriculture. These solutions are arrived at by various means, as indicated in the topics covered in the twenty chapters described below.

- Chapter 1 presents an overview of how AI helps to increase socio-economic and environmental sustainability in the Indian agricultural sector. It also highlights the AI practices incorporated by farmers in India with small and medium-sized agricultural lands.
- Chapter 2 describes the high efficacy of using remote sensing images and neural network models to generate accurate crop yield maps and offers proof of the significant superiority of neural network models over conventional methods.

- Chapter 3 discusses the use of intelligent irrigation systems, which have recently gained importance in terms of efficient cultivation of plants and the correct use of Earth's water. The use of machine learning and control methods in plant growth modeling and irrigation systems is also explained. The chapter ends with a discussion of current problems along with possible future implementation of new approaches to solve them.
- Chapter 4 provides insight into the opportunities presented by the use of robots in agriculture, known as agribots, and focuses on the advancements in different types of agribots in terms of sensing, mobility, path planning, and manipulation. It also talks about the status and progress of robots in Indian agriculture, concentrating on Indian-based robotic startups and case studies involving the use of robots in harvesting crops along with the challenges faced when deploying robots in the field.
- Chapter 5 delves into the Colombian palm oil (PO) industry. The contribution of this study is twofold: First, it provides a more comprehensive review of the PO industry technology literature based on Scopus and Clarivate Analytics, using the reporting checklist of preferred reporting items for systematic reviews and meta-analyses (PRISMA). Second, as far as the authors know, this is one of the first studies to address the technological solutions applied by Colombia's PO producers and aims to help fill this research gap.
- Chapter 6 presents a case on smart agriculture and discusses intelligent agriculture in a greenhouse-based multi-agent system (MAS), which is made up of several agents located in an environment that interact according to some defined relationships. In this work, each part of the greenhouse environment is represented by one or more agent, with each agent coordinating with other agents to achieve set goals. In addition, it discusses the society of agents in which two types of agents can be found: 1) reactive agents characterized by simple behavior, whose mission it is to perform tasks that do not require intelligent reasoning, and 2) cognitive or intelligent agents, which are tasked with performing more complex missions and require reasoning to make good decisions.
- Chapter 7 is a study on the use of automatic and intelligent methods in the management of irrigation of agricultural

land. Among these technologies are artificial intelligence and the Internet of Things (IoT), which are used to optimize the management of irrigation water in agricultural lands. The elements of the agricultural system and its environment are presented by things in direct contact with each other by relying on information and communication technology (ICT).

- Chapter 8 discusses how modern agriculture has become knowledge intensive and how improved access to and availability of information and communication technologies (ICTs), especially cell phones, computers, radio, internet, and social media, has created many more opportunities for multi-format information gathering, processing, storage, retrieval, management and sharing.
- Chapter 9 presents an overview of nanotechnology and nanosensors in forestry and agriculture, including its use in forest health protection, forest management, wood and paper processing, and chemotaxonomy. The nanotechnology sector has best applied this technology in precision farming by developing nanobionic plants by inserting nanosensors into living plants that can be utilized to communicate as infrared devices and for sensing objects in the plant's environment. Therefore, the nanobionics approach has opened a new vista into plant nanomaterial research. Some nanobionics approaches for agriculture and forestry development are also briefly discussed.
- Chapter 10 is all about mathematical models of the water resources management process of canals in the middle reaches of the Chirchik River, which were developed using simplified differential equations of Saint Venant in partial derivatives to model the necessary conditions for optimizing water distribution. An algorithm for solving the problem of optimal water resources management of distributed irrigation canals was also developed.
- Chapter 11 discusses various principles of reengineering of agricultural resources and throws light on open problems, challenges, and future trends.
- Chapter 12 shows how the supply chain management method is used for planning maintenance strategy, storing products, moving material through the organization and its distribution channel, which leads directly to maximum

profits through cost-saving fulfilment of orders. A simple supply chain acts as a bridge between demand and supply. Startups are bringing a new shape to the agri-supply chain by using new-age technologies like AI, machine learning, IoT and blockchain management, that procure directly from farm gates and supply to retailers.

- Chapter 13 discusses the need for an institutional approach of using digital techniques in modern agrarian production. This approach is illustrative of the synergy of economic, ecological, and social effectiveness as a progressive direction in which the development of a global economic system can be worked out. A general model was used to determine a new organization of the informational paradigm of agricultural activities based on the agility of the knowledge and analytical data being transferred into the value of information.

- Chapter 14 provides a comprehensive analysis of four aspects of AI implementation in treatment of wastewater: management, technology, reuse and economics of wastewater. It also provides an insight into the future prospects of the use of AI in the treatment of wastewater, which, in complex practical applications, simultaneously addresses pollutant removal, water reuse and management and cost-efficient challenges.

- Chapter 15 presents methods for assessing the impact of digital transformation risks on the business model of agricultural enterprises. Industry 4.0 is accompanied by the rapid transformation of several sectors under the influence of "breakthrough" digital innovations such as blockchain, IoT, AI, and augmented reality.

- Chapter 16 presents a unified systematic approach to the issue of modeling the dynamics of water management facilities. There is a wide range of mathematical models of individual objects of different complexity, which is why the choice of mathematical models that will describe the complex processes of water distribution in water management systems with the required degree of accuracy is a very problematic task.

- Chapter 17 showcases the use of blockchain technology that has become a phenomenon in recent years and is evolving into a form that institutionalized organizations can benefit from. The IoT integrates blockchain technology into the agricultural sector and provides the automation of the control mechanisms in the agricultural food supply chain. The study evaluated in this chapter utilizes technology in various forms, from farm to fork. Furthermore, a Fintech solution framework via blockchain created for digitalization of the agricultural commodity value chain is presented that secures the contract creation, transfer, and redemption (burn) processes.

- Chapter 18 discusses how new-age entrepreneurs are using technological innovations to address supply chain challenges and unlock value across it. India's startup agricultural ecosystem is mushrooming, with over 450 startups that are currently operational, over 50% of which are focused on making the supply chain more efficient by improving market linkages. Inputs play a crucial role in extracting higher yields. The existing delivery system is not appropriate due to poor supply, lack of subsidies, improper infrastructure, lack of farm credit, and poor delivery systems.

- Chapter 19 is about the adoption of blockchain technology in the Malaysian agriculture sector and proposes a framework of blockchain agriculture supply chain management. As the blockchain supply chain framework in the agriculture sector is still limited, social network theory tends to be used in the development of the framework. This chapter has collected quantitative survey and social network data from firms registered in the Federation of Malaysian Manufacturers that operate in the agriculture sector. The demographic profiles were analyzed through IBM SPSS 26 and the social network data was analyzed through Social Network Visualizer.

- Chapter 20 discusses the use of machine learning algorithms to study soil fertility, salinity, dynamics, and the relationship of soil organic carbon with the environment, spatial and temporal variation of soil water content, soil and water pollution, soil formation processes, soil classification, prediction, nutrient availability, etc.

Our intent in writing this book was to provide a foundation of comprehensive knowledge for others to build on; therefore, it is our sincerest hope that it will prove to be beneficial to people from different domains. We hope that you find it useful and engaging as you continue your journey to expand the sphere of human knowledge, if only by an inch.

We are thankful to all the authors and co-authors of every chapter who have contributed their knowledge in the form of quality manuscripts for the benefit of others.

The editors
Dr. Roheet Bhatnagar
Dr. Nitin Kumar Tripathi
Dr. Chandan Kumar Panda
Dr. Nitu Bhatnagar
April 2022

1

Scope and Recent Trends of Artificial Intelligence in Indian Agriculture

X. Anitha Mary[1], Vladimir Popov[2,3], Kumudha Raimond[4],
I. Johnson[5] and S. J. Vijay[6*]

[1]Department of Robotics Engineering, Karunya Institute of Technology and
Sciences, Coimbatore, Tamil Nadu, India
[2]Additive Manufacturing, Technion-Israel Institute of Technology, Haifa, Israel
[3]Ural Federal University, Ekaterinburg, Russia
[4]Department of Computer Science and Engineering, Karunya Institute of
Technology and Sciences, Coimbatore, Tamil Nadu, India
[5]Department of Plant Pathology, TamilNadu Agricultural University,
Coimbatore, India
[6]Department of Mechanical Engineering, Karunya Institute of Technology and
Sciences, Coimbatore, Tamil Nadu, India

Abstract

Agriculture is the economic backbone of India. About 6.4% of the total world's economy relies on agriculture [1]. Automation in agriculture is the emerging sector as there is an increase in food demand and employment. The traditional ways used by farmers are not sufficient to fulfill the demands and it is high time that newer technologies are implementing in the agricultural sector. Artificial Intelligence (AI) is one of the emerging and promising technologies where intelligence refers to developing and utilizing human-level thinking machines through learning algorithms programmed to solve critical problems. Artificial Intelligence plays an important role in supporting agriculture sectors with the objectives of boosting productivity, efficiency, and farmers' income. This chapter focuses on how AI helps in increasing the socioeconomic and environmental sustainability in the Indian agricultural sector. Also, it highlights the AI practices in India incorporated by farmers having small and medium-size agricultural lands.

Keywords: Indian agriculture, Artificial Intelligence, farmers

Corresponding author: vijayjoseph@karunya.edu

Roheet Bhatnagar, Nitin Kumar Tripathi, Nitu Bhatnagar and Chandan Kumar Panda (eds.)
The Digital Agricultural Revolution: Innovations and Challenges in Agriculture through
Technology Disruptions, (1–24) © 2022 Scrivener Publishing LLC

1.1   Introduction

Artificial Intelligence (AI) is a broad field of computer science that focuses on creating intelligent machines that can accomplish activities that would normally need human intelligence. Although AI is a multidisciplinary field with many methodologies, advances in machine learning (ML) and deep learning (DL) [4] are causing a paradigm shift in nearly every sector of the IT industry.

One of the oldest occupations in the world is farming and agriculture. It has a significant impact on the economy. Climate variations also play an influence in the agriculture lifecycle. Climate change is a result of increasing deforestation and pollution, making it difficult for farmers to make judgments about which crop to harvest. Nutrient insufficiency can also cause crops to be of poor quality [37]. Weed control has a significant impact and can lead to greater production costs. The above traditional farming can be replaced by using modern technology with AI.

1.2   Different Forms of AI

Agriculture is extremely important, and it is the primary source of income for almost 58% of India's population [2]. However, it lacks support and suffers from a variety of factors, such as groundwater depletion, erratic monsoons, droughts, plant diseases, and so on. To detect the relationship between influencing factors with crop yield and quality, a variety of tools and approaches have been identified. The impact of recent technological advancements in the field of AI is significant. Recently, large investors have begun to capitalize on the promise of these technologies for the benefit of Indian agriculture. Smart farming and precision agriculture (PA) are ground-breaking science and technological applications for agriculture growth. Farmers and other agricultural decision makers are increasingly using AI-based modeling as a decision tool to increase production efficiency.

Artificial Intelligence is silently entering Indian agriculture and impacting society to a greater extent. There are three forms of AI, namely Artificial Narrow Intelligence (ANI), Artificial General Intelligence (AGI), and Artificial Super Intelligence (ASI) [3] as shown in Figure 1.1 Artificial Narrow Intelligence as the name suggests uses computer programming to do a specific task. Artificial General Intelligence refers to a machine that can think like a human and perform huge tasks. Artificial Super Intelligence is

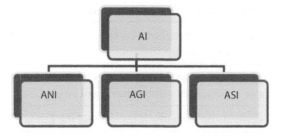

Figure 1.1 Different forms of AI [3].

designed to think beyond humans. Artificial Narrow Intelligence is mainly used in agriculture to do some specific tasks, such as identification of diseases in leaf, optimization in irrigation, the optimal moisture content in crops, and so on, using AI techniques. The different forms of AI are shown in Figure 1.1.

1.3   Different Technologies in AI

There are many subfields, such as ML, Artificial Neural Network (ANN), and DL, as shown in Figure 1.2. The distinguishing features of these subfields are shown in Table 1.1.

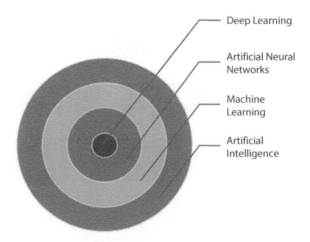

Figure 1.2 AI versus ML versus ANN versus DL.

Table 1.1 Distinguishing feature of subfields of AI.

AI	AI is a technology that allows us to build intelligent systems that mimic human intelligence.
ML	ML is an AI discipline that allows machines to learn from previous data or experiences without having to be explicitly programmed.
ANN	ANN depends on algorithms resembling the human brain.
DL	DL algorithms automatically build a hierarchy of data representations using the low- and high-level features.

1.3.1   Machine Learning

A subset of AI focuses on algorithm development by learning from experience and helps in the improvement of decision making with greater accuracy. The categories and the corresponding tasks are shown in Figure 1.3. Supervised, unsupervised, and reinforcement are the three main learning paradigms. Supervised is the most prevalent training paradigm for developing ML models for both classification and regression tasks [27]. It finds the relationship between the input and target variables. Some of the supervised learning algorithms are support vector machine (SVM), logistic regression, Decision Tree (DT), random forest, and so on. Unsupervised learning is often used for clustering and segmentation tasks. This method does not require any target variable to group the input data sets. Some of

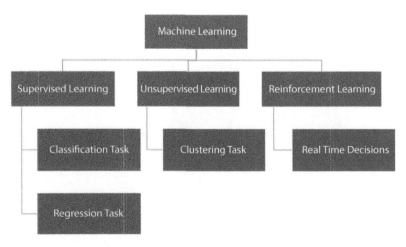

Figure 1.3 Types of machine learning.

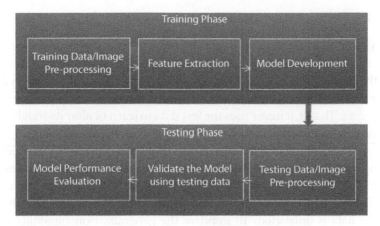

Figure 1.4 Generic methodology in building a model using machine learning algorithms.

the examples are K-means, hierarchical, density, grid clustering, and so on. Reinforcement learning corresponds to responding to the environment and deciding the right action to complete the assignment with maximum reward in a given application. It finds its applications in a real-time environment.

In ML, training is performed with a huge amount of data to get accurate decisions or predictions. The general steps involved in building an ML model are shown in Figure 1.4.

1.3.1.1   Data Pre-processing

It is a process of converting raw data into a usable and efficient format.

1.3.1.2   Feature Extraction

Before training a model, most applications need first transforming the data into a new representation. Applying pre-processing modifications to input data before presenting it to a network is almost always helpful, and the choice of pre-processing will be one of the most important variables in determining the final system's performance. The reduction of the dimensionality of the input data is another key method in which network performance can be enhanced, sometimes dramatically. To produce inputs for the network, dimensionality reductions entail creating linear or nonlinear combinations of the original variables. Feature extraction is the process of creating such input combinations, which are frequently referred to as features. The main motivation for dimensionality reduction is to help mitigate the worst impacts of high dimensionality.

1.3.1.3   Working With Data Sets

The most popular method is to split the original data into two or more data sets at random or using statistical approaches. A portion of the data is used to train the model, whereas a second subset is used to assess the model's accuracy. It is vital to remember that while in training mode, the model never sees the test data. That is, it never uses the test data to learn or alter its weights. The training data is a set of data that represent the data that the ML will consume to answer the problem it was created to tackle. In certain circumstances, the training data have been labeled—that is, it has been "tagged" with features and classification labels that the model will need to recognize. The model will have to extract such features and group them based on their similarity if the data is unlabeled. To improve the generalization capability of the model, the data set can be divided into three sets according to their standard deviation: training sets, validation sets, and testing sets. The validation set is used to verify the network's performance during the training phase, which in turn is useful to determine the best network setup and related parameters. Furthermore, a validation error is useful to avoid overfitting by determining the ideal point to stop the learning process.

1.3.1.4   Model Development

The ultimate goal of this stage is to create, train, and test the ML model. The learning process is continued until it provides an appropriate degree of accuracy on the training data. A set of statistical processing processes is referred to as an algorithm. The type of algorithm used is determined by the kind (labeled or unlabeled) and quantity of data in the training data set, as well as the problem to be solved. Different ML algorithms are used concerning labeled data. The ML algorithm adjusts weights and biases to give accurate results.

i. Support Vector Machine
Support vector machine finds out an optimum decision boundary to divide the linear data into different classes. It is also useful to classify nonlinear data by employing the concept of kernels to transform the input data into higher dimension data. The nonlinear data will be categorized into different classes in the new higher-dimensional space by finding out an optimum decision surface.

ii. Regression Algorithm
Regression methods, such as linear and logistic regression, are used to understand data relationships. Independent variables are used to predict

the value of a dependent variable using linear regression. When the dependent variable is binary, such as x or y, logistic regression can be employed. The dependency of crop yield overirrigation and fertilization is an example of linear regression. Using temperature, nitrogen, phosphorous, and potassium content in the soil, rainfall, pH of the soil as independent variables; yield can be forecasted using multiple regression.

iii. Decision Tree

The most powerful and widely used tool for classification and prediction is the DT algorithm. A DT is a tree structure that resembles a flowchart, with each leaf node representing the outcome, an inside node indicating a feature (or attribute), and a branch representing a decision rule. In a DT, the root node is the uppermost node. A Top-Down technique is used to classify the instances by sorting them down the tree from the root to a leaf node, with the leaf node provides the classification label to the given data set. This process is called recursive partitioning. Figure 1.5 shows an example of the application of the DT algorithm for the identification of leaf disease in cotton crops.

iv. K-means Clustering

It uses categorization to determine the likelihood of a data point belonging to one of two groups based on its proximity to other data points. The first

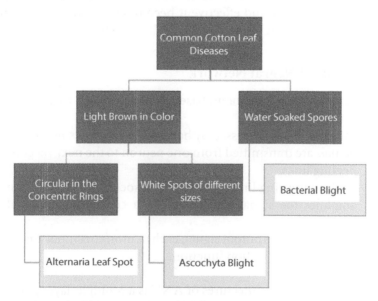

Figure 1.5 Cotton leaf disease using DT algorithm.

stage in the k-means clustering algorithm is to determine the number of clusters (K) that will be obtained as a final result. The cluster's centroids are then chosen at random from a set of k items or objects. Based on a distance metric, all remaining items (objects) are assigned to their nearest centroid (mostly Euclidean Distance Metric). The algorithm then calculates the new mean value of each cluster. The term "centroid update" cluster is used to build this stage. Now that the centers have been recalculated, each observation is evaluated once more to see if it is closer to a different cluster. The cluster updated means are used to reassign all of the objects. The cluster assignment and centroid update processes are done iteratively until the cluster assignments do not change anymore (until a convergence criterion is met). That is, the clusters created in the current iteration are identical to those obtained in the prior iteration. Generally, K-means clustering is used in predicting crop yields.

v. Association Algorithm

Association algorithms look for patterns and links in data, as well as frequently occurring "if-then" correlations known as association rules. These restrictions are comparable to data mining rules.

1.3.1.5   *Improving the Model With New Data*

The final stage is to apply the model to new data and, in the best-case scenario, see how accurate and effective it becomes over time. The source of the new data will be determined by the problem to be solved.

1.3.2   Artificial Neural Network

ANNs resembles the human brain based on the principle that:

- Information is processed by basic units known as neurons.
- Signals are transmitted from one neuron to the next via connecting links.
- Each connecting link has a weight associated with it, which amplifies the signal transmitted in a conventional neural network.
- To determine its output signal, each neuron's net input passes through the activation function.

One of the popular architectures of ANN is a Multiple-layer perceptron (MLP) which consists of input, hidden, and output layers. Multiple-layer perceptrons have been successfully trained in a supervised manner utilizing a widely used method known as the Error Back Propagation Algorithm to solve a variety of complex and diverse tasks. The input layer consists of nodes that receive information from external sources and passes this information to one or more hidden layers of computation nodes and an output layer of computation nodes. During the training phase, the output is calculated for every given input and compared with the desired output. Based on the error, the network is updated. During the testing phase, the network will calculate the output for any new input data. Each conclusion has a probability assigned to it. For the most part, ANN is thought to be a good answer to difficult situations. They solve intricate relationships between crop production and interconnected characteristics that linear systems can't solve. Artificial Neural Networks are computer programs that simulate the functioning of the human brain. Artificial Neural Network is a task-based strategy that instructs the system to work based on an internal task rather than a computationally programmed task.

1.3.2.1   ANN in Agriculture

The major advantage of neural networks is their ability to predict and anticipate via parallel thinking. Artificial Neural Network can be taught instead of being extensively programmed. Artificial Neural Network was employed by Gliever and Slaughter [30] to distinguish weeds from crops. Maier and Dandy [31] used ANNs to forecast water resources factors. Song and He [32] combined expert systems and ANNs to forecast crop nutrient levels. Comax (COtton Management eXpert), an expert system, was effectively integrated with Gossym, a computer model, and cotton crop growth was simulated. This expert system was created to work continuously in cotton crop fields throughout the year. Comax considers three field parameters: irrigation timing, nitrogen content in the field, and cotton crop development.

1.3.3   Deep Learning for Smart Agriculture

Images make up a significant portion of the data collected by remote sensing. Images can provide a complete view of agricultural landscapes in many circumstances, and they can help with a range of problems. As a result, imaging analysis is an important research field in the agricultural realm, and picture identification/classification is done using intelligent data analysis approaches [33]. One such approach is DL. A deep neural network is a network that has numerous hidden layers, each of which refines the preceding layer's output. Feature learning, or the automatic extraction of features from raw data, is a key advantage of DL. This architecture finds its applications in the computer vision field for image classification, object identification, picture segmentation, and so on.

Because of the more complicated models utilized in DL, which allow huge parallelization, it can tackle more complicated problems exceptionally well and quickly [34]. Many researchers used DL for fruit counting, predicting future parameters, such as yield production, soil moisture content, evapotranspiration, weed detection, weather prediction, and so on.

1.3.3.1   Data Pre-processing

A commonly used pre-processing step is image resizing to 60×60, 256×256, 128×128, and 96×96 pixels. Image pre-processing is also used to identify the region of interest through segmentation, background removal, conversion to grayscale, and so on.

1.3.3.2   Data Augmentation

Many computer vision tasks have shown that deep neural networks perform exceptionally well. However, to avoid overfitting, huge data have to be provided to perfectly model the training data. The goal of data augmentation techniques is to artificially increase the quantity of training images. By providing the model with a variety of data, it helps to improve the overall learning method and performance, as well as generalization capability. For small data sets, this augmentation method is critical for training DL models. Some of the popular data augmentation techniques are flipping, rotating, cropping, scaling, translation, Gaussian noise, color casting, and so on.

1.3.3.3   Different DL Models

Convolutional Neural Networks (CNNs) and Recurrent Neural Networks (RNNs) are two types of DL models that are driving development in different areas including the agricultural field. Many other increasingly sophisticated architectures, such as AlexNet, VGG-16, VGG-19, ResNet, Inception-V3, DenseNet, and so on, have been developed. To apply such architectures to smaller data sets, some regularization techniques, like data augmentation, dropout, batch normalization, transfer learning, and pre-training, are implemented.

1.4   AI With Big Data and Internet of Things

Policymakers and industry leaders are turning to technology factors like Internet of Things (IoT), big data, analytics, and cloud computing to help them deal with the demands of rising food demand and climate change. Farmers can use big data to get detailed information on patterns of rainfall, fertilizer requirements, and more. This allows them to make decisions on which crops to sow for maximum profit and when to harvest. Farm yields are improved when the appropriate selections are made. Sensors have been integrated into farming equipment by companies like John Deere. This kind of monitoring can be lifesaving for big farms, as it notifies users of tractor availability, service due dates, and fuel refill warnings. In essence, this maximizes the efficiency of farm equipment while also ensuring its long-term health [38].

IoT is truly a ground-breaking modern technology due to its dynamic nature. When AI is integrated with the IoT, predictive intelligence emerges. According to some experts, IoT and AI technologies can dramatically boost crop yields and maybe the only option to reach a better system. The technology has the potential to pave the way for ecologically friendly practices as well. Figure 1.6 shows the steps involved in advanced technologies.

Farmers must keep a sharp eye on their crops for symptoms of sickness and pollution in most farming operations. The procedure is simple at a macro level, but the eyes cannot see everything. Farmers can use modern IoT solutions, as well as AI and mobile computing, to automate the entire process, leaving the review to technology. Farmers can keep track of their crops. With the help of microsensors, farmers can keep an eye on an individual plant for signs of illness or disease. Furthermore, the system can display statistics remotely via a smartphone or similar device, allowing farmers to receive real-time notifications about the condition of their fields, presence of pests, diseases, and so on.

Farmers can better safeguard their crops from pests by combining AI control technologies and IoT sensors. Farmers can use a spot treatment

Figure 1.6 Steps involved in advanced technologies.

to treat individual plants and keep insects at bay. Simultaneously, fewer pollutants are released into the environment, particularly the soil beneath.

Aerial drones can evaluate and monitor crops in addition to—or perhaps instead of—IoT monitoring. The drones collect information about plants down to a single leaf using cameras and sensors placed inside. All of the acquired data, when fed into an ANN or ML solution, can produce a detailed image of a farmer's herd.

Earth observation satellites have recently made high spatiotemporal remote sensing data available. Satellite and aerial imaging technologies are particularly valuable for capturing effective sensory images to monitor the environment, floods, fires, droughts, and other natural disasters, as well as agricultural applications like mapping, crop evaluation, crop health, and drought prediction. It offers high-speed spatial data at the global level. Numerous agricultural and hydrological indices have been created from this distant data to define the state of the land surface, primarily vegetation, groundwater level, soil moisture, and so on, to monitor and detect the beginning, duration, and severity of drought.

Managing cattle and livestock is no easy task. Farmers must not only keep track of each animal's whereabouts, but they must also stay updated about their health. Farmers tie their cows with Fitbit-like IoT wristbands that monitor data in real-time to relieve some of the burdens. Animals will be benefitted from such wearable devices.

Experts can utilize the data acquired to develop predictive models and compare the performance to gain insights. The sharing of thousands of setups and pertinent facts in the farming world can lead to more efficient operations across the board. Agricultural specialists can exchange and consume a large quantity of knowledge, which includes anything from soil and seed tests to yield large production.

1.5   AI in the Lifecycle of the Agricultural Process

Despite modern technologies, instability in climate and unsustainable agriculture practices cause agricultural distress. The AI technology can help agriculture in the sectors [5] as shown in Figure 1.7.

1.5.1   Improving Crop Sowing and Productivity

Artificial Intelligence helps the farmers to determine the appropriate crop production in a favorable climate. An AI-based machinery helps in

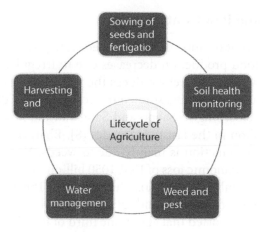

Figure 1.7 The lifecycle of the agriculture process.

sowing crops at equidistant intervals and optimal depths. For example, in Andhra Pradesh, AI-powered sowing mobile application helps the farmers to increase the yield by about 30% per hectare [39]. The pilot farming was launched with the combined effort of Microsoft and ICRISAT (International Crops Research Institute for the Semi-Arid Tropics) and was implemented in the Kurnool district in 2016. Machine learning with business intelligence tools helped the farmers and Government to use digital technologies with the dashboard providing SMS for seed sowing, optimal seed depth, land preparation, and weed management [6].

1.5.2   Soil Health Monitoring

Adequate amounts of moisture and nutrient content in the soil also contribute to the best yield. Soil health can be effectively monitored using distributed technology with DL and image recognition approach. Remote sensing techniques along with hyperspectral imaging and 3D laser scanning are also used for constructing crop matrices for better yield. The Indian Government introduced schemes like Soil Health Management (SHM) and Soil Health Card (SHC). The SHM scheme promotes judicious usage of chemical fertilizers, soil test recommendations, ensuring quality fertilizers, and so on. Each farmer is given SHC to make sure that a good harvest is possible by analyzing the soil quality. According to this scheme, the states like Madhya Pradesh, Rajasthan, Karnataka, and Uttar Pradesh [7] and nearly 45 million farmers got benefitted.

1.5.3   Weed and Pest Control

India needs 400 million tons of food to feed nearly 1.7 billion people by 2050 [12]. The food production decreases due to irregular climate which favors weed growth and thereby reduces the yield and quality of production. Many researchers in India studied the economic loss due to the presence of weeds. According to Sahoo and Saraswat, the loss was estimated to be INR 28 billion in the last two decades [8]. Bhan *et al.* [9] estimated that the 31.5% of reduction is mainly due to weeds. Varshney and Babu [10] estimated an economic loss of INR 1050 billion/year. Yogita *et al.* [11] estimated about 11 billion dollars lost due to weeds. The major crop which estimated economic losses is groundnuts, maize, soybean, wheat, rice, and so on [11, 28]. It is reported that about one third of total losses are because of weeds [13]. Despite efforts taken by weed management, weeds are considered to be a serious issue for different crops and other ecosystems. The main challenges faced by Indian farmers are as follows [36]:

(i)   managing weeds in small area cultivation,
(ii) inadequate labor and modern tools,
(iii) less information about weed biology,
(iv) impact of climate change on growth of weeds,
(v)   lack of knowledge in usage of herbicide which kills the weeds.

Various weed managements are prevailing, namely chemical, mechanical, biological, and cultural control. It is difficult to manage the weed effectively using single weed management. The use of integrated weed practices is suggested by many researchers [14–20] for major crops like rice, wheat, finger millet, maize, cotton, groundnut, and so on [29]. In a nutshell, it is proven that the herbicides combined with hand weeding help in removing weeds and increase crop production [21]. However, location-specific weed management with AI technology is necessary for Indian crops.

1.5.4   Water Management

In India, because of diverse climatic conditions, water management is not effective. Modern technologies are being used—thermal imaging camera, which monitors the crop determines whether it is getting adequate water. It is reported that water scarcity in India can lead to about 6% of the Gross Domestic Product (GDP) by 2030. The researchers also predicted that about 70% of groundwater is being pumped faster than estimated [23].

It is high time to look into the overpumping of groundwater. Artificial Intelligence coupled with image processing techniques helps in proper water management thereby increasing yield.

1.5.5 Crop Harvesting

It is reported that about 40% of the annual agricultural cost is being spent on labor employment. Nowadays, AI-based robots are being deployed to reduce labor costs. Artificial Intelligence also finds application in supply chain management [22] for crops.

1.6   Indian Agriculture and Smart Farming

As the population increases, the traditional methods of agriculture are not suitable, and adopting the latest technologies is essential for improving productivity and farmers' income. The revolution in the latest technologies like Big Data, Cloud Computing, Internet of Things, and Satellite, and Drone-based image analysis has made a big impact in many Indian industries from IT to health care. Nearly 450 start-ups from India are using the latest technologies like AI, ML, blockchain, big data, drones, and IoT with the main aim of increasing agricultural productivity [24]. Gobasco is a private concern in Lucknow which offers an online marketplace for best buying and selling supply goods. Gramophone in Indore provides chatbots for farmers, which help farmers to have better crop cycles. Jivabhumi, Bengaluru uses blockchain technology to bridge the gap between farmers and consumers. Digital farming is adopted in the states of Gujarat, Maharashtra, and Rajasthan by Agrostar, Pune, which helps farmers 24/7 to know the crop requirements along with required services [26].

According to the NASSCOM report 2019, smart farming is predicted to reach 23.14 billion dollars by 2022. The following are some of the smart farming applications:

- precision farming uses IoT sensors in the field, and farmers can view the data through mobile applications;
- agricultural drones manage large farms using airborne sensors, which are capable of collecting thermal and visual data;
- livestock monitoring helps to detect sick animals;
- smart greenhouses use solar-powered sensors, which help the farmer remotely turn on/off the lights, fan, monitor temperature, and humidity, and so on;

- smart irrigation uses a sprinkler system along with an alert system;
- farm management system for collecting and storing sensor data in the cloud and access through various devices and applications;
- apart from soil health monitoring, optimal seed sowing, water management, and weed management, AI also helps in identifying plant diseases.

1.6.1   Sensors for Smart Farming

Sensors collect data from crops, livestock, soil, and the atmosphere. The sensor data are supplied to a cloud-based IoT platform with prepro-grammed decision rules and models that determine the status of the studied object and highlight any flaw or requirement. Following the discovery of difficulties, the IoT platform's user and/or ML-driven components assess whether and which location-specific treatments are required. Various sensors used for smart farming are shown in Figure 1.8.

Electromagnetic sensors detect the ability of soil particles to conduct or acquire electrical charge using electric circuits. The electrical conductivity of the soil is immediately recorded in a logger after it becomes a member of the electromagnetic circuit. To measure electrical conductivity, contact

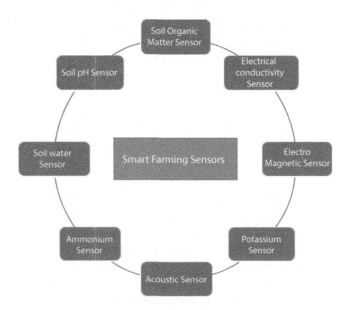

Figure 1.8 Various sensors for smart farming.

EC sensors use electrodes and make contact with the soil. The data, as well as the position information, are stored in a data logger. Contact EC sensors are highly common in precision agriculture because of their large area coverage and less prone to outside interference.

Optoelectronic devices allow for such interaction. In general, optoelectronic sensors use the properties of various materials to create a spectral signature. A common type of sensor in this category is the soil organic matter (SOM) sensor that uses the optical method.

An ion-selective electrode is used for some measurements. The activity of certain ions is detected by these electrodes. The mechanical resistance of the soil is measured by mechanical sensors. Airflow sensors are used to determine the air permeability of the soil. The sensor detects the pressure required to compress a specific volume of air into the soil at a specific depth.

Acoustic sensors: The change in noise level caused by the tool's interaction with the soil particles is used to evaluate soil texture. Soil pH sensors detect acidity and alkalinity in the soil, which can lead to fertility issues, stunted growth, oddly colored leaves, and poor plant health. Ammonium sensors detect exact ammonia and nitrogen concentration and nitrate sensors are devices that detect the presence of nitrate in the soil or water.

Potassium sensors: These devices monitor potassium levels in the soil to better understand the relationship between free potassium in soil nutrients reserves, soil texture, and root growth, which could lead to more efficient fertilizer use. Soil-water sensors are useful for detecting local energy and water balances, delivery of applied chemicals to plants and groundwater, irrigation management, and precision farming.

1.7   Advantages of Using AI in Agriculture

In agriculture, AI aids farmers in comprehending data insights, such as temperature, precipitation, wind speed, and solar power.

    i.   Essential plants can be produced, harvested, and marketed more efficiently with AI.

    ii.   The focus of AI implementation is on detecting defective crops and improving the chances of healthy crop production.

    iii.   Agro-based businesses have benefited from the advancement of AI technology.

    iv.   AI is being used in applications such as weather forecasting and automated machine adjustments.

Artificial Intelligence has the potential to improve crop management practices, allowing many tech companies to use advanced algorithms

1.8   Role of AI in Indian Agriculture

In India, adoption of modern technologies referred to as Agritech developments in various verticals like smart irrigation, weather technology solutions, and so on. The Government of India has initiated a new program called AGRI-UDAAN with the aim to boost innovations and entrepreneurship in India. Indian agriculture also attracts a foreign direct investment equity inflow of about 2.45 billion dollars (according to DIPP). To meet one-sixth of the total Indian economy, we need nearly half of India's land and huge labor.

Various AI and ML methods are employed in predictive agricultural analytics to anticipate the best time to sow seeds, receive alerts on upcoming pest attacks, and so on. Artificial Intelligence in agriculture enables the most efficient use of farming data, allowing types of equipment such as smart drones, autonomous tractors, soil sensors, and Agri-bots to support smart farming.

In the fiscal year 2019 to 2020, 133 agreements raised more than $1 billion for Indian agrifood tech start-ups. India's agricultural exports increased to $37.4 billion in 2019, and this is expected to rise further with improvements in the supply chain, as well as better storage and packaging. All of these measures will go a long way toward ensuring farmers receive fair pricing and reducing agrarian stress. Investments in technology are helping to boost agricultural output and productivity even further. Disruptive technologies, such as AI, are transforming Indian agriculture, and an increasing number of agri-tech businesses are developing and implementing AI-based solutions.

Artificial Intelligence has the potential to improve farm production, alleviate supply chain restrictions, and expand market access. It has the potential to benefit the entire agriculture value chain. By2026, AI in global agriculture is expected to be a $4 billion opportunity. The use of AI in agriculture in India might promote mechanization. By implementing precision agriculture, it would boost productivity. Agriculture technology businesses in India are attempting to combine AI-based technical solutions across a variety of use cases, including crop production and soil fertility monitoring, predictive agricultural analytics, and supply chain efficiency. Industry and government have teamed up to develop an AI-powered crop production forecast model that will provide farmers with real-time advice. To help raise crop output, improve soil yield, limit agricultural input waste, and warn of pest or disease outbreaks, the system uses AI-based prediction tools.

To offer correct information to farmers, the system incorporates remote sensing data from the Indian Space Research Organization (ISRO), data from soil health cards, weather predictions from the India Meteorological Department (IMD), and soil moisture and temperature analysis, among other things [35]. Similarly, a growing number of Indian start-ups are using AI-based agricultural solutions. A start-up has used data science, AI, and ML algorithms, as well as data sets from ISRO, to estimate crop damage and give compensation based on the amount of damage.

Even though the green revolution system in India made the nation self-sufficient in food grains, the agricultural sector should use modern technologies like AI, ML, and robotics. Many start-ups help in finding ways so that farmer receives various inputs and suggestions via mobile phones. CropIn is a company in Bengaluru that helps the farmers to know the quality of soil, assists the farmers to monitor the crops, and alerts them when the disease impends on the crops through a specific alert system. Deep Learning algorithm-based Graphical User Interface system has been developed by Intello labs situated in Bengaluru. It helps farmers to know crop health through image processing techniques. Microsoft India came out with a new AI-based App, which helps the farmer to sow the seeds at right time with the big data techniques by collecting climatic data over the past 30 years from 1986 to 2015.

Increased public and private investments, particularly from venture capitalists, are required to enable these AI technologies

1.9 Case Study in Plant Disease Identification Using AI Technology—Tomato and Potato Crops

The traditional method of plant disease identification through visual observations of the symptoms of plant leaves leads to a significant high degree of inaccuracy. Today modern tools incorporate graphical processing unit which includes ML-based algorithms which precisely detect the plant disease and assist the pathologist to easily identify the disease. Machine learning is the subset of AI that uses algorithms that predicts experience. Nowadays, a technology named DL using a large amount of processing layers made exponential growth in AI. The common diseases of tomato and potato crops are blackleg, early blight, late blight, stem rot, and ring rot. Figure 1.9 and Figure 1.10 show the late blight and leaf spot of tomato crop and the early blight and stem rot of potato crop, respectively.

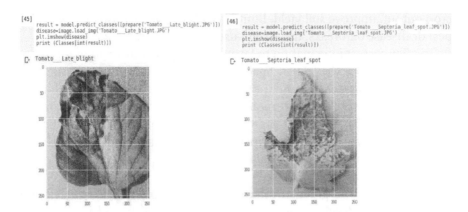

Figure 1.9 Late blight and leaf spot of tomato crop.

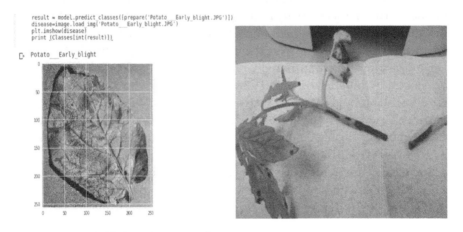

Figure 1.10 Early blight and stem rot of potato crop.

Apps are given for farmers to know the current status of the crop and get an opinion from the experts [25].

1.10   Challenges in AI

Practicing AI is difficult for the agriculture field. Even for a small field, the condition keeps changing from one area to another. Also, unpredicted weather conditions change soil quality. The presence of pests and diseases often visits the field [3]. Because no two environments are alike, it is difficult to deploy ML and DL-based AI models in the agricultural field although scientists are capable of developing programs for large sectors [35].

Moreover, the testing and validation of such models require more laborious than in other fields. As per Indian agriculture is concerned, the road is not smooth and it is up to the farmers, businessmen, and consumers to use the power of AI to increase production.

While IoT-enabled gadgets and sensors are not prohibitively expensive, buying in quantity can be costly. A proper local network must be set up in addition to the hardware to permit and handle a large amount of data and there comes the issue of data storage, which might be local or cloud-based.

To function, all new technologies necessitate the use of energy. Massive amounts of energy will be required to support a large-scale agricultural activity. Furthermore, many modern robots and solutions continue to operate on fossil fuels, damaging the environment. IoT and other current technologies are not a proper cure for environmental challenges without more sustainable energy or even renewable alternatives.

1.11   Conclusion

Artificial Intelligence helps farmers to increase the crop yield and quality of production. Many start-ups are growing to automate farming using modern technology. The main challenges in deploying AI and ML are unpredictable weather, frequent change in soil quality, the possibility of uncontrollable pests, and so on. It is imperative that any application of AI needs to be carefully designed and implemented which benefits the end-users. The use of AI in agriculture in India might promote mechanization. By implementing precision agriculture, it would boost productivity.

References

1. Pathan, M., Patel, N., Yagnik, H., Shah, M., Artificial cognition for applications in smart agriculture: A comprehensive review. *Artif. Intell. Agric.*, 4, 81–95, 2020.
2. Agriculture in India: Information About Indian Agriculture & Its Importance, IBEF, Last updated on Dec. 30, 2020, https://www.ibef.org/industry/agriculture-india.aspx.
3. Bhar, L.M., Ramasubramanian, V., Arora, A., Marwaha, S., Parsad, R., *Era of Artificial Intelligence: Prospects for Indian Agriculture*, Indian Farming, 69, 3, 2019.
4. Ferentinos, K.P., Deep learning models for plant disease detection and diagnosis. *Comput. Electron. Agric.*, 145, 311–318, 2018.

5. Artificial Intelligence in Indian Agriculture, 20 February 2020, https://www.ciiblog.in/technology/artificial-intelligence-in-indian-agriculture/#:~-:text=In%20Andhra%20Pradesh%2C%20India%2C%20with,per%20hectare%20has%20been%20seen.

6. Amarendra, ICRISAT develop app and dashboard to help farmers find right time to sow crops, August 25, 2016.

7. Anonymous: Soil health monitoring in India, 2017, https://www.icfa.org.in/assets/doc/reports/Soil_Health_Management_in_India.pdf.

8. Sahoo, K.M. and Saraswat, V.N., Magnitude of losses in the yields of major crops due to weed competition in India. *Pestic. Inf.*, 14, 1, 2–9, 1988.

9. Bhan, V.M., Sushilkumar, Raghuwanshi, M.S., Weed management in India. *Indian J. Plant Prot.*, 17, 171–202, 1999.

10. Varshney, J.G. and PrasadBabu, M.B.B., Future scenario of weed management in India. *Indian J. Weed Sci.*, 40, 1&2, 01–09, 2008.

11. Gharde, Y., Singh, P.K., Dubey, R.P., Gupta, P.K., Assessment of yield and economic losses in agriculture due to weeds in India, *Crop Protection*, 107, 12–18, 2018.

12. Rao, A.N., Singh, R.G., Mahajan, G., Wani, S.P., Weed research issues, challenges, and opportunities in India, *Crop Protection*, 134, Februrary 2018.

13. DWR, 2015. Vision 2050, Directorate of Weed Research. Indian Council of Agricultural Research, Jabalpur 482 004, Madhya Pradesh, 2015.

14. Singh, R., Das, T.K., Kaur, R., *et al.* Weed Management in Dryland Agriculture in India for Enhanced Resource Use Efficiency and Livelihood Security. *Proc. Natl. Acad. Sci., India, Sect. B Biol. Sci.*, 88, 1309–1322, 2018, https://doi.org/10.1007/s40011-016-0795-y.

15. Singh, B., Dhaka, A.K., Pannu, R.K., Kumar, S., Integrated weed management-a strategy for sustainable wheat production—A review. *Agric. Rev.*, 34, 243–255, 2013.

16. Rao, A.N., Wani, S.P., Ramesha, M., Ladha, J.K., Weeds and weed management of rice in Karnataka State, India. *Weed Technol.*, 29, 1–17, 2015a.

17. Sunitha, N. and Kalyani, D.L., Weed management in maize (Zea mays L.)—A review. *Agric. Rev.*, 33, 70–77, 2012.

18. Vijayakumar, M., Jayanthi, C., Kalpana, R., Ravisankar, D., Integrated weed management in sorghum [Sorghum bicolor (L.) Moench]—A review. *Agric. Rev.*, 35, 79–91, 2014.

19. Annadurai, K., Puppala, N., Angadi, S., Chinnusamy, C., Integrated weed management in the groundnut-based intercropping system—A review. *Agric. Rev.*, 31, 11–20, 2010.

20. Nithya, C., Chinnusamy, C., Ravisankar, D., Weed management in herbicide-tolerant transgenic cotton (*Gossypium hisrsutum* L.)—a review. *Int. J. Agric. Sci. Res.(IJASR)*, 3, 277–284, 2013.

21. Rao, A.N. and Nagamani, A., Integrated weed management in India—Revisited. *Indian J. Weed. Sci.*, 42, 1–10, 2010.

22. Agarwal, R.G., Water management key to sustainable agriculture growth in India New Delhi, Financial Express, Updated: Mar 14, 2019, 3:46 AM, https://www.financialexpress.com/opinion/water-management-key-to-sustainable-agriculture-growth-in-India/1515331/.

23. Timesnow, Global water crisis: Groundwater is being pumped 70% faster than expected in North India, research claims, New Delhi, 24 February 2019, https://www.timesnownews.com/mirror-now/in-focus/article/global-water-crisis-groundwater-is-being-pumped-70-faster-than-expected-in-north-india-research-claims/371528#:~:text=Scientists%20mentioned%20that%20the%20groundwater,than%20what%20was%20estimated%20earlier.&-text=Drying%20up%20of%20groundwater%20by,underground%20water%20is%20much%20higher.

24. Baruah, A., Artificial Intelligence in Indian Agriculture – An Industry and Startup Overview, Emerald, The AI Research and Advisory Company, 2019.

25. Mary, A., Evangeline, S., Minnang, M R., A beginners guide for machine learning models with python environment, lambert publication, Republic of Moldova, Chisinau-2068, 2019.

26. Digital Agriculture: Farmers in India are using AI to increase crop yields, Microsoft News Center India, 7 November, 2017, https://news.microsoft.com/en-in/features/ai-agriculture-icrisat-upl-india/.

27. Anonyms, Machine Learning, IBM Cloud Education, updated 15 July 2020.

28. Adisa, O., Botai, J., Adeola, A. et al., Application of artificial neural network for predicting maize production in South Africa. Sustainability, 11, 4, 1145–1227, 2019.

29. Chary, S., Mustaffha, S., Ismail, W.I.W., Determining the yield of the crop using artificial neural network method. Int. J. Eng. Adv. Technol., 9, 1, 2959–2965, 2019.

30. Gliever, C. and Slaughter, D.C., Crop verses weed recognition with artificial neural networks, ASAE paper., 01-3104, 2001, 1–12, 2001.

31. Maier, H.R., Dandy, G.C., Neural networks for the prediction and forecasting of water resources variables: a review of modelling issues and applications, Environmental Modelling & Software, 15, 1, 101–124, 2000.

32. Song, H. and He, Y., Crop nutrition diagnosis expert system based on artificial neural networks. third International Conference on Information Technology and Applications (ICITA'05), Sydney, NSW, 1 (2005), pp. 357–362, 2005.

33. Singh, A., Ganapathysubramanian, B., Singh, A.K., Sarkar, S., Machine learning for high-throughput stress phenotyping in plants. Trends Plant Sci., 21, 2, 110–124, 2016.

34. Pan, S.J. and Yang, Q., A survey on transfer learning. IEEE Trans. Knowl. Data Eng., 22, 10, 1345–1359, 2010.

35. Danziger, C., The Environmental Impacts of AI and IoT In Agriculture, aitrends, January 9, 2020, https://www.aitrends.com/ai-in-agriculture/the-environmental-impacts-of-ai-and-iot-in-agriculture/.

36. Abhishek, S., AI for farmers, Indian Express, Updated: November 26, 2020.

37. Jain, P., Artificial Intelligence in Agriculture: Using Modern Day AI to Solve Traditional Farming Problems, aAnalytics Vidhya, November 4, 2020, https://www.analyticsvidhya.com/blog/2020/11/artificial-intelligence-in-agriculture-using-modern-day-ai-to-solve-traditional-farming-problems/.

38. Big data and Agriculture: A Complete Guide, talend, 2020, https://www.talend.com/resources/big-data-agriculture/.

39. Dua, A.M., Artificial Intelligence in Indian Agriculture, Bhajan Global Impact Foundation, updated Feb 2020, http://bhajanfoundation.org/knowledge/artificial-intelligence-in-indian-agriculture/.

2

Comparative Evaluation of Neural Networks in Crop Yield Prediction of Paddy and Sugarcane Crop

K. Krupavathi[1]*, M. Raghu Babu[2] and A. Mani[3]

[1]Department of Irrigation and Drainage Engineering, Dr. NTR College of Agricultural Engineering, Bapatla, ANGRAU, India
[2]Department of Irrigation and Drainage Engineering, College of Agricultural Engineering, Madakasira, ANGRAU, India
[3]Department of Soil and Water Engineering, Dr. NTR College of Agricultural Engineering, Bapatla, ANGRAU, India

Abstract

Climate change causing extreme temperature events, erratic pattern of rainfall, droughts and floods poses serious limitations on agriculture, in turn requires regular crop monitoring and management of resources to get maximum yields. Food chain of the crops can be transformed by technological innovations, like mechanization, artificial intelligence and robotics, UAVs, sensors, Internet of Things (IoT), remote sensing, machine learning and deep learning in agriculture. The present study focused on ability of machine learning algorithm in integration with remote sensing in crop yield prediction of paddy and sugarcane crops at regional level. Crop-sensitive parameters extracted from high resolution LANDSAT 8 OLI imageries are used as neural network model inputs. The Feed Forward Back Propagating Neural Network (FFBPNN) models for crop yield were developed and calibrated in MATLAB environment. During training, the model perceptron's were trained with 75 of the 100 inputs upto10,000 epochs with 1 to 10 hidden neurons. Four performance indices (coefficient of multiple determination, R^2; MAE; RMSE and the average ratio between estimated yield to target crop yield [R_{ratio}]) were calculated to achieve optimum neural network. Accurate and stable results observed from the model for paddy with highest mean relative error as 6.166%

*Corresponding author: krupareddy572@gmail.com

Roheet Bhatnagar, Nitin Kumar Tripathi, Nitu Bhatnagar and Chandan Kumar Panda (eds.)
The Digital Agricultural Revolution: Innovations and Challenges in Agriculture through Technology Disruptions, (25–56) © 2022 Scrivener Publishing LLC

and the lowest relative error as −0.133%. The range of R^2 values were 0.946 and 0.967 for training and same for testing was 0.936 and 0.950 for paddy in *Kharif* and *Rabi* seasons, whereas for sugarcane the values are 0.916 and 0.924 during testing and training, respectively. The highest MAE was 0.178 for Paddy (*Rabi*). The R_{ratio} values showed the under crop yield estimation of sugarcane crop. The model's best performance was observed at [i+1] and [i+2] hidden nodes. The statistical analysis revealed that the reliability of the model in paddy yield estimation. However, slight under estimation of yield of the sugarcane crop indicates sensitivity of yield algorithms to crop input parameters. The results demonstrated the high efficacy of using remote sensing images and NN models to generate accurate crop yield maps and also revealed significant superiority of neural network models over conventional methods.

Keywords: Crop yield, remote sensing, neural networks, feed forward and back propagation, NDVI, APAR, crop water stress

2.1   Introduction

Climate change posing serious challenges on fresh water and good soil and are becoming serious limitations for agriculture around the world. Average raise in temperatures was causing more extreme heat throughout the year. Rainfall patterns are also shifted more intense storms of short spells and longer dry periods. Severe droughts tolled heavily on crops, and livestock. On the other hand, increased floods destroy crops and livestock, accelerate erosionof soil, pollute fresh water, and damage roads and bridges. Sea level rise is also the intensity of floods on farms and sea water intrusion in coastal regions. New pests are boosting up and damaging crops [1].

It is also important to know that climate change risks are not constant and not distributed equally neither in space nor in time. In turn, it requires regular crop monitoring and management of resources to get maximum yields. The monitoring of crops at regional level includes crop type mapping, cropping pattern recognition, crop condition estimation, crop yield estimation, estimation of evapotranspiration, irrigation scheduling, monitoring of water resources, uncertainty analysis, Identification of pest attack, soil mapping, and so on [2]. Although agriculture is a complex interlinked phenomenon, clear-cut success has been achieved with the technological interventions in decision-making processes and in shaping adaptation strategies with the changing scenarios. Technological innovations like mechanization, artificial intelligence and robotics, UAVs, sensors, Internet of Things (IoT), remote sensing, machine learning, deep learning, and their combinations in agriculture have the ability to transform food chain of the crops. The integration of local agricultural knowledge with remote sensing depends on the understanding of complex phenomena in agriculture [3].

Crop yield estimation at regional level plays crucial role in planning for food security of the population. This is of greater important task for some wide applications, including management of land and water management, crop planning, water use efficiency, crop losses, economy calculation, and so on. Traditional ground observation-based methods of yield estimation, such as visual examination and sampling survey, require continuous monitoring, and regular recording of crop parameters [4–6]. Spectral information from remote sensing images gives very accurate crop attributes that can be used for crop mapping and estimation. Further integration of machine learning algorithm with remote sensing provides explicit estimation of yield [7]. The present study focused on ability of machine learning algorithm in integration with remote sensing in crop yield prediction of paddy and sugarcane crops at regional level.

2.2   Introduction to Artificial Neural Networks

2.2.1   Overview of Artificial Neural Networks

An artificial neural network (ANN) is a wide class of flexible and simple mathematical model. It is capable to identify complex nonlinear relationships between input and output observed datasets. Neural network consists of a large number of "neurons," nonlinear computational elements, connected internally in a complex way and arranged into layers [7]. Artificial neural network simulates natural neural network in the brain. In the rain, the fundamental neural network is connected to each other by synapses. The neurons are basic components of the human brain are processing unit in the brain. The neurons are responsible for learning and retention of information. The sensory/observed data are the input to the network, processes it, and gave output for other neurons. In ANN, everything is designed to replicate this process. An ANN also consists of a bundle of neurons. Biological axon-dendrite connects each node to other nodes via links. All the data the variable name "X" enters in the system with a weight of "w" for generating a weighted value. Each link weight determines the strength of nodes influence on other node. This denotes the strength of a signal in the brain. An activation function that use the basic mathematical equations to determine input-output relation. The familiar activation functions in NN are logistic function, binary step function, rectified linear units, and hyperbolic tangent function. The ANN models are efficient;

particularly in solving the problem in the complex processes, which are difficult to describe using physical equations [8]. The ANN models are capable of modeling the complex nonlinear relationships, compared with a traditional linear regression model approach [9]. The ANN also has excellent fault tolerance and is fast and highly scalable with parallel processing. ANN models are similar to statistical models like generalized linear regression models, polynomial models, nonparametric models and discriminant analysis, principal component analysis, and other models in which the prediction of complicated phenomena is important than the explanation. On the other hand, NN models, like learning vector quantization, counter propagation, and self-organizing maps, are useful for data analysis. Some of the published work that provide insight about relation between statistics and NN are discussed.

2.2.2   Components of Neural Networks

The human brain on an average contains 86 billion neurons approximately [10]. A biological neuron consists of thin fibers, and those are known as dendrites. Dendrites receive incoming signals. The cell body, "soma" responsible for processing input signals and to decide firing/nonfiring of neurons to output signal. Processed signals output from neurons received by "axon" and passes it to relevant cells.

Artificial neuron called also as "perceptron" is a fundamental component of neural network, which is a mathematical function of a real-world problem with binary outputs. The neurons are systematically organized into two or more than two layers. One layer of neurons are connected to immediately preceding neurons layer and immediately succeeding neuron layer. The first (input) layer receives the external data, and the last (output) layer ultimately produces result. Each artificial neuron receives input from input layer, process the weights and sums and pass the sum through a nonlinear mathematical relation to produce output. In between them are one or more hidden layers (Figure 2.1). Weights are multiples of respective input values arranged in an array. To achieve a final value of prediction, bias is added to the weighted sum. The size of the correction values to adjust for errors by the model is known as a learning rate. Activation function decides whether or not a neuron is fired [11]. The neural network uses previous step output data values for the network training and minimizes the error between observed and estimated. The process readjusts the weights at each interaction of neuron. The training will stop after reaching the optimal learning rate [12, 13]. The higher learning rate reduces the time for training, and ultimate accuracy is low. Lower learning rate takes longer time and higher accuracy.

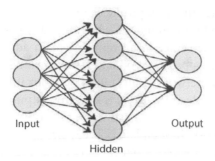

Input   Output

Hidden

Figure 2.1 Architecture of artificial neural network (original figure).

2.2.3 Types and Suitability of Neural Networks

The artificial neural networks are usually selected based on the mathematical functions and output parameters. Among the different types of artificial neural networks, some of the most important kinds of the neural networks are discussed in this section.

A feed-forward neural network (FFNN) is an artificial neural network and is one of the simple type of neural network. In which, the input data travels in only one direction no loop or cycle formation. In an FFNN, every neuron (perceptron) in one layer is connected with each node in the immediate layer. As a result, each and every node is fully connected. This systematic arrangement of FFNN generates output by output layer. The number of hidden layers may arrange in between input and output layers and do not have a connection with the outer environment. These neural networks may or may not have a hidden layer. Common applications are pattern recognition, speech recognition, data compression, computer vision, and so on. If an FFN network uses more than one hidden layer, it is called a deep feed-forward network. By adding more hidden layers, overfitting will be reduced and improved generalization. The synaptic operation order in a hidden neuron, the ANNs were classified as first order, second, third, or higher order [14]. The back loops are absent in the FFN network. To reduce the error value in prediction, the back propagation algorithm may be used. The weights between the input hidden and output layers can be adjusted by using back propagation algorithm through learning rate and momentum. Then, the error value is back propagated from output layer to the input layer [15]. Back propagation algorithm was adopting widely for forecasting problems with the networks [16, 17]. Radial Basis Network (RBN)s behave as feed forward networks using other functions (radial basis function) to activate the network. Radial Basis Networks determine the gap between the generated output and target output.

The logistic (sigmoid) function produces output value between 0 and 1. An RBN cannot be used for continuous value. Radial basis function considers the distance from the center to a point.The main advantage of RB neural networks is universal approximation and faster learning rate.

Recurrent neural network (RNN) uses previous information in current iterations. The principle of the RNN is keeping output and feeding the output back to input layer to help in estimating the output of the layer. In this type of neural network, hidden layers every neuron receives an input with a specific time delay. Recurrent neural network is required more time with low computational speed. These types can be used in time series anomaly detection, speech recognition, speech synthesis, and robot control. Long-/short-term memory networks (LSTM) use a memory cell that processes data in RNNs. Gate recurrent units (GRUs) are different from LSTMs with similar models and produce equally better results. Extreme learning machines (ELMs) determine the output weights by choosing hidden nodes randomly. Extreme learning machine networks learn the output weights in only one step, and assigned weights are never updated. These algorithms work faster than the other general NN algorithms.

Convolution neural networks (CNN) are primarily used for image classification, image clustering, time series forecasting and object recognition. Deconvolutional networks (DCN) are CNNs that work in anopposite process. The major drawbacks of conventional neural networks are low learning rate and all the parameters tuning iteratively. In Hopfield network (HN), every neuron in network is directly connected with other neurons. The HNs are used to save memories and patterns and also applied in optimization problems. A Kohonen neural network (KN) also known as self-organizing maps is an unsupervised algorithm. This is very useful for multidimensional scattered data. It gives output in one or two dimensions only, so it is treated as a method of dimensionality reduction. This self-organizing process has different phases. A small weight is initialized to each neuron. In the second phase, the close neuron is the "winning neuron," and the other neurons are connected to the winning neuron. The KN networks use more competitive learning than error correction learning.

2.3   Application of Neural Networks in Agriculture

2.3.1   Potential Applications of Neural Networks in Agriculture

Various ANN techniques are suitable to use in agriculture. The widely accepted neural network includes radial basisfunction neural network

(RBFNN), backpropagation neural network (BNN), convolutional neural network (CNN), recurrent neural network (RNN), and Adaptive Neuro-Fuzzy Inference System (ANFIS) for different applications. These NNs are also used in combination with remote sensing classification, rice mapping [17, 18]. Rice mapping is done by combining MS Sentinel 2 and Sentinel 1 SAR band using the LSTM network and dynamic time warping distance approach [19]. Detailed crop classification and mapping is the area for high scope of NN application [20, 21]. A ANN-based model combining a CNN and generative adversarial network (GAN) is used for crop classification with advantages of few data requirement and high flexibility [22]. A CNN-based approach with fused MODIS NDVI data, multitemporal Landsat, and synthetic phenological variable classifies a land accurately into small patches [23]. The methodology for crop classification using deep learning models was framed [24]. They proposed CNN model from multiple Landsat and Sentinel-1 images. Cropland was classified by a LSTMRNN model using Landsat imagery with high accuracy [25]. Wheat production was forecasted and compared the performance of different training methods using an ANN model [26].

Plant identification is done using deep learning neural networks and showed good performance [27, 28]. Deep learning algorithm is used for mango fruit identification and fruit classification [29]. Support vector regression (SVR) and genetic algorithm (GA)–based BPNN were combined to develop a spectral model for evaluating cultivated land quality based on MODIS-GPPs on late rice phenology [30]. SVM and ANN combined to predict crop with accuracy of 86.80% in India adopting the factors like temperature, rainfall, relative humidity, soil, and so on [31]. Five remote sensing (RS) data-derived parameters like VI, slope, vegetation dryness index, temperature, patch-fractal dimension, and road accessibility were used, and they found that cultivated land quality was significantly and nonlinearly correlated [32].

Machine learning methods were also used in pest classification of crops [33, 34]. The CNNs were used to identify the plant pests from leafs [35, 36], weed classification [37], crop quality evaluation [38], and field pest classification. Many agricultural-related research surveys were done to provide comprehensive results [39]. An ANN model used was for soil moisture estimation using temperature of soil, temperature of atmosphere, and RH. Artificial neural networks were adopted to predict the production of biofuel from cow manure and agricultural wastes at high accuracy [40]. The study helped in identifying favorable conditions to predict the behavior of biofuel production in a short time [41].

2.3.2   Significance of Neural Networks in Crop Yield Prediction

The factors that responsible for crop yields, like soil type, climate variables, water application, and crop management, are nonlinear and complex. Traditional statistic applications lead inaccurate results in yield estimation. There are several studies reported about crop yield estimation using neural networks in response to climate, soil, genotypes, and crop management practices. A design to train an ANN to forecast the soybean production demand in Brazil was framed by adopting a nonlinear autoregressive solution [42]. They concluded an increase of about 26.5% for 2017 compared with 2016. An ANN is used to predict soybean yield and production and to compare with time series analysis [43]. A crop yield model corresponding to soil-related parameters was developed [44] by training a BP neural network. Different vegetation indices and plant density were analyzed from UAV to analyze grain yield of corn crop by using an NN model [45].

Maize yield estimated using time series data of different satellites and also radar with a neural network with an R^2 of 0.69 [46]. Chlorophyll data were used to estimate productivity of corn crop [47] resulting in an r^2 of 0.73. Vegetation indices and crop height were correlated with maize yield to predict maize yield using neural networks [48, 49]. Corn grain yield was calculated with RS-based plant density, canopy cover, and VI using neural networks [50]. Sugarcane yield was estimated using feed forward and back propagation neural network with the crop attributes derived from remote sensing data. They observed stable results with R^2 values of 0.916 and 0.924 during testing and training, respectively [51]. Although there are many applications of the ANN in yield prediction, the problems are area specific and needs simplified neural networks.

2.4   Importance of Remote Sensing in Crop Yield Estimation

As remote sensing provides up-to-date, precise, and cost-effective information, remote sensing and GIS support agricultural production monitoring toward sustainable agricultural systems. The application of remote sensing technology agricultural operations requires high accuracy and reliable data with data quantitative processing facility [52]. For crop yield prediction, very highly accurate and reliable data are necessary. It was clear from the studies that even after a long time of research (more than 20 years), no regular crop yield estimation method suitable for a wide range crops was developed; however, a huge amount of work done was shown and is an important step in this field.

Remote sensing imageries have the potential to provide spatial information of features at any scale on earth at real-time basis. Remote sensing imageries have the potential not only in identification of crop classes but also in estimation of crop yield. A wide number of sensors data is useful for yield estimation of crops. Soil moisture, NDVI, surface temperature and rainfall data were considered for assessment of crop yield, using piecewise linear regression method with breakpoint, found predicted values very close to observed values (R^2 = 0.78) for corn and for soybean crop (R^2 = 0.86) [53]. Poststratified estimator of crop yield using satellite data (IRS-1B-LISS-II) along with crop yield data from crop cutting experiments for small area estimated crop yield at tehsil/block level with the existing sampling design [54]. A simple linear statistical relationship between normalized difference vegetation index and yield used for estimation of paddy, corn, wheat, and cotton crops was developed [55]. Corn yield scenarios was constructed from the AVHRR-based temperature condition index (TCI) and vegetation condition index (VCI) at approximately 42 days prior to harvest time [56]. Recent studies used low altitude helicopter and unmanned aerial vehicle (UAV) for field scale yield prediction. A study using UAV at 20 m height revealed that NDVI values were highly correlated with yield and total biomass at panicle initiation stage [57].

Although a large amount of research has been done on this, there is no particular best yield estimation method available [58, 59]. Training of neural network with RS data can be done to predict crop yield. It is also possible with big satellite data analytics also with neural network.

2.5   Derivation of Crop-Sensitive Parameters From Remote Sensing for Paddy and Sugarcane Crops

2.5.1   Study Area

The present study was carried out in Krishna Central Delta (KCD), a part of Krishna Eastern Delta in the Krishna district in the state of Andhra Pradesh, which is named after the holy river Krishna, bounded by the latitudes 16°37'15"N and 15°42'15"N and longitudes 80°34'0"E and 81°16'0"E. It constitutes the command area of Bandar canal and Krishna Eastern bank canal, which has an irrigated ayacut of 111223.83 ha in Krishna district. It irrigates about 18 mandals in Krishna district (Figure 2.2). In the *Kharif* season (July/August to November/December), the major crops grown are

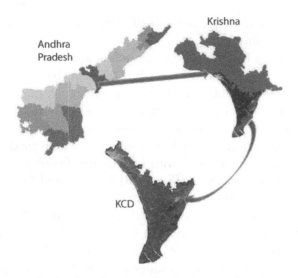

Figure 2.2 Location details of Krishna Central Delta (original figure).

paddy, sugarcane, turmeric, and vegetables, and the predominant crops grown during the *Rabi* season (December to March) are paddy, sugarcane, maize, pulses, and cauliflower. At the upper reaches, farmers are also cultivating in the summer season. Orchards are also grown specifically in south part of the study area. The main crop in *Kharif* is paddy in 95% of the study area. The various land use pattern of the study area is presented in Table 2.1. The major area is under agriculture (1539.342 km²) followed by aqua (402.971 km²) and horticulture (57.648 km²).

Table 2.1 Land use of the study area in the year 2014–2015.

S. no.	LULC class	Area (km²)	Percentage (%)
1	Agriculture	1539.342	69.1924
2	Water bodies/Aqua	402.971	18.11328
3	Other waste land	18.91	0.849992
4	Buildup	117.369	5.275659
5	Deciduous forest	88.487	3.977432
6	Plantation/orchard	57.648	2.591239

2.5.2   Materials and Methods

2.5.2.1   Data Acquisition and Crop Parameters Retrieval From Remote Sensing Images

Five RS indices, namely normalized difference vegetation index (NDVI), surface temperature (T_s), water stress index (WSI), absorbed photosynthetically active radiation (APAR), and averaged yield for the last 5 years, were selected. The first four parameters were retrieved from Landsat 8 remote sensing images. The average yield is calculated from statistical and ground truth data.

The spectral information from free available high-resolution optical Landsat 8 satellite images is used in the present study. Several researchers reported that estimates from Landsat were considerably more accurate in yield estimates and its variability during growth stages [60, 61]. The Landsat 8 level 1 images were downloaded from USGS Earth explorer. Digital numbers are changed to TOA reflectance data. The developed indices are as follows.

The NDVI is most important and efficient index of crop growing conditions [62, 63], which is the response index to greenness and vegetative cover High NDVI values that reflect greater greenness, similarly, low NDVI values reflect too stress or senescence and low vegetation. It is the normalized difference between the near infrared (NIR) and visible RED (R) reflectance bands.

$$NDVI = \frac{\rho_{NIR} - \rho_{RED}}{\rho_{NIR} + \rho_{RED}} \tag{2.1}$$

The next important parameter is solar radiation. The amount of light available for photosynthesis is known as photosynthetically active radiation (PAR) and ranges between 400 and 700 nanometers. Absorbed photo synthetically active radiation is the portion absorbed for photosynthesis by crop leaves.

$$APAR = PAR*FAPAR \tag{2.2}$$

Fraction of absorbed PAR (FAPAR) is related to absorbed PAR and can be used in the estimation of light use efficiency to estimate crop yields at the pixel level [64]. A linear, scale-invariant relationship between FAPAR and the NDVI was suggested by earlier scientists [65–67]. In the present study, computed FAPAR using NDVI, as suggested by [65] for Landsat images, is adopted in this study as:

$$FAPAR = 1.24 * NDVI - 0.168 \qquad (2.3)$$

Canopy surface temperature represents sunlight radiated onto leaves, and also, it is an indication of evaporation intensity. Surface temperature is calculated as

$$T_s = (BT / 1) + W * (BT / 14380) * \ln(\varepsilon) \qquad (2.4)$$

where, BT = Top of atmosphere brightness temperature (°C)
   W = Wavelength of emitted radiance
   ε = Land Surface Emissivity

Spectral radiance data were converted to top of atmosphere (TOA) brightness temperature by using the thermal constant (K_1 and K_2) values in Meta data file

$$BT = K_2 / \ln (K_1 / L_\lambda + 1) - 272.15 \qquad (2.5)$$

where BT = Top of atmosphere brightness temperature (°C), L_λ = Top of atmospherespectral radiance (Watts/($m^2 * sr * \mu m$)), K_1 = K_1 Band Constant, K_2 = K_2 Band Constant.

Crop Water Stress Index ($NDVI/T_s$) is taken as one of the indicators of crop yield. The water stress index (WSI or CWSI) quantifies moisture stress and relationship between plant temperature and stress [68]. Crop Water Stress Index was used for moisture deficit monitoring with best results and revealed that there was a close relationship in between WSI and crop water content [69].

The crop yield data (crop cutting data) are collected for 5 years. Five years of data are sufficient for estimates of yield potential for fully irrigated production systems [70] and is adopted for the present study. The crop yield per unit area of different crops for the years 2013 to 2017 is collected from Directorate of Economics and Statistics, Vijayawada. The location details of the data collected is in the form of survey numbers of revenue department. To know latitude and longitude and also to collect previous years' data at each crop cutting point ground truth is done by using EpiCollect (A mobile based App) (Figure 2.3).

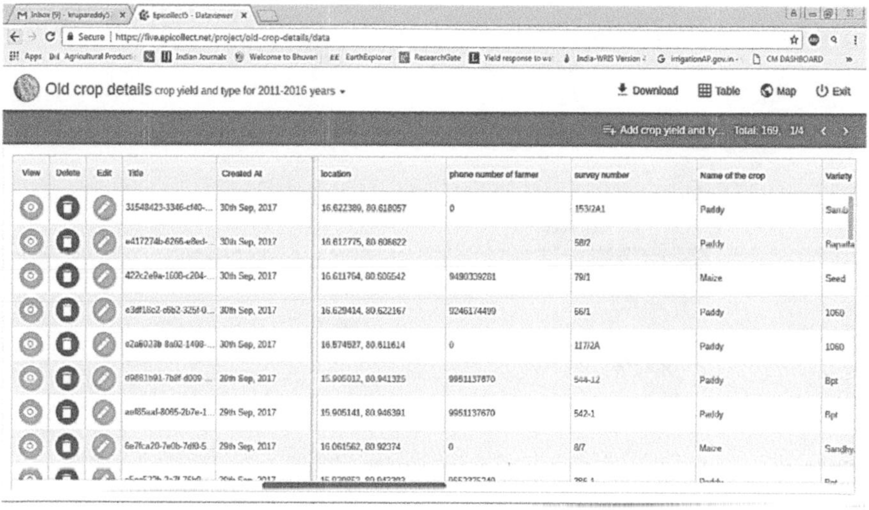

Figure 2.3 Illustration of collection of ground sample points using EpiCollect app (original figure).

2.5.3   Results and Conclusions

The parameters selected as input variables for neural network were derived for each season separately for all years. The APAR derived from Landsat 8 image on 14 October 2015 is shown in Figure 2.4. The spatial distribution of APAR values varied from 0.4369 to 0.7741. The higher APAR was observed at cropped area and was the lowest at water bodies. Similarly, the crop water stress index was derived and was presented in Figure 2.4 (a). The CWSI on the day of derived is shown in Figure 2.4 (b), which is a proxy for water stress. The CWSI varied from 0-1. The CWSI matched with irrigation canals. The CWSI is high in the areas where there is a low supply of irrigation water, especially in the lower parts of the area. Mandal wise-extracted mean crop yield parameters are presented in Table 2.2.

The selected yield parameter maps were derived from satellite images and were given as input to FFBP NN model. Time series NDVI, T_s, CSWI, and APAR maps were retrieved from remotely sensed images from transplanting to the harvesting stage of paddy crop. The values for the ground truth points of all parameters derived by remote sensing were extracted. Spatial distribution of sample points is shown in Figure 2.5. The attributes of abovementioned derived thematic maps are extracted for all the sample points and exported to Excel as .csv file (Figure 2.6) for preparation of input files to neural network structure.

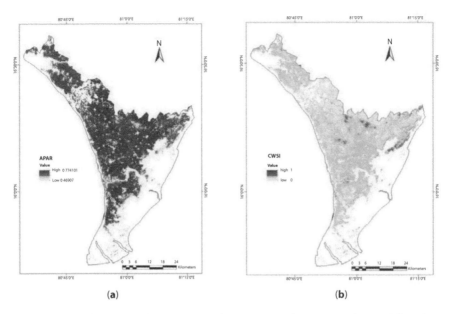

(a)   (b)

Figure 2.4 (a, b). APAR and CSWI maps of KCD on October 14, 2015 (original figure).

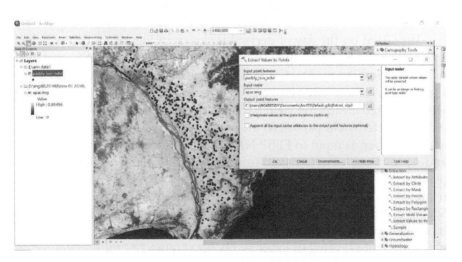

Figure 2.5 Synoptic view of spatial distribution of sample points of crop collected (original figure).

Table 2.2 Sample normalized input data of FFBPNN yield estimation model of paddy crop in *kharif* during 2015.

S. no.	Mandal name	NDVI	T_s	APAR	Water index	Normalized average yield
1	Vijayawada rural	0.542	0.831	0.775	0.354	0.674
2	Kankipadu	0.548	0.148	0.778	0.448	0.855
3	Challapalle	0.539	0.792	0.773	0.180	0.544
4	Pamarru	0.528	0.577	0.768	0.224	0.533
5	Vuyyuru	0.531	0.330	0.770	0.325	0.744
6	Movva	0.687	0.363	0.844	0.723	0.725
7	Thotlavalluru	0.687	0.439	0.844	0.686	0.450
8	Avanigada	0.563	0.454	0.785	0.359	0.000
9	Pamidimukkala	0.575	0.687	0.791	0.302	0.900
10	Guduru	0.459	0.767	0.735	0.000	0.915
11	Penamaluru	0.478	0.706	0.744	0.063	0.525
12	Koduru	0.748	0.482	0.874	0.821	0.900
13	Pamarru	0.771	0.390	0.885	0.929	0.619
14	Machilipatnam	0.533	0.452	0.771	0.284	0.921
15	Pedana	0.491	0.203	0.750	0.266	0.957
16	Mopidevi	0.496	0.790	0.752	0.080	0.544
17	Nagayalanka	0.511	0.521	0.760	0.203	0.750

Table 2.2 represents the maximum and minimum values of the normalized data. The average values of NDVI ranged from 0.459 to 0.687 for different mandals. Similarly, APAR and CWSI ranged from 0.750 to 0.874 and 0 to 0.929, respectively. Surface temperature and average yield were normalized. The normalized surface temperature was in the range of 0.148 for Kankipadu to 0.831 at Vijayawada rural. The highest normalized yield is at 0.957 at Pedana. The point wise normalized parameter values were used as input to the NN model.

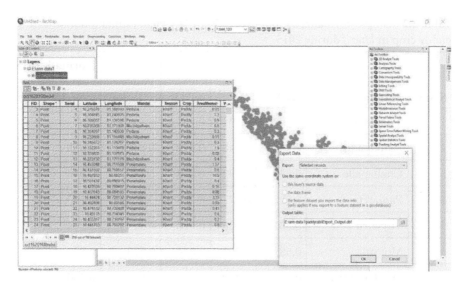

Figure 2.6 Exporting the attribute values of the points to excel (original figure).

2.6 Neural Network Model Development, Calibration and Validation

2.6.1 Materials and Methods

2.6.1.1 ANN Model Design

The data extracted from the abovementioned maps are divided into two data sets for training and testing to analyze network results and testing the models. The typical architecture of three-layered MLFF perceptron used is shown in Figure 2.7. The derived five yield factors, such as NDVI, surface temperature, APAR, crop water stress index, and average yields are taken as neurons for input layer. The output layer is one neuron, i.e., yield.

The hidden layer has a different number of hidden neurons and is tested for optimum number of neurons. The optimum number of neurons in hidden layer and parameters of the model is determined by trial and error method. W_{ij} is the connecting weight between i^{th} input layer neuron to the jth hidden layer neuron. The V_{jk} is weight between the jth hidden layer neuron and the kth output layer neuron (in this case k=1). Momentum and learning rate are two main parameters for training, which takes care of steepest-descent convergence [71]. The final weighting factors are used to simulate relationship between crop yield and corresponding crop growth factors. The final weighting factors generated by the network trained model

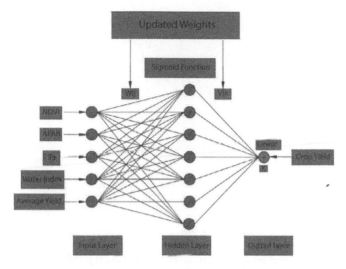

Figure 2.7 Architecture of the proposed FFBPNN model (original figure).

are saved for estimation of new data. The hidden layer neurons were varied between 1 and 30 in the developed models. Sigmoidal transfer function and linear activation functions are in hidden output layers. The code to develop the neural network is written in MATLAB programming language package.

The hidden layer receives data from the input neurons layer. In the hidden layer, inputs are multiplied by suitable weights and sums. The sigmoid transfer function was activated before the output layer. Mathematical expression linear transfer function is

$$x = \sum_{i=1}^{n} w_i x_i + b = w_1 x_1 + w_2 x_2 + w_3 x_3 + \ldots\ldots + w_n n + n \quad (2.5)$$

The output y is expressed as:

$$y = f(x) = f(\sum_{i-1}^{n}(w_i x_i + b) \quad (2.6)$$

where f is neuron activation or transfer function. The transfer function of each neuron in the network is a sigmoid transfer function and is given as

$$y = f(x) = \frac{1}{1 + e^{-x}} \quad (2.7)$$

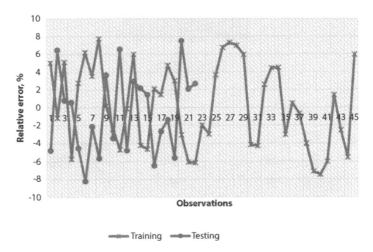

Figure 2.8 Relative error between observed and predicted crop yields of training and testing data during 2015 of paddy crop in *Kharif* season (original figure).

The neuron activation function was shown in Figure 2.8. The final form of the FFBPNN model with the substitution of weights is given as

$$Y = \frac{1}{1 + \exp[-(\sum_{j=1}^{q} V_{jk} H_{ij} - \gamma)]} \tag{2.8}$$

where Y = Yield per unit area, q = number of nodes in hidden layer, Vj = weight coefficient between j^{th} hidden and k^{th} output nodes, c = threshold of the output node.

2.6.1.2 Model Training

The trained ANN model recognizes the functional relationship between input parameters and desired outputs. The network training started with a random initiation of weights and proceeds and optimizes an error function (RMSE) [72, 73]. The generated weights by neural network saves and also remembers this functional relationship for further calculations. Yield estimation models are developed at the regional scale for paddy crops in *kharif* season. The right time stopping of the training of neural network is called because early stopping is an important step to avoid over fitting. To achieve this, the training, validation, and test set data were used to adjust the weights of neuron and bias, to stop the training process, and for external prediction respectively. Initially, 75% of the samples are selected randomly for the training, and the remaining 25% are used for testing to evaluate the model performance.

The data of different parameters have wide range of values. For uniformity and also to avoid the confusion of learning algorithm, all the input data are normalized before input layer to represent 0 as minimum and 1 as maximum values. The output results (yields) are converted back to the similar unit by a denormalization procedure. Learning rate, number of hidden nodes, and training tolerance were adjusted. The initial selected number of hidden nodes was equal to inputs i 1.

2.6.1.3   Model Validation

Four statistical parameters are used for performance analysis of the developed FFBPNN models, namely R^2, RMSE, MAE, and the R_{ratio}. These parameters are calculated using the testing data for finding out to optimize neural network. The criteria for optimum neural network are minimum RMSE, minimum MAE (Should be optimally 0), and the value of coefficient of determination is nearer to 1. The R_{ratio} is used to explain the models underprediction or overprediction of the simulated yield values. R_{ratio} that is less than 1 indicates underestimation, R_{ratio} that is more than 1 indicates overestimation. The relative error for each data point was also calculated. Additionally, the simulated values were plotted against the observed values and tested the statistical significance of parameters of regression analysis.

To achieve this, training, validation, and test set were used to adjust the weights and biases, to stop the training process and for external prediction, respectively. Initially, 75% of samples are randomly selected for training, and the remaining 25% are used for testing to evaluate the model performance. The selected four statistical parameters were used for performance analysis of the developed FFBPNN models. These parameters were calculated using the testing data for finding out optimized neural network. The normalized output results (yields) from the ANN model are converted into original values at the end. Relative error between the targeted and neural network model predicted yield values. All relative errors of the model obtained are smaller than 10% except for two readings. 85% of the relative errors between predicted and observed values are even smaller than 10%.

2.6.2   Results and Conclusions

Relative error between the targeted and neural network model predicted yield values is shown in Figure 2.8 for paddy and Figure 2.9 for sugarcane crop. Relative errors between the actual and neural network model

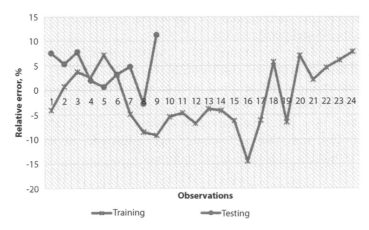

Figure 2.9 Relative error between observed and predicted crop yields of training and testing data during 2015 of sugarcane crop (original figure).

were calculated for all the values of observation. All relative errors of the model for paddy crop are smaller than 10% in case of paddy crop. Only two readings are above ±10% in the case of sugarcane crop. 85% of the relative errors between predicted and observed values are even smaller than 8%.

The normalized output results (yields) from the ANN model are converted into original values at the end. Mean Mandal wise average relative error between observed and model predicted crop yields are presented in Table 2.3. The highest mean error of a mandal was 6.166% (at Pedana). The lowest relative error was 0.133% (at Challapalle).

The statistical parameters of the training and testing for sugarcane were compared. The range of R^2 values were 0.946 and 0.967 for training and same for testing was 0.936 and 0.950 for paddy in *Kharif* and *Rabi* seasons (Table 2.4), whereas for sugarcane the values are 0.916 and 0.924 during testing and training, respectively. The highest MAE was 0.178 for Paddy (*Rabi*). The R_{ratio} values for paddy (*kharif*) crop were 1.063 and 1.065. The same for sugarcane, it is 1.006 and 0.556. The R_{ratio} values showed the underestimation of crop yield of sugarcane crop during testing. The RMSE values were 0.15 and 0.184 with sugarcane crop in the year 2015. The results indicated that the R^2 for testing is more than that for training, which means that the FFBPNN models performed better during testing. The simulations produced highly satisfactory output in all predictions. This indicates that a well-trained FFBPNN model can be successfully used for crop yield prediction.

Table 2.3 Sample and training result of FFBPNN yield prediction model of paddy crop in *Kharif* during 2015.

S. no.	Mandal name	Mean actual observed yield, kg/ha	FFBP NN predicted yield, kg/ha	Relative error (%)
1	Vijayawada rural	7440.96	7618.65	−2.388
2	Kankipadu	8028.28	8406.09	−4.706
3	Challapalle	6897.78	6906.95	−0.133
4	Pamarru	7617.60	7162.68	5.972
5	Vuyyuru	7595.52	7914.53	−4.20
6	Movva	7286.40	7623.40	−4.625
7	Thotlavalluru	6624.00	6485.03	2.098
8	Avanigada	5453.76	5374.90	1.446
9	Pamidimukkala	8765.76	8352.45	4.715
10	Guduru	8964.48	8513.84	5.027
11	Penamaluru	6853.62	6931.55	−1.137
12	Koduru	8854.08	8403.05	5.094
13	Pamarru	8589.12	9081.36	−5.731
14	Machilipatnam	8824.32	8582.00	2.746
15	Pedana	8311.36	7798.88	6.166
16	Mopidevi	6586.24	6354.08	3.525
17	Nagayalanka	7904.64	7890.10	0.184

Scatter plots of predicted yield and observed yield are shown in Figures 2.10 and 2.11. This shows that the points are equally distributed over 1:1 line and also in close agreement with an R^2 value of 0.9681 for paddy. There was wide scattering of yield points in case of sugarcane. There was an under estimation of yield in some cases of cane yield prediction. Although there was a deviation in crop yield prediction in few observations, the over-all accuracy of the model prediction was high. The R^2 value was high for

Table 2.4 Statistical analysis of neural network training and testing of season in different years.

Year	Training				Testing			
	RMSE	R_{ratio}	MAE	R^2	RMSE	R_{ratio}	MAE	R^2
Paddy (*Kharif*)	0.117	1.063	0.095	0.946	0.108	1.065	0.085	0.936
Paddy (*Rabi)*	0.125	0.987	0.108	0.967	0.317	0.620	0.178	0.950
Sugarcane	0.150	1.006	0.119	0.916	0.184	0.556	0.143	0.924

paddy compared with sugarcane crop. However, a slight underestimation of yield of the sugarcane crop indicates that sensitivity of yield algorithms to crop input parameters may be further improved by changing the input parameters.

It is also observed during the study that for the model, the RMSE decreased with increased number of hidden nodes from 1 to [i + 1], where "i" is the number of input layer nodes (i = 5). Further, R^2 increased and MAE decreased with the increased the number of hidden nodes from 1 to [i + 1], in all the years. The results are in accordance with researchers [74–76]. After 20 hidden nodes, the trails are conducted at a step of 10. After a number of trials with 100 to 10,000 epochs with each step of 100

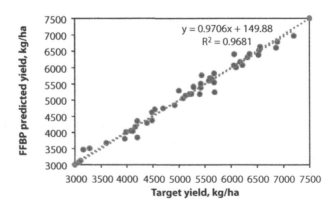

Figure 2.10 Scatter plots of actual and FFBP NN model predicted yield of sugarcane during 2015 (original figure).

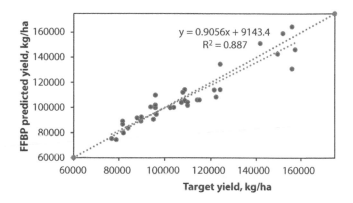

Figure 2.11 Scatter plots of actual and FFBP NN model predicted yield of sugarcane during 2015 (original figure).

up to 2000 and a step of 1000 up to 10000, better results are found at 1000 epochs for most of the cases. Although the performance increased after i+1, the computation time increased with increase in the number of nodes and epochs. The smaller the data sets, the lesser hidden nodes requirement and lower learning rates in the optimized model is observed [62]. The best performance of the models was observed at i+1 and i+2 hidden nodes. Statistical analysis revealed that the reliability of the model in crop yield estimation. The final predicted yield map of paddy and sugarcane during 2015 are shown in Figures 2.12 and 2.13. Paddy yields in the study area varied from 3.25 t/ha to 6.6 t/ha. The sugarcane yields were ranged between 70000 kg/ha and 125,000 kg/ha.

There was an underestimation of yield in some cases of cane yield prediction. Although there was a deviation in crop yield prediction in few observations, the overall accuracy of the model prediction was high. The model prediction accuracy may be further improved by changing the input parameters. Sugarcane crop is sensitive to leaf area index (LAI), and number of stalks per meter [77]. A stronger relationship exists between sugarcane yield and rainfall. Total soil available water is an important indicator of yield. Another important point, which differs yield prediction, is input parameter as average yield. In case of sugarcane, the input is given as average of plant and ratoon for the 3 years. The improvement of model was not attempted because of the nonavailability of the data on sugarcane crop-sensitive parameters, like the number of stalks per meter and total soil available water.

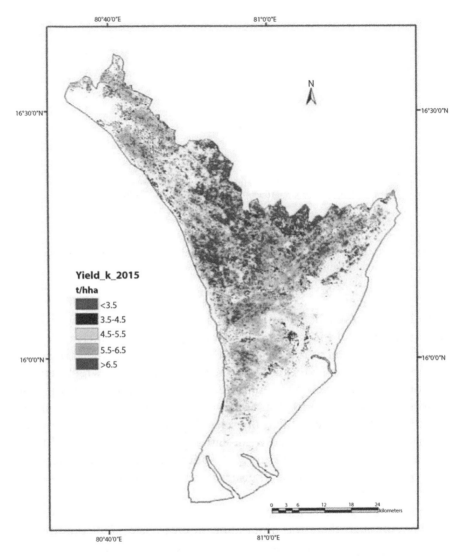

Figure 2.12 Final predicted yield map of paddy during 2015 (original figure).

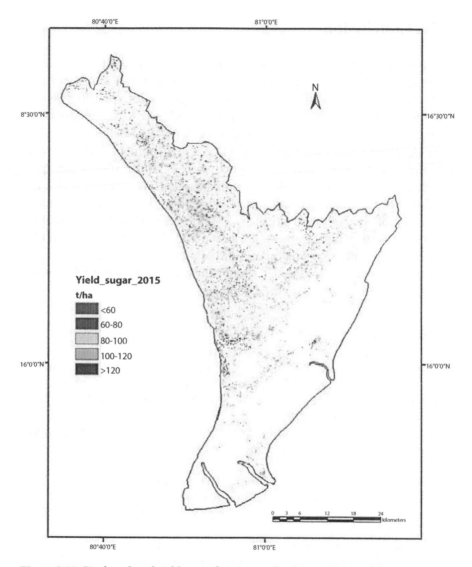

Figure 2.13 Final predicted yield map of sugarcane during 2015 (original figure).

2.7   Conclusion

The present study conducted with an aim to test the ability of machine learning algorithm in integration with remote sensing in crop yield prediction of paddy and sugarcane crops at regional level. Crop-sensitive parameters extracted from high-resolution LANDSAT 8 OLI imageries are used as neural network model inputs. The FFBPNN models for crop yield were developed and calibrated in MATLAB environment. During training, the model perceptrons were trained with 75 of the 100 inputs up to 10,000 epochs with 1 to 10 hidden neurons. Statistical analysis revealed the reliability of the model in paddy yield estimation. However, slight under estimation of yield of the sugarcane crop indicates sensitivity of yield algorithms to crop input parameters. It was concluded that there is a high efficacy of using remote sensing images and NN models to generate accurate crop yield maps and also revealed significant superiority of neural network models over conventional methods.

References

1. Adams, R.M., Hurd, B.H., Lenhart, S., Leary, N., Effects of global climate change on agriculture: an interpretative review. *Clim. Res.*, *11*, 1, 19–30, 1998.
2. Patel, P., Agriculture drones are finally cleared for takeoff [News]. *IEEE Spectr.*, *53*, 11, 13–14, 2016.
3. Tokekar, P., Vander Hook, J., Mulla, D., Isler, V., Sensor planning for a symbiotic UAV and UGV system for precision agriculture. *IEEE Trans. Rob.*, *32*, 6, 1498–1511, 2016.
4. Alsalam, B.H.Y., Morton, K., Campbell, D., Gonzalez, F., Autonomous UAV with vision based on-board decision making for remote sensing and precision agriculture, in: *2017 IEEE Aerospace Conference*, pp. 1–12, p. IEEE, 2017.
5. Gevaert, C.M., Suomalainen, J., Tang, J., Kooistra, L., Generation of spectral–temporal response surfaces by combining multispectral satellite and hyperspectral UAV imagery for precision agriculture applications. *IEEE J. Sel. Top. Appl. Earth Obs. Remote Sens.*, *8*, 6, 3140–3146, 2015.
6. Gómez-Candón, D., De Castro, A.I., López-Granados, F., Assessing the accuracy of mosaics from unmanned aerial vehicle (UAV) imagery for precision agriculture purposes in wheat. *Precis. Agric.*, *15*, 1, 44–56, 2014.
7. Sarle, W.S., Neural networks and statistical models, *Proceedings of the Nineteenth Annual SAS Users Group International Conference*, pp. 1538–1550, 1994.
8. Hsu, K.L., Gupta, H.V., Sorooshian, S., Artificial neural network modelling of the rainfall-runoff process. *Water Resour. Res.*, *31*, 10, 2517–2530, 1995.

9. Zou, J., Han, Y., So, S.S., Overview of artificial neural networks, in: *Artificial Neural Networks*, pp. 14–22, 2008.

10. Lent, R., Azevedo, F.A., Andrade-Moraes, C.H., Pinto, A.V., How many neurons do you have? Some dogmas of quantitative neuroscience under revision. *Eur. J. Neurosci.*, 35, 1, 1–9, 2012.

11. Wang, J., Tsapakis, I., Zhong, C., A space–time delay neural network model for travel time prediction. *Eng. Appl. Artif. Intell.*, 52, 145–160, 2016.

12. Demuth, H., Beale, M., Hagan, M., *Neural Network Toolbox User's Guide*, The MathWorks, Inc, Natick, MA, USA, 2017.

13. Park, J., Yi, D., Ji, S., A Novel Learning Rate Schedule in Optimization for Neural Networks and It's Convergence. *Symmetry*, 12, 660, 2020.

14. Mohamed, Z.E., Using the artificial neural networks for prediction and validating solar radiation. *J. Egypt. Math. Soc.*, 27, 1, 1–13, 2019.

15. Garg, B., Kirar, N., Menon, S., Sah, T., A performance comparison of different back propagation neural networks methods for forecasting wheat production. *CSI Trans. ICT*, 4, 2-4, 305–311, 2016.

16. Maladkar, K., *6 Types of Artificial Neural Networks Currently Being Used in Machine Learning*, analyticsindia, 2019. [Online]. Available: https://www.analyticsindiamag.com/..

17. Park, S., Im, J., Park, S., Yoo, C., Han, H., Rhee, J., Classification and mapping of paddy rice by combining Landsat and SAR time series data. *Remote Sens.*, 10, 3, 447, 2018.

18. Zhang, M., Lin, H., Wang, G., Sun, H., Fu, J., Mapping paddy rice using a convolutional neural network (CNN) with Landsat 8 datasets in the Dongting Lake Area, China. *Remote Sens.*, 10, 11, 1840, 2018.

19. Wang, M., Wang, J., Chen, L., Mapping Paddy Rice Using Weakly Supervised Long Short-Term Memory Network with Time Series Sentinel Optical and SAR Images. *Agriculture*, 10, 10, 483, 2020.

20. Wu, Y. and Xu, L., Crop Organ Segmentation and Disease Identification Based on Weakly Supervised Deep Neural Network. *Agronomy*, 9, 11, 737, 2019.

21. Pourdarbani, R., Sabzi, S., García-Amicis, V.M., García-Mateos, G., Molina-Martínez, J.M., Ruiz-Canales, A., Automatic classification of chickpea varieties using computer vision techniques. *Agronomy*, 9, 11, 672, 2019.

22. Li, Y. and Chao, X., ANN-Based Continual Classification in Agriculture. *Agriculture*, 10, 5, 178, 2020.

23. Zhang, M., Lin, H., Wang, G., Sun, H., Fu, J., Mapping paddy rice using a convolutional neural network (CNN) with Landsat 8 datasets in the Dongting Lake Area, China. *Remote Sens.*, 10, 11, 1840, 2018.

24. Kussul, N., Lavreniuk, M., Skakun, S., Shelestov, A., Deep learning classification of land cover and crop types using remote sensing data. *IEEE Geosci. Remote Sens. Lett.*, 14, 5, 778–782, 2017.

25. Sun, Z., Di, L., Fang, H., Using long short-term memory recurrent neural network in land cover classification on Landsat and Cropland data layer time series. *Int. J. Remote Sens.*, 40, 2, 593–614, 2019.

26. Garg, B., Kirar, N., Menon, S., Sah, T., A performance comparison of different back propagation neural networks methods for forecasting wheat production. *CSI Trans. ICT*, *4*, 2-4, 305–311, 2016.
27. Ghazi, M.M., Yanikoglu, B., Aptoula, E., Plant identification using deep neural networks via optimization of transfer learning parameters. *Neurocomputing*, *235*, 228–235, 2017.
28. Xie, C., Wang, R., Zhang, J., Chen, P., Dong, W., Li, R., Chen, H., Multi-level learning features for automatic classification of field crop pests. *Comput. Electron. Agric.*, *152*, 233–241, 2018.
29. Koirala, A., Walsh, K.B., Wang, Z., Anderson, N., Deep Learning for Mango (Mangiferaindica) Panicle Stage Classification. *Agronomy*, *10*, 1, 143, 2020.
30. Zhu, M., Liu, S., Xia, Z., Wang, G., Hu, Y., Liu, Z., Crop Growth Stage GPP-Driven Spectral Model for Evaluation of Cultivated Land Quality Using GA-BPNN. *Agriculture*, *10*, 8, 318, 2020.
31. Sharma, N., Chakrabarti, A., Balas, V.E., *Advances in Intelligent Systems and Computing*, vol. 1016, pp. 311–324, Springer, Singapore, 2020.
32. Liu, S., Peng, Y., Xia, Z., Hu, Y., Wang, G., Zhu, A.-X., Liu, Z., The GA-BPNN-Based Evaluation of Cultivated Land Quality in the PSR Framework Using Gaofen-1 Satellite Data. *Sensors*, *19*, 5127, 2019.
33. Martineau, M., Conte, D., Raveaux, R., Arnault, I., Munier, D., Venturini, G., A survey on image-based insect classification. *Pattern Recognit.*, *65*, 273–284, 2017.
34. Wang, J., Lin, C., Ji, L., Liang, A., A new automatic identification system of insect images at the order level. *Knowl. Based Syst.*, *33*, 102–110, 2012.
35. Ferentinos, K., Deep learning models for plant disease detection and diagnosis. *Comput. Electron. Agric.*, *145*, 311–318, 2018.
36. Lu, Y., Yi, S., Zeng, N., Liu, Y., Zhang, Y., Identification of rice diseases using deep convolutional neural networks. *Neurocomputing*, *267*, 378–384, 20172017.
37. Knoll, F.J., Czymmek, V., Harders, L.O., Hussmann, S., Real-time classification of weeds in organic carrot production using deep learning algorithms. *Comput. Electron. Agric.*, *167*, 105097, 2019.
38. Przybylak, A., Kozłowski, R., Osuch, E., Osuch, A., Rybacki, P., Przygodziński, P., Quality Evaluation of Potato Tubers Using Neural Image Analysis Method. *Agriculture*, *10*, 112, 2020.
39. Li, Y. and Yang, J., Few-shot cotton pest recognition and terminal realization. *Comput. Electron. Agric.*, *169*, 105240, 2020.
40. Chatterjee, S., Dey, N., Sen, S., Soil moisture quantity prediction using optimized neural supported model for sustainable agricultural applications. *Sustain. Comput. Inform. Syst.*, 28, 100279, 2018.
41. Almomani, F., Prediction of biogas production from chemically treated co-digested agricultural waste using artificial neural network. *Fuel*, 280, 118573, 2020.

42. Abraham, E.R., dos Reis, J.G.M., Colossetti, A.P., de Souza, A.E., Toloi, R.C., Neural Network System to Forecast the Soybean Exportation on Brazilian Port of Santos. *Advances in Production Management Systems. The Path to Intelligent, Collaborative and Sustainable Manufacturing*, pp. 83–90, 2017.

43. Abraham, E.R., Mendes dos Reis, J.G., Vendrametto, O., Oliveira Costa Neto, P.L.D., Carlo Toloi, R., Souza, A.E.D., Oliveira Morais, M.D., Time Series Prediction with Artificial Neural Networks: An Analysis Using Brazilian Soybean Production. *Agriculture*, 10, 10, 475, 2020.

44. Liu, G., Yang, X., Li, M., An Artificial Neural Network Model for Crop Yield Responding to Soil Parameters, in: *Advances in Neural Network*, vol. 3498, pp. 1017–1021, 2020.

45. García-Martínez, H., Flores-Magdaleno, H., Ascencio-Hernández, R., Khalil-Gardezi, A., Tijerina-Chávez, L., Mancilla-Villa, O.R., Vázquez-Peña, M.A., Corn Grain Yield Estimation from Vegetation Indices, Canopy Cover, Plant Density, and a Neural Network Using Multispectral and RGB Images Acquired with Unmanned Aerial Vehicles. *Agriculture*, 10, 7, 277, 2020.

46. Fieuzal, R., Marais Sicre, C., Baup, F., Estimation of corn yield using multi-temporal optical and radar satellite data and artificial neural networks. *Int. J. Appl. Earth Obs. Geoinf.*, 57, 14–23, 20172017.

47. Michelon, G.K., Menezes, P.L., de Bazzi, C.L., Jasse, E.P., Magalhães, P.S.G., Borges, L.F., Artificial neural networks to estimate the productivity of soybeans and corn by chlorophyll readings. *J. Plant Nutr.*, 41, 1285–1292, 2018.

48. Olson, D., Chatterjee, A., Franzen, D.W., Day, S.S., Relationship of Drone-Based Vegetation Indices with Corn and Sugarbeet Yields. *Agron. J.*, 111, 2545–2557, 2019.

49. Khaki, S., Khalilzadeh, Z., Wang, L., Predicting yield performance of parents in plant breeding: A neural collaborative filtering approach. *PloS One*, 15, 5, e0233382, 2020.

50. Jeong, J.H., Resop, J.P., Mueller, N.D., Fleisher, D.H., Yun, K., Butler, E.E., *et al.*, Random forests for global and regional crop yield predictions. *PloS One*, 11, e0156571, 2016.

51. Krupavathi, K., Raghu Babu, M., Mani, A., Parasad, P.R.K., Edukondal, L., Seed to Seed: Application of Remote Sensing in Complete Monitoring of Sugarcane Crop at Regional Level, in: *Research Trends in Agriculture Sciences*, vol. 25, pp. 35–59, Akinik publications, Delhi, India, 2020.

52. Ferencz, C., Bognár, P., Lichtenberger, J., Hamar, D., Tarcsai, G., Timár, G., Molnár, G., Pásztor, S., Steinbach, P., Székely, B., Ferencz, O.E., Ferencz-Árkos, I., Crop yield estimation by satellite remote sensing. *Int. J. Remote Sens.*, 25, 4113–4149, 2004.

53. Prasad, A.K., Chai, L., Singh, R.P., Kafatos, M., Crop yield estimation model for Iowa using remote sensing and surface parameters. *Int. J. Appl. Earth Obs. Geoinf.*, 8, 1, 26–33, 2006.

54. Singh, R. A. N. D. H. I. R., Semwal, D.P., Rai, A., Chhikara, R.S., Small area estimation of crop yield using remote sensing satellite data. *Int. J. Remote Sens.*, 23, 1, 49–56, 2002.

55. Quarmby, N.A., Milnes, M., Hindle, T.L., Silleos, N., The use of multi-temporal NDVI measurements from AVHRR data for crop yield estimation and prediction. *Int. J. Remote Sens.*, 14, 2, 199–210, 1993.

56. Unganai, L.S. and Kogan, F.N., Drought monitoring and corn yield estimation in Southern Africa from AVHRR data. *Remote Sens. Environ.*, 63, 3, 219–232, 1998.

57. Zhou, X., Zheng, H.B., Xu, X.Q., He, J.Y., Ge, X.K., Yao, X., Cheng, T., Zhu, Y., Cao, W.X., Tian, Y.C., "Predicting grain yield in rice using multi-temporal vegetation indices from UAV-based multispectral and digital imagery. *ISPRS J. Photogramm. Remote Sens.*, 130, 246–255, 2017.

58. Bastiaanssen, W.G. and Ali, S., A new crop yield forecasting model based on satellite measurements applied across the Indus Basin, Pakistan. *Agric. Ecosyst. Environ.*, 94, 3, 321–340, 2003.

59. Sapkota, T.B., Jat, M.L., Jat, R.K., Kapoor, P., Stirling, C., Yield estimation of food and non-food crops in smallholder production systems, in: *Methods for measuring greenhouse gas balances and evaluating mitigation options in smallholder agriculture*, pp. 163–174, 2016.

60. Hooda, R.S., Yadav, M., Kalubarme, M.H., Wheat production estimation using remote sensing data: An Indian experience, in: *Workshop Proceedings: Remote Sensing Support to Crop Yield Forecast and Area Estimates*, Stresa, Italy, vol. 30, pp. 85–89, 2006.

61. Kumhalova, J., Zemek, F., Novak, P., Brovkina, O., Mayerovaa, M., Use of Landsat images for yield evaluation within a small plot. *Plant Soil Environ.*, 60, 11, 501–506, 2014.

62. Kaul, M., Hill, R.L., Walthall, C., Artificial neural networks for corn and soybean yield prediction. *Agric. Syst.*, 85, 1, 1–18, 2005.

63. Jiang, D., Yang, X., Clinton, N., Wang, N., An artificial neural network model for estimating crop yields using remotely sensed information. *Int. J. Remote Sens.*, 25, 9, 1723–1732, 2004.

64. Patel, N.R., Bhattacharjee, B., Mohammed, A.J., Tanupriya, B., Saha, S.K., Remote sensing of regional yield assessment of wheat in Haryana, India. *Int. J. Remote Sens.*, 27, 19, 4071–4090, 2006.

65. Sims, D.A., Parallel adjustments in vegetation greenness and ecosystem CO_2 exchange in response to drought in a Southern California chaparral ecosystem. *Remote Sens. Environ.*, 103, 3, 289–303, 2005.

66. Peng, Z., Hu, M., Liu, Y., Application of RS and GIS Technique to Estimate Regional Water-saving Potentiality, 2007.

67. Singh, R.K. and Prajneshu, Artificial Neural Network Methodology for Modelling and Forecasting Maize Crop Yield. *Agric. Econ. Res. Rev.*, 21, 1, 152–156, 2008.

68. Poblete-Echeverría, C., Espinace, D., Sepúlveda-Reyes, D., Zúñiga, M., Sanchez, M., Analysis of crop water stress index (CWSI) for estimating

stem water potential in grapevines: Comparison between natural reference and baseline approaches, in: *VIII International Symposium on Irrigation of Horticultural Crops*, vol. 1150, pp. 189–194, 2015.

69. Gowda, P.H., Jose, L., Paul, D.C., Steve, R.C., Terry, A.E., Judy, H., Tolk, A., ET mapping for agricultural water management: present status and challenges. *Irrig. Sci.*, 26, 23–237, 2008.

70. Wart, J.V., Kersebaum, K.C., Peng, S., Milner, M., Cassman., K.G., Estimating crop yield potential at regional to national scales. *Field Crops Res.*, 143, 34–4, 2013.

71. Sirisha, A., Raghuwanshi, N.S., Mishra, A., Tiwari, M.K., Evapotranspiration Modeling Using Second-Order Neural Networks. *J. Hydrol. Eng.*, 19, 6, 1131–1140, 2014.

72. Martí, P. and Gasque, M., Ancillary data supply strategies for improvement of temperature-based ETo ANN models. *Agric. Water Manage.*, 97, 7, 939–955, 2010.

73. Tabari, H., Marofi, S., Sabziparvar, A.A., Estimation of daily pan evaporation using artificial neural network and multivariate nonlinear regression. *Irrig. Sci.*, 28, 5, 399–406, 2010.

74. Kumar, M., Raghuwanshi, N.S., Singh, R., Wallender, W.W., Pruitt, W.O., Estimating evapotranspiration using artificial neural network. *J. Irrig. Drain. Eng.*, 128, 4, 224–233, 2002.

75. Uno, Y., Prasher, S.O., Lacroix, R., Goel, P.K., Karimi, Y., Viau, A., Artificial neural networks to predict corn yield from Compact Airborne Spectrographic Imager data. *Comput. Electron. Agric.*, 47, 2, 149–161, 2005.

76. Prasad, A.K., Chai, L., Ramesh, P.S., Kafatos, M., Crop yield estimation model for Iowa using remote sensing and surface parameters. *Int. J. Appl. Earth Obs. Geoinf.*, 8, 26–33, 2006.

77. Simoes, M.D., Rocha, S.J.V., Lamparelli, R.A.C., Spectral variables, growth analysis and yield of sugarcane. *Sci. Agric.*, 62, 3, 199–207, 2005.

3

Smart Irrigation Systems Using Machine Learning and Control Theory

Meriç Çetin[1] and Selami Beyhan[2*]

[1]Pumukkale University, Department of Computer Engineering, Kinikli Campus, Denizli, Turkey
[2]Izmir Democracy University, Department of Electrical and Electronics Engineering, Uckuyular Dist., Gursel Aksel Blv., Karabağlar, Izmir, Turkey

Abstract

Intelligent irrigation systems have recently gained importance in terms of efficient cultivation of plants and the correct use of water on earth. Therefore, studies, such as plant growth modeling, irrigation modeling, and control continue, in this field. Plant growth modeling creates the infrastructure for the most accurate irrigation and fertilization activities in terms of crop yield. In addition, irrigation modeling and control is the efficient use of water resources to irrigate the entire plant system adequately. Machine learning (ML) methods are very suitable for modeling and prediction, and many studies have been done in the literature for plant growth modeling and irrigation. On the other hand, control theory methods ensure that the desired irrigation amount is made precisely. In addition, remote control approaches are an important step that facilitates irrigation systems. In this study, it is explained how ML and control methods are used in plant growth modeling and irrigation systems. In addition, current problems are discussed at the end then possible future implementation of the new approaches are explained at the end of the chapter.

Keywords: Smart irrigation systems, control theory, machine learning

Corresponding author: selami.beyhan@idu.edu.tr

Roheet Bhatnagar, Nitin Kumar Tripathi, Nitu Bhatnagar and Chandan Kumar Panda (eds.)
The Digital Agricultural Revolution: Innovations and Challenges in Agriculture through Technology Disruptions, (57–86) © 2022 Scrivener Publishing LLC

3.1   Machine Learning for Irrigation Systems

The models used for irrigation decision systems in the literature are investigated, and the transition to smart irrigation systems is evaluated through machine learning (ML) and control theory perspective. Machine learning is a definition given to computational models developed to improve existing experiences and predict future experiences to perform a task [1]. The purpose of the ML methods is to express the environment with complex dynamics in machine language with artificial learning methods and to form a decision-making mechanism. The general learning structure [2] used in control applications based on ML methods can be considered as shown in Figure 3.1. In this structure, the learning algorithm extracts the necessary information to decide on the unknown situations using the training set. Learning techniques used to create a knowledge base include ANN, statistics learning, FL, Decision Tree (DT), genetic algorithms (GAs) methods, and so on, can be listed.

The ML techniques are generally categorized as: (i) supervised learning, (ii) unsupervised learning and (iii) reinforcement learning (RL). The aim of supervised learning, which includes algorithms, such as random forests (RFs), DTs, Bayesian networks, and regression analysis, is to match the variables with the desired output [2]. Unsupervised learning includes methods, such as ANNs, GAs, deep learning (DL), and clustering, and it is used for exploratory data analysis [3]. Reinforcement learning, evaluated in the unsupervised learning category, is an approximate solution of dynamic programming used in ML [4].

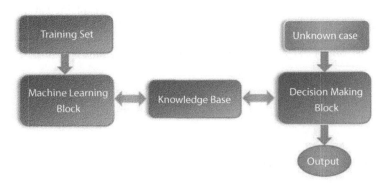

Figure 3.1 The general learning structure of ML systems.

In recent years, ML has started to be used extensively in multidisciplinary agricultural technologies. Many of these applications have focused on crop prediction, disease detection, crop quality, irrigation control, livestock management, water management, and soil management. Smart irrigation systems based on ML methods can be designed thanks to the models that are developed by including the parameters that form an effective irrigation system. Today, site-specific irrigation techniques that adapt to changing conditions are needed. Therefore, ML based applications that meet the improved accuracy and high efficiency criteria are increasing day by day. In this review, irrigation system applications based on ML techniques in the last years are systematically evaluated and summarized. The search procedure is limited to the following keywords to determine the conceptual limits of our review: RF, time series models (TSMs), regression trees, ANN, support vector machines (SVMs), adaptive-network based fuzzy inference systems, DL, RL, IoT-based automatic irrigation systems, wireless sensor networks, and so on.

It is important to evaluate the soil infiltration rate according to various infiltration models in irrigation systems. The performance of infiltration models in Kumar and Sihag [5] was compared using ML-based techniques (adaptive neuro-fuzzy inference system-ANFIS, and random forest regression-RF). In Goldstein et al. [6], periodic irrigation plans have been defined based on meteorology station, irrigation plan records, along with data collected with various sensors to monitor plant needs in real time. Different regression and classification algorithms were applied to the data set to design models predicting the periodic irrigation schedule. Among the compared models, gradient-boosted regression trees (GBRT) has been shown as the best regression model with 93% accuracy and Boosted Tree Classifier (BTC) has been shown as the best classification model with 95% accuracy. A similar study, which predicts evapotranspiration (ET_0) and offers ML models for proper irrigation planning, was proposed in Ponraj and Vigneswaran [7]. Multiple linear regression (MLR), RF and GBRT algorithms were compared for evapotranspiration forecast based on daily weather data. In Braga et al. [8], deep ML techniques, such as GBRT, RF and TSMs, have been evaluated to estimate the value of evapotranspiration. As a result of comparison, it was stated that multivariate models perform better than univariate techniques.

A water management mechanism based on the Hargreaves evapotranspiration (ET_0) expression has been presented in Torres et al. [9]. In that study, two different approaches were tested using statistical ML (multivariate relation vector machine [MVRVM] algorithm). These two methods are direct and indirect approaches. The difference of these two approaches is using weather parameter for computing the potential evapotranspiration (ET_o) with historical data. For comparing these methods, artificial neural network (ANN) has been used. After comparison, indirect approach has given more stable and robust results than direct method. In the study by Irukula [10], reinforcement learning method was used to make the crop system model adaptable, and it was aimed to minimize water use based on daily sensor data. In addition to this, a simulation model has been developed for corn crops by using crop parameters and environmental parameters in Decision Support System (DSS) structure. Furthermore, water usage has been reduced by using the Q learning algorithm to optimize daily irrigation.

Karandish and Simunek [11] have presented a smart system that estimates soil moisture based on weather forecasts and field data collected via a sensor node. Thanks to a proposed novel algorithm, the features of the decision support system on the server and node side were developed. By using this algorithm, optimum water usage is ensured and effective irrigation strategies can be developed.

In Navarro-Hell *et al.* [12], SIDSS which means Smart Irrigation Decision Support System has been mentioned and developed. The ML method (ANFIS-Adaptive-Network Based Fuzzy Inference Systems) used in this study estimates how much water is needed for plantation with the help of soil measurements and weather parameters collected by the nodes in the fields. In Sun *et al.* [13], reinforcement learning–based irrigation control method has been presented. The learning phase consists of simulations using real-data from the sensors. Because of the limited data, neural network models have been used for learning process.

An intelligent IoT-based automatic irrigation system was presented in Shekhar *et al.* [14]. In this system, which the farmer accesses the server via mobile phone, k-nn ML algorithm was run on Raspberry Pi3 to predict soil condition parameters and driven by the water pump Arduino according to the control signal. In the study by Kwok and Sun [15], by the help of ML, automatic irrigation system is developed in a large area, which contains different kinds of plants. The system consists of two parts as software and hardware. In the hardware part, the camera is used to take the pictures of the plant for plant recognition and software part, identification and classification of images and analysis of data is dealt by using the database, which includes soil moisture levels. The aim is to help people handle the irrigation system easily. In Goap *et al.* [16], several parameters (such as UV, soil moisture, air temperature, soil temperature, humidity, rainfall forecast, etc.) have been estimated to achieve optimum water usage targets by support vector regression (SVR) and k-means clustering-based smart irrigation management system.

In Keswani *et al.* [17], the water estimation based on ANN has been obtained using data from sensors in the independent IoT system. Similarly, an application conducted in India used a radial-based function-type neural network to estimate soil moisture hourly [18]. In Binas *et al.* [19], a development of optimization problem. which consists of environmental parameters and yields conditions, was presented using reinforcement learning. In Jha *et al.* [20], various agricultural applications carried out with methods, such as IoT, wireless communication, ML, Artificial Intelligence (AI), and DL are mentioned. In Suntaranont *et al.* [21], an irrigation DSS has been proposed to estimate the future level of water by using the ANN. In Sidhu *et al.* [22], traditional ML techniques have been designed to manage the water usage for production of rice. In addition, these techniques were compared using common regression performance parameters. Sharma *et al.* [2] have proposed a review about how agricultural topics are dealt with ML algorithms. In Fernández-López [23], a new approach has been proposed, which provides accurate and cost-effective estimated models for evapotranspiration with ML methods using only meteorological data.

In addition to traditional irrigation systems, there are also models using renewable energy sources. It is possible to power smart irrigation systems with renewable energy sources (RES). In Adenugba *et al.* [24], it was examined how to control and monitor such a system using IoT sensors and environmental data. In this context, the data collected through the web platform, developed to monitor the system remotely, were used in the radial-based function network (RBFN), and environmental conditions were estimated. In addition, computer vision and Fuzzy Logic Controller (FLC) were used for variable rate irrigation in a cultivated field in Chang and Lin [25]. In the study by Geetha and Priya [26], in smart agricultural irrigation, an expert irrigation planning has been proposed using WSNs, GSM, Android phone and fuzzy logic (FL) to optimize water use.

The findings of this review show that different ML-based technologies used for estimation and classification in the irrigation systems increase productivity in irrigation systems and overcome various difficulties, such as crop yield, soil, and disease management. Table 3.1 shows the abbreviations for ML techniques, and Table 3.2 summarizes the recent ML practices of the irrigation systems mentioned above.

Table 3.1 Abbreviations of machine learning techniques.

Abbreviation	Description
AN FIS	Adaptive Neuro-Fuzzy Inference System
RF	Random Forest
GBRT	Gradient Boosted Regression Tree
BTC	Boosted Tree Classifier
MLR	Multiple Linear Regression
TSM	Time Series Models
MVRVM	Multivariate Relevance Vector Machine
RL	Reinforcement Learning
SVM	Support Vector Machine
PLRS	Partial Least Square Regression
Knn	K-nearest neighbor
SVR	Support Vector Regression
FL	Fuzzy Logic
ANN	Artificial Neural Network
DT	Decision Tree
CaRT	Classification and Regression Tree
MV	Machine Vision

3.2   Control Theory for Irrigation Systems

In this section, classical and advanced control methods applied to irrigation systems are investigated. Studies involving Proportional-Integral-Derivative (PID) control, FLC, Sliding-Mode Control (SMC), and Model Predictive Control (MPC) methods, neural-network control, primarily on-off control, are included. Model predictive control method has been preferred frequently because of its predictive and robust structure. The remote control strategies are also added because of ease application of designed control methods. Nowadays, eventhough the LAN/WLAN/WSN-based

Table 3.2 Recent machine learning practices of the irrigation systems.

Reference	Machine learning algorithm	Findings
[5]	ANFIS, RF	The proposed model is simple and suitable for field use. When ANFIS and RF performance were compared, it was seen that RF was more powerful in representing the soil infiltration rate.
[6]	GBRT, BTC	In predicting irrigation decisions, it is presented that nonparametric GBRT and BTC are more accurate than linear regression models, with 93% and 95% success rates, respectively.
[7]	MLR, GBRT, RF	The pre-processed gradient boost regression model has been found to be more successful in predicting reference evapotranspiration (ETo) than MLR, RF models.
[8]	GBRT, RF, TSM	It was stated that multivariate models perform better than univariate techniques.
[9]	MVRMV	Indirect approach has been observed to give more stable and robust results compared with the direct method.
[10]	RL	Thanks to the proposed RL controller, almost 40% decrease in water consumption was achieved compared with the constant irrigation method.
[11]	MLR, ANFIS, SVM	Both ANFIS and SVM models performed well when there was lack of input data and for water stress conditions.
[12]	ANFIS, PLSR	It has been concluded that the use of ML techniques can predict the irrigation needs of a crop by using the weather and soil variables.

(Continued)

Table 3.2 Recent machine learning practices of the irrigation systems. (*Continued*)

Reference	Machine learning algorithm	Findings
[13]	RL	Given both crop yield and water expense for geographic locations and crop types, net return has increased significantly.
[14]	Knn	The developed smart IoT-based automatic irrigation system has reduced water use and dependence on human resources.
[16]	SVR, KMC	The combined usage of the SVR and k-means approaches lower error and higher accuracy than their separate usage.
[17]	ANN, FL	It was stated that the gradient descent-based optimization approach with variable learning rate in soil moisture content estimation is more successful than ANN.
[18]	ANN, FL	Fuzzy logic-based irrigation control compensated for water loss through evapotranspiration, taking into account air, soil, water, and crop data.
[19]	RL	Reinforcement learning approach can be used to achieve yield maximization under harsh environmental conditions (limited space, over-temperature or water supply limitations).
[20]	ANN	It is recommended to build an IoT and ML-based system to automate practices in agriculture.
[21]	ANN, FL	The water level has been predicted with high accuracy.
[22]	SVR, DT, RF	In the ML models, irrigation demand for the crop is calculated using weather parameters.

(*Continued*)

Table 3.2 Recent machine learning practices of the irrigation systems. (*Continued*)

Reference	Machine learning algorithm	Findings
[2]	RL	The proposed ML framework for sustainable agricultural supply chains (ASCs) provide analytical data for decision-making structure.
[23]	SVR, CaRT, ANN, K*, M5 algorithms	It has been stated that the classification based on the K* algorithm used to estimate ET_o is more successful than ANN.
[24]	RBFN	The applicability of the IoT based approach has been proven for the smart irrigation system powered by solar energy and water saving has been achieved with the developed AI algorithm.
[25]	FL, MV	An average of 90% or higher classification success was achieved in real-time experimental results.
[26]	FL	The proposed system offers low manual labor cost and effective usage for irrigation with android application in real-time applications.

remote control approaches are constructed more; GSM/GPS-based remote control methods have been extensively applied from the beginning.

3.2.1   Application Literature

Control methods are interdisciplinary approaches developed to control the dynamic systems and have important role in complex decision-making processes. Irrigation control systems can be designed as open-loop or closed-loop controller mechanism as shown in Figure 3.2.

Although open loop controllers have less costs, they do not offer the most appropriate solution to the irrigation problem, because they cannot respond to disturbances. However, closed-loop controllers have a feedback mechanism that ensures the irrigation process continues correctly. Today,

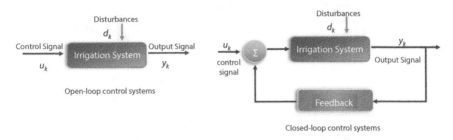

Figure 3.2 The control mechanisms of the irrigation systems.

closed-loop automatic irrigation control systems are preferred for the sustainable usage of water resources [27]. In such a closed-loop system, measuring various variables that determine the plant water content is helpful in calculating the next irrigation amount. Some of the irrigation control techniques mentioned in the literature are related to physical models in terms of various factors, such as crop phenology, soil physics, and hydrology [28, 29]. Irrigation decisions are mostly based on inferences associated with these models. In addition, "on-off," rule-based, model-based, optimal, adaptive, predictive, heuristic, remote methods or decision support mechanisms are also used for the irrigation systems.

Decision support systems (DSSs) are used extensively to maximize efficiency in irrigation and water conservation issues. The DSSs, which have an application area in environmental management issues, were first introduced in 1985 for the water resources management [30]. Advanced technology tools related to smart management of water resources through a multiagent approach or a fuzzy approach have been presented in van Oel *et al.* and Chen and Paydar [31, 32], respectively. An application of automatic irrigation system to improve irrigation was designed using the fuzzy decision support system in Giusti and Marsili-Libelli [33]. In a study by Torres-Sanchez *et al.* [34], an alternative to traditional irrigation management through automatic learning systems has been proposed, and various learning techniques have been examined to determine goodness or error according to expert decision.

In applications where on-off control is used, the output of controller is changed between limit values according to the error. Many traditional methods used for irrigation control are not effective because they are based on on-off control methods [35]. In addition to the on-off methods, new approach in designing the sensor with precision modified Proportional-Integral-Derivative (PID) controller has been achieved in Goodchild *et al.* [36] and association between dielectric tensiometer and PID controller in irrigation system can be explained in a clear way on daily water usage. In Goodchild *et al.* [37], modified PID controller has been used. The observations have shown that PID controller has given quick responses under unexpected conditions. In a study by Harper [38], by simulating the one-dimensional water usage, bang-bang controller, and PID controller was compared and PID controller gave better solution in usage of water, but it jeopardized moisture of soil. A fixing idea is to change the target of the controller to get rid of the damage on plants. In a study by Levidow *et al.* [39], the main topic is the developing new insight that enables to decrease the usage of water in irrigation systems when reaching the maximum efficiency on the production and crop quality.

The structure of artificial neural network, which is frequently preferred for applications, such as classification, estimation, clustering, regression, is also used in irrigation system applications. There are many artificial neural network-based irrigation system applications in the literature. Some of these are: prediction applications that work integrated with IoT systems [18, 21], renewable energy-based applications [40], wireless communication applications [41], ML applications [42, 43], and deep learning applications [20]. Fuzzy systems, which have great applicability in the agricultural field, are often preferred to solve the problem in irrigation [44]. In systems requiring variable speed irrigation, fuzzy models can be used to increase efficiency. Fuzzy models provided more flexible results than traditional methods thanks to the decision, control, diagnosis, and classification capabilities. Therefore, irrigation planning through fuzzy models is considered to be very effective [45]. The fuzzy logic method used in Kia *et al.* [35] was compared with the two methods, which are on-off with hysterics, simple on-off controllers, respectively. This paper also stated that FLC is easier to usage and less expensive in irrigation systems. In fuzzy inference system proposed by Almeida *et al.* [46], environmental factors, such as the usage of water, drought, the index of water exploration, the density of population, the index of wastewater treatment, were examined. In Mendes *et al.* [47], it is stated that an intelligent precision irrigation can be done using fuzzy inference system and central pivot irrigation system maps can be created with remote sensing measurements and accessing methods. In Patil *et al.* [48], by collecting and using sensors data from soil moisture and leaf wetness in fuzzy logic controller system, reduction of water usage was aimed. An irrigation control mechanism based on fuzzy logic using weather data was presented in Mohapatra *et al.* [18].

Many studies have shown that conventional methods (on-off or PID controllers) are not suitable for effective control of the irrigation systems [49, 50]. In recent years, model-based control strategies (predictive control, adaptive control) have been proposed to overcome this [29, 51, 52]. The model predictive control strategy aims to minimize a cost function to estimate the mathematical evolution of the system [53]. The preference of model-based methods in the control of irrigation systems has led to the development of sensitive agricultural practices [54, 55]. In Delgoda *et al.* [29], a robust model predictive mechanism has been designed for irrigation control. Using that model, both the uncertainty in the weather forecast has been mitigated, and direct measurements of variables have been included in the model. To achieve the desired root zone soil moisture deficit in difficult conditions, the new approach on model predictive control is proposed with real-time data in Guo and You [56]. A central model predictive controller was proposed in Shahdany *et al.* [57] to manage water with both surface irrigation methods and modern irrigation systems. As others, the aim is in Lozoya *et al.* [58] to reduce the water used by using the automatic irrigation system in real time. The difference is that applying the water in an appropriate time in right places by controlling some parameters, which are moisture of the soil and climatic factors. Set-point tracking and incorporated input output constraints in soil moisture are became an important parameters to construct the model predictive controller in Saleem *et al.* [59] unlike other papers which mentioned above. The parameters in dynamics of the soil and gained data models have been used to form a model for uncertainties in estimated errors on evapotranspiration and precipitation in Shang *et al.* [52, 60]. Moreover using the past data, new design of uncertainties have been developed and used to train. Besides, heuristic approaches are also used to model the water balance [61]. For example, a heuristic algorithm for designing a pressurized water distribution network has been proposed in Gonçalves *et al.* [62]. There are also studies that propose sliding-mode control to regulate the water content in soil using the Richards equation among model-based applications [63].

Generally, in irrigation systems, the process is considered as a closed-loop feedback control problem as shown in Figure 3.3. Model-based controllers are needed in closed loop control system due to factors such as climate factor, plant type, irrigation methods, variable system parameters, where, the controller is directly depend on the control algorithm through feedback mechanism. For more precise results in the irrigation systems, considering a closed-loop structure that summarizes the abovementioned literature, adaptive mechanisms can be incorporated into the feedback structure.

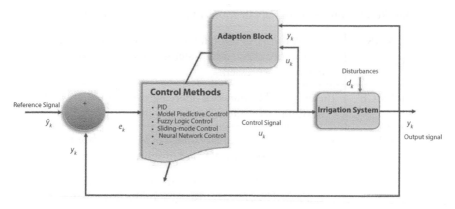

Figure 3.3 Control diagram of the irrigation system.

The abbreviations of control theory techniques are given in Table 3.3 and the findings of the control theory applications in irrigation systems are summarized in Table 3.4.

Table 3.3 Abbreviations of control theory techniques.

Abbreviation	Description
DSS	Decision Support System
MAS	Multi Agent Simulation
FMCE	Fuzzy Multi-Criteria Evaluation
FDSS	Fuzzy Decision Support System
FLC	Fuzzy Logic Control
PID	Proportional-Integral-Derivative
LaNN	Laguerre Neural Networks
GA	Genetic Algorithm
FDMM	Fuzzy Decision-Making Method
FIS	Fuzzy Inference System
MPC	Model Predictive Control
SMC	Sliding Mode Control
MH	Meta-Heuristic

Table 3.4 Recent control theory applications of the irrigation systems.

[31]	MAS	By using the MAS model, the variability between water availability affected by water use in a river basin is correctly expressed.
[32]	FMCE	The proposed framework offered greater simplicity and flexibility to evaluate land suitability.
[33]	FDSS	The performance and advantage of FDSS has been verified according to IRRINET and in some cases has increased.
[34]	DSS	In terms of performance, the amount of irrigation estimated by DSS against agronomist was calculated with less than 9% error per week for the most critical periods of the system.
[35]	FLC	The designed controller effectively estimated the amount of water consumed by plants at different depths. For this, irrigation model, evapotranspiration functions, environmental conditions, soil type, plant type and the other factors affecting greenhouse irrigation was taken into consideration.
[36]	PID	It is concluded that the PID controller has water saving potential in irrigation system design.
[37]	PID	The designed controller fully adapted to factors such as controller deactivation, insufficient irrigation or changes in environmental conditions.
[38]	PID	PID controller was used less water than the other method. However, optimization of the PID parameters present the current barrier to implementation of this technology.
[40]	ANN	The developed system has reduced daily water and energy consumption by 38%.
[41]	LaNN	The proposed LaNN-based sensor model saved approximately 50% on hardware.
[46]	FDMM	Fuzzy inference system has been found to be suitable for defining the reuse trend of water.
[50]	PID	The performance and robustness of the proposed control methods have been proven by simulation results.

(Continued)

Table 3.4 Recent control theory applications of the irrigation systems. (*Continued*)

[42]	MV	Using neural intelligent water drops feature selection, superior prediction performance was obtained compared to other feature selection methods.
[43]	ANN, GA	This designed framework, which accelerates the network convergence and improves the prediction accuracy is suitable for drip irrigation systems.
[44]	FDMM	It has been shown that the FDMM has many advantages such as communication reliability, control accuracy
[45]	FMCA	It has been observed that the fuzzy decision support system is useful due to its features such as its interactive structure and flexibility.
[47]	FIS	It is stated that an intelligent precision irrigation can be done using fuzzy inference system and central pivot irrigation system maps can be created with remote sensing measurements and accessing methods.
[51]	MPC	The MPC simulation results are similar to the results obtained using the fully centralized PI controller.
[29]	MPC	It is possible to include direct measurements of several variables in the MPC through system identification. Uncertainty in weather forecasts can be reduced with the MPC technique.
[52]	MPC	The controller has been compared with traditional strategies. According to the results, soil moisture remained above the safety level with less water consumption.
[56]	MPC	The proposed approach is effective in implementing a data driven real-time irrigation control system.
[57]	MPC	The designed controller has been shown to successfully regulate water levels.
[58]	MPC	As the use of MPC in the irrigation system provides high control efficiency, water consumption can be reduced significantly.
[59]	MPC	Real-time irrigation planning was carried out using measured climate data, including system model and water limitations.

(*Continued*)

Table 3.4 Recent control theory applications of the irrigation systems. (*Continued*)

[62]	MH	It has been presented that the Shuffled Complex Evolution algorithm and EDOSIM model are advantageous for the optimization of the fields.
[63]	SMC	The results show that external disturbances caused by water evaporation are completely rejected.

3.2.2   An Evaluation of Machine Learning–Based Irrigation Control Applications

Although traditional methods were initially preferred for irrigation system control, the insufficiency of these methods or their inability to adapt to technology has led to the development of different approaches over time. In the literature, applications based on prediction have been developed with models, including soil content, weather, labor, and even economic parameters. However, if there is uncertainty in the system model whose dynamics are expected to be precise, the exact mathematical model for the system cannot be designed. Instead, various predictions are performed based on measured variables by system identification models. The accuracy of the model depends on the correlation between data, which is a limitation of diagnostic-based approaches. In this case, the validity of the model cannot be trusted. Recently, ML approaches have become popular, instead of working with weak system models in irrigation systems as in every field. Such models combined with classical control methods can provide more accurate predictions. If there is a scenario with several uncertainties, reinforcement learning approaches based on rewarding-punishment mechanism may be preferred, where more experiments are needed to learn irrigation dynamics. Although smart irrigation or agriculture control applications based on reinforcement learning are currently limited, it will be possible to find many applications combined with deep networks in the near future.

3.2.3   Remote Control Extensions

The use of site-specific irrigation techniques that can adapt to changing conditions is extremely important in terms of increasing efficiency and reducing environmental impacts. For this purpose, distributed sensor-based and site-specific irrigation systems are being developed. Remote controlled irrigation systems have advantages, such as saving water and increasing the quality and yield. However, problems may arise in these systems, such as sensor, irrigation control, interface, software and seamless integration of communication. Remote controlled irrigation systems in the literature are generally as in Figure 3.4.

In this structure, information collected from the agricultural field with all sensors is converted into discrete data, which can be used in the control process by analog to digital converter (ADC). Then, the output signals obtained with the intelligent control block trigger the related actuator in automatic-mode. In new applications, intelligent irrigation control with integrated sensor networks is an increasing trend. The following section includes a literature about these studies.

In Kim *et al.* [64], the equipment of variable rate irrigation system, design, and communication system of sensors, which works with software for real time system, is mentioned. Irrigation machines are controlled by a programmable logic controller, which updates location of sprinklers from Global Positioning Systems (GPS) and communicate with the main computer via wireless system. Bluetooth is the communication type between sensor network and main computer. Field sensor stations are distributed in the yield production area. The field sensors monitor the product status at regular intervals and send information to the base station. In addition to these, this study is focused on a new software to stabilize remote access to field status, real-time control system, observing the variable-rate

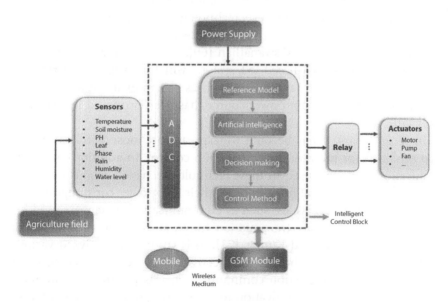

Figure 3.4 Remote control diagram of the irrigation system.

irrigation controller in site-specific management. In Hong *et al.* [65], by the use of integrated control strategy, comparison between conventional timer control, which fundamentally works with a timer for watering the yields and soil moisture control is focused in this paper. By using components, such as wireless sensor network, microcontroller, programmable logic controller, Bluetooth module used in the integrated control strategy, multiple information about the microclimate in the greenhouse has been detected, and thus, adaptable decisions have been created in real time. In Aleotti *et al.* [66], an automatic precision irrigation system has been designed. This structure consists of decision support system, embedded IoT devices, server, mobile application for user interaction, and linear irrigation machines.

The main idea in IoT-based irrigation system is that the devices are communicating with each other, sharing the data and using the data that is collected by sensor information unit for watching its behavior. In Nawandar and Satpute [67], an IoT-based automatic irrigation system was presented for efficient irrigation process. In this study, Message Queqe Telemetry Transport (MQTT), which is light-weight messaging protocol for power devices and sensors and HTTP systems, has helped users to monitor the system condition even if it is far away. In Rajkumar *et al.* [68], basic definitions and working principles of IoT technologies were explained, and applications of IoT technologies based on agriculture were focused and compared with other survey papers. In addition to these, a novel irrigation system has been built by high-level technology for crop production. Cloud computing-based agricultural network technology applications were examined in Mekala and Viswanathan [69]. In addition, a Global Mobile Communication (GSM)-based IoT system, which makes smart irrigation according to the input parameters, such as soil moisture level, environmental temperature, main power source, has been proposed in Krishnan *et al.* [70].

In recent years, it has become widespread to choose wireless sensors and actuators for monitoring in irrigation control. In addition, the communication protocols used in these technologies have become a popular standard for agricultural fields because their low-power consumption [27, 71, 72]. The technical issues, such as communication of sensors used for monitoring greenhouses, transmission range, and sensor selection, were reviewed in Kochhar and Kumar [73]. This study also analyzed various models adopted in greenhouses for effective integration and management of WSN. Magnetic induction communication was proposed as an alternative to EM wave communication for WSN in Parameswaran *et al.* [74] to overcome the difficulties that may occur in wireless sensor networks.

In González-Briones *et al.* [75], using a multiagent system developed on the cloud computing framework, all simulation processes, data collection, crop tracking, and user interaction have been managed. In Mehra *et al.* [76], the optimum control action was provided based on the parameters of an intelligent IoT system developed using deep neural networks. In Mehra *et al.* [77], a regression algorithm was used, which estimates the daily amount of water required for irrigation based on the data provided from various sensors. A similar agricultural monitoring system based on IoT was presented in Bauer and Aschenbruck [78]. The decision support system presented in Viani *et al.* [79] aimed to reduce water waste and increase crop yield according to weather conditions and actual water needs. The communication type is very important for a wireless sensor network [80] because some issues, such as the transmission of data, the connectivity of the network, the reliability, and the performance of the system, are shaped by the type of communication.

Some of the known major communication wireless protocols are Wi-Fi, Bluetooth, ZigBee, GPRS3G4G technology, LoRa, SigFox, NB-IoT, MQTT, LoWPAN, LTE Cat-NB1, LTE Cat M1, and so on [81, 82]. The controller, communication type and measured values of the mentioned remote control extensions are summarized in Table 3.5.

The descriptions of the abbreviations used in this table are as follows: SM, soil moisture; ST, soil temperature; AT, air temperature; H, humidty; P, precipitation; WD, wind direction; WS, wind speed; SR, solar radiation; SI, solar irradiation; GMSD, geographic, meteorological and soil data; VM, vegetation map; SNL, soil nutrition levels; WL, water level; WIR, water inflow rate; SWC, soil water content; E, evapotranspiration; WF, weather forecast; LDR, Light Dependent Resistor; RD, rain drop; LAI, Leaf Area Index; SWP, soil water potential; WS, water stress.

3.3   Conclusion and Future Directions

When developments are examined since the 1970s, the applications that started with on-off control for the first time can now be done in a predictive way. The application of crop growth modeling and weather forecasting improves the irrigation decision systems, but more systematic and precise models are expected to be developed. The water need and growth models of a crop can be constructed by mathematical modeling and system identification. True mathematical model needs all the information about crop biology, such as accurate knowledge about type of seed, soil ingredients, microorganizms, evapotranspiration, precipitation, weather, and other

Table 3.5 Aforementioned remote control extensions for irrigation systems.

Reference	Controller	Communication type	Measured data
[64]	PLC	Bluetooth	SM, ST, AT, H, P, WS, WD, SR
[65]	PLC, microcontroller	Bluetooth	AT, H, SM, SR
[66]	Embedded IoT device	4G network connection	GMSD, VM
[67]	ANN	MQTT	SM, AT, H
[68]	Microcontroller	Wifi	SM, AT, H
[69]	Microcontroller	Lifi	pH, AT, H, SNL, WL
[70]	Microcontroller	GSM	SM, AT, H
[71]	identification based control	Wifi	SM, AT, WIR
[27]	PID, MPC	Not described	SWC, E, AT, WF
[76]	Microcontroller	UART Serial Communication	ST, H, WL, LDR, pH
[77]	microcontroller	GSM	WIR, RD, C, SM, AT
[78]	microcontroller	MQTT	AT, H, SI, LAI
[79]	FLC	Wifi	E, SWP, WS, AT

disturbances, such that those must be known for each crop and the field. In lack of information case, true mathematical model can not be designed, instead system identification models can be consulted. In the system identification, according to the available input-output measurements, the constructed model can predict the output based on the identification model. However, its accuracy depends on the amount of information provided and correlation between the input-output data. In case of unknown disturbances, the correlation is broken down, and the system identification model loses its validity. On the other hand, there exist also limitations because there are no continuous measurements for the years from the same area and crop. To obtain accurate identification model, there are more data required and bias terms to model unknown disturbances. In general, instead of using linear or weak nonlinear models, a well-designed neural-network and support vector machine, or deep neural networks must be designed for crop growth or irrigation decision models. Those models can provide more accurate predictions for the control methods. Because of the reward-punishment–based learning structure of the reinforcement learning models, there is no need much knowledge about the irrigation systems but it needs more experiments to learn the irrigation dynamics. In this context, in the near future, it is expected that the deep neural networks based deep-reinforcement learning approaches will be used for the irrigation systems that can be seen in the timeline of Figure 3.5.

In lack of information case mentioned above, mathematical models can still be constructed however, the accuracy of mathematical model can be less than desired level. To build a true mathematical model, we need an experimental field and crop for modeling. However in practice, the obtained model can not be used around the world because of the required measurement sensors. Therefore, the current models disregard some of these inputs and make estimations under some accuracy. In the future, it is expected that more sensor devices will be available, then true mathematical models can be obtained, which needs some years to be developed. Without explicit modeling of irrigation systems, adaptive control and generalized MPC can be used for the control of irrigation systems. However, these control methods generate a system identification model to approximate the system dynamics or control dynamics. Therefore, because of the lack of information, the control accuracy is not expected well because of unknown disturbances. After the available sensors that measures the disturbances, the online identification-based control methods will be accurate as expected.

The available methods based on the mathematical or identification model assume that true predictions exist for the evapotranspiration and precipitation. However, these variables are based on weather conditions where true predictions on the weather conditions are difficult to obtain in general. There are numerous time-series prediction methods to forecast weather conditions but the accuracy of the predictions remains still under desired level. Nowadays, although deep networks are used to forecast weather conditions, there are more input information required all over the world that changes the air dynamics. In the future, it is expected that an accurate air map will be constructed, and the accuracy of the forecast models will be improved. After that, many systematic approaches will be utilized by true weather forecasting.

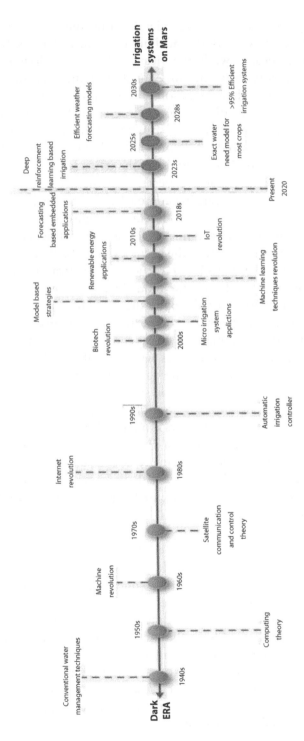

Figure 3.5 Time-line of irrigation decision systems.

Climate change because of global warming, precipitation uncertainty, soil type, water resources, national agricultural policies, economic, and sociocultural factors determine the approaches of countries to irrigation decision systems. In an effective irrigation planning, timing, amount of irrigation, and its application are important for crop yield and quality. Today, it is possible to reduce water consumption and increase irrigation performance in agriculture thanks to the use of existing technologies, such as control theory approaches, artificial intelligence applications, internet of things, big data processing, remote sensing, smart systems, renewable energy sources. According to our inferences from this survey, it is best to use a remote irrigation decision system that includes decision support system to analyze water requirements and effectively manages water resources with dynamical planning. To achieve a satisfactory performance with this control mechanism, the following should be considered: weather forecast (precipitation, temperature, humidity, evaporation factors) using advanced models, the effect of climate change on crop yields, plant water consumption, yield prediction, farmers' competencies, seasonal irrigation timing, infrastructure, contribution of uncertainties in economic factors. Using ML, deep learning and control theory approaches, a sustainable and dynamically manageable irrigation decision strategy can be created, sensor and IoT-based data analysis can be performed. Thus, irrigation decision models can be optimized for efficient use of resources and maximizing technological investments.

References

1. Mohri, M., Rostamizadeh, A., Talwalkar, A., *Foundations of machine learning, Second edition,* Cambridge, MA, MIT Press, 2018.
2. Sharma, R., Kamble, S.S., Gunasekaran, A., Kumar, V., Kumar, A., A systematic literature review on machine learning applications for sustainable agriculture supply chain performance. *Comput. Oper. Res.,* 119, 1–17, 104926, 2020.
3. Jordan, M., II and Mitchell, T.M., Machine learning: Trends, perspectives, and prospects. *Science,* 349, 6245, 255–260, 2015.
4. Sutton, R.S., Barto, A.G. *et al., Introduction to reinforcement learning,* vol. 135, 1em plus 0.5em minus 0.4em MIT Press, Cambridge, 1998.
5. Kumar, M. and Sihag, P., Assessment of infiltration rate of soil using empirical and machine learning-based models. *Irrig. Drain.,* 68, 3, 588–601, 2019.
6. Goldstein, A., Fink, L., Meitin, A., Bohadana, S., Lutenberg, O., Ravid, G., Applying machine learning on sensor data for irrigation recommendations:

revealing the agronomists tacit knowledge, in: *Precision agriculture*, vol. 19, pp. 421–444, 2018.

7. Ponraj, A.S. and Vigneswaran, T., Daily evapotranspiration prediction using gradient boost regression model for irrigation planning. *J. Supercomput.*, 76, 5732–5744, 2020.

8. Braga, D.J.F., da Silva, T.L.C., Rocha, A., Coutinho, G., Magalhães, R.P., Guerra, P.T., de Macêdo, J.A., Barbosa, S.D., Time series forecasting to support irrigation management. *J. Inf. Data Manage.*, 10, 2, 66–80, 2019.

9. Torres, A.F., Walker, W.R., McKee, M., Forecasting daily potential evapotranspiration using machine learning and limited climatic data. *Agr. Water Manage.*, 98, 4, 553–562, 2011.

10. Irukula, S., *Reinforcement learning based controller for precision irrigation*, Ph.D. dissertation, Texas A&M University, 2015.

11. Karandish, F. and Simunek, J., A comparison of numerical and machine-learning modeling of soil water content with limited input data. *J. Hydrol.*, 543, 892–909, 2016.

12. Navarro-Hellin, H., Martinez-del Rincon, J., Domingo-Miguel, R., Torres-Sánchez, R., A decision support system for managing irrigation in agriculture. *Comput. Electron. Agr.*, 124, 121–131, 2016.

13. Sun, L., Yang, Y., Hu, J., Porter, D., Marek, T., Hillyer, C., Reinforcement learning control for water-efficient agricultural irrigation, in: *2017 IEEE International Symposium on Parallel and Distributed Processing with Applications and 2017 IEEE International Conference on Ubiquitous Computing and Communications (ISPA/IUCC)*, 1em plus 0.5em minus 0.4em, IEEE, pp. 1334–1341, 2017.

14. Shekhar, Y., Dagur, E., Mishra, S., Sankaranarayanan, S., Intelligent iot based automated irrigation system. *Int. J. Appl. Eng. Res.*, 12, 18, 7306–7320, 2017.

15. Kwok, J. and Sun, Y., A smart iot-based irrigation system with automated plant recognition using deep learning, in: *Proceedings of the 10th International Conference on Computer Modeling and Simulation*, pp. 87–91, 2018.

16. Goap, A., Sharma, D., Shukla, A., Krishna, C.R., An iot based smart irrigation management system using machine learning and open source technologies. *Comput. Electron. Agr.*, 155, 41–49, 2018.

17. Keswani, B., Mohapatra, A.G., Mohanty, A., Khanna, A., Rodrigues, J.J., Gupta, D., de Albuquerque, V.H.C., Adapting weather conditions based iot enabled smart irrigation technique in precision agriculture mechanisms. *Neural Comput. Appl.*, 31, 1, 277–292, 2019.

18. Mohapatra, A.G., Lenka, S.K., Keswani, B., Neural network and fuzzy logic based smart dss model for irrigation notification and control in precision agriculture. *Proceedings of the National Academy of Sciences, India Section A: Physical Sciences*, vol. 89, pp. 67–76, 2019.

19. Binas, J., Luginbuehl, L., Bengio, Y., Reinforcement learning for sustainable agriculture, in: *ICML 2019 Workshop Climate Change: How Can AI Help*, 2019.

20. Jha, K., Doshi, A., Patel, P., Shah, M., A comprehensive review on automation in agriculture using artificial intelligence. *Artif. Intell. Agric.*, 2, 1–12, 2019.

21. Suntaranont, B., Aramkul, S., Kaewmoracharoen, M., Champrasert, P., "Water irrigation decision support system for practical weir adjustment using artificial intelligence and machine learning techniques. *Sustainability*, 12, 5, 1763, 2020.

22. Sidhu, R.K., Kumar, R., Rana, P.S., Machine learning based crop water demand forecasting using minimum climatological data. *Multimed. Tools Appl.*, 79, 13109–13124, 2020.

23. Fernández-López, A., Marin-Sánchez, D., Garcia-Mateos, G., Ruiz-Canales, A., Molina-Martinez, J.M., A machine learning method to estimate reference evapotranspiration using soil moisture sensors. *Appl. Sci.*, 10, 6, 1912, 2020.

24. Adenugba, F., Misra, S., Maskeliūnas, R., Damaševičius, R., Kazanavičius, E., Smart irrigation system for environmental sustainability in africa: An internet of everything (ioe) approach. *Math. Biosci. Eng*, 16, 5490–5503, 2019.

25. Chang, C.-L. and Lin, K.-M., Smart agricultural machine with a computer vision-based weeding and variable-rate irrigation scheme. *Robotics*, 7, 3, 38, 2018.

26. Geetha, S. and Priya, R.S., Smart agriculture irrigation control using wireless sensor networks. *Asian J. Inf. Technol.*, 15, 19, 3780–3786, 2016.

27. Romero, R., Muriel, J., Garcia, I., de la Peña, D.M., Research on automatic irrigation control: State of the art and recent results. *Agr. Water Manage.*, 114, 59–66, 2012.

28. Jones, J.W., Hoogenboom, G., Porter, C.H., Boote, K.J., Batchelor, W.D., Hunt, L., Wilkens, P.W., Singh, U., Gijsman, A.J., Ritchie, J.T., The dssat cropping system model. *Eur. J. Agron.*, 18, 3-4, 235–265, 2003.

29. Delgoda, D., Malano, H., , S. K. Saleem, and Irrigation control based on model predictive control (mpc): Formulation of theory and validation using weather forecast data and aquacrop model. *Environ. Modelling & Software*, 78, 40–53, 2016.

30. Guariso, G. and Soncini-Sessa, R., Decision support systems for water management: The lake como case study. *Eur. J. Operational Res.*, 21, 3, 295–306, 1985.

31. van Oel, P.R., Krol, M.S., Hoekstra, A.Y., Taddei, R.R., Feedback mechanisms between water availability and water use in a semi-arid river basin: A spatially explicit multi-agent simulation approach. *Environ. Model. Software*, 25, 4, 433–443, 2010.

32. Chen, Y. and Paydar, Z., Evaluation of potential irrigation expansion using a spatial fuzzy multi-criteria decision framework. *Environ. Model. Software*, 38, 147–157, 2012.

33. Giusti, E. and Marsili-Libelli, S., A fuzzy decision support system for irrigation and water conservation in agriculture. *Environ. Model. Software*, 63, 73–86, 2015.

34. Torres-Sanchez, R., Navarro-Hellin, H., Guillamon-Frutos, A., San-Segundo, R., Ruiz-Abellón, M.C., Domingo-Miguel, R., A decision support system for

irrigation management: Analysis and implementation of different learning techniques. *Water*, 12, 2, 548, 2020.

35. Kia, P.J., Far, A.T., Omid, M., Alimardani, R., Naderloo, L. *et al.*, Intelligent control based fuzzy logic for automation of greenhouse irrigation system and evaluation in relation to conventional systems. *World Appl. Sci. J.*, 6, 1, 16–23, 2009.

36. Goodchild, M.S., Jenkins, M.D., Whalley, W.R., Watts, C.W., A novel dielectric tensiometer enabling precision pid-based irrigation control of polytunnel-grown strawberries in coir. *Biosyst. Eng.*, 165, 70–76, 2018.

37. Goodchild, M., Kühn, K., Jenkins, M., Burek, K., Button, A., A method for precision closed-loop irrigation using a modified pid control algorithm. *Sens. Transducers*, 188, 5, 61, 2015.

38. Harper, S., *Real-time control of soil moisture for efficient irrigation*, Ph.D. dissertation, Massachusetts Institute of Technology, 2017.

39. Levidow, L., Zaccaria, D., Maia, R., Vivas, E., Todorovic, M., Scardigno, A., Improving water-efficient irrigation: Prospects and difficulties of innovative practices. *Agr. Water Manage.*, 146, 84–94, 2014.

40. Dursun, M. and Özden, S., An efficient improved photovoltaic irrigation system with artificial neural network based modeling of soil moisture distribution–a case study in turkey. *Comput. Electron. Agr.*, 102, 120–126, 2014.

41. Patra, J.C., Meher, P.K., Chakraborty, G., Development of laguerre neural-network-based intelligent sensors for wireless sensor networks. *IEEE Trans. Instrum. Meas.*, 60, 3, 725–734, 2010.

42. Hendrawan, Y. and Murase, H., Neural-intelligent water drops algorithm to select relevant textural features for developing precision irrigation system using machine vision. *Comput. Electron. Agr.*, 77, 2, 214–228, 2011.

43. Gu, J., Yin, G., Huang, P., Guo, J., Chen, L., An improved back propagation neural network prediction model for subsurface drip irrigation system. *Comput. Electr. Eng.*, 60, 58–65, 2017.

44. Wei, Z., Yong, H., Fei, L., Congcong, M., Yuewei, C., The fuzzy decision-making method of irrigation amount based on et and soil water potential, in: *2011 International Conference on Electronics, Communications and Control (ICECC)*, 1em plus 0.5em minus 0.4em, IEEE, pp. 2927–2931, 2011.

45. Raju, K.S. and Kumar, D.N., Fuzzy multicriterion decision making in irrigation planning. *Irrig. Drain.: J. Int. Commission Irrigation Drainage*, 54, 4, 455–465, 2005.

46. Almeida, G., Vieira, J., Marques, A.S., Kiperstok, A., Cardoso, A., Estimating the potential water reuse based on fuzzy reasoning. *J. Environ. Manage.*, 128, 883–892, 2013.

47. Mendes, W.R., Araújo, F.M.U., Dutta, R., Heeren, D.M., Fuzzy control system for variable rate irrigation using remote sensing. *Exp. Syst. Appl.*, 124, 13–24, 2019.

48. Patil, P., Kulkarni, U., Desai, B., Benagi, V., Naragund, V., Fuzzy logic based irrigation control system using wireless sensor network for precision agriculture. *Agro-Informatics and Precision Agriculture (AIPA)*, 2012.
49. Van Overloop, P.-J., *Model predictive control on open water systems*, Delft, The Netherlands: Delft Univ. Press, 2006.
50. Feliu-Batlle, V., Perez, R.R., Rodriguez, L.S., Fractional robust control of main irrigation canals with variable dynamic parameters. *Control Eng. Pract.*, 15, 6, 673–686, 2007.
51. Wahlin, B.T., Performance of model predictive control on asce test canal 1. *J. I. Drain. Eng.*, 130, 3, 227–238, 2004.
52. Shang, C., Chen, W.-H., Stroock, A.D., You, F., Robust model predictive control of irrigation systems with active uncertainty learning and data analytics. *IEEE Trans. Control Syst. Technol.*, 28, 4, 1493–1504, 2019.
53. Camacho, E.F. and Alba, C.B., Model predictive control. Springer Science & Business Media, Springer, London, 2013.
54. Chetty, V., Woodbury, N., Warnick, S., Farming as feedback control, in: *2014 American Control Conference*, 1em plus 0.5em minus 0.4em, IEEE, pp. 2688–2693, 2014.
55. Elsadek, E., Elnemr, M., A. Elsheikha, *Use of automatic control to improve the performance of field irrigation systems*, Ph.D. dissertation, Faculty of Agriculture, Damietta University, 2018.
56. Guo, C. and You, F., A data-driven real-time irrigation control method based on model predictive control, in: *2018 IEEE Conference on Decision and Control (CDC)*, 1em plus 0.5em minus 0.4em, IEEE, pp. 2599–2604, 2018.
57. Shahdany, S.H., Taghvaeian, S., Maestre, J., Firoozfar, A., Developing a centralized automatic control system to increase flexibility of water delivery within predictable and unpredictable irrigation water demands. *Comput. Electron. Agr.*, 163, 104862, 2019.
58. Lozoya, C., Mendoza, C., Mejia, L., Quintana, J., Mendoza, G., Bustillos, M., Arras, O., Solis, L., Model predictive control for closed-loop irrigation. *IFAC Proceedings Volumes*, vol. 47, pp. 4429–4434, 2014.
59. Saleem, S.K., Delgoda, D., Ooi, S.K., Dassanayake, K.B., Liu, L., Halgamuge, M., Malano, H., Model predictive control for real-time irrigation scheduling. *IFAC Proceedings Volumes*, vol. 46, pp. 299–304, 2013.
60. Shang, C., Chen, W.-H., You, F., Robust constrained model predictive control of irrigation systems based on data-driven uncertainty set constructions, in: *2019 American Control Conference (ACC)*, 1em plus 0.5em minus 0.4em, IEEE, pp. 1–6, 2019.
61. Akbari, M., Gheysari, M., Mostafazadeh-Fard, B., Shayannejad, M., Surface irrigation simulation-optimization model based on meta-heuristic algorithms. *Agr. Water Manage.*, 201, 46–57, 2018.
62. Gonçalves, G.M., Gouveia, L., Pato, M.V., An improved decomposition-based heuristic to design a water distribution network for an irrigation system. *Ann. Oper. Res.*, 219, 1, 141–167, 2014.

63. Molina, N., II and Cunha, J.P.V., A distributed parameter approach for sliding mode control of soil irrigation. *IFAC-PapersOnLine*, vol. 50, pp. 2714–2719, 2017.
64. Kim, Y., Evans, R.G., Iversen, W.M., Remote sensing and control of an irrigation system using a distributed wireless sensor network. *IEEE Trans. Instrum. Meas.*, 57, 7, 1379–1387, 2008.
65. Hong, G.-Z. and Hsieh, C.-L., Application of integrated control strategy and bluetooth for irrigating romaine lettuce in greenhouse. *IFAC-PapersOnLine*, vol. 49, pp. 381–386, 2016.
66. Aleotti, J., Amoretti, M., Nicoli, A., Caselli, S., A smart precision-agriculture platform for linear irrigation systems, in: *2018 26th International Conference on Software, Telecommunications and Computer Networks (SoftCOM)*, 1em plus 0.5em minus 0.4em, IEEE, pp. 1–6, 2018.
67. Nawandar, N.K. and Satpute, V.R., IoT based low cost and intelligent module for smart irrigation system. *Comput. Electron. Agr.*, 162, 979–990, 2019.
68. Rajkumar, M.N., Abinaya, S., Kumar, V.V., Intelligent irrigation systemâ€"an iot based approach, in: *2017 International Conference on Innovations in Green Energy and Healthcare Technologies (IGEHT)*, 1em plus 0.5em minus 0.4em, IEEE, pp. 1–5, 2017.
69. Mekala, M.S. and Viswanathan, P., A survey: Smart agriculture iot with cloud computing, in: *2017 international conference on microelectronic devices, circuits and systems (ICMDCS)*, 1em plus 0.5em minus 0.4em, IEEE, pp. 1–7, 2017.
70. Krishnan, R.S., Julie, E.G., Robinson, Y.H., Raja, S., Kumar, R., Thong, P.H. et al., Fuzzy logic based smart irrigation system using internet of things. *J. Clean. Prod.*, 252, 119902, 2020.
71. Ooi, S.K., Mareels, I., Cooley, N., Dunn, G., Thoms, G., A systems engineering approach to viticulture on-farm irrigation. *IFAC Proceedings Volumes*, vol. 41, pp. 9569–9574, 2008.
72. Patel, N. and Desai, N., Wi-fi module and wireless sensor net-work based automated irrigation system. *System*, 2, 4, 70–76, 2015.
73. Kochhar, A. and Kumar, N., Wireless sensor networks for greenhouses: An end-to-end review. *Comput. Electron. Agr.*, 163, 104877, 2019.
74. Parameswaran, V., Zhou, H., Zhang, Z., Irrigation control using wireless underground sensor networks, in: *2012 Sixth International Conference on Sensing Technology (ICST)*, 1em plus 0.5em minus 0.4em, IEEE, pp. 653–659, 2012.
75. González-Briones, A., Mezquita, Y., Castellanos-Garzón, J.A., Prieto, J., Corchado, J.M., Intelligent multi-agent system for water reduction in automotive irrigation processes. *Proc. Comput. Sci.*, 151, 971–976, 2019.
76. Mehra, M., Saxena, S., Sankaranarayanan, S., Tom, R.J., Veeramanikandan, M., Iot based hydroponics system using deep neural networks. *Comput. Electron. Agr.*, 155, 473–486, 2018.
77. Kumar, A., Surendra, A., Mohan, H., Valliappan, K.M., Kirthika, N., Internet of things based smart irrigation using regression algorithm, in:

2017 International Conference on Intelligent Computing, Instrumentation and Control Technologies (ICICICT), 1em plus 0.5em minus 0.4em, IEEE, pp. 1652–1657, 2017.

78. Bauer, J. and Aschenbruck, N., Design and implementation of an agricultural monitoring system for smart farming, in: *2018 IoT Vertical and Topical Summit on Agriculture-Tuscany (IOT Tuscany)*, 1em plus 0.5em minus 0.4em, IEEE, pp. 1–6, 2018.

79. Viani, F., Bertolli, M., Salucci, M., Polo, A., Low-cost wireless monitoring and decision support for water saving in agriculture. *IEEE Sens. J.*, 17, 13, 4299–4309, 2017.

80. Kothawade, S.N., Furkhan, S.M., Raoof, A., Mhaske, K.S., Efficient water management for greenland using soil moisture sensor, in: *2016 IEEE 1st International Conference on Power Electronics, Intelligent Control and Energy Systems (ICPEICES)*, 1em plus 0.5em minus 0.4em, IEEE, pp. 1–4, 2016.

81. Abioye, E.A., Abidin, M.S.Z., Mahmud, M.S.A., Buyamin, S., Ishak, M.H., II, Abd Rahman, M.K., II, Otuoze, A.O., Onotu, P., Ramli, M.S.A., A review on monitoring and advanced control strategies for precision irrigation. *Comput. Electron. Agr.*, 173, 105441, 2020.

82. Glória, A., Dionisio, C., Simões, G., Cardoso, J., Sebastião, P., Water management for sustainable irrigation systems using internet-of-things. *Sensors*, 20, 5, 1402, 2020.

4

Enabling Technologies for Future Robotic Agriculture Systems: A Case Study in Indian Scenario

X. Anitha Mary[1], Kannan Mani[2], Kumudha Raimond[3*],
Johnson I.[4] and Dinesh Kumar P.[5]

[1]Department of Robotics Engineering, Karunya Institute of Technology and Sciences,
Coimbatore, Tamil Nadu, India
[2]Department of Entomology, Chemistry, and Nematology, Institute of Plant
Protection, Agricultural Research Organization, Volcani Research Center,
Derech HaMaccabim, Rishon LeZion, Israel
[3]Department of Computer Science Engineering, Karunya Institute of Technology
and Sciences, Coimbatore, Tamil Nadu, India
[4]Department of Plant Pathology, Tamil Nadu Agricultural University,
Coimbatore, Tamil Nadu, India
[5]Department of Electrical Engineering, National Chung Hsing University,
Taichung, Taiwan

Abstract

Robotics and automation transform global industries and paved an impact on large economic sectors. Today's agriculture methodology needs improvement due to the pressure of global population growth, unpredictable climatic changes, and the impact of migration. However, the traditional agricultural methods are facing challenges to provide enough food supply for the growing population. There is an urgent need to incorporate computing technologies to automate traditional farming practices. So, this chapter is divided into four sections—(1) opportunities of robots in agriculture where we discuss the need for robots in the current scenario of increasing population and demand for labor to do the agricultural task; (2) advancement in agribots, which is focused on different types of agricultural robots in terms of sensing, mobility, path planning, and manipulation; (3) status

*Corresponding author: kumudha@karunya.edu

Roheet Bhatnagar, Nitin Kumar Tripathi, Nitu Bhatnagar and Chandan Kumar Panda (eds.)
The Digital Agricultural Revolution: Innovations and Challenges in Agriculture through
Technology Disruptions, (87–108) © 2022 Scrivener Publishing LLC

and progress of robots in Indian agriculture, which concentrates on Indian-based robot start-up and case studies of using robots in harvesting crops; (4) challenges in the deployment of robots in the field.

Keywords: Robots, types, precision agriculture, smart farming, technologies, UAV

4.1   Need for Robotics in Agriculture

The requirement for agricultural products is surging at an incredible rate. According to the prediction made by the UN [21], the world's population would grow from 7.3 billion today to 9.7 billion in 2050. Also, in India, nearly 40% of the national farm cost is given for wages and another labor cost [4, 5]. The current farming practices, such as ploughing, seeding, cultivating, harvesting, and so on, need a lot of human labor and a lot of natural resources. The farmers also spend much amount on the preparation of fields and crops. The farmers will face serious problems to meet the food demand. It is reported that [1] in the Dharwad district of Karnataka, India, the farmers were given low cost for various tasks in the field. The situation has led to the shortage of laborers and food for the growing population. It is essential to exploit modern technologies to bring a solution to this global problem. The most impressive technology, which is progressing speedily, is robotics for automating the tasks of the laborers efficiently at less cost [8], thereby achieving labor-saving and efficient large-scale agriculture.

Robotics in agriculture is highly predominant in modern agriculture development. Robots along with the latest technologies, like sensors, Internet of Things (IoT), satellite images, cloud computing, and machine learning, have made a big impact in performing agricultural activities. Such intelligent and autonomous robots help in automating the slow, repetitive, and touch manual tasks and improve the crop yield and lower the costs associated with fertilizer, irrigation, pesticides, and so on. To deal with labor and food shortages cost-effectively, farmers are now concentrating on modern technologies like the IoT, field sensors, data analytics, and Artificial Intelligence (AI).

Other benefits include:

- reduction of environmental footprint through pollution monitoring at ground level;
- reduction of crops' exposure to herbicides through proper navigation in the farm and spray herbicides at the targeted locations to eliminate weeds;

- perform touch manual tasks, such as moving plants in large greenhouses, to address the labor shortage problem;
- mass harvesting of crops and fruits [23];
- perform accurate planting of crops for optimal plant growth;
- improve farm management by consistent and parallel tasks [23].

4.2 Different Types of Agricultural Bots

Based on agricultural usage, the robots are broadly classified into three types (Figure 4.1), namely

1. field robots/unmanned ground vehicles (UGVs), used for doing the task in the field such as planting and harvesting crops, irrigating and plucking weeds;
2. aerial robots or unmanned aerial vehicles (UAVs) or drones, which are incorporated with computer vision and image processing helps in monitoring the real-time fields, data collection, and so on;
3. livestock robots are mainly used for monitoring the location and movement of the animal in the field.

4.2.1 Field Robots

Field robots can automate various agricultural activities and are completely independent in carrying out the tasks [17, 63]. These robots can be used in

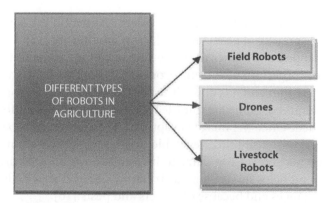

Figure 4.1 Different types of robots in agriculture.

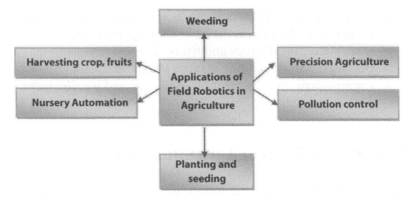

Figure 4.2 Various tasks of field robot.

small farms or vineyards and greenhouses. The robot application in agriculture is mainly focused on harvesting, weeding, seedling, and disease identification. The various tasks of field robots are shown in Figure 4.2.

In precision agriculture (PA), field robots are used to monitor the humidity, temperature level, fertilizer level, and other biological factors in soil. As part of pollution monitoring, the field robots help in measuring the carbon dioxide that is emitted during soil respiration and nitrous oxide that is emitted by the soil microbes. It is also useful to control weeds by spraying herbicides at the targeted locations. Some of the repetitive and laborious tasks, such as crop and fruit harvesting, planting, disease detection, can be automated using field robots to improve the speed and accuracy and to lower the laborers cost.

4.2.2   Drones

These help PA in applications like crop height estimation [9], soil and field analysis [10] spraying of pesticides [11], crop monitoring [12]. Usually, the fields are mapped at a higher resolution for seedlings and also to identify the unsuccessful germination using drones [13]. But the challenges here are some crops are thin and it is difficult to see from above, so high-resolution images are required. Some are thick leaves so such high-resolution images are not needed. Once the image is captured, then either pixel-based classification [14] or density slice vegetable index [15] is used to improve the classification accuracy. Crop damage investigation is another area where drone mapping helps in viewing its structural changes especially because of weather changes and because of insects and pests [16].

4.2.3 Livestock Drones

These are used to monitor the behavior of animals or herbs in pastures. Body temperature is an important parameter in screening the animal with infectious diseases.

4.2.4 Multirobot System

An important emerging trend is the development of Multirobot Systems (MRS)/fleets to execute the tasks in a collaborative manner [18, 20]. This configuration will be helpful to execute complicated tasks that need coordination from multiple locations of the farm or to carry out repetitive simple tasks in less time. Such robot systems are applicable for both greenhouse farming and outdoor agriculture and proved to be more efficient, flexible, and fault-tolerant. Some of the applications need heterogeneous robots, with diverse capabilities.

Some of the benefits of MRS are as follows:

- accomplish the same task of a single UGV by a team of homogeneous/heterogeneous robots, but of lightweight, which can move freely in the ground;
- robust because of the availability of few robots despite the failure of few other robots in the fleet;
- it can be adapted for various applications according to the need.

However, with more robots, overall system complexity and cost will increase. Such systems will be more beneficial only when applied to high-value crops [20].

4.3 Existing Agricultural Robots

Agricultural robots are helpful to increase production yields in various ways in the form of drones, autonomous tractors, arms. Agricultural robots and other related types of machinery vary widely based on the type of application, agricultural land, and requirements. Unmanned ground robots may not be suitable for all agricultural lands, such as wide and open areas, whereas suitable for small areas, as well as greenhouses. Besides, mobile robots cannot be used in all extreme conditions due to their sensitivity toward climate, water, and soil type. So, application-specific robots are to be designed based on the environment, land, and climate.

Autonomous tractors are being used in harsh environments, in less protected zone toward electronic instruments, and muddy soil because of their greater ability to traverse inside the muddy soil. However, because of its structure, it can be used only in wide agricultural fields. So, mobile robots can be designed for small farms and greenhouses. Drones are more suitable to cover open areas at reasonable elevation [19].

According to a recent study by NASA [2], the increase in carbon dioxide will boost the crop yield by increasing the photosynthesis rate but it hurts the crop yield by lowering the water transpiration for plants. It is necessary to monitor the emission level at the permissible limit. Herbicides are sprayed uniformly in the traditional method of weed management; however, it has the disadvantages of using large herbicides and does not eliminate weeds with 100% accuracy. Agricultural robots help in controlling the weed. These robots use advanced technologies, like AI, to target the weed plant. Blue River Technology [3] has used a robot sprayer inbuilt with deep machine learning to identify weeds and crops. The robot sprayer uses a high-resolution camera to scan the field, and an intelligent algorithm using neural network guides the robot to hit only the weed. It is reported that the entire process of capturing image, processing, and decision output takes only a few milliseconds, which helps the farmer to scan the field easily within few hours.

Based on the concept of the manipulator, to automate the fruit picking without injuring the fruits, a harvesting device is proposed in Kootstra *et al.* [22]. The proposed advanced vision system can detect the fruit's position in 2 seconds and harvest it in approximately 16 seconds. Field robots are being designed for selective harvesting in greenhouses, orchards, and open fields. Although such robots are not commercially successful, a lot of pre-commercial R&D initiatives have been taken to develop robots for strawberry harvesting—"Agrobot", "Octonion," "Dogtooth," and "Shibuya Seiki" and tomato harvesting—"Panasonic," "MetroMotion-GroW," "RootAI." Few open field harvesting robots are commercially available, such as Sparter from Cerescon for asparagus and "RoboVeg" for broccoli harvesting [23].

The world's first multirobot vision-based weed management system is Robot Fleets for Highly Effective Agricultural and Forestry Management (RHEA), designed by combining ground and aerial vehicles. In this proposed approach, the objective is to reduce the plant intake, which in turn will improve the crop quality and decrease the cost and environmental pollution. Through this system, the robots can identify the location accurately to apply the pesticides' incorrect measure [18, 20].

Multirobot Systems can also be used to carry out continuous tasks in harsh conditions, which cannot be executed by humans. One such application is the environmental monitoring of greenhouses.

4.4   Precision Agriculture and Robotics

Precision agriculture farming procedures frequently necessitate [50]:

(1) Repetitive tasks—The same PA responsibilities were repeated several times during the day.
(2) Intensive data gathering—Sensors are used for data collection from the soil, water management, plant growth, pests, climatic conditions.
(3) Awareness and foresight—For a variety of situations, instruments for agricultural awareness and prediction are available.
(4) Safety and security are important—PA installations frequently necessitate safeguarding measures.

Precision agriculture robotics assists in the automation of the aforementioned farming activities and may have positive impacts in terms of energy, time, and cost savings, as well as an improvement in total production.

Tillage, harvesting, pest detection and control, and seed sowing might all benefit from the newest robotics technologies in combination with existing tools, such as GIS applications and drones. Furthermore, robots are outfitted with a variety of sensors that enable the collecting of critical production data, such as soil moisture, soil temperature, soil quality, and so on.

Because of the introduction of unique and technologically superior robots, the PA robot market is seeing a growth in investments globally. Agricultural robots, also known as agribots, are progressively being implemented around the world to help farmers and boost production by assisting in operations, such as harvesting and scouting.

AgRobotics' AutoProbe is a PA robotic device that provides current soil services to boost crop output and cost savings. In comparison to any other commercially available equipment, it also provides efficient, consistent, and accurate soil analysis. In comparison to semiautomatic or manual sampling, this automated technology obtains samples in less time. BoniRob is a field robot that works independently with a global positioning system (GPS) and agro-sensors.

It can navigate on its own and find the GPS location of individual plants before mapping and recording their positions. This device is capable of continuously determining and monitoring plant growth statuses.

4.5 Technologies for Smart Farming

An approach of creating data about the farms and analyzing to make planned and effective decisions that are appropriate is the foundation of Agriculture 4.0. Generally, farmers used to make decisions based on their prior expertise by visiting the fields and inspecting the crops. Advanced management systems are providing practical answers in the framework of Smart Farming. Furthermore, although few farmers gained extensive knowledge through years of fieldwork, the technological revolutions are providing a systematic approach to handle unexpected matters, which are difficult to identify through visual examination during routine checks. Young farmers are more optimistic than older farmers when it comes to using contemporary agricultural equipment.

4.5.1 Concepts of Internet of Things

Sensors and related equipment are used in the agricultural environment to transform each aspect of work carried out in farms into a useful form of information are referred to as IoT. According to reports, between 10% and 15% of US farmers are utilizing IoT solutions on their farms, which span 1200 million hectares and 250,000 farms [51]. Internet of Things is expected to enhance agricultural output by 70% by 2050 with new approaches. Furthermore, because of a population increase of roughly nine thousand million people, the world food supply must be increased by 60% by 2050 [52, 53]. The main benefit of using IoT has increased crop yields at a lower cost. According to OnFarm research, a moderate farm that uses IoT shows a 1.75% increase in output, reduces the cost of energy in every hectare from 17 to 32 dollars, and saves 8% on irrigation water [54].

4.5.2 Big Data

The ever-increasing volume of data accessible for field management necessitates the deployment of some sort of automated mechanism for extracting operational data from bulk data. However, it is debatable if the current amount of data received from the agricultural fields has yet to meet the level regarded to be big data. Kunisch [55] stated that big data in agriculture is only relevant in certain conditions depends on the extent of utilization of technology in each farm. Nonetheless, the Proagrica research [57] verified that big data is increasingly being used in agriculture. Kamilaris *et al.* [56] highlighted 34 papers in which big data was applied to agriculture. In smart farming, Wolfert *et al.* [58] have written a survey article on the applications of big data. The consortium of International Agricultural Research Centers has developed a big data platform to handle issues in Agriculture at a larger scale than ever before [59].

4.5.3   Cyber Physical System

A cyber-physical system is one in which computation is integrated with physical processes. Embedded systems and networks are useful to continuously monitor and regulate physical processes [60]. As a result, a CPS is made up of the process, hardware, and software. The physical device is made up of embedded hardware, whereas the virtual device is made up of software. Sensors, controllers, computers, data acquisition devices, communication networks, and other components make up the physical device. The virtual device is made up of mathematical representations that reflect the behavior of the real device, as well as the essential algorithms.

4.5.4   Cloud Computing

Managing large information necessitates specialized processing and storage capabilities, and cloud computing approaches provide convenient, quick, cost-effective, and secure solutions. Could Computing is defined by the National Institute of Standards and Technology as "a methodology for offering convenient, on-demand network access to a shared pool of programmable computer resources" [61, 62].

4.6   Impact of AI and Robotics in Agriculture

Artificial Intelligence is the latest technology that is being practiced in agriculture to take it to a new level. Crop production has improved in terms of yield with the advent use of technology. Various high-tech computer-based systems have been developed to identify a variety of critical factors, such as weed, yield, quality, and so on [29]. The design of robots for agriculture is to incorporate AI for agriculture applications. The agriculture sector is experiencing a crisis as the world population grows, AI, on the other hand, can deliver a suitable solution. Farmers have been able to increase productivity with fewer resources, improve the quality of their output, and reduce the time it takes for their harvested crops to reach the market. Farmers are expected to get benefitted the usage of 75 million linked devices by 2020. By 2050, a normal farm is expected to produce 4.1 million points of data each day.

Artificial Intelligence allows farmers to gather a colossal amount of information from public and government websites, evaluate it and give farmers answers to a variety of difficult issues, as well as a smarter irrigation system that results in higher yields for farmers [30]. As a result of AI, farming will soon be discovered to be a blend of technology and biological skills, which will not only deliver a better quality outcome for all farmers but will also cut their losses and loads. AI can be used in agriculture to automate operations, decrease hazards, and make farming easier and more effective for farmers.

Hybrid Seed selection with quality [31] gives the maximum yield with AI. Natural language techniques help the user in the identification of seeds reacting to climatic conditions.

They are mostly geared for shopping, travel, and media, but agriculture has made use of this capability by supporting farmers in receiving answers to their unanswered queries, as well as providing guidance and varied recommendations.

In agricultural production and administration, robotics has played a significant role. Because traditional farming machinery was inefficient, researchers have begun focusing on technology to build autonomous agricultural implements. Robots should independently take care of effective farming with respective irrigation and weeding.

Agriculture absorbs 85% of the world's available freshwater resources. And this fraction is progressively rising in tandem with population expansion and rising food demand. As a result, we need to develop more effective technologies to make sure that the water resources are efficiently used in irrigation. Automatic irrigation scheduling systems have replaced manual irrigation based on soil water monitoring. While implementing autonomous irrigation equipment, the plant evapotranspiration was taken into account, which was based on many climatic characteristics. The various irrigation systems to build a system that uses fewer resources were explained [32].

Fertility meters and PH meters are set up on the field to detect the proportion of the primary ingredients of the soil, such as potassium, phosphorous, and nitrogen, to measure the fertility of the soil. Automatic drip irrigation is facilitated using wireless technology in the farms. This strategy ensures the soil's fertility as well as the efficient use of water resources.

The production is enhanced through smart irrigation-based technology without employing many human resources by automatically measuring and predicting the land parameters. The irrigator pump is turned ON/OFF according to the microcontroller's instructions. Nodes in the farms can communicate and share data as well as with the server or cloud using machine to machine (M2M) technology [33].

Here an automated robotic model for detecting moisture content and temperature using Arduino and Raspberry Pi3 boards is created. Data are acquired regularly and sent to the Arduino microcontroller for further converting the input from analog to digital form. The signal is transferred to the Raspberry Pi 3, which is then transmitted to Arduino to activate the automatic irrigation. The resource will supply the water based on the demand, and it will also update and store the sensor results. Soil moisture content can be determined using soil moisture sensors by deploying it near the root portion of the crop. It accurately determines the level and transmits the data to the controller [34]. Irrigation will be carried out only on demand if the soil moisture content is below a certain threshold. Sensors read the moisture content and permit the controllers only if it is below the set level [35]. The placement of sensors is critical to the successful use of irrigation robots. A single sensor can be used to control irrigation in multiple field zones. It is also possible to use numerous sensors to irrigate different zones. To verify whether the crops receive a sufficient amount of water, sensors should be placed in the root zone of the crops [36].

Based on a study made by Academicians at the Indian Council for Agricultural Research, India is losing a revenue of value $11 billion every year because of the presence of weeds. This loss is more than the budget allocated for agriculture in the 2017 to 2018 financial year. It is vital to eradicate these weeds; otherwise, they will not only take up precious land but would also have a detrimental impact on the yield [37].

We must distinguish between crop seedlings and weeds before designing an automated weed management system. In rice cultivation, the method of using agricultural robots to eradicate weeds and inventing methods of managing robot postures in case of uneven fields. The robot's position is managed, and the weeds are suppressed using Laser Range Fielder (LRF) technology [38]. The robotic weed control system [39, 40] incorporates various visual systems. The color-based vision was used to discriminate every weed from the others. To guide the robot across the rows, the gray-level vision was used to build a row structure. Among these, color-based vision is vital. A unique algorithm was used to create the row recognition system, which has a precision of 2 cm.

4.7   Unmanned Aerial Vehicles (UAV) in Agriculture

Wireless Sensor Networks (WSNs) are used in the development of the UAV (WSN). The WSN's data allow the UAS to improve its usage, such as limiting its spraying of synthetic substances to certain areas. Because ecological conditions are constantly changing, the control circle must almost surely respond as quickly as it is possible [41, 42]. Unmanned aerial vehicles are mostly used in PA for tasks, such as soil and field analysis, crop monitoring, crop height estimations, pesticide spraying, and so forth. In the following years, the agricultural drone market is predicted to rise by more than 38%. Because of rising population numbers and changing climate patterns, it is expected that the need for efficient agriculture would only grow [43]. Farmers have been using drones as substance sprayers for several years, and they are regarded as effective and important in foggy climates. It is also helpful to solve the accessibility problem of tall crops, such as maize in the field.

Yaduraju [44] used drones to spray synthetic compounds on crops, with the drones for horticulture applications. These drones were used in conjunction with remote sensor networks, which were placed on the crops in the field and controlled the application of synthetic substances. Drones were only able to spray because of the data collected by these remote sensors. Xue *et al.* [45] created a programmable flying prayer framework based on a UAV.

Xue *et al.* [46] evaluated Digital Photography from Model Aircraft for Crop Biomass and Nitrogen Status Remote Sensing. In their research, they developed an aerobatic model airplane for taking photographs using a customer-supplied electronic camera, and they used colored canvases to alter the images.

Sonaa *et al.* [47] showed how a UAV with multispectral vision may be used to guide soil and harvest for precision farming. A low-cost multispectral imaging system was designed and built for crop monitoring. It is made up of a microprocessor and two cameras that are embedded in the drone. One camera detects infrared light, whereas the other is a standard RGB camera. The health of the plants can be determined using the acquired images and calculating the NDVI [48]. Yield mapping, one of the most important aspects of the unprecedented advancements in precision cultivating frameworks, allows the farmer to view spatial variation over the field perceptive zone for future actions and the outcome of previous sessions, management. Grainflow sensor, grain moisture content sensor, GPS antenna.

4.8   Agricultural Manipulators

Electromechanical parts that form a continuous chain are called manipulators in which the base is attached to the ground and the end tool is positioned in the workspace. Normally, in agriculture, the end effectors are moved to a particular spot to interact with the object. These end effectors can be designed with contact or noncontact based. Contact or noncontact interactions are possible. Using the suitable end effector, a manipulator may be adapted to a variety of agricultural activities.

Soft end effectors are an excellent way to handle deformable items. Some fruits and vegetables, such as apples and eggplants, can be picked with suction end effectors, but some plants require a hand emulator, not only for mechanical capabilities but also for detecting touch and applying the appropriate pressure. Many harvesting tasks can be performed with a soft gripper carried by a rigid manipulator that provides accuracy and force [64].

4.9   Ethical Impact of Robotics and AI

Engineers working on systems should be aware of potential ethical issues to consider, such as avoiding misuse and allowing for human scrutiny of the algorithms and systems' functionality. The systems should be able to make ethical decisions on their own to limit the danger of undesirable conduct. The magnitude of any erroneous decisions made without human intervention grows as the number of autonomous systems that work together grows.

According to several reports, the usage of robots will increase, especially industrial robots. Robots and autonomous systems, on the other hand, are projected to be widely used in society in the next years [26, 27]. A service robot is a robot that performs helpful tasks for humans or equipment in a semiautonomous or fully autonomous manner, excluding industrial automation applications [28]. Industrial robots have had a significant impact for several years. Engineers working on AI systems must be aware of any ethical issues that must be considered [29]. To limit the possibility of undesirable conduct, autonomous systems should be able to make ethical decisions, according to a report by the National Transportation Safety Board. More jobs are created as a result of the adoption of information technology and automation, according to a new report by the Department of Labor.

4.10   Scope of Agribots in India

Currently, developing countries like India are facing problems in labor shortage and most of the operations like the placement of seed at equal distancing, nutrient management, seedbed preparation, tillage, and transplantation are still done manually. One of the major issues influencing output is the occurrence of disease in horticulture crops. Due to a lack of knowledge about the illness, manual crop monitoring is arduous and prone to errors. Additionally, about 33% of total losses are due to the presence of weeds (source: Weed Science Research). Besides, bulk harvesting is the traditional method usually followed in India. One of the latest developments, which answer the above-stated problems, is by using agricultural autonomous robots and mobilerobot. Recently, only in few parts of India, agricultural autonomous robots are being used in a controlled environment for picking tomatoes, cucumbers, mushrooms, and so on.

At Green Robot lab, Bengaluru, India focuses on smart machines for harvesting cotton and horticulture crops. "Green Robot," a prototype has been designed to detect and pluck cotton bolls individually with an average speed of 2 seconds/cotton boll without running through the plant's branches. It could be used to harvest strawberries, grapes, and even weeds. This prototype is the first of its kind in India. These machines can also be used to perform labor-demanding tasks, such as weeding, pruning, and spraying.

Agribot, designed by BIT students, is used to increase productivity by automating the field works like harvesting, spraying, seeding, and removal of weeds. Researchers from IIT Kharagpur have developed a robotic arm to pick cotton using 3D machine vision techniques [25]. Further, a researcher in India has designed a mobile robot with vision sensors for disease identification in a greenhouse.

In a study by Bikram *et al.* [24], a novel robotic coconut tree climber and harvester called "Amaran" is proposed. It's made out of a ring-shaped structure that houses a robotic arm and a cutter. It can be operated using a wireless interface, either by an operator or by an App. According to trial data, it can climb up to 15.2 meters with a circumference of 0.66 to 0.92 meters with trunk inclinations of up to 30 degrees [24].

It is now possible for autonomous robot vehicles to continuously monitor the crop canopy and identify the pest and diseases at early stages. With the advancement in computer vision, the actual position of the weeds can be identified. Variable-rate technologies are currently used to maintain soil health by detecting nitrogen and potassium level in real time using IoT.

4.11   Challenges in the Deployment of Robots

Autonomous mobile robots are made functional by incorporating suitable electronic and communication systems based on the application to carry out agricultural tasks. The design is getting complicated to meet the current requirements, which in turn affects its reliability and increases the cost. The current challenge is to build a cost-effective and reliable robotic system with minimum hardware and software.

Another most common issue is robustness where the current agribots are not robust to withstand the adverse climatic and soil conditions, such as rain, dew, extreme temperatures, muddy soil, and so on [21]. Besides, to deploy a useful commercial robot platform, the innovators need to be aware and address the design issues, such as robustness and reliability, managing the power system, user-friendliness [21], and integration with the latest technologies to perform intelligent autonomous tasks.

Despite the tremendous amount of research, robots are still not available commercially, which is dedicated to complex field environments, such as Indian fields [6]. The robots used in a controlled environment cannot be adopted to an uncontrolled environment and such robots are still in the development stage [7].

Although field robots are advancing, it is difficult to automate faster and accurate fruit harvesting and picking. Plants in multi-annual crops should not be injured while harvesting. High-value crops require selective harvesting, which is one of the most time-consuming and costly activities [23]. Irrespective of the crop type, harvesting needs a plucking hand on a manipulator that has to be flexible to move in the right direction by overcoming all the obstacles and wind to localize and pick the fruit accurately without damage. Besides, it should be integrated with an advanced vision system to overcome the challenges, such as changing light intensity, accurate detection, and localization, color, texture of the fruit, and so on. [22]. Although many innovative solutions are being provided by hi-tech companies and R&D Institutions on selective harvesting robots, it is still a challenge because it does not meet the expected success rate and speed and because of large levels of variation and inadequate data [23]. Besides, the design will be farm- and crop-specific whether it is a high-value crop or multiannual crop.

In India, the farmers have very few farms ranging from 10 to 400 acres [1]. First, there is a lack of sufficient laborers to do various field tasks. Deploying weed control robots has the biggest challenge to identify weed from crops since both are plants. Second, the crop plants are mechanically planted almost in a structured manner but the weeds will grow in random patterns so adopting robotic machines is difficult as they injure the nearby crop plants unknowingly. Another challenge was the battery life of the multirotor, which ranges from few minutes to an hour [1] as a result, it is not possible to cover the entire field. With drones, the challenges faced are hardware components integrating with software, modeling of a dynamic system, and its implementation.

4.12   Future Scope of Robotics in Agriculture

Artificial Intelligence will be useful in predicting weather and other agricultural circumstances, such as land quality, groundwater, crop cycle, and pest assault, among others. Most of the farmers' fears will be alleviated by precise projection or prediction using AI technology. Artificial Intelligence–powered sensors are extremely beneficial for extracting critical agricultural data. The information will help improve output. These sensors have a lot of potential in agriculture. Data, such as soil quality, weather, and groundwater level, among other things, can be derived by agriculture scientists and used to optimize the cultivation process. To collect data, AI-enabled sensors can be integrated into robotic harvesting equipment. The most difficult aspect of farming is crop damage caused by natural disasters, such as pest attacks. The majority of the time, farmers lose their crops owing to a lack of sufficient information. In this cyber age, technology might be beneficial to farmers in protecting their crops from cyber-attacks. In this case, AI-assisted image recognition will be advantageous. Drones have been used by several companies to monitor production and detect insect infestations. Such procedures have previously proven to be useful, motivating the development of a system to monitor and protect crops. The revolution in AI can help the world to face the biggest challenge of providing food for an extra two billion people by 2050.

By the middle of the century, the United Nations forecasts that we will need to raise food production by 50%. Agricultural productivity tripled from 1960 to 2015, as the world's population grew from three billion to seven billion people [49]. Although the usage of herbicides, fertilizers, and machinery was beneficial, a large part of the development may be attributed to ploughing additional land by clearing forests and diverting water. In the coming years, AI will undoubtedly change agriculture and the economy. Farmers have been able to comprehend numerous forms of hybrid cultivations that would produce more cash in a shorter period. The right application of AI in agriculture will aid in the agricultural process, as well as generate a market environment. There is a lot of food waste around the world, and with the right algorithms, this problem may be overcome, saving time and money while also promoting long-term development. Agriculture has a better probability of adopting digital transformation than other industries. However, it all hinges on a vast amount of data that are impossible to get because of the production process, which only happens one or two times a year. Farmers, on the other hand, are adapting to the shifting landscape by applying AI to bring digital transformation to agriculture.

4.13   Conclusion

In recent years, robots have developed themselves in agriculture. This chapter focused mainly on the different types of agricultural robots, the need, and scope of the robot, and their challenges. Precision agriculture aims to use a variety of technologies to learn about crop spatial and temporal variability. Ground robots are used to treat plants preciously, and aerial robots are used to produce field maps for identifying irrigation shortfalls or weeds, among other technologies. Furthermore, Robo-agriculture has been incorporated into greenhouse agriculture. The UAVs and UGVs are the most commonly used robots in agriculture. Aerial robots are commonly used to gain field knowledge by taking advantage of their altitude. Although fixed-wing UAVs were the first agricultural aerial robots, multi-rotors are becoming more popular due to their versatility. Robots that work on the ground are usually utilized to work on crops. The most common configurations are caterpillar and wheeled robots, with the chosen navigation and position algorithms being the critical challenges. Other designs, like spherical or bioinspired robots and multirobot systems, are gaining power than single robot systems.

References

1. Jerry, J., AgRobots: A glimpse into Futuristic Farming, 26 May 2020. https://iit-techambit.in/agrobots-a-glimpse-into-futuristic-farming/.
2. Hille, K., Rising Carbon Dioxide Levels Will Help and Hurt Crops, 2016.
3. PyTorch ML framework is now used for weed control: United States (USA)• Agriculture•, India, Aug 13, 2020. https://indiaai.gov.in/news/pytorch-ml-frame-work-is-now-used-for-weed-control.
4. Food and Agriculture Organization of the United Nations (FAO), How to Feed the World 2050. High-Level Expert Forum, 2009.

5. Golan, E., Kuchler, F., Mitchell, L., Economic research service, us department of agriculture. *Agric. Econ. Rep.*, 793, 2000.

6. Urrea, C. and Muñoz, J., Path tracking of mobile robot in crops. *J. Intell. Robot. Syst.*, 80, 2, 193–205, 2015.

7. Bac, C.W., Hemming, J., vanHenten, E.J., Robust pixel-based classification of obstacles for robotic harvesting of sweet-pepper. *Comput. Electron. Agric.*, 96, 148–162, August 2013.

8. Talaviya, T., Shah, D., Patel, N., Yagnik, H., Shah, M., Implementation of artificial intelligence in agriculture for optimisation of irrigation and application of pesticides and herbicides. *Artif. Intell. Agric.*, 4, 58–73, 2020.

9. Anthony, D., Elbaum, S., Lorenz, A., Detweiler, C., On crop height estimation with UAVs. In *2014 IEEE/RSJ International Conference on Intelligent Robots and Systems,* IEEE, pp. 4805–4812, 2014.

10. Primicerio, J., Di Gennaro, S.F., Fiorillo, E., Genesio, L., Lugato, E., Matese, A., Vaccari, F.P., A flexible unmanned aerial vehicle for precision agriculture. *Precis. Agric.*, 13, 4, 517–523, 2012.

11. Huang, Y., Hoffmann, W.C., Lan, Y., Wu, W., Fritz, B.K., Development of a spray system for an unmanned aerial vehicle platform. *Appl. Eng. Agric.*, 25, 6, 803–809, 2009.

12. Bendig, J., Bolten, A., Bareth, G., Introducing a low-cost mini-UAV for thermal-and multispectral-imaging. *Int. Arch. Photogramm. Remote Sens. Spat. Inf. Sci*, 39, 345–349, 2012.

13. Sankaran, S., Khot, L.R., Carter, A.H., Field-based crop phenotyping: Multispectral aerial imaging for evaluation of winter wheat emergence and spring stand. *Comput. Electron. Agric.*, 118, 372–379, 2015.

14. Venkateswarlu, N.B. and Raju, P.S.V.S.K., Fast iso data clustering algorithms. *Pattern Recognit.*, 25, 3, 335–342, 1992.

15. Knight, A.W., Tindall, D.R., Wilson, B.A., A multitemporal multiple density slice method for wetland mapping across the state of Queensland, Australia. *Int. J. Remote Sens.*, 30, 13, 3365–3392, 2009.

16. Puri, V., Nayyar, A., Raja, L., Agriculture drones: A modern breakthrough in precision agriculture Machine Learning and Software Systems. *J. Stat. Manage. Syst.*, 20, 4, 507–518, 2017.

17. Gonzalez-de-Santos, P., Fernández, R., Sepúlveda, D., Navas, E., Emmi, L., Armada, M., Field Robots for Intelligent Farms—Inhering Features from Industry. *Agronomy*, 10, 11, 1638, 2020.

18. Mahmud, M.S.A., Abidin, M.S.Z., Emmanuel, A.A., Hasan, H.S., Robotics and automation in agriculture: Present and future applications. *Appl. Model. Simul.*, 4, 130–140, 2020.

19. Emmi, L., Gonzalez-de-Soto, M., Pajares, G., Gonzalez-de-Santos, P., New trends in robotics for agriculture: integration and assessment of a real fleet of robots. *Sci. World J.*, 2014.

20. Rubio, F., Valero, F., Llopis-Albert, C., A review of mobile robots: Concepts, methods, theoretical framework, and applications. *Int. J. Adv. Robotic Systems*, 16, 2, 1729881419839596, 2019.
21. Onishi, Y., Yoshida, T., Kurita, H., Fukao, T., Arihara, H., Iwai, A., An automated fruit harvesting robot by using deep learning. *Robomech J.*, 6, 1, 1–8, 2019.
22. Kootstra, G., Wang, X., Blok, P. M., Hemming, J., & Van Henten, E., Selective harvesting robotics: current research, trends, and future directions. *Curr. Robot. Rep.*, 1–10, 2021.
23. Megalingam, R.K., Manoharan, S.K., Mohandas, S.M., Vadivel, S.R.R., Gangireddy, R., Ghanta, S., Kumar, K.S., Teja, P.S., Sivanantham, V., Amaran: An Unmanned Robotic Coconut Tree Climber and Harvester. *IEEE/ASME Trans. Mechatron.*, 26, 1, 288–299, 2020.
24. Jyoti, B., Chandel, N.S., Agarwal, K.N., Application of Robotics in Agriculture: An Indian Perspective. *8th Asian-Australasian Conference on Precision Agriculture*, 2019.
25. IFR. (2016). World Robotics Report, in: *International Federation of Robotics*, 2016.
26. Taxonomy and definitions for terms related to driving automation systems for on-road motor vehicles, in: *SAE J3016 Standard 2016 (SAE International)*, SAE. (2016, Available at: http://standards.sae.org/j3016_201609/.
27. Robotics, D. S., IFR International Federation of Robotics–service robots. International Federation of Robotics. *Service Robots*, 2017. Available at: http://www.ifr.org/service-robots/.
28. Liakos, K., Busato, P., Moshou, D., Pearson, S., Bochtis, D., Machine Learning in Agriculture: A Review. *Sensors*, 18, 8, 2674, 2018. 10.3390/s18082674.
29. Panpatte, D.G., Artificial intelligence in agriculture: An emerging era of research, in: *Intutional Science*, Anand Agricultural University, pp. 1–8, 2018.
30. Ferguson, R.B., Shapiro, C.A., Hergert, G.W., Kranz, W.L., Klocke, N.L., Krull, D.H., Nitrogen and Irrigation Management Practices to Minimize Nitrate Leaching from Irrigated Corn, in: *Jpa*, vol. 4, p. 186, 1991.
31. Robotics, W., Executive summary world robotics 2016 industrial robots. *Int. Fed. Robot.*, 2016.
32. Kumar, G., Research paper on water irrigation by using wireless sensor network, in: *International Journal of Scientific Engineering and Technology, IEERT Conference Paper*, pp. 123–125, 2014.
33. Shekhar, Y., Dagur, E., Mishra, S., Tom, R.J., Veeramanikandan, M., Sankaranarayanan, S., Intelligent IoT based automated irrigation system. *Int. J. Appl. Eng. Res.*, 12, 18, 7306–7320, 2017.
34. Dukes, M.D., Shedd, M., Cardenas-Lailhacar, B., Smart Irrigation Controllers: How Do Soil Moisture Sensor (SMS) Irrigation Controllers Work?. EDIS, 2, 2009.
35. Yong, W., Shuaishuai, L., Li, L., Minzan, L., Ming, L., Arvanitis, K. G., ... & Sigrimis, N., Smart sensors from ground to cloud and web intelligence. *IFAC-PapersOnLine*, 51, 17, 31–38, 2018.

36. Rajpal, A., Jain, S., Khare, N., Shukla, A.K., *Proc. of the International Conference on Science and Engineering*, pp. 94–96, 2011.
37. Bak, T. and Jakobsen, H., Agricultural robotic platform with four-wheel steering for weed detection. *Biosyst. Eng.*, 87, 2125–2136, 2003.
38. Nakai, S. and Yamada, Y., Development of a Weed Suppression Robot for Rice Cultivation: Weed Suppression and Posture Control. *Int. J. Electr. Comput. Electr. Commun. Eng.*, 8, 12, 1658–1662, 2014.
39. Fennimore, S.A., Slaughter, D.C., Siemens, M.C., Leon, R.G., Saber, M.N., Technology for Automation of Weed Control in Specialty Crops. *Weed Technol.*, 30, 04, 823–837, 2016.
40. Ahirwar, S., Swarnkar, R., Bhukya, S., Namwade, G., Application of drone in agriculture. *Int. J. Curr. Microbiol. App. Sci.*, 8, 1, 2500–2505, 2019.
41. Abdullahi, H.S., Mahieddine, F., Sheriff, R.E., Technology impact on agricultural productivity: A review of precision agriculture using unmanned aerial vehicles. In *International conference on wireless and satellite systems,* pp. 388–400, Springer, Cham, 2015.
42. Costa, F.G., Ueyama, J., Braun, T., Pessin, G., Osorio, F.S., Vargas, P.A., The use of unmanned aerial vehicles and wireless sensor network in agricultural applications, in: *2012 IEEE International Geoscience and Remote Sensing Symposium*, 2012.
43. Puri, V., Nayyar, A., Raja, L., Agriculture drones: a modern breakthrough in precision agriculture journal of Statistics and Management Systems. 20, 4, 507–518, 2017.
44. Yaduraju, N.T. (Ed.), *Weed Science for Sustainable Agriculture, Environment and Biodiversity: Proceedings of the Plenary and Lead Papers of the 25th Asian-Pacific Weed Science Society Conference*, Indian Society of Weed Science, Madhya Pradesh, India, 2015.
45. Xue, X., Lan, Y., Sun, Z., Chang, C., Hoffmann, W.C., Develop an unmanned aerial vehicle based automatic aerial spraying system compute. *Electron. Agric.*, 128, 58–66, 2016.
46. Hunt, E.R., Cavigelli, M., Daughtry, C.S.T., Mcmurtrey, J., Walthall, C.L., Evaluation of digital photography from model aircraft for remote sensing of crop biomass and nitrogen status. *Precis. Agric.*, 6, 359–378, 2005.
47. Sonaa, G., Passonia, D., Pintoa, L., Pagliaria, D., Masseroni, D., Ortuani, B., Facchib, A., UAV multispectral survey to map soil and crop for precision farming applications. *The international archives of the photogrammetry, remote sensing, and spatial information sciences*, vol. 9, pp. 1023–102, 2016.
48. Close, De Oca, A.M., Arreola, L., Flores, A., Sanchez, J., Flores, G., Low-cost multispectral imaging system for crop monitoring 2018. *International Conference on Unmanned Aircraft Systems (ICUAS)*, 2018.
49. Talaviya, T., Shah, D., Patel, N., Yagnik, H., Shah, M., Implementation of artificial intelligence in agriculture for optimization of irrigation and application of pesticides and herbicides. *Artif. Intell. Agric.*, 4, 58–73, 2020.

50. Valero, C., Krus, A., Barreiro, P., Diezma, B., Garrido-Izard, M., Hernández, N., ... Pulignani, G., Teaching precision farming and entrepreneurship for European students: Sparkle online course. In *Precision agriculture'21*, pp. 177–190, Wageningen Academic Publishers, 2021.

51. Dutta, P. K. and Mitra, S., Application of Agricultural Drones and IoT to Understand Food Supply Chain During Post COVID-19. *Agric. Inform.: Autom. Using IoT Mach. Learn.*, 67–87, 2021.

52. Sarni, W., Mariani, J., Kaji, J., From Dirt to Data: The Second Green Revolution and IoT. Deloitte insights. Available online: https://www2.deloitte.com/ insights/us/en/deloitte-review/issue-18/second-greenrevolution-and-internet-of-things.html#endnote-sup-9 (accessed on 18 September 2019).

53. Myklevy, M., Doherty, P., Makower, J., *The New Grand Strategy*, p. 271, St. Martin's Press, New York, NY, USA, 2016.

54. Gralla, P., Precision agriculture yields higher profits, lower risks. Hewlett Packard Enterprise, 2018.

55. Kunisch, M., Big Data in Agriculture—Perspectives for a Service Organization. *Landtechnik*, 71, 1–3. [CrossRef], 2016.

56. Kamilaris, A., Kartakoullis, A., Prenafeta-Boldú, F.X., A review on the practice of big data analysis in agriculture. *Comput. Electron. Agric.*, 143, 23–37. [CrossRef], 2017.

57. Coble, K. H., Mishra, A. K., Ferrell, S., Griffin, T. Big data in agriculture: A challenge for the future. *Appl. Econ. Perspect. Policy*, 40, 1, 79–96, 2018.

58. Wolfert, S., Ge, L., Verdouw, C., Bogaardt, M.-J., Big Data in Smart Farming—A review. *Agric. Syst.*, 153, 69–80. [CrossRef], 2017.

59. Platform, C. B. D., Big Data Coordination Platform: Full Proposal 2017–2022, 2016.

60. Lee, E.A., Cyber-Physical Systems: Design Challenges, in: *Proceedings of the 11th IEEE International Symposium on Object and Component-Oriented Real-Time Distributed Computing (ISORC)*, pp. 363–369, 5–7 May 2008.

61. Mell, P. and Grance, T., The NIST definition of cloud computing, 2011.

62. Jadcja, Y. and Modi, K., Cloud computing concepts, architecture, and challenges, in: *Proceedings of the 2012 International Conference on Computing, Electronics and Electrical Technologies (ICCEET)*, Kumaracoil, India, pp. 877–880, 21–22 March 2012.

63. Gonzalez-de-Santos, P., Fernández, R., Sepúlveda, D., Navas, E., Emmi, L., Armada, M., Field Robots for Intelligent Farms—Inhering Features from Industry. *Agronomy*, 10, 11, 1638, 2020.

64. Pratt, G.A. and Williamson, M.M., Series elastic actuators, in: *Proceedings of the 1995 IEEE/RSJ International Conference on Intelligent Robots and Systems. Human-Robot Interaction and Cooperative Robots*, vol. 1, Pittsburgh, PA, USA, p. 399, 5–9 August 1995.

5

The Applications of Industry 4.0 (I4.0) Technologies in the Palm Oil Industry in Colombia (Latin America)

James Pérez-Morón* and Ana Susana Cantillo-Orozco

School of Business, Universidad Tecnológica de Bolívar,
Cartagena de Indias, Colombia

Abstract

Seven percent of world palm oil (PO) production comes from Latin America (LATAM), 15% certified as sustainable PO with the adoption of the Round Table model for Sustainable Palm Oil (RSPO), pointing to sustainable agriculture that contributes to hunger reduction and a reduction of dependence on hydrocarbons for energy. Colombia is the fourth global producer of PO and the first one in LATAM and expects to produce over two million tons in 161 municipalities and 21 departments in 2021.

This document will focus on the Colombian PO industry. The contribution of this study is twofold: First, it provides a more comprehensive review of the PO industry technology literature based on Scopus and Clarivate Analytics, using the reporting checklist of preferred reporting items for systematic reviews and meta-analyses (PRISMA). Second, as far as the authors know, this is one of the first studies to address the technological solutions applied by Colombia's PO producers and aims to help fill this research gap.

Evidence for the use of Internet of Things (IoT), big data (BD), and cloud computing in the Colombian PO industry was found in the extraction plants, in crop and pest management, in the use of seeds with smart tags, and in biofuel generation from PO, positioning it as a country with multiple lessons to offer to the PO industry.

Keywords: Palm oil, agroindustry, technologies, sustainable, Industry 4.0, Colombia

*Corresponding author: jperez@utb.edu.co

Roheet Bhatnagar, Nitin Kumar Tripathi, Nitu Bhatnagar and Chandan Kumar Panda (eds.)
The Digital Agricultural Revolution: Innovations and Challenges in Agriculture through Technology Disruptions, (109–142) © 2022 Scrivener Publishing LLC

5.1   Introduction

The 2030 Agenda for Sustainable Development (SD) acknowledges the vital role of the Agriculture, Sustainability, and People (ASP) triad [1]. It promotes an inclusive and sustainable agriculture sector (the main economic sector in many countries worldwide) that seeks to enrich the living standards of ten billion people by 2050 [2] by providing more nutritious food to meet food security needs while being environmentally friendly [3, 124]. However, 9 years into the 2030 Agenda, the COVID-19 pandemic has worsened food security and nutrition, setting bigger challenges to achieving SD Goal 2 (Zero Hunger) Targets 2.1 and 2.2 [4].

The use of Industry 4.0 (I4.0) technologies in agriculture, including BD [5], cloud computing [6], Internet of Things (IoT) [6, 7], machine learning [5, 8], drones [6], sensors [5, 9], robotics and artificial intelligence [10, 11], 3D printing, Geographic Information System (GIS), Global Positioning System (GPS), cyber security, digital twins, augmented reality, among others [7, 12, 13 101–108, 122], will allow it to work with recent innovations in the industrial sector [8, 14, 64–66, 68–70] and address climate change, food security, sustainability, and farm productivity and profit [9, 94–100].

Palm oil is the world's most valuable oil crop [15], a versatile/important source of edible oil, a potential raw material for biofuel production [16], and the most efficient oil crop produced, with palm producing 3.8 tons per hectare, rape seed and sunflower 0.8, and soy 0.5 [16]. Global PO production has grown from 15.2 million Tons (MT) in 1995 to 75.4 MT in 2020. This volume is mainly produced by Southeast Asian countries, such as Indonesia (58%—43,500 MT) and Malaysia (26%—19,900 MT). Colombia is ranked fourth (2%—1,559 MT) and leads production in the Americas [25]. Other parts of the worlds have also seen an increase in PO production, including Thailand (4%—3,100 MT) and Nigeria (2%—1,280 MT). Table 5.1 summarizes the top 10 PO-producing countries worldwide.

However, just a small portion of producers are net exporters [18]. Indonesia and Malaysia combined represent 90% of the world's exports as shown in Table 5.2, whereas the remaining countries account for no more than 3% [18 , 49, 51, 54].

Historically, PO was mainly consumed by traditional producer countries, like Colombia, Indonesia, Papua New Guinea, and Honduras [17]. However, consumption has shifted to many non-producing and industrialized countries where PO has multiple applications, both edible and non-edible. Palm oil is the most widely consumed oil worldwide, and its global consumption has quadrupled, from 14.6 MT in 1995 to 70.5 MT in 2018.

Table 5.1 Top 10 PO world production.

Rank	Country	Percent of world production (%)	Production (1000 MT)
1	Indonesia	58	43,500
2	Malaysia	26	19,900
3	Thailand	4	3,100
4	Colombia	2	1,559
5	Nigeria	2	1,280
6	Guatemala	1	865
7	Ecuador	1	615
8	Honduras	1	580
9	Papua New Guinea	1	561
10	Brazil	1	540

Source: Original Table.

Table 5.2 Top 10 PO world exports 2020.

World exports 51,338 (1000 MT)			
Rank	Country	Percent of world exports (%)	Exports (1000 MT)
1	Indonesia	56	28,850
2	Malaysia	34	17,275
3	Guatemala	2	850
4	Colombia	1	725
5	Papua Nueva Guinea	1	750
6	Honduras	1	400
7	Thailand	1	325
8	Other	1	300
9	Ecuador	1	265
10	Cote d'Ivoire	0	2 30

Source: Original Table.

The top 3 PO global importers (together consuming 45% of global imports) are India (17%—8,700 MT), China (14%—6,900 MT), and the European Union (14%—6,800 MT). Table 5.3 shows the top 10 global importers.

Palm oil (PO) helps attain SDG 1 No Poverty by reducing rural poverty, SDG 2 Zero Hunger by producing the most versatile and efficient vegetable oil in the world, SDG 8 Decent Work and Economic Growth by generating income above the poverty line, SDG 10 Reduced Inequality by decreasing inequality between urban and rural populations, and SDG 13 Climate Action by promoting forest conservation and sustainable production [19–22], and the global expansion of PO production, especially in South East Asia, LATAM, and West Africa [21], has led to a wide variety of concerns related to ecosystem integrity, such as, greenhouse emissions (GHG), forests of high conservation value (HCV), waste generation, High Carbon Stock Forests (HCS), habitat degradation, deforestation (PO generates an annual loss of 270,000 hectares of forests, in contrast with 380,000 from lumber, 480,000 from soy and 2,710,000 from livestock farming) [24, 73–82], biodiversity, and land use change (LUC) [21, 23].

Table 5.3 Top 10 palm oil world imports 2020.

World imports 49,931 (1000 MT)			
Rank	**Country**	**Percent of world imports (%)**	**Imports (1000 MT)**
1	India	17	8.700
2	China	14	6,900
3	European Union	14	6,800
4	Pakistan	7	3,450
5	Bangladesh	3	1,650
6	Other	3	1,650
7	United States	3	1,450
8	Philippines	2	1,225
9	Egypt	2	1,200
10	Kenya	2	1,050

Source: Original Table.

These serious concerns have required coordinated responses to arrive at sustainably produced PO: (1) In 2004, several companies and non-governmental organizations (NGOs) established the first global sustainability standard to certify the production and use of sustainable PO and founded the RSPO, a multi-stakeholder initiative that brings together actors from each link of the global value chain [20, 26, 58, 60–62]. Some other examples of sustainable PO standards are the International Sustainability & Carbon Certification (ISCC), the Indonesian Sustainable Palm Oil (ISPO), Malaysian Sustainable Palm Oil (MSPO), and the North American Sustainable Palm Oil Network created by the USA and Canada [27, 83–92].

There have been several review articles on PO and I4.0 published between 2000 and 2021 [28, 29, 31–36, 50, 52–54]. Although informative, these articles only reviewed a portion of the literature. Thus, the first contribution of this research is to offer a more complete review of PO industry technologies by following the reporting checklist of the PRISMA [37, 38].

Another limitation of the previous work is that it excludes the application of I4.0 technologies in the LATAM PO industry from the research [41–46]. The novelty of this work lies in addressing the use of I4.0 technologies in the Colombian PO industry, which can provide lessons for other Latin and Central American PO producers, such as Brazil, Mexico, and Chile, and seeks to help fill this research gap.

The review in this research is lead by this research question: Research on Industry 4.0 in the global PO industry is still immature. However, the Colombian PO industry has been implementing these technologies. *What have been the results of the use of these new technologies in the Colombian PO Industry?*

The rest of this study is organized as follows: The method used for the literature review is discussed in section 2. The third section is focused on summarizing the findings of prior studies. Future research direction is outlined in the following section. The final section provides a summary of findings and conclusions.

5.2   Methodology

5.2.1   Sample Selection

Following the method used by previous reviews [39, 40], this study used Scopus and Clarivate Analytics, as well as their reference lists, to determine 79 focal documents released in the fields of PO and I4.0 from 2000 to 2021, restricted to articles included in the Social Science Citation Index

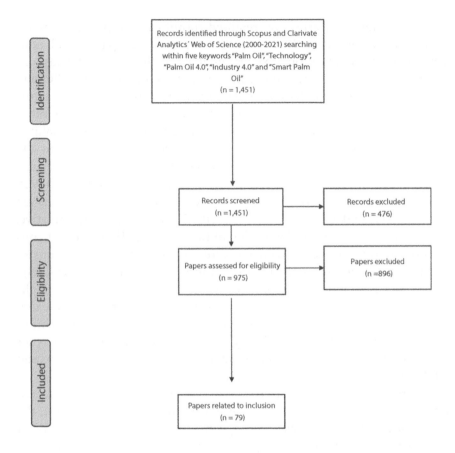

Figure 5.1 PRISMA analysis. Source: Original.

(SSCI) [39]. These 79 focal articles belonged to the following domains, among others: environmental sciences, ecology, business economics, science technology, energy fuels, and agriculture.

To include all studies relevant to the field, the authors adopted a systematic four-step process as described below. First, the authors used keywords, including *Palm Oil, Industry 4.0, Palm Oil 4.0, Palm Oil and Technology, and Smart Palm Oil.* The study identified and combined keyword synonyms for a more comprehensive search. The authors search used both "free terms" and "index terms" funnelled using the OR Boolean operator and the proximity operator W/n "within." The maximum distance between keywords was four words to ensure a closer relationship between the keywords selected in the results.

Using the chosen keywords, the search returned 1,451 articles published in journals. The authors then independently reviewed these articles and

Table 5.4 Focal articles selected.

Journal name	Articles	Reference
Agricultural Economics	2	(Krishna *et al.*, 2019; Ruml and Qaim, 2021)
Agricultural Economics-Zemedelska Ekonomika	1	(Zahri *et al.*, 2019)
Agricultural Systems	2	(Aguilar-Gallegos *et al.*, 2015; Hounkonnou *et al.*, 2018)
Annual Review of Resource Economics, Vol./ 5	1	(Byerlee and Deininger, 2013)
Applied Geography	1	(Portillo-Quintero and Smith, 2018)
Biofuels-UK	1	(Souza *et al.*, 2018)
Biotechnology For Biofuels	1	(Amin *et al.*, 2017)
Bulletin of Indonesian Economic Studies	1	(Gaskell, 2015)
Business Strategy and the Environment	1	(Gueneau, 2018)
Computers & Operations Research	1	(Abdul-Hamid *et al.*, 2020)
Energy	2	(Umar *et al.*, 2014; Harahap *et al.*, 2019)
Energy & Environment	2	(Olusola *et al.*, 2009; John, 2010)
Energy Policy	5	(Quintero *et al.*, 2012; Kelly-Yong *et al.*, 2007; Abdullah *et al.*, 2009); Takahashi and Ortega, 2010; Yusoff *et al.*, 2013)
Energy Sources Part B-Economics Planning and Policy	1	(Sakulsuraekkapong and Pairintra, 2018)

(*Continued*)

Table 5.4 Focal articles selected. (*Continued*)

Journal name	Articles	Reference
Engineering Studies	1	(Mackenzie, 2013)
Environmental Management	1	(Rodthong *et al.*, 2020)
Environmental Research Letters	1	(Correa *et al.*, 2020)
Environmental Science and Pollution Research	1	(Sarkar *et al.*, 2020)
European Journal of Development Research	1	(Bachtold *et al.*, 2020)
Food and Bioproducts Processing	1	(Ghani *et al.*, 2019)
Food Policy	1	(Ramirez *et al.*, 2018)
Food Quality and Preference	1	(Hartmann *et al.*, 2018)
Forest Policy and Economics	1	(Varkkey *et al.*, 2018)
Global Environmental Change- Human and Policy Dimensions	1	(Newton *et al.*, 2013)
Health Promotion International	1	(Downs *et al.*, 2015)
Historia Agraria	1	(Clare, 2012)
IEEE Access	1	(Ul-Haq *et al.*, 2020)
International Journal of Primatology	1	(Luncz *et al.*, 2017)
International Journal of The Commons	1	(Surahman *et al.*, 2019)
Journal of Agrarian Change	2	(Castellanos-Navarrete and Jansen, 2018; Neimark and Healy, 2018)
Journal of Agrarian Change	1	(Euler *et al.*, 2016)
Journal of Cleaner Production	5	(Hansen *et al.*, 2015; Murakami *et al.*, 2015; Bautista *et al.*, 2019; Koistinen *et al.*, 2019; Er *et al.*, 2012)

(*Continued*)

Table 5.4 Focal articles selected. (*Continued*)

Journal name	Articles	Reference
Journal of Environmental Economics and Management	1	(Rudolf *et al.*, 2020)
Journal of Evolutionary Economics	1	(Wong, 2016)
Journal of Medical Systems	1	(Selanikio *et al.*, 2002)
Journal of Peasant Studies	2	(Cardenas, 2012; Radjawali *et al.*, 2017)
Journal of Rural Studies	1	(Martin *et al.*, 2015)
Journal of SouthEast Asian Studies	1	(Robins, 2020)
Journal of Technology Transfer	1	(Lebdioui *et al.*, 2020)
Land Use Policy	1	(Ruysschaert and Hufty, 2020)
Production Planning & Control	1	(Shukla and Tiwari, 2017)
Public Health Nutrition	1	(Shankar *et al.*, 2017)
Regional Environmental Change	1	(Uckert *et al.*, 2015)
Renewable & Sustainable Energy Reviews	4	(How *et al.*, 2019; Xu *et al.*, 2020; Shehu and Clarke, 2020; Zhao *et al.*, 2020)
Renewable Energy	1	(Umar *et al.*, 2018)
Resources Consideration and Recycling	1	(Capaz *et al.*, 2021)
Royal Society Open Science	1	(Proffitt *et al.*, 2018)
Scientific World Journal	1	(Amin *et al.*, 2013)
Sustainability	7	(Srichaichana *et al.*, 2019; Aghamohammadi *et al.*, 2016; Gallemore and Jespersen, 2019; Aziz *et al.*, 2020, Nasution *et al* 2020; Permpool *et al.*, 2021; Ho *et al.*, 2020)

(*Continued*)

Table 5.4 Focal articles selected. (*Continued*)

Journal name	Articles	Reference
Sustainable Production and Consumption	2	(Munasinghe *et al.*, 2019; Leong *et al.*, 2019)
Technological and Economic Development Economy	1	(Wong and Govindaraju, 2012)
Technology in Society	1	(Adejuwon *et al.*, 2016)
Technovation	1	(Hansen and Ockwell, 2014)
World Development	1	(Bishop, 2018)
Zoo Biology	1	(Pearson *et al.*, 2014)
Total Number of Journal Articles	79 from 55 Journals	

Source: Original.

discussed the relevance of the articles and which ones to exclude from the final sample. Given the aim of this study, the authors consciously excluded 476 documents that did not explicitly discuss PO- and I4.0-related concepts.

The resulting list of 975 documents was refined by selecting journals from 2000 to 2021 with an SSCI impact factor to ensure high-quality data, which led to the exclusion of 896 articles (see Figure 5.1).

This iterative process resulted in a final set of 79 focal articles (see Table 5.4).

This study filtered the data in the final database using criteria, such as authors, journals, numbers of citations, references, and publication years, and excluded the following documents: articles published in letters, editorials, note, incorrect affiliations, inaccessible abstracts, and wrong titles. The authors used the VOSviewer software to visualize bibliometric maps. Based on the initial sample of 79 articles, and for deeper analysis, three additional lists were created using Scopus and Clarivate Analytics features: (1) 5,337 references of the 79 focal documents, (2) 1,167 publications that cited the 79 focal documents, and (3) 1,094 references to these 79 publications.

5.3 Results Analysis

Based on the 79 focal articles selected, using criteria, such as categories, publication years, authors, countries/regions, number of citations,

Table 5.5 includes the top 10 journals publishing the focal articles, citations, and impact factor from 2000 to 2021. From 2000 to 2010, only six articles/7.59% of the total were published (one in 2002, one in 2007, two in 2009, and two in 2010), several years saw zero publications in the field (2000, 2001, 2003 to 2006, 2008). The second decade of the century has seen increased publications starting with five articles in 2012 (6.32%) to 16 articles in 2020 (20.25%), which was the most prolific year. The first 3 months of 2021 added three articles to the list (Figure 5.2).

The following figure provides the top ten research areas. Environmental sciences ecology is ranked first with 33 records (41.77%), business economics has 22 (27.84%), science technology has 21 (26.58%), energy fuels has 15 (18.98%), and engineering has 13 (16.45%). The remaining categories contribute between 1% and 7% (Figure 5.3).

As for the countries/regions with most publications, Malaysia is ranked first with 19 articles (24.05%), followed by England with 14 articles (17.72%), USA with 12 (15.19%), Thailand with 9 (11.39%), and Germany with 7 (8.86%). Brazil is the Latin American country with the most publications (5, 6.32%) followed by Colombia with 4 (5.06%). Surprisingly, the

Table 5.5 Top 10 journals publishing the focal articles, citations, and impact factor 2019.

Rank	N	Outlets of focal articles	No. of citations	Impact factor 2019
1	7	Sustainability	32	2.57
2	5	Energy Policy	333	5.04
3	5	Journal of Cleaner Production	117	7.24
4	4	Renewable Sustainable Energy Reviews	12	12.11
5	2	Agricultural Economics	30	2.26
6	2	Agricultural Systems	45	4.21
7	2	Energy	56	6.08
8	2	Energy Environment	2	1.77
9	2	Journal of Agrarian Change	13	1.98
10	2	Journal of Peasant Studies	41	5.17

Note: N = Number of articles.
Source: Original.

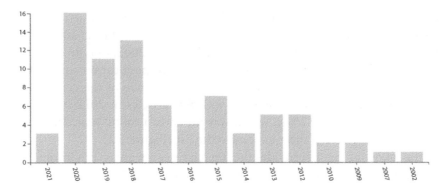

Figure 5.2 Publication years analysis. Source: Clarivate Analytics.

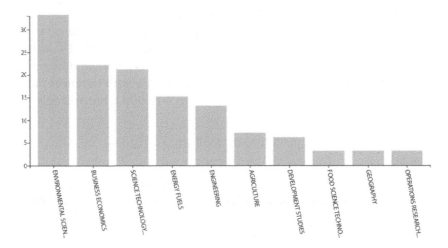

Figure 5.3 Top 10 research areas. Source: Clarivate Analytics.

top 2 PO importers, India with three articles (3.79%) and China with none, have few publications in the field. The preferred language for most of the 79 articles is English with 78 publications (98.73%), the remaining article is in Spanish [71] and covers Costa Rica.

Table 5.6 shows the most influential publications in the field of PO and I4.0 and its historical roots—the most cited references. The work of Kelly-Yong et al. [28] is the number 1 article with the most citations (168). Here, the authors highlight the availability of PO biomass to be transformed into hydrogen. Second place goes to the seminal article by Abdullah et al. [29], where the authors show Malaysia current scenario of both the biodiesel program and biofuel policies.

Although the agricultural sector is not an ally to I4.0, the sector can achieve higher yields through technology and the implementation of

Table 5.6 Top 10 most-cited focal articles.

Rank	Citations	Focal articles
1	169	Kelly-Yong (2007)
2	95	Abdullah *et al.* (2009)
3	63	Hansen *et al.* (2015)
4	60	Newton *et al.* (2013)
5	50	Hartmann *et al.* (2018)
6	48	Euler *et al.* (2016)
7	43	Aguilar-Gallegos *et al.* (2015)
8	43	Hansen *et al.* (2014)
9	36	Murakami *et al.* (2015)
10	32	Umar *et al.* (2014)

Source: Original.

artificial intelligence (AI) techniques [116] in decision-making processes. At the same time, Mohd and Arenas [109] explain how geospatial and information technology (IT) contribute to the modernization of PO plantations. Along these same lines, technical remote sensing to obtain geospatial information, and the use of field platforms, aerial and space sensors and devices, are techniques that enable monitoring crop conditions.

I4.0 implies digital innovations in industry and companies with a mixture of disruptive new technologies. In the study by Rozo-García [110], a review of the concept is made based on the "fusion of physical systems, digital systems, and biological systems to generate an intelligent production network."

Therefore, according to Abdul-Hamid *et al* and Zulqarnain *et al.* [111, 118], current technologies are the IoT, BD, and cloud computing, and these in turn relate to a chain of concepts and methods that enable the changes demanded by society and the administrative production processes of 21st century industries. These are in evidence in the technological instruments demanded to improve land use, as exemplified by Parody and Zapata [112], which is a system to increase production while reducing costs and environmental impacts, known as Precision Agriculture (PA), integrating information and technological tools to process crop resources and inputs optimally and efficiently.

Geospatial and IT support the modernization of oil palm plantations, and remote sensing is used to obtain geospatial information from sensors and devices that are not in direct contact with the targets. In this context, the PO agribusiness in Colombia has experience with the application of significant innovations (see Figure 5.4).

In this vein, Adamchuk *et al.* [119] refer to Malaysia and Indonesia as pioneers in the integration of technologies like GPS, sensors, and Geographic Information Systems (GIS) in agronomic database management systems, which are sets of mechanisms that increase efficiency in fertilizer use, productivity, and environmental variable tracking. For Shang *et al.* [120], digital agriculture, smart agriculture, or agriculture 4.0, addresses the use of new technologies for agricultural processes.

According to The Organization for Economic Co-operation and Development [121], digital tools provide opportunities that result in better policies for the sector. From a government point of view, they aid with the design and implementation of data-based policies, and digital technologies can help regulators minimize public costs and monitor producers. Governments can also use them to improve administrative functions.

Complementing this, precision agriculture or site-specific crop management, uses GPS technologies, information technologies, agricultural management and economic knowledge, and sensors among others [121].

5.3.1   Data Visualization

The authors used VOSviewer software for creating maps based on Clarivate Analytics/Scopus data and for visualizing and exploring them, specifically these are the maps the author selected: cooccurrence, coauthorship, citation, and cocitation.

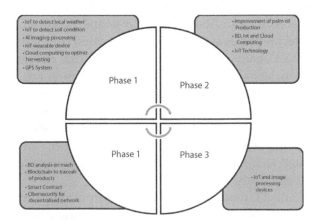

Figure 5.4 Technologies used for PO management. Source: Original.

5.3.2   Cooccurrence

First, the authors chose this type of analysis, including all keywords and full counting as the counting method, which means that cooccurrence link has the same weight. From the 631 keywords extracted from all focal documents, the authors selected 121 that had two minimum occurrences. The top 3 clusters are PO in blue, technology in red, and sustainability in purple on the map (Figure 5.5), the most used keywords are PO (22 occurrences and a total link strength (TLS) of 108), sustainability (15 occurrences and a TLS of 89), renewable energy (10 occurrences and a TLS of 67), biomass (8 occurrences and a TLS of 58).

5.3.3   Coauthorship

This analysis reviews the existing links between the authors and where they are from. For each of the 32 authors divided in 20 clusters, the strength of coauthorship links with other will be shown. Of 41 countries, Malaysia is the most productive (19 articles come from that region, which is 24.05% of the total), followed by England (14 records—17.72%), USA (12 records—15.19%, Thailand (9 records—11.39%), and Germany (7 records-8.86%). The first two Latin-American countries in this list are Brazil (5 records—6.32%9 and Colombia (4 records—5.06%) (Figure 5.6).

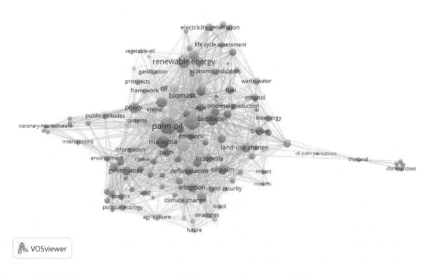

Figure 5.5 Word cooccurrence map (full counting). Source: VOSviewer.

Figure 5.6 Map of authors. Source: VOSviewer.

The four Colombian records include Correa *et al.* [93] where the authors speak about sustainable biofuel production alternatives in the region; Bautista *et al.* [72] predicted that the government policies are vital to rise biodiesel production; Ramirez *et al.* [56] discussed patterns in which small- and medium-sized producers are included in agricultural food clusters in Peru (mango) and Colombia PO, and finally [47], the most cited document of these four articles with 27 citations discussed liquid biofuel production systems that would include small farms in their supply chains and how to make them more competitive. None of them is part of the top 10 most cited articles, which represents a challenge for researchers in Colombia. As far as authors can tell, this research is one of the first that covers I4.0 and its applications in the Colombian PO industry.

5.3.4   Citation

For this type of analysis, the authors chose "documents" as the unit of analysis. Of the 79 focal articles, the authors chose a threshold of a minimum of one citation per document. Sixty-eight met the threshold. Umar *et al* and Aghamohammadi *et al.* [57, 63] have five which is the highest link between authors, followed by Abdullah *et al.*, Euler *et al.*, How *et al.* [29, 32, and 59] with three links each (Figure 5.7). The average citation per article is 15.03. 1,187 times have been cited the focal articles, 1,167 without self-citations, above 98% of the total.

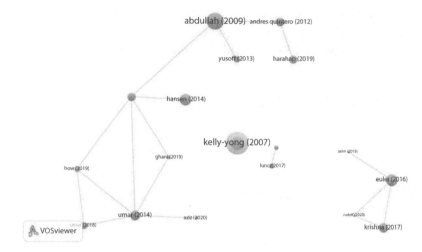

Figure 5.7 Citations. Source: VOSviewer.

5.3.5   Cocitation

For the cocitation analysis, the authors selected "cited references" as unit of analysis, and full counting as the counting method. Of 5,041 cited references, 223 met the threshold, a minimum number of citations of a cited reference was set to two (Figure 5.8). Of the 79 focal articles, 1,112 times have been cocited one or more times, 1,099 times without self-citation.

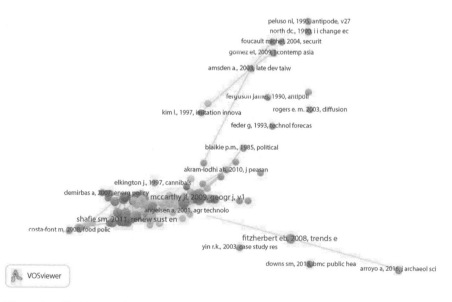

Figure 5.8 Cocitations. Source: VOSviewer.

The top 5 of the most cocited authors are: Hansen and Ockwell [34] with 43 cocitations, Cardenas [67] with 32 cocitations, Takahashi and Ortega [55] with 29 cocitations, and Byerlee and Deininger [48] with 18 cocitations.

5.4   Colombia PO Industry

According to Fedepalma [129], 559,582 hectares were planted with oil palm in Colombia, an increase of 3.4% compared with 2018. Thirteen percent of this area, or 73,577 hectares, was under development and 87%, or 486,006 hectares, was in production (Figure 5.9).

Colombian yields are broken down as follows [129]:

1. PO: In 2019, the average national yield was 3.15 t/ha. The southwestern zone yielded 2.73 t/ha, with the northern zone at −17.1%, eastern zone at −10.5%, and central zone at −7.4%.
2. Fruit: In 2019, the average national yield was 14.42 t/ha. The eastern and northern zones were both above 14.6 t/ha.
3. Extraction Rate: crude PO extraction (OER) was 21.8%. It was 22.6% in the eastern zone (22.6%). The palm kernel extraction rate was 4.36%.

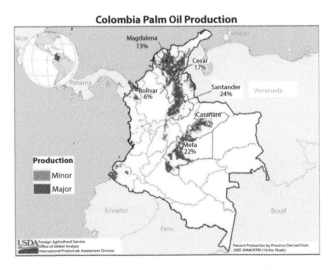

Figure 5.9 Colombia PO production. Source: U.S. Department of Agriculture.

It is crucial to comprehend the distribution of palm crops in the country for analysis in terms of technological advances, thus Fedepalma [129] presents the way in which Fedepalma has divided the country's palm plantations into four zones (Table 5.7), which shows how these zones are made

Table 5.7 Colombia's palm oil plantations.

Zones	Departaments	Municipalities
Northern Zone:	Antioquia (North) Atlántico Bolívar (North) Cesar (North) Chocó Córdoba Guajira Magdalena Sucre	Sonson, Yondo, Chigorodó, Turbo, Carepa, Mutata, Repelón, Piojo, San Pablo, Río Viejo, Arenal, Morales, Mahates, Regidor, María La Baja, Norosí, Arjona, Simití, Zambrano, Santa Catalina, El Peñón, Cantagallo, Becerril, La Gloria, Chimichagua, Valledupar, San Martín, Pelaya, La Paz, La Jagua de Ibirico, San Diego, Río de Oro, Pailitas, Agustín Codazzi, Astrea, El Copey, Aguachica, Chiriguaná, Bosconia, Curumaní, El Paso, Tamalameque, Riosucio, Cienaga de Oro, Puerto Libertador, Montería, Lorica, Momíl, Puerto Escondido, Buenavista, Tierralta, San Juan del Cesar, Fonseca, Villanueva, Barrancas, Distracción, Riohacha, Dibulla, Zona Bananera, Algarrobo, Cienaga, El Reten, Ariguaní, Pueblo Viejo, Sabanas de San Ángel, El Piñón, Fundación, Salamina, Aracataca, Pivijay, Tolúviejo, San Onofre, San Marcos.
Central Zone:	Antioquia (South) Bolívar (South) Caldas Cesar (South) Cundinamarca Norte de Santander Santander Tolima	Oleaginosas, El Zulia, Tibú, La Esperanza, Sardinata, Cúcuta, Santiago, San Vicente de Chucurí, Sabana de Torres, Rionegro, Puerto Wilches, San Martín, San Alberto, Simití, San Pablo, Barrancabermeja, Betulia, Puerto Parra, Simacota, El Carmen de Chucuri, Chimitarra, Flandes.

(Continued)

Table 5.7 Colombia's palm oil plantations. (*Continued*)

Zones	Departaments	Municipalities
Eastern Zone:	Arauca Casanare Cundinamarca Meta Vichada	Tame, Maní, Orocué, Villanueva, Yopal, San Luis de Palenque, Nunchia, Tauramena, Mani, Hato Corozal, Aguazul, Monterrey, Acacías, Barranca de Upía, Cabuyaro, Castilla la Nueva, Mapiripán, Puerto Gaitán, San Carlos de Guaroa, Villavicencio, Puerto Lopez, Granada, Guamal, San Juan de Arama, Puerto Rico, Mapiripan, San Martín, Fuente de Oro, Restrepo, San Martín, Puerto Concordia, Barranca de Upia, Cumaral, Puerto Lleras, Vista Hermosa, Santa Roalia, Cumaral
Southwestern Zone:	Cauca Caquetá Nariño	Guapi, Belén de los Andaquies, Magui Payan, San Andrés de Tumaco

Source: Original.

up, from general (departments) to specific or detailed (municipalities). The top 5 Colombian departments with the highest palm production are: Meta, with 32% of total oil produced, Santander with 20%, Magdalena 13%, Cesar 12%, and Casanare 6%. Figure 5.10 summarizes the palm areas indicating departments and municipalities.

Similarly, mechanisms for the dissemination of digital agricultural technologies should be comprehended at the system, as well as farm level [120]. For the Colombian palm sector, this takes place through the Oil Palm Research Center Corporation (Cenipalma), whose higher purpose states "we promote the sustainable development of the agroindustry and the well-being of Colombian palm growers with science, technology and innovation."

By way of illustration, the tables below present the technological achievements per oil palm production zone. Table 5.8 synthesizes some technologies used for management of oil palm in Colombia.

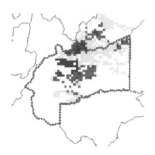

Meta 32% of total oil, palm production

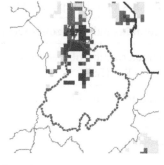

Santander 20% of total oil, palm production

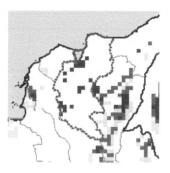

Magdalena 13% of total oil, palm production

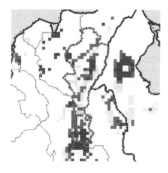

Cesar 12% of total oil, palm production

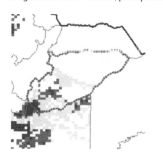

Casanare 6% of total oil, palm production

Figure 5.10 Top 5 Colombian departments with the highest palm oil production. Source: U.S. Department of Agriculture.

The work done by the National Federation of Oil Palm Growers (Fedepalma) to improve the phytosanitary status should also be highlighted, based on technological surveillance of genetic materials and technologies to ensure crop health.

Table 5.8 Colombia's palm oil technologies.

Colombia's palm oil zones technologies
Characterization of spectral signatures of adult oil palms affected by Basal Stipe Rot (BSR)
Methodology for obtaining the crop water stress index—CWSI for oil palm in adult stage
Agroclimatic Platform. Agroclimatic Monitoring Extension Module—MXM
Normalized Difference Vegetation Index-NDVI as an indicator of nitrogen content
Satellite images for land use change analysis
Movil Cenispace: application to capture information in the plantation through Personal Digital Agendas (PDA)
Integration of georeferenced regional information for regional pest campaign
Regional analysis through hostpost map (Hot spot) of biodiversity
Using the methane gas released from Wastewater Treatment Systems (WWTS) for electric power generation and reduce GHG
Integrated use of solid biomass for composting
Usage of bag filters and electrostatic precipitators for the control of atmospheric emission
Development and commissioning of the Geopalma Plantación information system, designed in accordance with the cultivation requirements, competitive and with permanent updating of the system.
Remote Sensors that allow the development of tools for the identification and mitigation of limiting conditions in the crop
Smart tags in the plants to provide real time information

Source: Original.

5.5   The PO Industry and the Circular Economy

Agribusiness refers to the transformation of agricultural, forestry, and pisci-culture products [28, 30] with the possibility to improve the agricultural economy [130]. Using other terms, Lalić *et al.* [125] define agricultural production according to the biological characteristics of plants and animals, which require a longer period to transform inputs into final value [126].

The palm industry involves planting, harvesting, and oil production, together with approaches for dealing with environmental and economic problems, and this constitutes a move toward an implementation of the "Circular Economy." For Abdul-Hamid et al. [111], this is a reality of Industry 4.0, which makes use of the circular economy for social, economic, and environmental benefits. This is why, for [113], part of this adoption of a production model based on resource use and environmental protection, focusing on eliminating waste and transforming it into resources, is an economic concept, or, in other words, a circular economy [117]. Thus, the circular economy model is based on the sustainable production of goods and services [114].

The PO industry in Colombia is framed, according to Galindo and Romero [115], by environmentally and economically sustainable palm cultivation, in line with principle 5 of the RSPO, which includes recycling, mitigation of negative environmental impacts, and energy efficiency [123].

Colombia's National Circular Economy Strategy (NCES) proposes actions to generate new business models that incorporate waste and materials management and efficient resource, water and energy use, hand in hand with changes in the population's lifestyle. Strategies are proposed according to lines of action, which promote productive transformation based on circularity, technological innovation, and collaboration under new business models.

Biodiesel, as a fuel, is a viable means to replace fossil fuels that cause ozone depletion and environmental degradation. It is also a renewable fuel that gives off fewer emissions when burned [117, 127, 128].

5.6   Conclusion

The purpose of the authors was to appraise the literature on PO technologies using PRISMA and bibliometric analysis, as the first step for research into the field. The authors organized scientific literature on PO technologies published between 2000 and 2021 in Scopus and Clarivate Analytics and provided valuable insights.

This study revealed that the most cited document, with 169 over 14 years citations was Kelly-Yong et al. [28], and that the journals with the most cited papers were Sustainability with seven documents, Energy Policy and Journal of Cleaner Production with five documents each. 20.25% of the articles were published in 2020 (the most productive year). 2000 and 2001 had zero publications.

This study highlighted that PO was the most common keyword (22 occurrences) and connect strongly with other keywords (a TLS of 258), such as sustainability (15 occurrences), renewable energy (10 occurrences), as well as biodiesel, biomass, and technology with nine occurrences each. Malaysia is the country whose authors have the most publications with 19 (24.05% of the total), followed by England and USA with 14 and 12 publications, respectively.

It is interesting to note that Colombia is not in the top 10 countries, which sets a challenge for researchers in the region to have a more active research role and produce further knowledge on this field in the following years. The novelty of this study lies in addressing the application of I4.0 technologies in the Colombian PO industry. In our view, these results constitute an initial step toward enhancing our understanding of I4.0 and its applicability in Colombian PO industry, and to further this, the authors intend to visit each zone plantation to analyze deeper the technologies used there. Hopefully, this work will be beneficial for future studies on I4.0 and Colombian PO industry.

Colombia has implemented technological solutions that guarantee productivity in different areas and the development of competitive agribusinesses that are crucial for generating employment and income opportunities and contribute to improving the quality of and demand for agricultural products. There is a need to improve services that integrate technology into precision or on-site economic processes, considering the current environmental, social, and economic impact of the agribusiness sector. Fedepalma and Cenipalma generate systematic actions and processes for sustainable intensification that combine I4.0 with zone-based research and an implementation of technological changes that have a positive impact on the sector's positioning. Palm oil biodiesel is an important alternative fuel for society, contributes to a reduction in harmful emissions, and generates income and green jobs. For Colombia, it is vital to have a sustainable agribusiness, which will make the PO industry more competitive and viable over time.

5.7   Further Recommendations for the Colombian PO Industry

All actors of the Colombian PO sector need to keep on working hand in hand to promote the implementation of good environmental practices for the development of the PO industry, avoiding deforestation and environmental impacts, as well as conserving natural resources. The authors propose that further research may be undertaken in the following areas: implementation of high-efficiency technologies in the Colombian PO industry to comply with sustainability certifications applicable to PO, and to plan and manage water resources, important for the sustainability of the industry. There is also a need to have a more active research and development system to make sure that the evolution of the Colombian PO industry.

Acknowledgments

The authors extend their gratitude to Dr. Denise McWilliams, Crop Assessment Analyst and Global Market Analysis at the International Production Assessment Division of the USDA, for her valuable support. Needless to say, this does not imply that she endorses the analyses in this publication.

References

1. Food and Agriculture Organization of the United Nations, Transforming the World Through Food and Agriculture. *FAO and the 2030 Agenda for Sustainable Development*, 2021, http://www.fao.org/3/ca5299en/ca5299en.pdf.
2. Food and Agriculture Organization of the United Nations, *The Future of Food and Agriculture. Trends and Challenges*, Food and Agriculture Organization, 2017, http://www.fao.org/3/a-i6583e.pdf.
3. Hobbs, P.R., Conservation agriculture: what is it and why is it important for future sustainable food production? *J. Agric. Sci.*, 145, 2, 127, 2007.
4. United Nations, Goal 2: Zero Hunger. [Online], in: *United Nations Sustainable Development*, 2021, Available at: https://www.un.org/sustainabledevelopment/hunger.
5. Bhatnagar, R., Machine Learning and Big Data Processing: A Technological Perspective and Review, in: *Advances in Intelligent Systems and Computing*, pp. 468–478, 2018.
6. Ozdogan, B., Gacar, A., Aktas, H., Digital agriculture practices in the context of agriculture 4.0. *J. Economics, Finance Accounting (JEFA)*, 4, 2, 184–191, 2017.
7. Klerkx, L., Jakku, E., Labarthe, P., A review of social science on digital agriculture, smart farming, and agriculture 4.0: New contributions and a future research agenda. *NJAS – Wagen. J. Life Sc.*, 90–91,, 100315, 2019.
8. Weltzien, C., Digital Agriculture or Why Agriculture 4.0 Still Offers Only Modest Returns. *Landtechnik*, 71, 2, 66–68, 2016.

9. Himesh, S., Prakasa Rao, E.V.S., Gouda, K.C., Ramesh, K.V., Rakesh, V., Mohapatra, G.N., Digital revolution and Big Data: a new revolution in agriculture. *CAB Rev.*, 13, 21, 1–7, 2018.

10. Harold, E., Woodard, J., Glos, M., Verteramo, L., *Digital Agriculture in New York State: Report and Recommendations*, Cornell University, Ithaca, NY, 2016.

11. Şerdean, M., Şerdean, F., Mândru, D., E.C., An Overview of Grippers in Agriculture Robotic Systems, in: *New Advances in Mechanisms, Mechanical Transmissions and Robotics. Mechanisms and Machine Science*, vol. 88, Lovasz, I. Maniu, I. Doroftei, M. Ivanescu, C.M. Gruescu (Eds.), MTM & Robotics, Springer, Cham, 2020.

12. Jiang, Z., Guo, Y., Wang, Z., Digital twin to improve the virtual-real integration of industrial IoT. *J. Ind. Inf. Integr.*, 22, 100196, 2021.

13. Palmara, G., Frascella, F., Roppolo, I., Chiappone, A., Chiadò, A., Functional 3D printing: Approaches and bio applications. *Biosens. Bioelectron.*, 175, 1–16, 1 March 2021.

14. Zambon, I., Cecchini, M., Egidi, G., Saporito, M.G., Colantoni, A., Revolution 4.0: Industry vs. Agriculture in a Future Development for SMEs. *Processes-Special Issue Process Industry 4.0: Application Research to Small and Medium-Sized Enterprises (SME).* 7, 1, 36, 2019.

15. Corley, R. H. V., & Tinker, P. B. *The Oil Palm*, 1–627, Wiley Blackwell, United Kingdom, 2015. ISBN: 9781405189392

16. Henderson, J. and Osborne, D.J., The oil palm in all our lives: how this came about. *Endeavour*, 24, 2, 63–68, 2000.

17. World Bank, Commodities and export projections division economic analysis and projections department, in: *Palm Oil Handbook*, 1981.

18. Lai, O., Phuah, E., Lee, Y., Basiron, Y., Palm Oil, in: *Bailey's Industrial Oil and Fat Products*, pp. 1–101, 2020.

19. Refinitiv, Palm Oil Supply and Demand Outlook. Half year report 2021. 1, 1–14, 2021. https://www.cpopc.org/wp-content/uploads/2021/07/2021_PALM-OIL-SUPPLY-AND-DEMAND-OUTLOOK-REPORT-WITH-REFINITIV-1.pdf

20. Federación Nacional de Cultivadores de Palma de Aceite, Fedepalma, European Palm Oil Alliance (EPOA), *The Palm Oil Story, facts and figures*, Federación Nacional de Cultivadores de Palma de Aceite, Fedepalma, 2019, https://palmoilalliance.eu/wp-content/uploads/2019/10/Brochure-Palm-Oil-Story-2019-FINAL.pdf.

21. Hansen, S.B., Padfield, R., Syayuti, K., Evers, S., Zakariah, Z., Mastura, S., Trends in global palm oil sustainability research. *J. Clean. Prod.*, 100, 140–149, 2015.

22. European Palm Oil Alliance, International Institute for Sustainable Development-IISD, *What is sustainable development?*, European Palm Oil Alliance, 2014, http://www.iisd.org/sd/.

23. Gonzales-Delgado, A., Barajas-Solano, A., Leon-Pulido, J., Evaluating the Sustainability, and Inherent Safety of a Crude Palm Oil Production Process in North-Colombia. *Appl. Sci.*, 11, 3, 1046, 2021.

24. Gatti, R.C., Liang, J., Velichevskaya, A., Zhou, M., Sustainable palm oil may not be so sustainable. *Sci. Total Environ.*, 652, 48–51. PMID: 30359800. 2018.

25. Fedepalma-Federación Nacional de Cultivadores de aceite palma, Contexto y perspectivas económicas de la agroindustria de la palma de aceite en Colombia, in: *Context and economic perspectives of the oil palm agribusiness in Colombia*, 2019, https://web.fedepalma.org/sites/default/files/files/Contexto-perspectivas-economicas-agroindustria-palmadeaceite.PDF.

26. Genoud, C., Access to land and the Round Table on Sustainable Palm Oil in Colombia. *Globalizations*, 109, 18, 1–18, Taylor and Francis, 2020.

27. Murad, S.M.A., Hashim, H., Jusoh, M., Zakaria, Z.Y., Integration of Roundtable on Sustainable Palm Oil-Environmental Sustainability Index for the Development of Quantitative Environmental Sustainability Index. *Chem. Eng. Trans.*, 83, 169 174, 2021.

28. Kelly-Yong, T., Lee, K., Mohamed, A., Bhatia, S., Potential of hydrogen from oil palm biomass as a source of renewable energy worldwide. *Energy Policy*, 35, 11, 5692–5701, 2007.

29. Abdullah, A., Salamatinia, B., Mootabadi, H., Bhatia, S., Status, and policies on biodiesel industry in Malaysia as the world's leading producer of palm oil. *Energy Policy*, 37, 12, 5440–5448, 2009.

30. Newton, P., Agrawal, A., Wollenberg, L., Enhancing the sustainability of commodity supply chains in tropical forest and agricultural landscapes. *Glob. Environ. Change*, 23, 6, 1761–1772, 2013.

31. Hartmann, C., Hieke, S., Taper, C., Siegrist, M., European consumer healthiness evaluation of Tree-from' labelled food products. *Food Qual. Prefer.*, 68, 377–378, 2018.

32. Euler, M., Schwarze, S., Siregar, H., Qaim., M., Oil Palm Expansion among Smallholder Farmers in Sumatra, Indonesia. *J. Agric. Econ.*, 67, 3, 658–676, 2016.

33. Aguilar-Gallegos, N., Munoz-Rodriguez, M., Santoyo-Cortes, H., Aguilar-Avila, J., Klerkx, L., Information networks that generate economic value: A study on clusters of adopters of new or improved technologies and practices among oil palm growers in Mexico. *Agric. Syst.*, 135, 122–132, 2015.

34. Hansen, U. and Ockwell, D., Learning and technological capability building in emerging economies: The case of the biomass power equipment industry in Malaysia. *Technovation*, 34, 10, 617–630, 2014.

35. Ruml, A. and Qaim, M., New evidence regarding the effects of contract farming on agricultural labor use. *Agric. Econ.*, 52, 1, 51–66, 2021.

36. Robins, J., Shallow roots: The early oil palm industry in Southeast Asia, 1848-1940. *J. SouthEast Asian Stud.*, 51, 4, 538–560, 2020.

37. Liberati, A., Altman, D., Tetzlaff, J., Mulrow, C., Gøtzsche, P., Ioannidis, J., Moher, D., The PRISMA statement for reporting systematic reviews & meta-analyses of studies that evaluate healthcare interventions: Explanation & elaboration. *PloS Med.*, 6, 7, e1000100, 2009.

38. Kumar, A., Paul, J., Unnithan, A.B., "Masstige" marketing: A review, synthesis, and research agenda. *J. Bus. Res.*, 113(C), 384–398, Elsevier, 2019.

39. Randhawa, K., Wilden, R., Hohberger, J., A Bibliometric Review of Open Innovation: Setting a Research Agenda. *J. Prod. Innov. Manage.*, 33, 6, 750–772, 2016.

40. Pearson, E.L., Lowry, R., Dorrian, J., Litchfield, C., Evaluating the Conservation Impact of an Innovative Zoo-Based Educational Campaign: 'Don't Palm Us Off' for Orang-utan conservation. *Zoo Biol.*, 33, 3, 184–196, 2014.

41. Martin, S., Rieple, A., Chang, J., Boniface, B., Ahmed, A., Small farmers, and sustainability: institutional barriers to investment and innovation in the Malaysian palm oil industry in Sabah. *J. Rural Stud.*, 40, 46–58, 2015.

42. Uckert, G., Hoffmann, H., Graef, F., Grundmann, P., Sieber, S., Increase without spatial extension: productivity in small-scale palm oil production in Africa-the case of Kigoma, Tanzania. *Reg. Environ. Change*, 15, 1229–1241, 2015.

43. Varkkey, H., Tyson, A., Choiruzzad, S., Palm oil intensification and expansion in Indonesia and Malaysia: environmental and socio-political factors influencing policy. *For. Policy Econ.*, 92, 148–159, 2018, ISSN 1389-9341.

44. Umar, M., Urmee, T., Jennings, P., Policy framework and industry roadmap model for sustainable oil palm biomass electricity generation in Malaysia. *Renew. Energy*, 128(PA), 275–284, Elsevier, 2018.

45. Shukla, M. and Tiwari, M., Big-Data Analytics Framework for Incorporating Smallholders in Sustainable Palm Oil Production. *Prod. Plan. Control*, Taylor and Francis, 28, 1365–1377, 2017.

46. Murakami, F., Sulzbach, A., Pereira, G., Borchardt, M., Sellitto, M., How the Brazilian government can use public policies to induce recycling and still save money? *J. Clean. Prod.*, 96, 94–101, 2015.

47. Quintero, J., Felix, E., Rincon, L., Crisspin, M., Baca, J., Khwaja, Y., Cardona, C., Social and techno-economical analysis of biodiesel production in Peru. *Energy Policy.*, 43, 427–435, 2012.

48. Byerlee, D. and Deininger, K., Growing resource scarcity and global farmland investment. *Annu. Rev. Resour. Econ.*, 5, 13–34, 2013.

49. Abdul-Hamid, A., Ali, M., Tseng, M., Lan, S., Kumar, M., Impeding challenges on industry 4.0 in circular economy: palm oil industry in Malaysia. *Comput. Oper. Res.*, 123, 1–14, 2020.

50. Amin, L., Jahi, J., Nor, A., Stakeholders' attitude to genetically modified foods and medicine scientific. *Sci. World J.*, 2013, 1–14, 2013, Article ID 516742.

51. Krishna, V., Euler, M., Siregar, H., Qaim, M., Differential livelihood impacts of oil palm expansion in Indonesia. *Agric. Econ.*, 48, 5, 639–653, 2017.

52. Munasinghe, M., Jayasinghe, P., Deraniyagala, Y., Matlaba, V., Dos santos, J., Maneschy, M., Mota, J., Value-supply chain analysis (vsca) of crude palm oil production in Brasil, focusing on economic, environmental, and social sustainability. *Sustain. Prod. Consum.*, 17, 1–37, 2019.

53. Souza, S., Seabra, J., Nogueira, L., Feedstocks for biodiesel production: Brazilian and global perspectives. *Biofuels-UK*, 9, 455–478, Taylor and Francis, 2018.

54. Gaskell, J., The role of markets, technology, and policy in generating palm-oil demand in Indonesia. *Bull. Indones. Econ. Stud.*, Taylor and Francis, 51, 29–45, 2015.

55. Takahashi, F. and Ortega, E., Assessing the sustainability of Brazilian oleaginous crops - possible raw material to produce biodiesel. *Energy Policy.*, 38, 2446–2454, 2010.

56. Ramirez, M., Bernal, P., Clarke, I., Hernandez, I., The role of social networks in the inclusion of small-scale producers in agri-food developing clusters. *Food Policy.*, 77, 1–12, 2018.

57. Umar, M., Jennings, P., Urmee, T., Sustainable electricity generation from oil palm biomass wastes in Malaysia: an industry survey. *Energy.*, 67, 496–505, 2014.

58. Mackenzie, A., The economic principles of industrial synthetic biology: cosmogony, metabolism, and commodities. *Eng. Stud.*, 5, 74–589, 2013.

59. How, B., Ngan, S., Hong, B., lam, H., Ng, W., Yusup, S., Ghani, W., Kansha, Y., Chan, Y., Cheah, K., Shahbaz, M., Singh, H., Yusuf, N., Shuhaili, A., Rambli, J., An outlook of Malaysian biomass industry commercialisation: perspectives and challenges. *Renew. Sust. Energ. Rev.*, 113, 1–19, 2019.

60. Srichaichana, J., Trisurat, Y., Ongsomwang, S., Land use and land cover scenarios for optimum water yield and sediment retention ecosystem services in klong u-Tapao watershed, Songkhla, Thailand. *Sustainability*, 11, 1–22, 2019.

61. Harahap, F., Silveira, S., Khatiwada, D., Cost competitiveness of palm oil biodiesel production in Indonesia. *Energy.*, 170, 62–72 , Oxford, 2019.

62. Castellanos-Navarrete, A. and Jansen, K., Oil palm expansion a challenge to agroecology? Smallholders practising industrial farming in Mexico. *J. Agrar. Change*, 18, 1, 132–155, 2018.

63. Aghamohammadi, N., Reginald, S., Shamiri, A., Zinatizadeh, A., Wong, L., Sulaiman, N., An investigation of sustainable power generation from oil palm biomass: a case study in Sarawak. *Sustainability*, 8, 1–19, 2016.

64. Bishop, C., Ex post evaluation of technology diffusion in the African palm oil sector: the Caltech expeller in Cameroon, Benin, and Liberia. *World Dev.*, 112, 233–243, 2018.

65. Downs, S., Thow, A., Ghosh-Jerath, S., Leeder, S., Aligning food-processing policies to promote healthier fat consumption in India. *Health Promot. Int.*, 30, 595–605, 2015.

66. Wong, C. and Govindaraju, V., Technology stocks and economic performance of government-linked companies: the case of Malaysia. *Technol. Econ. Dev. Eco.*, 18, 248–261, 2012.

67. Cardenas, R., Green multiculturalism: articulations of ethnic and environmental politics in a Colombian 'black community'. *J. Peasant Stud.*, 39, 309–333, 2012.

68. Gueneau, S., Neoliberalism and the emergence of private sustainability initiatives: the case of the Brazilian cattle value chain. *Bus. Strateg. Environ.*, 27, 240–251, 2018.

69. Shankar, B., Thaiprasert, N., Gheewala, S., Smith, R., Policies for healthy and sustainable edible oil consumption: a stakeholder analysis for Thailand. *Public Health Nutr.*, 20, 1–9, 2017.

70. Radjawali, I., Pye, O., Flitner, M., Recognition through reconnaissance? Using drones for counter-mapping in Indonesia. *J. Peasant Stud.*, 44, 1–17, 2017.

71. Clare, P., Power and environment: oil palm production in the pacific region of Costa Rica, 1950-2007. *Hist. Agrar.*, 56, 135–166, 2012.

72. Bautista, S., Espinoza, A., Narvaez, P., Camargo, M., Morel, L., System dynamics approach for sustainability assessment of biodiesel production in Colombia. Baseline simulation. *J. Clean. Prod.*, 213, 1–20, 2019.

73. Olusola, J., Adediran, M., Oluseyi, A., Ajao, U., Processing of triglycerides to diesel range hydrocarbon fuels: easily practicable small-scale approach. *Energy Environ.*, 20.21, 8–1, 1325–1341, 2009.

74. Koistinen, K., Upham, P., Bogel, P., Stakeholder signalling and strategic niche management: the case of aviation biokerosene. *J. Clean. Prod.*, 225, 72–81, 2019.

75. Wong, C., Evolutionary targeting for inclusive development. *J. Evol. Econ.*, 18, 151–156, 2016.

76. Portillo-Quintero, C. and Smith, V., Emerging trends of tropical dry forests loss in north & central america during 2001-2013: the role of contextual and underlying drivers. *Appl. Geogr.*, 94, 5583, 58–70, 2018.

77. Amin, L., Hashim, H., Mahadi, Z., Ibrahim, M., Ismail, K., Determinants of stakeholders' attitudes towards biodiesel. *Biotechnol. Biofuels*, 10, 1–17, 2017.

78. Ghani, W., Salleh, M., Adam, S., Shafri, H., Shaharum, S., Lim, K., Rubinsin, N., lam, H., Hasan, A., Samsatli, S., Tapia, J., Khezri, R., Jaye, I., Martinez-Hernandez, E., Sustainable bioeconomy that delivers the environment-food-energy-water nexus objectives: the status in Malaysia. *Food Bioprod. Process.*, 118, 167–186, 2019.

79. Neimark, B. and Healy, T., Small-scale commodity frontiers: the bioeconomy value chain of castor oil in Madagascar. *J. Agrar. Change*, 18, 2, 1–27, 2018.

80. Luncz, L., Svensson, M., Haslam, M., Malaivijitnond, S., Proffitt, T., Gumert, M., Technological response of wild macaques (macaca fascicularis) to anthropogenic change. *Int. J. Primatol.*, 38, 872–880, Springer, 2017.

81. Yusoff, M., Abdullah, A., Sultana, S., Ahmad, M., Prospects, and status of B5 biodiesel implementation in Malaysia. *Energy Policy.*, 62, 456–462, 2013.

82. Ehr, A., Mol, A., Van Koppen, C., Ecological modernization in selected Malaysian industrial sectors: political modernization and sector variations. *J. Clean. Prod.*, 24, 66–75, 2012.

83. Rodthong, W., Kuwornu, J., Datta, A., Anal, A., Tsusaka, T., Factors influencing the intensity of adoption of the roundtable on sustainable palm oil

practices by smallholder farmers in Thailand. *Environ. Manage.*, 66, 3, 377–394, 2020.

84. Gallemore, C. and Jespersen, K., Offsetting, insetting, or both? Current trends in sustainable palm oil certification. *Sustainability.*, 11, 1–15, 2019.

85. Leong, H., Leong, H., Foo, D., Ng, L., Andiappan, V., Hybrid approach for carbon-constrained planning of bioenergy supply chain network. *Sustain. Prod. Consum.*, 237, 1–14, 2019.

86. Xu, H., Lee, U., Wang, M., Life-cycle energy use and greenhouse gas emissions of palm fatty acid distillate derived renewable diesel. *Renew. Sust. Energ. Rev.*, 134, 1–17, 2020.

87. Shehu, B. and Clarke, M., Successful and sustainable crop-based biodiesel programme in Nigeria through ecological optimisation and intersectoral policy realignment. *Renew. Sust. Energ. Rev.*, 134, 1–12, 2020.

88. Lebdioui, A., Lee, K., Pietrobelli, C., Local-foreign technology interface, resource-based development, and industrial policy: how Chile and Malaysia are escaping the middle-income trap. *J. Technol. Transf.*, 46, 660–685, Springer, 2020.

89. Bachtold, S., Bastide, J., Lundsgaard-Hansen, L., Assembling drones, activists, and oil palms: implications of a multi-stakeholder land platform for state formation in Myanmar. *Eur. J. Dev. Res.*, 32, 359–378, 2020.

90. Proffitt, T., Luncz, V., Malaivijitnond, S., Gumert, M., Svensson, M., Haslam, M., Analysis of wild macaque stone tools used to crack oil palm nuts. *R. Soc. Open Sci.*, 5, 1–16, 2018.

91. Sakulsuraekkapong, J., Thepa, S., Pairintra, R., Improvement of biodiesel's policy in Thailand. *Energy Sources Part B- Econ. Plan. Policy.*, 13, 1–7, 2018.

92. Aziz, N., Hanafiah, M., Gheewala, S., Ismail, H., Bioenergy for a cleaner future: a case study of sustainable biogas supply chain in the Malaysian energy sector. *Sustainability.*, 12, 1–24, 2020.

93. Correa, D., Beyer, H., Possingham, H., Garcia-Ulloa, J., Ghazoul, J., Schenk, P., Freeing land from biofuel production through microalgal cultivation in the neotropical Region. *Environ. Res. Lett.*, 15, 1–14, 2020.

94. Zahri, I., Wildayana, E., Ak, A., Adriani, D., Harun, M., Impact of conversion from rice farms to oil palm plantations on socio-economic aspects of ex-migrants in Indonesia. *Agric. Econ.*, 65, 579–586, 2019.

95. Surahman, A., Shivakoti, G., Soni, P., Climate change mitigation through sustainable degraded peatlands management in Central Kalimantan, Indonesia. *Int. J. Commons.*, 13, 859–866, 2019.

96. Zhao, Q., Cai, X., Mischo, W., Ma, L., How do the research and public communities view biofuel development? *Renew. Sust. Energ. Rev.*, 133, 1–12, 2020.

97. Nasution, M., Wulandari, A., Ahamed, T., Noguchi, R., Alternative pome treatment technology in the implementation of roundtable on sustainable palm oil, Indonesian sustainable palm oil (ISPO), and Malaysian sustainable palm oil (MSPO) standards using lca and ahp methods. *Sustainability*, 12, 1–16, 2020.

98. Ul-Haq, A., Jalal, M., Sindi, H., Ahmad, S., Energy scenario in south Asia: analytical assessment and policy implications. *IEEE Access*, 8, 156190–156207, 2020.

99. Sarkar, M., Begum, R., Pereira, J., Impacts of climate change on oil palm production in Malaysia. *Environ. Sci. Pollut. Res.*, 27, 1–11, Springer, 2020.

100. Adejuwon, O., Ilori, M., Taiwo, K., Technology adoption and the challenges of inclusive participation in economic activities: evidence from small scale oil palm fruit processors in southwestern Nigeria. *Technol. Soc*, 47, C, 111–120, 2016.

101. Selanikio, J., Kemmer, T., Bovill, M., Geisler, K., Mobile computing in the humanitarian assistance setting: an introduction and some first steps. *J. Med. Syst.*, 26, 113–125, 2002.

102. Capaz, R., Posada, J., Osseweijer, P., Seabra, J., Carbon footprint of alternative jet fuels produced in Brasil: exploring different approaches. *Resour. Conserv. Recy.*, 166, 872–879, 2021.

103. Permpool, N., Mahmood, A., Ghani, H., Gheewala, S., Eco-efficiency assessment of bio-based diesel substitutes: a case study in Thailand. *Sustainability.*, 13, 1–10, 2021.

104. Ruysschaert, D. and Hufty, M., Building an effective coalition to improve forest policy: lessons from the coastal tripa peat swamp rainforest, Sumatra, Indonesia. *Land Use Policy.*, 99, 1–8, 2020.

105. Rudolf, K., Romero, M., Asnawi, R., Irawan, B., Wollni, M., Effects of information and seedling provision on tree planting and survival in smallholder oil palm plantations. *J. Environ. Econ. Manage.*, 104, 1–26, 2020.

106. Ho, B., Azahari, B., Bin, M., Talebi, A., Ng, C., Tajarudin, H., Ismail, N., Green technology approach for reinforcement of calcium chloride cured sodium alginate films by isolated bacteria from palm oil mill effluent (pome). *Sustainability*, 12, 1–13, 2020.

107. Hounkonnou, D., Brouwers, J., Van Huis, A., Jiggins, J., Kossou, D., Roling, N., Sakyi-Dawson, O., Traore, M., Triggering regime change: a comparative analysis of the performance of innovation platforms that attempted to change the institutional context for nine agricultural domains in West Africa. *Agric. Syst.*, 165, 296–309, 2018.

108. John, G., High temperature gasification technology prospects for palm wastes in Tanzania. *Energy Environ.*, 21, 21–28, 2010.

109. Mohd Shafri, H. and Arenas París, C., Métodos de inteligencia artificial (IA) para aplicaciones de teledetección de palma de aceite. *Rev. Palmas*, 40, 185–193, 2019.

110. Rozo-García, F., "Revisión de las tecnologías presentes en la industria 4.0.", *Rev. UIS Ingenierías*, 19, 2, 177–192, 2020.

111. Abdul-Hamid, A.-Q., Helmi Ali, M., Tseng, M.-L., Lan, S., & Kumar, M. Impeding Challenges on Industry 4.0 in Circular Economy: Palm oil industry in Malaysia. Computers & Operations Research, 123 105052, Elsevier, BV, 2020. ISSN: 0305-0548.

112. Parody, A.M. and Zapata, E., Agricultura de precisión en Colombia utilizando teledetección de alta resolución. *Suelos Ecuatoriales*, 48, 1 y 2, 41–49, 2018.

113. Rodríguez-Martín, A., Palomo-Zurdo, R., González-Sánchez, F., CIRIEC-España. *Rev. Economía Publica, Soc. y Cooperativa*, 99, 233–272, 2020.

114. Arroyo, F., Economía Circular Como Factor De Desarrollo Sustentable Del Sector Productivo. *INNOVA Res. J.*, 3, 12, 78–98, 2018.

115. Galindo, T. and Romero, H., Compostaje de subproductos de la agroindustria de palma de aceite en Colombia: estado del arte y perspectivas de investigación Centro de Investigación en Palma de Aceite—Cenipalma. *Boletín Técnico*, 31, 1–53, 2012. https://publicaciones.fedepalma.org/index.php/boletines/article/view/10642/10629

116. Moreno, G., Inteligencia artificial: herramienta al servicio de la agroindustria en Colombia. *Universitas Científica*, 21, 1, 32–35, 2020.

117. Geissdoerfer, M., Savaget, P., Bocken, N., Jan, E., The Circular Economy—A New Sustainability Paradigm?. *J. Clean. Prod.*, 143, 757–768, 2017.

118. Zulqarnain, A., Yusoff, M.H.M., Nazir, M.H., Zahid, I., Ameen, M., Sher, F., Floresyona, D., Budi Nursanto, E., A Comprehensive Review on Oil Extraction and Biodiesel Production Technologies. *Sustainability*, 13, 1–28, 2021.

119. Adamchuk, V., II, Lund, E.D., Reed, T.M., Ferguson, R.B., Evaluation of an on-the-go technology for soil pH mapping. *Precis. Agric.*, 8, 3, 139–149, 2007.

120. Shang, L., Heckelei, T., Gerullis, M., Börner, J., Rasch, S., Adoption and diffusion of digital farming technologies - integrating farm-level evidence and system interaction. *Agric. Syst.*, 190, 1–17, Elsevier, 2021.

121. The Organization for Economic Co-operation and Development—OECD, *Digital Opportunities for Better Agricultural Policies*, OECD Publishing, Paris, 2019.

122. Paustian, M. and Theuvsen, L., Adoption of precision agriculture technologies by German crop farmers. *Precis. Agric.*, 18, 5, 701–716, 2016.

123. Instituto de Estudios para el Desarrollo y la Paz – INDEPAZ. AgroIndustria de la Palma de Aceite- preguntas frecuentes sobre impacto y sostenibilidad. 1, 1–32, 2013, http://www.indepaz.org.co/wp-content/uploads/2018/08/Agroindustria_de_la_Palma_de_Aceite-Preguntas_Frecuentes-Indepaz-2013.pdf.

124. Da Silva, C., Baker, D., Shepherd, A., Jenane, C., Miranda, S., Food and Agriculture Organizations of the United Nations-FAO, in: *Agroindustrias para el desarrollo*, Food and Agriculture Organizations of the United Nations-FAO, 2013.

125. Lalić, S., Perić, N., Jovanović, D., The accounting treatment of the biological process of transformation. *Res. J. Agric. Sci.*, 44, 3, 233–239, 2012.

126. Wilkinson, J. and Rocha, R., Tendencias de las agroindustrias, patrones e impactos en el desarrollo, in: *FAO. Agroindustrias para el desarrollo*, pp. 51–102, 2013.

127. Ishola, F., Adelekan, D., Mamudu, A., Abodunrin, T., Aworinde, A., Olatunji, O., Akinlabi, S., Biodiesel production from palm olein: A sustainable bio-resource for Nigeria. *Heliyon*, 6, 4, e03725, 2020.

128. Yusoff, M., Zulkifli, N., Sukiman, N., Chyuan, O., Hassan, M., Hasnul, M., Zakaria, M., Sustainability of Palm Biodiesel in Transportation: A Review on Biofuel Standard, Policy and International Collaboration between Malaysia and Colombia. *Bioenergy Res.*, 14, 43–60, 2020.

129. International Institute for Sustainable Development-IISD. Report of the World Commission on Environment and Development: Our Common Future, IISD, 2014. https://sustainabledevelopment.un.org/content/documents/5987our-common-future.pdf

130. Ali, J., Reed, M., Saghaian, S., Determinants of product innovation in food and agribusiness small and medium enterprises: evidence from enterprise survey data of India. *Int. Food Agribusiness Manage. Rev.*, 24, 5, 1–20, 2021.

6

Intelligent Multiagent System for Agricultural Management Processes (Case Study: Greenhouse)

Djamel Saba*, Youcef Sahli and Abdelkader Hadidi

Unité de Recherche en Energies Renouvelables en Milieu Saharien, URERMS, Centre de Développement des Energies Renouvelables, CDER, Adrar, Alegria

Abstract

Agriculture is generally defined as the action of food, fodder, fiber, and fuel production by the plants and animals ranching. It presents currently the most important profession in the world and more common where it employs about 42% of the workers in the globe. Then, smart agriculture can be defined as a system that relies on advanced technology to grow food sustainably and cleanly, and rationalize the use of natural resources, especially water, and one of its most important characteristics is its dependence on management systems and information analysis to make the best possible production decisions at the lowest costs. However, a smart farm has good potential to supply more production and permit sustainable agriculture based on resource-efficient approaches. This document presents intelligent agriculture in a greenhouse based on multiagent systems (MAS). The MAS constitutes several agents located in an environment and interaction according to some defined relationships. In this work, each greenhouse environment part is represented by one or more agents. Each agent coordinates with the other agents to achieve set goals. In addition, in the society of agents, two types of agents can be found, reactive agents, which are characterized by simple behavior, their missions are to perform tasks that do not require intelligent reasoning and cognitive or intelligent agents, and the other are tasked to perform more complex missions and require reasoning to make good decisions.

Keywords: Multiagent system, agriculture, artificial intelligence, distributed system, Java, Jade, passive and active agent

---

*Corresponding author: saba_djamel@yahoo.fr

Roheet Bhatnagar, Nitin Kumar Tripathi, Nitu Bhatnagar and Chandan Kumar Panda (eds.) *The Digital Agricultural Revolution: Innovations and Challenges in Agriculture through Technology Disruptions*, (143–170) © 2022 Scrivener Publishing LLC

Abbreviations

ABM	Agent-Based Model
ACL	Agent Communication Language
AI	Artificial intelligence
BDI	Beliefs-Desires-Intentions
DAI	Distributed Artificial Intelligence
DPS	Distributed Problem Solving
FIPA	Foundation for Intelligent Physical Agents
IoT	Internet of Things
KQML	Knowledge Query and Manipulation Language
MAS	Multi-Agent Systems
PAI	Parallel Artificial Intelligence
FAO	Food and Agriculture Organization

6.1   Introduction

In recent years, the applications of information technology and artificial intelligence have been widely spreading [1, 2], where it has been applied to most areas of life, such as the management of electrical energy in buildings and workplaces [4, 5], forecasting the consumption and production of electrical energy, the management of homes and cities [6–8], and the management of agricultural systems [3]. It also used many methods and means to develop these solutions, such as multiagent systems (MAS), neural networks, ontology [9], big data, and machine learning.

The concept of modern agriculture began to appear in the beginning of the 18th century, in a short time, this concept permits to a serious revolution of agricultural production in most countries, so new and innovative agricultural methods were followed, which would greatly increase agricultural output, and through this system, resources were exploited [10]. Ideally available agricultural methods, and one of the agricultural methods that have appeared in that period and after are to change the crop cycle system from three to four crops, and the processes of propagation of excellent quality crops (selective crossbreeding) have become industrialized, in addition to the introduction of automatic tractors for plowing. The land used plowing process instead, which was done with the use of animals, and many things were used, which would protect the crop from damage, such as keenness to cultivate types of crops that have the ability to resist diseases and use of many natural materials as natural fertilizers, including animal dung, wood ash, and crushed bones to increase the soil effectiveness and provide it with nutrients.

Smart agriculture presents a current technique that is founded on the integration of current technology in the food cultivation according to different ways, including those used in traditional agriculture. It permits a rationalization of natural resources exploitation, especially water, and one of its most prominent features is their management systems and information analysis that make the best decisions, which permit the optimal production with the lowest possible cost, such as irrigation, pest control, soil monitoring, and crop monitoring [11].

Modern agricultural methods have evolved with scientific progress and the development of new energy sources. In the early 20th century, an average farmer used to produce enough crops for his family only, now, a farmer is able to produce an agricultural crop sufficient for dozens of families, and some argue that the use of modern agricultural technology has not only contributed to this effect in a way [12], it is also positive for the agricultural field and even has a role in the advancement of urban development and the industrial revolution development. The possibility of obtaining a good output from crops with a few workers led to the provision of these hands and directs them to other sectors, such as this industry.

The worldwide population is augmented day by day, and with this great increase in the population, concerns about providing food, achieving food security for the earth's population, and preserving arable lands, especially with the exacerbation of climate change problems, depletion of oil resources, as well as the water and soil pollution have also been augmented. To cope with the actual situation, it is necessary to increase the produced food quantity while preserving the environment, exploiting natural resources rationally and rehabilitee the traditional agricultural methods introducing the actual technology. The American "Iron Oaks" company is the first to model a farm wherein it is the robots that play the role of the farmers, by carrying out many tasks, instead of humans [13]. The agricultural company presented products obtained using robots, "Angus" farmer is charged by the most important operations in the farm; it uses an ingenious arm that glides in big aquariums planted with several types of plants. However, the learning program which gives the operating orders to the robot for identifying the plants that have pest or disease signs permits it to remove them from the aquariums before their propagations.

Multiagent system is currently a very active and widely applied field, where the models are increasingly used to simulate the evolution of different types of systems [14, 15]. Not only modellers, researchers in thematic disciplines (economics, ecology, agronomy, forestry, and animal husbandry), political decision makers, the international scientific community but also users (planners, actors, negotiators, consultants, farmers) are increasingly attentive to the contribution of MAS in the field of common resource management and decision support. Multiagent system is suitable for modeling decision-making processes on the management of natural resources, in particular at the exploitation of energy resources scale [16–19]. They are considered as an alternative to classical mathematical models because they take into account the modes of coordination and the actors' strategies. They are very appropriate to simulate the management of the shared resources. They can be used for learning processes by creating role plays focused on natural resource management. This approach puts the actors in a negotiating situation. Multiagent system allows the representation of the interaction between individuals, spaces, and their environment and thus promotes the simultaneous study of social, technical, and ecological dynamics.

6.2   Modern Agricultural Methods

Modern agriculture aims to increase productivity and obtain the highest possible material return, and there are several basic methods, including the following [20]:

a.   **Tillage:** a farmer can plow his land using many methods to improve their production, and it varies according to the reasons they employed of each of them. Therefore, and for improving the production, it is mandatory that a farmer process use in an appropriate way. There are three different main of plowing land, namely [20]:

   • **Primary tillage:** this plowing type concerns with dismantling the earthy clusters in the ground and reintegrating the organic materials present in them, and this plowing type has an important impact on the soil aeration and agricultural crop residues ridding, and the initial plowing of the soil extends to a depth ranging between 15 and 60 cm. This can be done using many hand tools, such as a shovel, or by using some industrial tools, such as a hand plow, or even some heavy industrial machines, such as a mechanical tractor.

   • **Secondary tillage:** This plowing type, also called shallow tillage, aims to reduce the particle size of the superficial soil. This type is applied to soil depths of 8 to 15 cm. The tools can be served to realize this plowing type, such as a manual earth comb, disc combs, and toothed combs as industrial equipment.

- **Agricultural tillage:** this plowing type is done after crop planting, where its goal is to get rid of any undesirable plants growing in the cultivated zone, and it has importance in ventilating the compacted soil, and any type of hand shovel can be used to do this type of plowing. Also, it is also possible to use the bare hand, or even some type of equipment, such as knives.

b. **Monoculture:** It is defined as the cultivation of one type of crop for multiple years on the same land, and this type of modern farming techniques appeared after the availability of low-price nitrogen fertilizers so that it was possible to compensate for what the soil might be missing from the important elements as a result of practicing this method and to compare it with the method of cultivation It is imperative to know the advantages and disadvantages of using monoculture.

Monoculture is characterized by the ability to grow each type of crop in the soil that suits it, there are certain types that are commensurate with the nature of the soil on the slopes, and there are other types that prefer to grow in soils in wet areas, whereas some types of crops, such as white corn, prefer in dry soils. It also has the ability to adjust the level of soil fertility and allocate it to suit one type of crop more than to allocate it to suit all crops in periodic cultivation, and the use of the monoculture method helps to avoid the process failure of cultivating other types of new crops and allows farm owners to create a flexible agricultural plan to meet the changes that may arise in different years, according to the different needs of various crops [21].

Despite the advantages of the monoculture process, it is not without disadvantages, some of which can be cited as follows [15]:

- Monoculture demands the use of great quantities of fertilizers, to catch up the nitrogen insufficiency in the soil due to the growth of unique crop types.
- This type of cultivation may disturb the soil structure and erode it.
- The use of monoculture leads to the use of preventive and curative measures for agricultural crops, such as total reliance on chemical pesticides and soil fumigation, whereas many of these measures can be dispensed within the periodic cultivation processes.
- Monoculture requires more management skills to be successful than cyclic cultivation.

The irrigation process can be defined as the water supply to the agricultural crops and plants in all their growth stages. Starting from planting them until their harvest, irrigation has a very important effect on plants and agricultural crops in the good irrigation case; it positively affects the quality and quantity of the crops. In addition to meeting the market requirements of each season, it is not related to rain uniquely to obtain the best plant growth, and avert threats that can occur during dry seasons, so the agriculture of drylands becomes possible exploiting irrigation systems [16].

6.3   Internet of Things Applications in Smart Agriculture

Can be found the following applications:

- **Precision agriculture:** it means controlling the crops using the technologies of information and communication, distant command and control systems, autonomous machines, and so on to obtain precise data, which are used subsequently to investigate and direction of agriculture for improving and increasing of quality and quantity of production with a possible lowest cost. For example, remote sensors placed in the fields allow farmers to obtain detailed terrain and resource maps in the farmer area and other measured parameters, such as soil acidity, temperature, and humidity, which can permit the prediction of weather patterns for days and weeks to come. Precision agriculture using the Internet of things (IoT) permits to perform best decisions, which logically means best agricultural production, in addition to the data collection and analysis. It permits the monitoring of the agriculture and also serves to forecast the more exact quantity and type of pesticides necessary to avoid their excessive and incorrect use, as well as the optimum water use in the irrigation [20].
- **The use of drones:** to assure better monitoring permitting the best possible farming evaluation, it is used to photograph the corps and permits to map the agricultural lands, to spray crops using pesticides precisely, rapidly and safely, to carry out measures of air quality and their components. As well as the sender of the harvested instantly information to pass for the analysis stage and finally the directing of farmers to implement best possible measures [20].

- **Vertical farming and emerging crops:** the introduction of vertical farming and recent developments in the technology of using artificial lighting in agriculture (LED lighting) will expand the range of crops that can be grown by following hydroponics, water diet, and other controlled ecosystems, and leafy greens and vegetables will grow [22]. Other and fruit widely apply that technology.
- **Three-dimensional technology:** this technology will produce complex bodies of daily foodstuffs with high nutritional value, and this technology will produce more food on demand and permit to reduce their waste.
- **Printed food:** the nanosensors that will be used on a large scale in the future will be able to collect a wide range of information, such as soil data and humidity levels.

Internet of things technology offers important advantages to greenhouse farmers, it permits the monitoring of air pressure, humidity and temperature, and lighting, as well as the water consumption during all exploitation period within the greenhouse and according to an electronic gateway that allows the farmers to receive information in case of the occurrence of a change in the monitored parameters. In addition, it permits to control and command of all devices, allowing an adjustment of monitored parameters, for example, control the level of lighting by open or close windows via the Internet [20].

6.4 Artificial Intelligence

6.4.1 Overview of AI

In 1956, AI was considered as an academic discipline [20]. Thereafter, it lived many optimism waves in the next year, which tracked by the loss of funding sources, that considered a big disappointment, (referred to as the "AI winter"), and it succeeds later by new approaches, victory, and renewed funding sources. In most of their history, AI research has fended on subfields, which often do not succeed to communicate between them.

These subdomains are based on technical considerations, such as particular objectives (for example, "s robots" or "machine learning"), the use of particular tools ("logic" or neural networks artificial), or deep philosophical differences [23]. The subfields are also based on social factors (particular institutions or the work of particular researchers).

The traditional problems and/or goals of AI research groups the knowledge representation, reasoning, learning, planning, perception, natural language processing, and the capacity to manipulate and displace objects. Generally, intelligence presents one of the principal long-term goals in this field. The used approaches include several methods, such as computational intelligence, statistical and traditional AI symbolism. Various tools that were employed include mathematical and optimization models and artificial neural networks based on probability, statistic, and economic methods. The AI area straddles some domains: engineering, psychology, physics, mathematics, linguistics, and so on.

This research area was based on the claim that human intelligence "can be described with such precision that a machine can be made to simulate it." Many people cusp that AI progresses relentlessly presents a veritable danger for humanity and other people believe that AI progress can introduce a veritable mass unemployment risk.

AI sometimes recognized by machine intelligence, presents simulated intelligence using machines, contrary to human intelligence [24, 25]. In reality, the appellation "artificial intelligence" is employed to machines and/or computers that mimic "cognitive" functions that are recognized linked to the human mind, such as "learning," "problem solving" or else the identification of elements, statistical forecasting or the simulation of meaning, such as sight. However, there are many definitions of AI. The first approach consists of integrating into it all the applications, which claim or have claimed to be AI [24, 25]. A list which ultimately includes all of what falls within the perimeter of human intelligence: the ability to maintain interpersonal relationships, language (understand, speak, analyze), coordination of movements, empathy, spirituality, logic, musical abilities, the ability to manage daily actions (accomplish daily tasks, reading ...), the ability to apprehend, analyze, and move around in one's environment, the senses (sight, hearing, taste, touch, smell). Then, in a professional context, AI is also interested in other types of tasks: forecasting, data representation, task automation, and self-learning.

In addition, with machines becoming more preferment, the operations and/or tasks that are considered as requisite "intelligence" from AI definition are omitted, this is an action called as AI effect. In the same context, one from Tesler's Theorem theories that "AI is anything that has not been done yet." For example, character recognition is often excluded from things considered AI because it has become a mainstream technology, which is ironic [26]. After all, any mature AI technology that displays 100% efficiency would precisely fall outside the scope of AI. In other words, according to this approach, AI would not remain AI as long as it made mistakes.

According to this school of thought, the modern machine abilities that nowadays considered AI comprise human voice understanding and recognition, games (such as chess, card games, and Go...etc.), self-driving cars, intelligent routing in content distribution networks. Artificial intelligence can be classified into three system types: analytical, human-inspired, and humanized AI.

Analytical AI possesses characteristics concordance to cognitive intelligence, which uses the learning according to experience to report future decisions [26]. Human-inspired AI includes cognitive and electronic intelligence elements, comprehends human emotions, and takes them into consideration in their decision making. Finally, humanized AI presents all characteristics of both previously explained system types (i.e., Cognitive, Emotional, and Social Intelligence), also it can be self-aware and its interactions.

6.4.2   Branches of DAI

The basic idea of DAI is to harness multiple intelligent entities to solve a complex problem. However, designing the solution using these entities can be done in several ways [23]. Each method of solving has its problems and challenges. As a result, DAI has been developed in three different tracks:

- **DPS:** this branch consists of problem division into a set of subproblems. Then, the subproblems are attributed to different entities to solve them. Then, it can synthesize the partial solutions to find the final solution. Taking the example of a landscaping and grounds maintenance problem, this problem can be solved by breaking it down into a set of subproblem, such as maintaining arable land, planting, and caring for trees (gardening), treating trees against diseases, and insects, protecting and maintaining tree tools (tensioner, tractor, shears, etc.), and so on. Each subproblem is assigned to a specialized entity. By carrying out the various tasks, one can solve the main problem, which is grounds maintenance. Note that this example only gives a simplified representation of this approach. In reality, a lot of problems can arise when one wants to adopt DPS, the problems dealt with by this branch are essential: how can the problem be divided into subproblems? How can the knowledge of the problem be shared among the solving entities? How can be synthesizing partial solutions to find the global solution? The projection of these questions on the previous example leads us to ask questions like: on what basis did be decompose the main problem into the aforementioned subproblem? Assuming it is discovered while treating tree diseases that require the performance of specific gardening tasks (removing weeds in the garden, pruning trees, avoiding planting, etc), how can this knowledge be shared between different entities? How can the different tasks be organized to accomplish the main objective?

- **MAS:** in this branch, there is a group of intelligent behavioral entities that must collaborate to solve a common problem. Each entity has its own purpose and its own plans. For example, in the landscaping case and grounds maintenance problem mentioned earlier, there is a need to design problem solving as task-specific entities (one for the maintenance task). An entity specializing in tool maintenance, for example, has its own objective (keeping tools in good condition) and has plans to achieve this objective (regular maintenance, malfunction diagnosis, troubleshooting tools). Compared with the previous approach, there is neither an a priori decomposition of the problem nor a general approach to solving it. The problem solution is appeared because of the interaction of these entities. As a result, the problems in this branch consist mainly in the coordination between the entities and the latter organization for the problem's effective resolution.

- **PAI:** consists of proposing solutions to take advantage of parallel machines in the field of AI. Several techniques have appeared in this track, such as the realization of machines (hardware) adapted to the execution of intelligent software. Several machines have been designed for this purpose, such as Connection Machine (CM-2), Semantic Network Array Processor, and IXM2 (Associative Memory Processor). In addition, this track proposes new paradigms for the development of intelligent systems. In fact, parallel machines offer the possibility of processing knowledge bases on a large scale in real time. Case-based reasoning, for example, requires the power of parallel machines to be able to save and process a large number of stored cases. In addition, this branch offers the development of languages (such as Parallel Prolog), allowing the implementation of parallel algorithms.

6.4.3   The Differences Between MAS and Computing Paradigms

Multiagent systems represent a new paradigm in software development. This paradigm is based on new concepts different from those known in different fields of computing. However, the similarities between the concepts of this new paradigm and the other concepts are a source of confusion. This confusion is amplified especially when one speaks of concepts of domains directly related to the MAS, such as expert systems, distributed systems, and object-oriented software.

- **The differences between MAS and object-oriented software:** the key concept of object-oriented programming is the notion of object. This latter is deemed the agent ancestor, and the similarity between the two concepts makes it possible to extend object-oriented programming languages to support agents. However, by neglecting the differences between the two concepts, one risks underutilizing the agent's power. In fact, the first difference between agents and objects is autonomy. An agent is autonomous from the object. The autonomy of an agent is the capacity to realize their objective without the intervention of another agent or other agents. In object-oriented programming, an object execution is considered as a response method to a message by the sending of another object, if an object reception a message, it is should take a response to this received message by executing the method. On the other hand, an agent does not have to execute a method as a response to another agent. The decision to execute a method is made only by the executing agent. In addition to autonomy, an agent is characterized by flexibility in relation to objects. The flexibility of agents is inherited from AI. This characteristic refers to the agent's ability to change his behavior depending on the situation. In the case of object-oriented software, an object always performs the same method in response to a received message. As a result, generating the same situation (receiving a message) implies the same behavior (executing a specific method). On the other hand, an agent executes different behaviors according to the situation (for example, when an agent is asked to perform a given behavior, the agent may perform the behavior, or they may refuse to perform it if the situation does not allow).

An object-oriented program has a single thread of control. As a result, at any given time, only one method can be found running. When a method calls on a method of another object, the new method can be implemented. In the case of MAS, agents run concurrently. Indeed, each agent has its control wire.

Despite the existence of some extensions of object-oriented programming, where these differences are not fully identified (such as the control case in concurrent object-oriented programming), it is noted that these extensions are not inherent characteristics of basic object-oriented programming.

- **The differences between ADS and expert systems:** MAS shares the original domain AI with expert systems. In fact, an agent can be considered as an expert who specialized in the performance of a given task. However, the differences between the two technologies can be summed up in two essential aspects: environmental situation and sociability. In fact, an expert system interacts with a domain expert. It is the latter that introduces knowledge to systems (facts). In addition, the system presents the results of its execution to the expert. On the other hand, an agent interacts directly with the environment. Considering the example of an expert system in the medical field, the doctor must introduce the patient's symptoms to the system and the system presents the doctor with the diagnosis and/or the medical prescription. The philosophy of an agent designed for the same problem is totally different. It is obligatory for an agent to be equipped with sensors, which are capable to perceive all patient symptoms. In addition, the agent must act directly on the patient's body (by injecting drugs, for example). The second aspect that makes the difference between MAS and expert systems is the social aspect. On the other hand, with expert systems, the agents interact with each other to solve the problem.

- **The differences between MAS and distributed systems:** MAS is a paradigm for Distributed Systems Development. However, this new paradigm has brought novelties compared with other paradigms for the development of distributed systems. The differences between MAS and distributed systems essentially boil down to autonomy and flexibility. Ordinary distributed systems are made up of a collection of interacting classical computer systems. As a result, these systems will not be stand-alone or flexible.

6.5 MAS

6.5.1 Overview of MAS

The MAS system can present as a system that is made up of several agents, and it presents by a regrouping of these interacting agents. In fact, this definition has adopted one of the concept "system" definitions (according to the systemic approach), which consists of a set of interacting elements. However, a more in-depth analysis shows us the limits of this definition. For example, this definition does not answer the following questions:

- Is a MAS made up of agents only?
- What is the interaction nature that can exist between the agents?
- What are the relationships between the agents that make up the system?

Ferber defined MAS as "a set made up of [27, 28]:

- An E environment: that is, space generally having a metric.
- A set of objects O located: that is to say for any object, it is possible, at a given moment, to associate a position in E. These objects are passive, that is to say, that they can be perceived, created, destroyed, and modified by agents.
- A set of agents, which are particular objects (that is,), which represent the system's active entities.
- A set of relations R which unite objects (and therefore agents) between them.
- A set of Op operations allowing agents of A to perceive, produce, consume, transform and manipulate objects of O.
- Operators are responsible for representing the application of these operations and the world's reaction to this attempted modification."

An agent can be defined as:

- An entity that perceives its environment and acts on it;
- An informatics system existing in a dynamic environment that can perceive and control it autonomously by performing the tasks or achieving the objectives for which this system was designed;

- An entity that continually performs three functions: perceiving the environment conditions, acting to affect, reasoning to determine actions;
- An independent entity, abstract or real, capable of acting both on itself and on its environment, that can communicate with other agents;
- A proactive, reactive, and autonomous system.

Although definitions of the concept of agent vary, it can be observed that there are some common characteristics among the definitions presented. Indeed, factors can be determined by their characteristics. Then, the properties of an agent are as follows:

- **Autonomous:** the decision making on his behavior is only based on his perceptions, knowledge, and world representation (an agent can be dependent and autonomous).
- **Proactive:** generates its goals, takes initiative to meet its goals, not directed only by events.
- **Flexible:** reactive and adaptive.
- **Social:** ability to interact to achieve goals, to help other agents in their activities.
- **Ability:** to perceive the environment and to act.

Agents can be classified into two main categories according to their behavior and granularity. This notion of granularity is very subjective; it expresses the "reasoning" complexity of an agent to separate "intelligent" agents and less "intelligent" agents, can be speaking of cognitive agents and reactive agents.

- **Cognitive:** they can anticipate, foresee the future, memorize things ... they think.
- **Reagents:** they react directly to the perceived environment, by impulse.
- **Hybrid:** a combination of two, it is designed to combine reactive capacities with cognitive capacities, which allow it to adapt its behavior in real time to the evolution of its universe. A hybrid agent is made up of several layers arranged in a hierarchy.

An agent is seen as a set of roles, which can be distinguished in three levels:

- **Individual roles:** which are the different behaviors that agents are able to strategically hold, regardless of choosing to hold them.
- **Relational roles:** which concern how they choose to interact with another (by activating or deactivating individual roles), with respect for the mutual dependencies of their individual roles.
- **Organizational roles:** or how agents can manage their interactions to become or remain organized (by activating or deactivating relational roles).

6.5.2   MAS Simulation

The term computer simulation refers to two main classes of applications: 1) the techniques that can be used when a statistical or mathematical model raises estimation, analysis, or visualization problems for which the analytical approach is insufficient; 2) the methods that are used when a model is built with the primary aim of imitating the details of a real mechanism or process. It is possible to identify five main issues when creating MAS:

- First, the problem of action: how can a set of agents act simultaneously in a shared environment, and how does this environment interact in return with the agents? The underlying questions are among those of the environment representation by the agents, the collaboration between agents and MAS planning.
- Then, the agent problematic and his relation to the world, which is represented by the cognitive model available to the agent. The individual of a MAS company must be able to implement the actions that best meet his objectives. This decision-making capacity is linked to a "mental state" that reflects the agent's perceptions, representations, beliefs and a certain number of "psychic" parameters (desires, tendencies, etc.). The individual issue of his relationship to the world also covers the notion of the agent's commitment to a third-party agent.
- MAS also goes through the nature study of interactions, as a source of possibilities on the one hand and constraints on the other. The issue of interaction is concerned with the means of interaction (which language? which medium?) and with

the analysis and forms of the design of interactions between agents. The concepts of collaboration and cooperation (taking cooperation as collaboration + coordination of actions + conflict resolution) are central here.

- Can be discussing the problem of adaptation in terms of individual adaptation or learning on the one hand and collective adaptation or evolution on the other.
- Finally, there remains the effective realization question and the MAS implementation, in particular by structuring the programming languages into several types ranging from the L5 type language, or the language of formalization and specification, to the L1 type language, which is the actual implementation language. Between the two, can be finding the language of communication between agents, of environment laws description, and knowledge representation.

By taking up the five previous issues can be describing some architectural elements of MAS:

- Agents must have multi-party decision and planning systems. Decision theories are a separate field of study on this subject. In the category of interactions with the environment, another recurrent problem of agent systems is that of pathfinding (with its best known algorithm, the A * algorithm).
- Agents must be endowed with a cognitive model: There too, several models exist, one of the most classic being the BDI model. It considers on the one hand the set of agent beliefs about his environment, which are the result of his knowledge and his perceptions, and on the other hand a set of objectives (Desires). By crossing these two sets, can be obtaining a new set of intentions which can then be translated directly into actions.
- The agent system is characterized by the availability of a communication system and several specialized languages for this purpose: KQML, FIPA-ACL. This latter standard is based in particular on the theory of speech acts, dear to John Searle.
- The MAS effective implementation, if it is not strictly speaking part of system architecture, deserves to be evoked through the example of many programming languages which have been developed for research in AI. The LISP language will be mentioned in particular.

6.6   Design and Implementation

6.6.1   Conception of the Solution

This section can be starting with an existing study, and then can be naming all the agents with a description of each. The next step concerns the scenario presentation and finally, can be introducing in the implementation phase.

6.6.1.1   The Existing Study

For the present chapter, we have selected the Adrar region to study. Adrar Wilaya is an Algerian state, located in the extreme south-west of the country, in the Sahara, it is sparsely populated, with regard to its area (427,368 km^2) (Figure 6.1). It far away (1500 km) from the capital of Algeria (Algiers), Adrar common is the capital of the Adrar Wilaya.

This Wilaya is limited by the Wilaya of El-Bayadh in the north, in the west bay the Wilaya of Tindouf, in the north-west by the Wilaya of Bechar, and bordered in the South and South-west by Mali and Mauritania coun tries, respectively, as well as in the south east by the Wilaya of Tamanrasset. Adrar Wilaya is an agricultural state; that became famous thanks to its high number of palmiers and its traditional irrigation system called "Fouggara."

Two climates predominate in Adrar: Pre-Saharan from Timimoun to the west of Bechar. Saharan, from Timimoun to Timiaouine in the south. The daytime temperatures register significant variations. They go seasonally from 45°C to (shade) in summer, to 0°C in winter.

Figure 6.1 Geographical position and location of Adrar Wilaya.

6.6.1.2   Agents List

It is important to divide the study system and its surroundings into a set of important sections. The division takes place in general and only with a strategy related to the tasks that must be accomplished to achieve the main goal of running agriculture in an automatic (smart) manner (Table 6.1).

Table 6.1 Extract from system agents.

Section	Description
Climate data	It is related to climatic factors that can positively or negatively affect the agricultural system such as wind speed, humidity …etc.
Energy	It is related to the electrical energy needed by the devices used in the agricultural system, such as the water extraction device, the spray and watering device, the ventilation and lighting devices, the window opening devices and the vents and other electrical devices. In addition, renewable energy sources can be used, especially for areas far from electrical networks.
Water	It is related to the process of watering the crops, which should be in an organized and economical way, according to the needs of crops.
Plant	It relates to the type of plants, their characteristics, and the conditions that must be met to ensure the good growth of plants, such as the amount of light and water.
Floor	It is related to the soil quality, such as the degree of salinity, the amount of fertilizer and water that must be provided to the plants
Construction	It concerns the greenhouse properties such as the number of windows, height, ...etc.
Sensors	Concerns all the sensors that are necessary for data recovery, for example, temperature sensor, humidity sensor
Actuator	Concerning all the actuators that can perform actions, have been distinguished different types of actuators such as sprinkler or irrigation pumps, fans.
Farmer	It concerns the farmer, who in some cases accomplishes some tasks manually or semi-automatically.

Table 6.2 Extract agents from the solution.

Agent	Type
Climate Data Agent	Reactive agent
Energy Agent	Reactive agent
Water Agent	Reactive agent
Plant Agent	Reactive agent
Floor Agent	Reactive agent
Construction Agent	Reactive agent
Sensors Agent	Reactive agent
Actuator Agent	Reactive agent
Farmer Agent	Reactive agent
Management Agent	Cognitive agent

From the list of sections presented in the previous table, it can be concluded that the agency of agents, which is necessary to accomplish the objectives programmed before (Table 6.2).

6.6.2   Introduction to the System Implementation

6.6.2.1   Environment

An agent cannot exist without an environment and without MAS. The group of agents is working on their environment which in turn acts on the agents. This structure can be centralized and it is represented as a monolithic block. In the next case, it can speak of a distributed environment. What distinguishes a distributed environment from a centralized environment is based on four points:

- The cell state depends on the other cells which surround it.
- The agents' perception generally extends beyond a cell, which means that it is not possible to send to the agent only the state information of the cell on which he is located.
- Agents move from cell to cell, which means managing the links that agents have with a particular cell.
- Signals can spread from cell to cell. This propagation takes a certain time and it is then necessary to synchronize the movement of signals with the agents' movements.

6.6.2.2   Group Communication (Multicast)

Subscription to a mailing list and reception of all messages associated with it (use of multicast sockets). If several lists exist, it is possible to structure them in the form of a list or a tree structure. This last case is considered much more flexible. Likewise, a shared object can manage the list of subjects and add some at the request of a user. A special case of multicast communication is broadcast communication. Broadcast communication consists of sending a message to all the agents of MAS. This permits, for example, the presence indication of an agent to others. This type of communication is very easy to implement if you have a multicast communication layer.

6.6.2.3   Message Transport

Message transport is an important point in MAS, where agents dialogue only by message exchange, so the performance of message transport directly influences MAS performance. It has been mentioned the transport methods likely to be used for direct communication between two agents, for multicast communication, it has been add other points:

- Various subjects management of mailing lists;
- Message broadcasting from a hardware point of view: you can use the direct message transport layer or use multicast protocols, where it is necessary to be able to give an address (equivalent to the IP address for the machines) to all the agents present in the system. It is also necessary to be able to route messages so that any agent can communicate with any other agent. Several solutions are possible to solve this problem:
- A single distributes object which assigns addresses (CORBA object for example) and which manages the routing of messages;
- An Ethernet network type architecture (it seems to me), with routers (gateway) at different levels. This architecture can be self-configurable (based in part on the machine's IP addresses) or be configured by initialization files.

6.6.2.4   Data Exchange Format

a. **XML:** used to describe data structures as well as to represent data. This, therefore, allows the XML language to be a good candidate for the exchange of data between the agents of MAS. Several solutions are presented all the same for the exchange of data with XML: The data which one exchanges does not have a fixed structure (a priori), it is thus necessary:

- Either describes the data structure in the XML document then construct an object which can accommodate this information;
- Either defines a library of objects that are likely to be exchanged, and refers to this library when exchanging information. Both solutions appear possible and each solution has its disadvantages and advantages. Finally, it should be noted that the use of different languages leads to other problems, especially on base types: an integer does not have the same range of values in all languages, etc.

b. **KQML:** is a language that makes it possible to define a uniform means of communication between the actors of MAS. This language, unlike XML describes the form in which the data is exchanged (the pseudo-lisp) but also the content, i.e. the information to be put in the message. Even if one uses XML for the form, for the message contents it can be interesting to look at what was done with KQML, the sender name, the recipient,...etc.

c. **FIPA-ACL:** KQML seems to be losing ground in favor of another language which is FIPA-ACL which is semantically richer. Theoretical, FIPA-ACL is inspired by the theory of speech acts; from a more technical point of view, the message is also a string of characters possessing a syntax - like LISP - (pairs of parentheses) beginning with a performative name and followed by a list of attribute-value pairs. In addition, FIPA-ACL is based on the definition of two sets:

   - A set of primitive acts of communication, to which are added the other acts of communication that can be obtained by the composition of these basic acts.
   - A set of predefined messages that all agents can understand.
   - **KIF (Knowledge Interchange Format):** agents need to understand the content of the messages they receive. This is possible through KIF.

6.6.2.5   Cooperation

There are several points of view on cooperation, depending on whether one considers that cooperation is an attitude of agents who decide to work together or whether one poses as an observer who interprets behavior a posteriori.

- **Cooperation as an intentional attitude:** cooperation is characteristic of an attitude (posture) of agents. Agents are said to cooperate if they engage in common action after identifying and adopting a common goal.
- **Cooperation from the observer's point of view:** cooperation is considered as an activity qualification of a set of agents by an external observer who would not have access to the agent's mental states.

6.6.2.6 Coordination

Coordination of actions is necessary for four main reasons:

- Agents need information and results that only other agents can provide;
- Resources are limited, it is then necessary to coordinate the attitudes of agents to avoid possible access collisions;
- It can be seeking to optimize costs by eliminating unnecessary actions and avoiding redundancies of action;
- It can be want to allow agents with distinct objectives but dependent on each other to meet these objectives and accomplish their work, possibly taking advantage of this dependence.

6.6.2.7 Negotiation

Negotiation is an activity of exchanging information between agents to reach a mutually acceptable compromise. Different approaches have been developed drawing on the rich diversity of human negotiations in various contexts. One of the most used protocols for negotiation is based on an organizational metaphor, where the contract network protocol has been one of the most used approaches in MAS.

6.7   Analysis and Discussion

MAS offer many advantages in the development of agricultural systems more specifically agricultural greenhouses. In fact, the agent paradigm is considered the ideal paradigm for the development of these agricultural systems. The power of MAS is an interaction consequence of different fields (AI, software engineering, and distributed systems). Among the advantages of MAS that can be mentioned are as follows:

- **Modularity:** MAS is made up of a set of entities (agents). Each agent is conceived as an autonomous entity independent of the others. Agent autonomy means that each agent has control over their state and behavior. The interaction between the agents is based primarily on the exchange of messages. As a result, the coupling between the agents is weak. In addition, several basic concepts of MAS contribute to their modularity. Among these concepts, can be cited in particular the concept of "organization." In fact, multi-agent organizations are generally modeled by sub-organizations (groups, coalitions, hierarchies, etc.). As a result, systems developed taking this approach will be more modular.
- **Reusability:** reusability is a modularity direct consequence of MAS. In fact, modularity makes it possible to reuse certain components of one software. In the case of MAS, reusability can be applied at several levels. Of course, the agent is designed to be a brick that can be reused whenever possible. For example, designing a workshop as a MAS consisting of producing agents, transporting agents and managing agents offers the possibility of reusing certain agents in other systems. A transporter agent, in this case, can be used in the development of supply chains or road traffic simulation systems. In addition, agents can also be designed in a modular fashion. Thus, the components of one agent can be reused to develop another agent. The reasoning mechanism of the agent is a component independent of the scope. It is, therefore, possible to develop a single mechanism and then reuse it for the development of agents. At the macro level, developers can reuse agent interaction models designed as protocols or patterns.
- **Ease of maintenance:** the modular development of MAS simplifies the maintenance of these systems. MAS are designed as independent entities with weak coupling. As a result, changing one entity has a low impact on other entities. In the case of corrective maintenance, this modification is for the purpose of correcting an existing system.

For example, the discovery of an error in an agent only involves modifying that agent. Likewise, the evolution of models and multi-agent approaches implies the modification of existing systems. However, this change affects only the system affected part. This change is entered under the type of evolutionary maintenance.

- **Reliability:** is the ability of a system to continue operating despite the occurrence of failures or errors in one or more of these parts. Multiagent systems can contribute to software reliability through agent autonomy. In fact, an agent is an autonomous entity in the sense that it can achieve its objectives without the intervention of other entities. As a result, an agent can achieve their goals even if another agent has failed. In addition, flexibility allows an agent to change his behavior in unpredictable situations.
- **Efficiency:** software effectiveness is measured by the resources consumed to solve a problem. MAS represents a distributed execution model where resources are distributed. This sharing allows a rational use of resources. In addition, certain types of agents allow better use of certain resources. For example, mobile agents decrease the bandwidth used to achieve the goal. It is known that the data size is more important than the processing size. Processing transfer is less expensive than data transfer. Mobile agents are based on this philosophy, where a specific agent is moved from one place to another (Mobil agent principle).
- **Adaptation to reality:** the agent paradigm allows faithful modeling of real phenomena. The characteristics of agents, such as autonomy, flexibility and sociability, represent intrinsic characteristics of several real systems (such as biological systems, human societies, insect colonies, etc.). Consequently, the adoption of this paradigm makes it possible to represent the system's essential characteristics.
- **Sophisticated modes of interaction:** MAS supports sophisticated modes of interaction such as negotiation, cooperation, and collaboration. The complexity of interactions allows the modeling and development of complex systems where interaction is a fundamental characteristic. An example of these systems is electronic commerce systems, the simulation of social phenomena and logistics chains.

6.8   Conclusion

The growth in world population has arrived at a height increase rate of three people every second, which present in almost 260,000 people per day, according to FAO, the world population reaches 8 and 9 billion in 2025 and 2050, respectively.

After this increase in population, the preoccupation concerning the provide in food, universal food security, and preservation of arable lands, taking into consideration the climate change problem, water and soil pollution and fossil resources depletion.

To meet these challenges relating to the growth of the world population, the farmers shall raise their production by taking into consideration the environmental preservation and oil resources depletion and rationalizing the integration and exploitation of natural resources. In addition, the farmers cannot do it alone, and traditional methods do not enable them to do so. Thanks to data management and analysis systems, modern technologies have very helped to meet the world food needs and remote control technologies. Also, the integration and exploitation of the most important technologies possible nowadays, such as robotics, AI, and IoT permit promoting agriculture and render them more productive, as well as less harmful to the environment and consumption of earth's resources.

Smart agriculture presents a system supported by advanced technologies used in the food grown to ensure sustainable and clean growth that exploits natural resources. Among these features, its reliance on the management and analysis systems of information permits the better possible decisions to achieve the best possible production at the lowest possible costs. In addition, a smart farm has the ability to give more crop production according to a sustainable way based on resource-efficient approaches.

Despite the advantages of MAS, this paradigm faces several challenges, which present the results of agent characteristics and MAS, where agent behavior characteristic is unpredictable, so the validation of the developed systems represents a real problem:

- the formulation of problems, the allocation of resources to the different entities and the synthesis of the results;
- the interaction between agents (when and how) and reasoning about other agents during the interaction process;
- ensuring consistency in behavior by ensuring a compromise between local actions and distributed processing and by eliminating undesirable effects.

- MAS engineering by proposing methods, techniques to facilitate the development task.

MAS, despite their interest, raise several problems:

- An important problem concerns the definition of a model, which assures the modeler that the computer tool indeed implements the model that the modeler has described and that the consequences observed during the simulation are directly model consequences and not the product. Unwanted computer system behavior.
- Another big problem is the explosion in the number of communications between agents for the ADM organization, therefore, the significant increase in communications. It often happens that an SMA application is slower to run than an unstarted application.

References

1. Saba, D., Sahli, Y., Hadidi, A., The Role of Artificial Intelligence in Company's Decision Making, in: Enabling AI Applications in Data Science. Studies in Computational Intelligence, Hassanien AE., Taha M.H.N. and Khalifa N.E.M. (eds), Springer, Switzerland, 911, pp. 287–314, 2021.
2. Saba, D., Sahli, Y., Maouedj, R., Hadidi, A., Medjahed, M. Ben, Towards Artificial Intelligence: Concepts, Applications, and Innovations, in: Enabling AI Applications in Data Science. Studies in Computational Intelligence, Hassanien, AE., Taha, M.H.N. and Khalifa, N.E.M. (eds.), 911. Springer, Switzerland, pp. 103–146, 2021.
3. Hadidi, A., Saba, D., Sahli, Y., The Role of Artificial Neuron Networks in Intelligent Agriculture (Case Study: Greenhouse). In: Artificial Intelligence for Sustainable Development: Theory, Practice and Future Applications. Studies in Computational Intelligence, Hassanien A., Bhatnagar R. and Darwish A. (eds), 912, Springer, Switzerland, pp. 45–67, 2021.
4. Saba, D., Laallam, F.Z., Degha, H.E., Berbaoui, B., Maouedj, R., Design and Development of an Intelligent Ontology-Based Solution for Energy Management in the Home. In: Machine Learning Paradigms: Theory and Application. Studies in Computational Intelligence, Hassanien A. (ed.), 801, Springer, Switzerland, pp. 135–167, 2019.

5. Degha, H.E., Zohra Laallam, F., Said, B., Saba, D., Onto-SB: Human Profile Ontology for Energy Efficiency in Smart Building. *Proc. - PAIS 2018 Int. Conf. Pattern Anal. Intell. Syst*, 2018.

6. Saba, D., Sahli, Y., Berbaoui, B., Maouedj, R., Towards Smart Cities: Challenges, Components, and Architectures. Iin: Toward Social Internet of Things (SIoT): Enabling Technologies, Architectures and Applications. Studies in Computational Intelligence, Hassanien A., Bhatnag R., Khalifa N. and Taha M. (eds.), 846, Springer, Switzerland, pp. 249–286, 2020.

7. Saba, D., Maouedj, R., Berbaoui, B., Contribution to the development of an energy management solution in a green smart home (EMSGSH). *ACM Int. Conf. Proceeding Ser.*, 5, 1–7, 2018.

8. Saba, D., Sahli, Y., Maouedj, R., Hadidi, A., Medjahed, M. Ben, Contribution to the Realization of a Smart and Sustainable Home , in: Artificial Intelligence for Sustainable Development: Theory, Practice and Future Applications. Studies in Computational Intelligence, vol. 912. Springer, Switzerland, pp. 261–290, 2021.

9. Saba, D., Sahli, Y., Hadidi, A., An ontology based energy management for smart home. *Sustain. Comput. Inform. Syst.*, 31, 100591, 2021.

10. Gras, C. and Cáceres, D.M., Technology, nature's appropriation and capital accumulation in modern agriculture. *Curr. Opin. Environ. Sustain.*, 45, 1–9, 2020.

11. Ratnaparkhi, S., Khan, S., Arya, C., Khapre, S., Singh, P., Diwakar, M., Shankar, A., Smart agriculture sensors in IOT: A review. *Mater. Today Proc.*, 2020. https://doi.org/10.1016/j.matpr.2020.11.138 is in press

12. Renuka, N., Guldhe, A., Prasanna, R., Singh, P., Bux, F., Microalgae as multi-functional options in modern agriculture: current trends, prospects and challenges. *Biotechnol. Adv.*, 36, 4, 1255–1273, 2018.

13. theguardian, 2018, https://www.theguardian.com/profile/noah-smithNoah Smith : America's first autonomous robot farm replaces humans with 'incredibly intelligent' machines. Available at: https://www.theguardian.com/us-news/2018/oct/08/robot-farm-iron-ox-california [Accessed 01/12/2021]

14. Saba, D., Laallam, F.Z., Berbaoui, B., and Abanda, F.H., An Energy Management Approach in Hybrid Energy System Based on Agent's Coordination. in: Proceedings of the International Conference on Advanced Intelligent Systems and Informatics 2016. AISI 2016. Advances in Intelligent Systems and Computing, Hassanien A., Shaalan K., Gaber T., Azar A., Tolba M. (eds.), vol. 533, Springer, Switzerland, pp. 299–309, 2017.

15. Saba, D., Laallam, F.Z., Berbaoui, B., Contribution to Energy Management in Hybrid Energy Systems Based on Agents Coordination. *Int. J. Inf. Commun. Eng.*, 10, 9, 1249–1255, 2016.

16. Saba, D., Laallam, F.Z., Hadidi, A.E., Berbaoui, B., Contribution to the Management of Energy in the Systems Multi Renewable Sources with Energy by the Application of the Multi Agents Systems "mAS". *Energy Proc.*, 74, 616–623, 2015.

17. Saba, D., Laallam, F.Z., Hadidi, A.E., Berbaoui, B., Optimization of a Multi-source System with Renewable Energy Based on Ontology. *Energy Proc.*, 74, 608–615, 2015.

18. Saba, D., Zohra Laallam, F., Belmili, H., Henry Abanda, F., Bouraiou, A., Development of an ontology-based generic optimisation tool for the design of hybrid energy systemsDevelopment of an ontology-based generic optimisation tool for the design of hybrid energy systems. *Int. J. Comput. Appl. Technol.*, 55, 3, 232–243, 2017.

19. Saba, D., Sahli, Y., Maouedj, R., and Hadidi, A., *Energy management based on internet of things*, In: Al-Emran M. and Shaalan K. (Eds.) Recent Advances in Technology Acceptance Models and Theories. Studies in Systems, Decision and Control, vol 335. Springer Nature, Switzerland, pp. 349-372, 2021.

20. Li, Y., Li, T., Zhao, D., Wang, Z., Liao, Y., Different tillage practices change assembly, composition, and co-occurrence patterns of wheat rhizosphere diazotrophs. *Sci. Total Environ.*, 767, 144252, 2020.

21. MacLaren, C., Labuschagne, J., Swanepoel, P.A., Tillage practices affect weeds differently in monoculture vs. crop rotation. *Soil Tillage Res.*, 205, 104795, 2021.

22. de Oliveira, F.B., Forbes, H., Schaefer, D., Syed, J.M., Lean Principles in Vertical Farming: A Case Study. *Proc. CIRP*, 93, 712–717, 2020.

23. Saba, D., Sahli, Y., Abanda, F.H., Maouedj, R., Tidjar, B., Development of new ontological solution for an energy intelligent management in Adrar city. *Sustain. Comput. Inform. Syst.*, 21, 189–203, 2019.

24. Saba, D., Berbaoui, B., Degha, H.E., Laallam, F.Z., *A generic optimization solution for hybrid energy systems based on agent coordination*. in: Proceedings of the International Conference on Advanced Intelligent Systems and Informatics 2017. AISI 2017. Advances in Intelligent Systems and Computing, Hassanien A., Shaalan K., Gaber T. and Tolba M. (eds), vol. 639, Springer Nature, Switzerland, pp. 527–536, 2018.

25. Saba, D., Degha, H.E., Berbaoui, B., Laallam, F.Z., Maouedj, R., Contribution to the modeling and simulation of multiagent systems for energy saving in the habitat. *Proc. 2017 Int. Conf. Math. Inf. Technol. ICMIT 2017*, 2018-January, 2018.

26. Saba, D., Degha, H.E., Berbaoui, B., Maouedj, R., Development of an Ontology Based Solution for Energy Saving Through a Smart Home in the City of Adrar in Algeria. in: The International Conference on Advanced Machine Learning Technologies and Applications (AMLTA2018). AMLTA 2018. Advances in Intelligent Systems and Computing, Hassanien A., Tolba M., Elhoseny M. and Mostafa M. (eds.), vol 723. Springer, Switzerland, pp. 531–541, 2018.

27. Ferber, J., Gutknecht, O., Michel, F., From Agents to Organizations: an Organizational View of Multi-Agent Systems, in: *Lecture Notes in Computer Science*, vol. 2935, pp. 214–230, 2003.

28. Ferber, J., *Les systemes multi-agents : un aperçu general: Tech. Sci. Informatiques* LIRMM, Université Montpellier II, France, 16, 8, 979–1012, 1997.

Smart Irrigation System for Smart Agricultural Using IoT: Concepts, Architecture, and Applications

Abdelkader Hadidi, Djamel Saba* and Youcef Sahli

Unité de Recherche en Energies Renouvelables en Milieu Saharien, URERMS, Centre de Développement des Energies Renouvelables, CDER, Adrar, Alegria

Abstract

Water is an important element for plant growth and agriculture in general. It is used first for the planting process of some plants and also for the watering for other plants to ensure normal growth and acceptable production. In the past, irrigation was done by traditional methods, by creating waterways above the ground. However, using this type of method requires considerable effort and time to set up, it also requires a large amount of water. These irrigation methods are feasible in the case of small or medium crops, but they become unnecessary in the case of the use of large agricultural areas. With a sharp increase in the world population, it becomes necessary to increase productivity through large-scale cultivation, so the use of traditional methods of irrigation has become inefficient. Therefore, it is helpful to find or develop more efficient and effective watering methods and means. In this context, this research paper presents a study on the use of automatic and intelligent methods in the management of irrigation of agricultural land. Among these technologies, the artificial intelligence and Internet of Things (IoT), which are used to optimize the manage irrigation water in agricultural lands. The elements of the agricultural system and its environment are presented by things that are in direct contact by relying on information and communication technology (ICT). Communication between things goal is to exchange information and cooperate with each other to realizing the main goal, it is a well-managed watering operation of the farms. On the basis of this technology, it is possible to obtain more production with less effort and less financial investment. Finally, this work

Corresponding author: saba_djamel@yahoo.fr

Roheet Bhatnagar, Nitin Kumar Tripathi, Nitu Bhatnagar and Chandan Kumar Panda (eds.)
The Digital Agricultural Revolution: Innovations and Challenges in Agriculture through Technology Disruptions, (171–198) © 2022 Scrivener Publishing LLC

can be considered as a reference and a knowledge base for students, professor-researchers and farmers.

Keywords: Decision making, smart irrigation, Internet of Things, big data, smart agricultural

7.1   Introduction

The increasingly widespread computerization of human activities is an ongoing endeavor that began with the advent of computers [1]. There is a growing need for humans to use machines, robots, and objects capable of providing services with little or no human intervention [2]. Where the computer has been integrated into various objects in everyday life. In addition, with Internet availability, objects can communicate with each other in record time [3, 4]. In this context, research is directed toward the concept of the connection between things, as well as to the Internet, to ensure automatic and intelligent management of agriculture [5].

The definition that can be kept of the Internet of Things (IoT) mainly consists of connecting physical things to the Internet, which allows data to be exchanged among the physical and virtual worlds via information technologies and communication [6]. Then, the birth of the IoT phenomenon paved the way for developing applications and models for collaboration and data sharing, which was not possible before. In this context, the question of collaboration and data sharing in the IoT world has been the subject of several studies: Saba *et al.* [7] focused on the management of energy in multi-source energy systems, depending on the coordination and the cooperation between cognitive and reactive agents [8, 9]. This work was then developed by other works, where more scenarios were presented, and the tasks of each element (agent) of the system were presented [10, 11]. Saba *et al.* [12] have moved toward the creation of the knowledge bases that are necessary for the completion of the tasks associated with the objects. It is also used for the recognition of messages exchanged between objects (solving the problem of semantics). In recent years, there has been a very large increase in the number of connected devices (things) [13]. According to recent statistics, they have grown to be one and a half times as numerous as the world's population [14]. The existence of a link between an object and the Internet is the main basis for the functioning of the IoT. Thus, for this relationship to meet the needs of the user, it is necessary to adopt a new communication system based on collaboration and sharing, especially when it ends up with a large number of devices connected from different regions [15].

Smart home applications have been growing in popularity for several years. They are not only practical but also often save energy [16, 17]. At the same time, the automation of processes creates independence—the mind remains free for other things [18]. The situation is similar with smart irrigation systems, which extend the area around the house to the garden and here offer extremely useful solutions. Smart watering is among the new technologies adopted by smart cities in the development of crops and the preservation of plant life cycles [19]. It is an intelligent and automatic irrigation system, which takes into account the elements favoring the saving of irrigation resources via the information provided by permanently connected objects and which form a base according to an intelligent algorithm that decides the start or stop of the watering operation.

Our work is part of smart irrigation projects based on the IoT [20]. Agriculture is an important component of the livelihoods of all individuals, because it provides food for humans and animals and contributes effectively to the economies of countries, especially if the crops are of good quality and quantity [21]. However, to achieve important agricultural results, it would provide many conditions including irrigation, which in turn requires a good management method.

Some of the basic problems encountered by guardians and land and farm owners include the following:

- lack of hydraulic resources and high costs to guarantee irrigation water;
- irrigation by conventional methods, causing irrational management of effort, time, and natural resources;
- the problem of water supply for each plant, something that requires special care in cultivated land;
- Overwatering and unorganized and inadequate watering, which lead to the depreciation of water reserves in an accelerated manner, and also result in the plantation quality deterioration.

This is why, today, it is necessary for farmers and supervisory authorities to adopt and use new technologies.

7.2   Irrigation Systems

Irrigation is the operation of artificially bringing water for plants so that crops can grow better and thus obtain more product, in the event of a shortage of water, especially in dry areas [22]. Irrigation can also have other applications:

- The contribution of fertilizers either to the soil or, by sprinkling, to the leaves (foliar fertilization); in hydroponics, irrigation is totally confused with fertilization;
- The fight against frost, by sprinkling water on the foliage (orchards, vineyards) can make it possible to gain a few precious degrees of temperature during spring frosts, or even, in some cases, by flooding.

7.2.1   Agricultural Irrigation Techniques

Currently, there are many irrigation techniques, including surface, micro, and sprinkler irrigation [23]. Choosing the right irrigation technique or more efficient technical knowledge is complicated. From a water conservation point of view, the choice is simple, as water storage increases when switching from surface to sprinkler and from sprinkler to precision irrigation. However, the success of the irrigation technology will depend greatly on the location and circumstantial factors, as well as the type of irrigation used. The current irrigation technology must be evaluated very carefully before switching to another technology. Finally, the most appropriate and cost-effective irrigation technique can be found by knowing the percentage value of field efficiency (Table 7.1) [24].

7.2.2   Surface Irrigation Systems

What distinguishes surface irrigation from other irrigation techniques is that water flows freely under the influence of gravity and the means of transport and distribution on agricultural areas [25].

- **Surface run-off irrigation:** irrigation water is provided by surface runoff from field trenches without real control of dams or other methods that limit the movement of water [26]. This approach is often compared with violent flooding. Although these methods are interesting for their low initial cost and the required work, they are not because of their low efficiency. This method is generally used in hilly terrain when it is not possible to create planks, ponds, or rays and where the water supply is adequate (Figure 7.1).

Table 7.1 Value in% of field efficiency [33].

Irrigation systems	Field efficiency (in %)
Surface irrigation systems	
Furrow irrigation (inclined)	50-80
With the reuse of downstream water	60-90
Furrow irrigation (horizontal)	65-95
Irrigation by plank	50-80
Flat basins	80-95
Sprinkling (except pivots)	
Sprinkling with displacement	60-85
Side Roll	60-85
Movable barrel	55-75
Sprays (hose feed)	75-95
Sprays (channel feed)	75-95
Pivots	
Sprinklers drummer with end gun	75-90
Spray gun without end	75-95
LEPA system without end barrel	80-95
Micro-irrigation systems	
Surface drip	70-95
Buried drip (SDI)	75-95
Micro sprinklers	70-95

- **Panel irrigation:** woody irrigation is the provision of water to tall, sloping, and rectangular lands with drainage conditions at the low end of the land. The panels are arranged toward the largest slope, 30 to 65 feet wide, and 300 to 1300 feet long with small embankments of land between slides to direct the water [27]. So he made the ground level between the panels to facilitate the movement of water. Bed irrigation

Figure 7.1 Runoff irrigation.

is suitable for most types of crops and soils, but soils with a slow infiltration rate and crops that tolerate ponds for long periods are preferred.

- **Sparkling irrigation:** with other surface irrigation techniques, water covers the entire plot of land, whereas gully irrigation covers only a fifth or half of the area. Different lines can be placed in the depressed area direction. Small, shallow grooves, called corrugations, are usually used for dense crops such as low grains and alfalfa. Unit flux is greatly reduced, and this technique can be practiced with slopes of up to 12% if the lines are laid according to contour lines with flux dimensions so that they are noncorrosive. If the lines are not placed along the contour lines, the maximum recommended slope is 3% or less. With this irrigation type, the wetted area can be reduced, as well as evaporation. Sunlight provides more possibilities for irrigation to manage irrigation more efficiently when conditions on the plot vary during the season. However, furrow irrigation is not always as effective as it can stimulate runoff. Various methods, such as two-flow or wave irrigation, can be used to reduce runoff [28].

- **Irrigation in ponds:** ponds are generally rectangular in shape, level, and surrounded by a dam to prevent runoff. In general, reservoir reservoirs are neither directed nor controlled and can be effective if a large flow is provided to quickly cover the plot [29]. Some crops and soils are not suitable for pond irrigation and are best suited for poor soil leaching and dense crops with deep roots [30].

7.2.3   Sprinkler Irrigation

Sprinkler irrigation has several methods of use for irrigating any type of crop, soil, and terrain [21]. They can be effective under soil or topographic conditions where there are no surface irrigation ways. In the general case, systems are selected according to the type of ramps that are linked with various types of sprinklers. This type of irrigation is considered to be efficient but it has disadvantages because of labor requirements and investment costs. This type is used in hand-lifted ramps for the smallest investment but very high labor requirements. This system can only be used in crops with low development. The side drum booms use the irrigation line as a pivot for large diameter wheels 40 feet apart. Driven by a heat engine, it requires less labor than a manual movement. To obtain the best possible efficiency, the choice of sprinklers should be proportional to soil conditions. Front ramps use structures similar to those on the hubs but in the field move parallel to themselves. In the case of full coverage, sprinklers are installed on the entire plot to be irrigated and all or only a few of them operate at the same time (Figure 7.2).

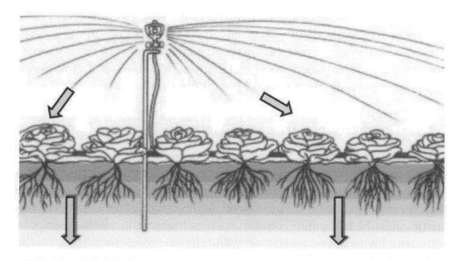

Figure 7.2 Sprinkler irrigation.

7.2.4   Micro-Irrigation Systems

Micro-irrigation is an irrigation technique that brings water to the soil slowly, with high frequency [31]. Properly designed, a micro-irrigation installation can increase yields and reduce the need for water, fertilizers, and labor. Micro-irrigation comprises drip, micro, and underground drip. Then, the micro-sprinklers comprise the mini-diffusers, the micro-diffusers, and the misters correspond to small distributors. With this technique, the small area wetted by the dispenser is easily and accurately controlled and can have different shapes corresponding to the types of watering chosen. Micro-sprinkler irrigation systems allow control of antifreeze, greater flexibility during irrigation, and sensitivity to clogging holes. However, the drip irrigation system helps to bring in water and irrigation of a soil portion [32]. It has advantages because water is supplied directly or near the root zone of plants, thus reducing losses by percolation and reducing or eliminating the wet surface allowing the water to evaporate and eliminate losses by runoff. It also reduces the use of water by weeds and works at extremely low pressure. Micro-irrigation systems water at high frequency, thus creating optimal soil moisture conditions for the plant. With proper management, micro-irrigation saves water because it is only supplied in small quantities in the root zone, thus avoiding loss due to deep percolation. Additionally, while the well-designed drip irrigation system is very efficient, it requires very little labor. There is also an increase in crop yields as the temporary high level of soil moisture needed to meet the transpiration requirements of the plant is maintained.

The main disadvantages of micro-irrigation are high upfront costs and the risk of system disruption, especially to distributors [34]. In some cases, work can be very important during the degradation of some fixation components by rodents, where good installation, operation, and continuous regulation can eliminate many problems of this kind.

7.2.5   Comparison of Irrigation Methods

One of the most popular alternatives to saving water is switching from surface to sprinkler irrigation. The reasons for this shift are that surface irrigation techniques are inherently less efficient and more labor-intensive than sprinkler irrigation [35]. However, before making this switch, various factors must be taken into account, such as impacts on yields, savings in water, employment, energy, economy, and climatic conditions. Then, for the choice to be good, it is best that the person responsible for implementing the watering system is aware of the pros and cons of each type. It also has advantages and disadvantages of one irrigation technique over the other. All of these must be taken into consideration before the change to efficient technology. If the irrigation system is not particularly suitable for a particular situation, it may not be more efficient or save more water than the original irrigation method. The expected water savings from one irrigation method to another is equal to the difference between the field efficiency values for these two methods.

7.2.6   Efficiency of Irrigation Systems

Terms are given to describe the effective performance of an irrigation system. Competency is determined in the field or during input:

$$Ef = 100 \ Ws/Wd \qquad (7.1)$$

With:
   Ws, water reserved in the soil at the root zone;
   Wd, water brought to the field.

The field efficiency takes into account all losses due to evaporation or runoff from the surface of canals or lines, all leaks from sprinklers or drip tubes, infiltration outside the root zone, water from wind-borne sprinklers, evaporation of fine droplets in the air and runoff out of the field [33] (Table 7.1).

Differences between the efficiencies of different irrigation systems result from variations in runoff, deep percolations and sometimes evaporation. However, the difference does not result from changes in the amount of water consumed by the plant (transpiration). For example, switching from furrow irrigation with 65% efficiency to a high-performance buried drip irrigation system with 90% efficiency will result in water savings of 25%. This is mainly the result of a reduction in the percolation of water at depth and runoff, two very important elements in the case of furrow irrigation. Buried drip irrigation also decreases evaporation because, compared with furrow irrigation, water is brought below the soil surface, which thus, remains dry [36]. However, in either case, there is no difference in the amount of water consumed for the development of the plant. E, the evaporation component of ET (evapotranspiration) can change but not T, the component of transpiration.

When making a decision to change the irrigation method, the expected water supply is equal to the product of the difference in the efficiency value of the two methods. An increase in efficiency by 10% will reduce the amount of water required to achieve the same results as the first method by 10% if the new system is operating properly. It is the quality of its facility installation, management, and improvement that will ultimately determine the actual level of efficiency. These are especially important when a farmer chooses to change the current irrigation method to a new method with more water consumption.

7.3   IoT

The term Internet of Things has recently spread across all platforms and different media, its importance in our daily life can be talked about [3]. The IoT is known as the ability of devices to communicate and coordinate with each other via the Internet so that they do all things without any human intervention [4]. The goal of IoT is to create and improve processes in various sectors by providing business models that contribute to raising business efficiency, reducing costs, enhancing innovation, creating new job opportunities, increasing profitability, and providing new insights to organizations in their operations that contribute to providing innovative solutions, whether for individuals or companies and in various vital sectors, such as industry, mining, energy, water, transportation, health, education, tourism, agriculture, environment, security, entertainment and welfare, and many other sectors to improve the quality of life [37]. According to the recent years' statistics, IoT has reached 12 billion connected devices in 2019 and is expected to reach 25 billion connected devices in 2025, as companies will be among the most beneficiaries by 2024. It is expected that IoT revenues will reach about $1.1 trillion in 2025.

7.3.1   IoT History

In 1999, a technology expert at MIT, "Kevin Ashton," presented the IoT proposal in an illustrative lecture at his workplace at Proctor & Gamble, where he thought of using RFID chips in the supply system [37]. In 2010, IoT technology began to gain some popularity among individuals and organizations through many smart applications on the web, such as the Google "StreetView" service that not only provides 360-degree images but also stores a large amount of data. This service has been considered a new strategy for not only indexing the Internet but also indexing the physical world. In that year, the State of China announced that it would make the IoT a priority in its 5-year plan "LPWAN."

7.3.2   IoT Architecture

The IoT system consists of four basic components: (1) sensors, (2) communication devices, (3) data processing systems, (4) user interface (Figure 7.3) [38].

- **Sensors/devices:** sensors collect data where it can be simple (like temperature) or complex (like video broadcast systems). It is also possible to group the sensors or the sensors can be part of a device that does more than just feel things. For example, a mobile phone contains multiple sensors (camera, GPS, etc.).
- **Communication devices:** after collecting the data encrypted by the sensors, it is sent to the cloud, which is an advanced system for storing data on the Internet. To view this information, many methods and means are used, such as satellites, phones, and so on, and the Wi-Fi network.
- **Data processing system:** the processing data may be as simple (for example, verifying the temperature is within a certain range), or it may be very complex processing, such as video playback.

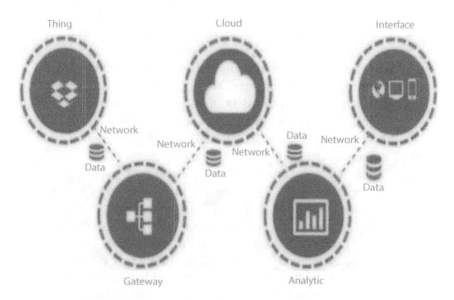

Figure 7.3 IoT system components diagram.

- **User interface:** after completing the processing process, the data become usable and useful for achieving a certain purpose (for example, alerting the user about a temperature rise in a place by e-mail or by sending text messages). In this context, it is possible to rely on the IoT to achieve the previous goal, where the user can remotely adjust the temperature in the storage warehouse through a program available on the phone. Some actions are performed automatically. Instead of waiting for the temperature to set, the system can do it automatically with preset rules. Instead of just calling you to alert you of a hacker, the IoT system can also notify the relevant authorities automatically.

7.3.3   Examples of Uses for the IoT

- Smart cities: It is possible to benefit from the IoT by applying intelligence technology to cities, and thus it is possible to suggest solutions for traffic jams, control the lighting of a place, cameras for protection, and others [19].
- Smart buildings: smart meters are the most popular and widely used of all uses [39, 40]. By using the IoT, it is possible to control all household appliances (such as washing machines, refrigerators, ovens, air conditioning, and heating).
- Wearables: There are also smart watches that are used a lot, and there are electronic bracelets that are used for many purposes, quarantine, security guard, or disease monitoring, especially for heart patients and other diseases that threaten the safety and health of humans and the entire disease record, in addition to medicines and the doctor who follows him. There are also smart glasses that support virtual reality and augmented reality.
- Connected cars: Transportation means, such as airplanes, cars, and buses, have become equipped with IoT technology, thanks to which, it is possible to communicate with any device connected to the Internet as it helps them to drive, monitor road conditions, avoid traffic congestion, maintain a distance safety on the road, adhere to the specified speed, and prevent theft, and in the event of accidents, the user can communicate with the nearest security point and send website for quick help.

7.3.4   IoT Importance in Different Sectors

- **Education:** it is possible to rely on the IoT to provide lessons and lectures remotely. The IoT can also be used to create three-dimensional models that help in simplifying the explanation of materials in new ways, such as simulation, and this technology also helps in developing educational applications for developing knowledge and innovation.
- **Industry:** the IoT helps the industrial method by using robots and monitoring industrial processes and information provided by equipment, measuring and controlling the operational status of equipment and setting maintenance schedules, and automatically updating machine software.
- **Farming:** it consists of many tasks, such as tracking irrigation systems, weather monitoring, crops monitoring, pests, and hazards monitoring and percentage of salts. It is also possible to add monitoring of forests and agricultural lands through very sophisticated surveillance devices, such as drones.
- **Transport:** it is represented in the tracking of the transportation field by analyzing the route data for the means of transport, and transport stations can also be equipped with devices to track the number of passengers present in each station through programs installed on mobile phones, where, for example, the driver is alerted about the number of people likely to be loaded or downloaded at each station.
- **Tourism:** by providing tourists with information about tourist sites and the best way to reach them, as well as the amenities and supplies available, such as hotels, restaurants, and various services. Generally, the information systems used by the tourist are equipped with the feature of multilingualism, and this is so that it is easy for every tourist to understand it.
- **Environment:** it consists of monitoring the extent of pollution, monitoring natural resources, biological diversity, and environmental reserves, linking them all with environmental protection, and issuing an immediate alert to the nearest periodicity to take immediate action in the event of a problem or danger.
- **IoT and cybersecurity:** It is very important to provide the necessary protection against hacking attacks and data breaches, especially with a large number of connected devices (IoT).

7.4   IoT Applications in Agriculture

The application of technology, such as the IoT, in agriculture could have a positive impact [41]. Then, to feed a large number of people in the world, it is necessary to increase agricultural production by modernizing the methods used. However, IoT technology-based smart agriculture will reduce waste and improve yields. Smart agriculture is about carrying out agricultural activities by relying on modern technologies, because the introduction of these techniques makes the yields better. In addition to that, smart farming is based on the IoT, systems are being built to monitor farms from anywhere and anytime with the help of sensors (temperature, light, humidity). Finally, smart farming based on the IoT is efficient and attractive compared with traditional farming. With regard to the environment, smart agriculture has many advantages, among which is the rational use of water.

7.4.1   Precision Cultivation

It is represented in practicing agricultural activity, but with more precision and control. In this approach to farm management, one of the main components is the use of information technology and many elements, such as sensors and robots [42].

7.4.2   Agricultural Unmanned Aircraft

Technology has evolved over time, and drones are the best example of this. Agriculture is one of the fields in which drone technology has been applied for the purpose of tracking agricultural lands in a timely and accurate manner. Drones are used in agriculture to promote various agricultural practices, crop health assessment, irrigation, crop monitoring, crop spraying with chemical pesticides, cultivation, and soil analysis [43]. The main benefits of using drones include crop photography and integrated geographic information system mapping. Advantages of applying these technologies include ease of use, time savings, and potential for increased returns. From the drone data, insights can be gleaned on plant health indicators, plant counts and yield prediction, plant height measurement, field water mapping, and chlorophyll measurement.

7.4.3   Livestock Control

The use of IoT technology allows collecting data related to agricultural activity, as this information helps them, for example, to identify sick animals, to know the degree of plant growth, the dangers of fires and floods, to determine the location of livestock [44].

7.4.4   Smart Greenhouses

It is a type of agriculture carried out with the aim of obtaining products outside its normal season, and better yields can be obtained by providing climatic conditions conducive to good growth and in record time. Greenhouses maintain environmental standards through manual or automatic intervention. The manual intervention leads to loss of production and energy and cost increase [45]. With the help of the IoT, it is possible to monitor climate data because sensors are used. After that, a cloud server can be used to remotely access the system when it is connected using the IoT. This eliminates the need for manual monitoring within the greenhouse, and the cloud server enables data processing and implementation of control measures. This design also provides cost-effective solutions and the best approach to growers with minimal manual intervention. In recent years, with technological development, modern and affordable greenhouses are being built using solar powered sensors. The IoT sensors in the greenhouse provide data on climatic factors, and through their analysis and treatment, appropriate decisions can be taken [46].

7.5   IoT and Water Management

The agricultural fields have the first place in achieving most of the human needs of food, as the need increases with the increase of people and there is a decrease in the areas suitable for agriculture and there is scarcity of water and the rest of the resources needed for this. Therefore, for that, agriculture becomes more tender in quantity and quality and with higher quality and at the lowest possible cost, and the decisions made by farmers are about it, they need to be able to match their crop management requirements to reduce waste and reduce the overall costs. One of the important elements that should be given priority is good water management [47]. For example, IoT applications can overcome these challenges by allowing farmers to benefit because data are collected, analyzed, and the best decisions are made from different types of sensors and monitoring systems, improving the productivity of their crops through remote monitoring and decision making based on actual data [48]. Among the benefits of the IoT applications for managing agricultural irrigation water are the following:

- sensing soil moisture and nutrients;
- monitoring of water management for optimal cultivation;
- classification of various fertilizers based on soil quality (soil chemistry);
- choosing the appropriate time for planting and harvesting.

There are many factors that affect the quality of the agricultural product and one of these is water, the optimal management of water management plays an important role in ensuring that an acceptable quantity of crops at the right time is salt. Around water management, the following can be cited:

- collecting data on water in real time by means of sensors, which allow first to predict and on the second hand to take appropriate decisions;
- work procedures depend on sensor data to turn on and off the water supply, taking into consideration irrigation needs and resource availability;
- rapidly detect water leaks and faults in pipelines to address problems in a timely manner.

7.6   Introduction to the Implementation

This part is dedicated to the implementation of a solution-based IoT irrigation solution, its concern is an intelligent sprinkler system. It must control the watering according to the soil temperature and humidity. This study being the case of an agricultural environment (land, greenhouse, or others), the specifications are defined as follows (Figure 7.4):

- store the water in a tank for possible use;
- receive a message each time there is a need for watering;
- start the watering from your smartphone;
- fill the watering tank after each watering.

Achieving these specifications requires the use of modules such as GSM, the Arduino UNO board, sensors, and so on [49].

- **Arduino UNO:** is an electronic card based on "Atmega328P" microcontroller. There are several other types like the MEGA,

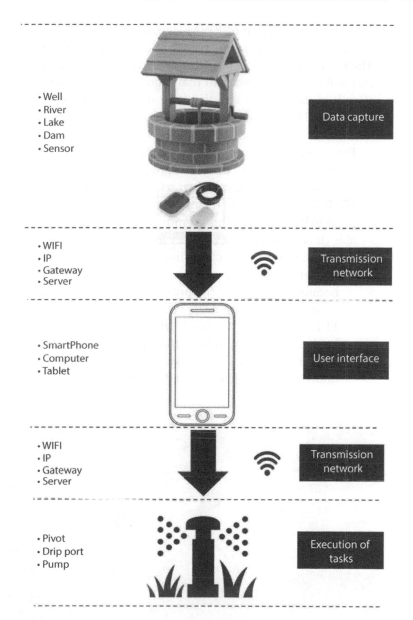

Figure 7.4 Presentation of the specifications.

DUO, and so on. The program is stored and executed by the microcontroller for various tasks [50]. The main advantage of Arduino cards is their ease of use. In addition, function libraries are also provided for the use of common input outputs: management of discrete I/O, management of ADC

converters, generation of PWM signals, operation of TWI/
I2C bus, operation of servomotors, and so on (Figure 7.5).

- **The microcontroller (1):** the brain of the card. It is the one
  that will receive the program that is going to create and will
  store it in its memory and then run it. Thanks to this program, it will know how to do the things that are needed. It is
  made up of some elements:
  - **Processor:** this is the microcontroller principal component.
    It is the one that will execute the program that will be given
    to him for processing. It is often referred to as the CPU.
  - **Flash memory:** this is the one that will contain the pro-
    gram to be executed. This memory is erasable and rewrit-
    able (it is the same as a USB key for example).
  - **RAM:** this is the so-called live memory; it will contain
    the variables of our program. It is said to be "volatile"
    because it is erased if the power to the microcontroller
    is cut (as on a computer).
  - **EEPROM:** this is the hard drive of the microcontrol-
    ler. You can record information that needs to survive
    over time, even if the card has to be stopped. Recorded
    information is not lost when the console is powered off.

Figure 7.5 Arduino board.

- ○ **Power supply (2 and 3):** as the microcontroller operates at 5V, the card can be supplied with 5V from the USB port (in 2) or by an external power supply (in 3) which is between 7V and 12V. This voltage must be continuous and can for example be supplied by a 9V battery. A regulator is then responsible for reducing the voltage to 5V for the proper functioning of the card. No danger of grilling everything, you must respect the interval of 7V to 15V.
- • **Display (4):** the three "white dots" circled in red (4) are LEDs whose size is of the order of a millimeter. These LEDs serve two purposes:
  - ○ **The one at the top of the frame:** it is connected to a pin of the microcontroller and will be used to test the equipment.
  - ○ **Two LEDs at the bottom of the frame:** are used to visualize the activity on the serial channel (one for transmission and the other for reception). The program is downloaded into the microcontroller in this way, which can be seen flashing during the download.
  - ○ **Connections (5 and 6):** the Arduino board does not have components that can be used for a program, put a by the LED connected to pin 13 of the microcontroller, it is necessary to add them. But to do this, you have to connect them to the card. This is where the card's connection comes in (in 5 and 5).
  - ○ **Soil humidity sensor:** is the used equipment that permits the acquisition of soil humidity data. This value can be analyzed and necessary measures can be taken for the ideal growth of crops. This is why the module has a support that is planted directly on the ground where electrodes are attached through which the resistance of the ground is, therefore, measured by the water concentration. Contains a switch to change between analog and digital output. Able to read specific soil moisture data (analog) or very wet or very dry soil information depending on the threshold (digital).
- • **Water level detector:** it can be used to detect the volume of water in the tank; through this information, an appropriate decision can be taken.
- • **Micro water pump with USB connector:** the use of a pump is necessary for this project. A small, flow adjustable pump

has been selected and is designed to fully submerge fresh-water and saltwater. It is made of plastic with the following characteristics:

- o A DC 3.5-9v input voltage;
- o The power of 1-3 w;
- o Flow: Max. 200L/H (44GPH);

- Arduino software: Arduino software is an integrated development space (IDE) that allows us to write, compile and send code to the circuit board of the same name (Arduino board). Its interface is presented in a simple and structured way (Figure 7.6).

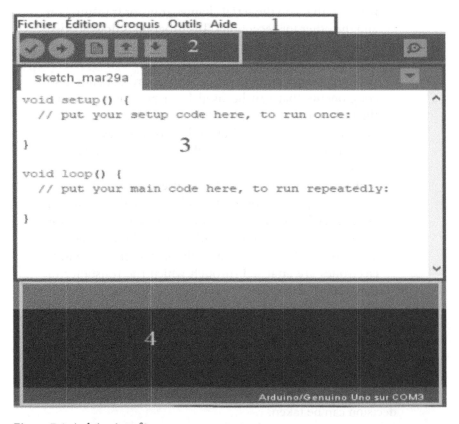

Figure 7.6 Arduino interface.

1) these are the software configuration options.
2) the buttons that will be used when programming the card.
3) this block will contain the program to be created.
4) it is important because it will help us to correct errors in this program it is the debugger.

- AT commands: are some of the textual commands used to manage the modems or GSM modules. These commands always start with the letters "AT" and must end with a carriage return. AT: Attention code. It is the prefix of a command line that tells the modem that command or sequence of commands is going to be sent (Table 7.2).

Table 7.2 AT commands dedicated to the SMS service.

Command	Description
AT + CSMS	Select messaging service
AT + CPMS	Select your memory area for the SMS storage
AT + CMGF	Selection of the SMS format (PDU or TEXT)
AT + CSCA	Definition of the address of the messaging
AT + CSDH	Displays in TEXT mode the configuration of the SMS
AT + CSAS	Save the settings
AT + CRES	Restoration of default settings
AT + CNMI	Indication of a new SMS
AT + CMGL	Lists SMS stored in memory
AT + CMGR	Reading an SMS
AT + CMGS	Send an SMS
AT + CMSS	Sends an SMS stored in memory
AT + CMGW	Writing an SMS
AT + CMGD	Delete an SMS

7.7   Analysis and Discussion

Because of the high rates of poverty and food shortages in the world, especially in Africa, due to climate change and weather fluctuations harmful to crops, as according to the latest statistics, the number of people affected by hunger has reached to an estimated 821 million, which is an attractive high number and needs studies and researches for urgent solutions. So, it has become imperative to work on finding techniques and means that will secure adequate food supplies and bypass the threats of climate change and harsh environmental conditions. To produce edible food at affordable prices for the world's population is constantly increasing while the world faces many challenges.

Climate change has caused an increase in the frequency of droughts and high temperatures and has made an impact on crops, the livestock sector, and fishing. Many countries found themselves in a race against time to achieve food security.

Perhaps, the most important reason is that most of these countries do not benefit from the technological innovations available in the field of agriculture, especially water management. Most of the agriculture in many countries still depend on traditional practices and are at the mercy of unexpected environmental changes.

To face the coming challenges, modifying the water management activity has become an urgent necessity, which must go hand in hand with diversification processes in production sources, by using advanced agricultural technologies and innovative solutions for artificial intelligence, such as IoT applications, which are adopted by peasants in developed countries [3]. Netherlands is a small European country, with a high population density (more than 1,300 inhabitants per square mile) and limited resources, but it managed to attract the world's attention in the agricultural field, and it is considered among the countries that have benefited from advanced technologies. Netherlands has taken steps toward embracing the latest agricultural technologies, and among the advanced methods on which the agricultural sector relies are, for example, unmanned tractors, drones, and smart sensors that provide data on water content, plant growth, and soil chemistry. Numerous high-tech greenhouses have been established, which control the climate, growing crops around the clock, and in all types of weather.

Apart from low energy consumption, the technology enables the selection of specific light spectrums, depending on the plant quality and energy required for good growth [51]. The results, compared with outdoor cultivation, are impressive, for example, 300 grams of lettuce is grown under the LED system and in the red and blue spectrum, during 4 weeks, as opposed to 8 to 12 weeks in the field, in addition to the high nutritional quality of the crops.

7.8 Conclusion

The purpose of intelligent watering is to save water by conditioning the watering (the action) on the basis of meteorological information's acquisition. Then, an intelligent solution is a system that collects information from sensors to build an image of the real world (in this case, the water needs of plants). This information is then processed and analyzed to act with a so-called intelligent action, which may, in turn, modify the real world. Smart sprinklers combine centralized sprinkler technology and soil moisture sensors with the goals of significantly reducing water consumption and preserving the look of green spaces compared to expected. The performance of intelligent irrigation is based on its ability to regularly adjust the quantities of water supplied. This requires having not only humidity probes connected but also remote-controlled solenoid valve controllers. The addition of connected water meters makes it possible to maximize water savings by detecting hidden leaks and to have more accurate management by instantaneous or regular flow control. An additional weather station, local or remote, provides an agronomic understanding by matching the quantities of water supplied.

This work has allowed us to make a state of art in different areas of research, namely agriculture, irrigation, and automatic sprinkler systems. In addition, the implementation of an IoT system for irrigation water management has allowed us to learn and operate several platforms, tools and development languages, among others the Arduino, Java platforms and Android.

Through programming and possibly a link to additional sensors, the devices control the water supply fully automatically. Then, thanks to the schedule, the watering can take place at a time that is optimal for the plants and not necessarily during your working hours. For example, if the system is turned on in the early hours of the morning, the water evaporates less quickly and the leaves cannot burn due to the hot glass effect. The third advantage is certainly the water savings. In combination with the sensors, irrigation only takes place when the soil is dry or when it is not raining. Thus, the plants grow better, because they are always supplied with sufficient water, but not too much.

In the coming years, there will be a drastic change in the way you live and work, thanks to the IoT technology, which will make everything possible, if true, especially with the increase in Internet speeds and the bandwidth provided by the 5G communication technology. However, the dilemma of security and protection of privacy remains one of the biggest problems facing the IoT. Many devices suffer from software bugs, making them vulnerable to hacking, tracking their location, eavesdropping, and blackmailing users.

References

1. Saba, D., Sahli, Y., Hadidi, A., The Role of Artificial Intelligence in Company's Decision Making. in: *Enabling AI Applications in Data Science. Studies in Computational Intelligence*, Hassanien AE., Taha M.H.N. and Khalifa N.E.M. (Eds), vol 911, Springer, Switzerland, pp. 287–314, 2021.
2. Polak, M., Tanzer, N.K., Bauernhofer, K., and Andersson, G., Disorder-specific internet-based cognitive-behavioral therapy. In: treating panic disorder, comorbid symptoms and improving quality of life: A meta-analytic evaluation of randomized controlled trials, *Internet Interv.*, vol 24, 100364, 2021.
3. Saba, D., Sahli, Y., Maouedj, R., Hadidi, A., Medjahed, M. Ben, Towards Artificial Intelligence: Concepts, Applications, and Innovations, in: *Enabling AI Applications in Data Science. Studies in Computational Intelligence*, Hassanien, AE., Taha, M.H.N. and Khalifa, N.E.M. (Eds.), vol 911. Springer, Switzerland, pp. 103–146, 2021.
4. Saba, D., Sahli, Y., Berbaoui, B., Maouedj, R., Towards Smart Cities: Challenges, Components, and Architectures, in: *Studies in Computational Intelligence: Toward Social Internet of Things (SIoT): Enabling Technologies, Architectures and Applications*, A.E. Hassanien, R. Bhatnagar, N.E.M. Khalifa, M.H.N. Taha (Eds.), pp. 249–286, Springer, Cham, 2020.
5. Nayak, J., Vakula, K., Dinesh, P., Naik, B., Pelusi, D., Intelligent food processing: Journey from artificial neural network to deep learning. *Comput. Sci. Rev.*, **38**, 100297, 2020.
6. Hussein, M., Zorkany, M., Neamat, S., A., K., Design and Implementation of IoT Platform for Real Time Systems. In: Hassanien A., Tolba M., Elhoseny M. and Mostafa M. (Eds) The International Conference on Advanced Machine Learning Technologies and Applications (AMLTA2018). AMLTA 2018. Advances in Intelligent Systems and Computing, vol 723. Springer, Switzerland, pp. 171–180, 2018.
7. Saba, D., Laallam, F.Z., Hadidi, A.E., Berbaoui, B., Contribution to the Management of Energy in the Systems Multi Renewable Sources with Energy by the Application of the Multi Agents Systems "mAS.", *Energy Proc.*, 74, 616–623, 2015.
8. Saba, D., Berbaoui, B., Degha, H.E., Laallam, F.Z., A Generic Optimization Solution for Hybrid Energy Systems Based on Agent Coordination, in: *Advances in Intelligent Systems and Computing*, A.E. Hassanien, K. Shaalan,

T. Gaber, M.F. Tolba, (Eds.), pp. 527–536, Springer, Cham, Cairo - Egypte, 2018.

9. Saba, D., Degha, H.E., Berbaoui, B., Laallam, F.Z., Maouedj, R., Contribution to the modeling and simulation of multi-agent systems for energy saving in the habitat. *Int. Conf. Math. Inf. Technol.*, p. 1, 2017.

10. Saba, D., Laallam, F.Z., Berbaoui, B., Contribution to Energy Management in Hybrid Energy Systems Based on Agents Coordination. *Int. J. Inf. Commun. Eng.*, 10, 9, 1249–1255, 2016.

11. Saba, D., Laallam, F.Z., Berbaoui, B., Fonbeyin, H.A., An energy management approach in hybrid energy system based on agent's coordination. *2nd Int. Conf. Adv. Intell. Syst. Informatics*, p. 533, 2016.

12. Saba, D., Zohra Laallam, F., Belmili, H., Henry Abanda, F., Bouraiou, A., Development of an ontology-based generic optimisation tool for the design of hybrid energy systems. *Int. J. Comput. Appl. Technol.*, 55, 3, 232–243, 2017.

13. Rebouças Filho, P.P., Gomes, S.L., e Nascimento, N.M.M., Medeiros, C.M.S., Outay, F., de Albuquerque, V.H.C., Energy production predication via Internet of Thing based machine learning system. *Futur. Gener. Comput. Syst*, 97, 180–193, 2019.

14. Worldometer, *Population by Country*. Available at: https://www.worldometers.info/world-population/population-by-country/ by United Nations, Department of Economic and Social Affairs, Population Division, 2021 [Accessed December 02, 2021].

15. Shahid, N. and Aneja, S., Internet of Things: Vision, application areas and research challenges. *Proc. Int. Conf. IoT Soc. Mobile, Anal. Cloud, I-SMAC 2017*, 2017.

16. Saba, D., Sahli, Y., Maouedj, R., Hadidi, A., Medjahed, M. Ben, Contribution to the Realization of a Smart and Sustainable Home, in: *Artificial Intelligence for Sustainable Development: Theory, Practice and Future Applications. Studies in Computational Intelligence*, Hassanien A., Bhatnagar R. and Darwish A. (Eds), vol 912, Springer, Switzerland, pp. 261-290, 2021.

17. Saba, D., Sahli, Y., Abanda, F.H., Maouedj, R., Tidjar, B., Development of new ontological solution for an energy intelligent management in Adrar city. *Sustain. Comput. Inform. Syst.*, 21, 189–203, 2019.

18. Saba, D., Sahli, Y., Hadidi, A., An ontology based energy management for smart home. *Sustain. Comput. Inform. Syst.*, 31, 100591, 2021.

19. Saba, D., Degha, H.E., Berbaoui, B., Maouedj, R., *Development of an Ontology Based Solution for Energy Saving Through a Smart Home in the City of Adrar in Algeria*, pp. 531–541, Springer, Cham, 2018.

20. Eltohamy, K.M., Liu, C., Khan, S., Niyungeko, C., Jin, Y., Hosseini, S.H., Li, F., Liang, X., An internet-based smart irrigation approach for limiting phosphorus release from organic fertilizer-amended paddy soil. *J. Cleaner Prod.*, 293, 126254, 2021.

21. Salleh, S.Z., Awang Kechik, A., Yusoff, A.H., Taib, M.A.A., Mohamad Nor, M., Mohamad, M., Tan, T.G., Ali, A., Masri, M.N., Mohamed, J.J., Zakaria,

S.K., Boon, J.G., Budiman, F., and Teo, P. Ter, Recycling food, agricultural, industrial wastes as pore-forming agents for sustainable porous ceramic production: A review. *J. Clean. Prod.*, 306, 127264, 2021.

22. Mohammed Wazed, S., Hughes, B.R., O'Connor, D., Kaiser Calautit, J., A review of sustainable solar irrigation systems for Sub-Saharan Africa. *Renewable Sustainable Energy Rev.*, 81, 1206–1225, 2018.

23. Njuki, E. and Bravo-Ureta, B.E., Irrigation water use and technical efficiencies: Accounting for technological and environmental heterogeneity in U.S. agriculture using random parameters. *Water Resour. Econ.*, 24, 1–12, 2018.

24. Jiang, L.M., Lak, B., Eijsvogels, L.M., Wesselink, P., and Van Der Sluis, L.W.M., Comparison of the cleaning efficacy of different final irrigation techniques, *J. Endod.*, 38, 6, 838–841, 2012.

25. Pereira, L.S., Surface Irrigation Systems, in: *Sustainability of Irrigated Agriculture*, 1996.

26. Yazdi, M.N., Sample, D.J., Scott, D., Owen, J.S., Ketabchy, M., Alamdari, N., Water quality characterization of storm and irrigation runoff from a container nursery. *Sci. Total Environ.*, 667, 166–178, 2019.

27. Zinkernagel, J., Maestre-Valero, J.F., Seresti, S.Y., Intrigliolo, D.S., New technologies and practical approaches to improve irrigation management of open field vegetable crops. *Agric. Water Manage.*, 242, 106404, 2020.

28. Jia, D., Dai, X., Xie, Y., He, M., Alternate furrow irrigation improves grain yield and nitrogen use efficiency in winter wheat. *Agric. Water Manage.*, 244, 106606, 2021.

29. Oda, T., Moriwaki, K., Tanigaki, K., Nomura, Y., Sumi, T., Irrigation ponds in the past, present, and future: A case study of the Higashi Harima Region, Hyogo Prefecture, Japan. *J. Hydro-Environ. Res.*, 26, 19–24, 2019.

30. Vico, G., Tamburino, L., Rigby, J.R., Designing on-farm irrigation ponds for high and stable yield for different climates and risk-coping attitudes. *J. Hydrol.*, 584, 124634, 2020.

31. Reddy, P.P. and Reddy, P.P., Micro Irrigation, in: *Sustainable Intensification of Crop Production*, 2016.

32. Bansal, G., Mahajan, A., Verma, A., Bandhu Singh, D., A review on materialistic approach to drip irrigation system. *Mater. Today Proc*, 46, 10712–10717, 2021.

33. FAO. Brouwer, C., Prins, K., Heibloem, M.: Irrigation Water Management: Irrigation Scheduling. Available at: https://www.fao.org/3/T7202E/t7202e00.htm#Contents [Accessed 12 December 2021].

34. Zhai, L., Lü, L., Dong, Z., Zhang, L., Zhang, J., Jia, X., Zhang, Z., The water-saving potential of using micro-sprinkling irrigation for winter wheat production on the North China Plain. *J. Integr. Agric.*, 20, 6, 1687–1700, 2021.

35. Cakmakci, T. and Sahin, U., Productivity and heavy metal pollution management in a silage maize field with reduced recycled wastewater applications with different irrigation methods. *J. Environ. Manage.*, 291, 112602, 2021.

36. Rouzaneh, D., Yazdanpanah, M., Jahromi, A.B., Evaluating micro-irrigation system performance through assessment of farmers' satisfaction: implications for adoption, longevity, and water use efficiency. *Agric. Water Manage.*, 246, 106655, 2021.

37. Atlam, H.F., El-Din Hemdan, E., Alenezi, A., Alassafi, M.O., Wills, G.B., Internet of Things Forensics: A Review. *Internet Things*, 11, 100220, 2020.

38. Patel, K.K., Patel, S.M., Scholar, P.G., Internet of Things-IOT: Definition, Characteristics, Architecture, Enabling Technologies, Application & Future Challenges. *Int. J. Eng. Sci. Comput.*, 6, 6122–6131, 2016.

39. Saba, D., Laallam, F.Z., Degha, H.E., Berbaoui, B., and Maouedj, R. (2019) Design and Development of an Intelligent Ontology-Based Solution for Energy Management in the Home. In: Hassanien A. (Eds) Machine Learning Paradigms: Theory and Application. Studies in Computational Intelligence, vol 801. Springer, Switzerland, pp. 135–167.

40. Saba, D., Maouedj, R., Berbaoui, B., Contribution to the development of an energy management solution in a green smart home (EMSGSH). *Proc. 7th Int. Conf. Softw. Eng. New Technol. - ICSENT 2018*, pp. 1–7, 2018.

41. Hadidi, A., Saba, D., Sahli, Y., *The Role of Artificial Neuron Networks in Intelligent Agriculture* (Case Study: Greenhouse). in: *Artificial Intelligence for Sustainable Development: Theory, Practice and Future Applications. Studies in Computational Intelligence*, Hassanien A., Bhatnagar R. and Darwish A. (Eds), vol. 912, Springer, Switzerland, pp. 45–67, 2021.

42. Foreignaffairs, *The Precision Agriculture Revolution* Making the Modern Farmer, 2015, Available at: https://www.foreignaffairs.com/articles/united-states/2015-04-20/precision-agriculture-revolution.byhttps://www.foreignaffairs.com/articles/united-states/2015-04-20/precision-agriculture-revolution#author-info"Jess Lowenberg-DeBoer, Purdue University, https://en.wikipedia.org/wiki/West_Lafayette,_Indiana"West Lafayette, https://en.wikipedia.org/wiki/Indiana, Indiana, United States [Accessed December 02, 2021]

43. Fischer, J.W., Greiner, K., Lutman, M.W., Webber, B.L., Vercauteren, K.C., Use of unmanned aircraft systems (UAS) and multispectral imagery for quantifying agricultural areas damaged by wild pigs. *Crop Prot.*, 125, 104865, 2019.

44. Wang, Y.-C., Han, M.-F., Jia, T.-P., Hu, X.-R., Zhu, H.-Q., Tong, Z., Lin, Y.-T., Wang, C., Liu, D.-Z., Peng, Y.-Z., Wang, G., Meng, J., Zhai, Z.-X., Zhang, Y., Deng, J.-G., Hsi, H.-C., Emissions, measurement, and control of odor in livestock farms: A review. *Sci. Total Environ.*, 776, 145735, 2021.

45. Castañeda-Miranda, A., Castaño, V.M., Smart frost control in greenhouses by neural networks models. *Comput. Electron. Agric.*, 137, 102–114, 2017.

46. Seethalakshmi, E., Shunmugam, M., Pavaiyarkarasi, R., Joseph, S., Edward paulraj, J., An automated irrigation system for optimized greenhouse using IoT. *Mater. Today Proc.*, 2021. https://doi.org/10.1016/j.matpr.2020.12.636 is in press

47. Perumal, T., Sulaiman, M.N., Leong, C.Y., Internet of Things (IoT) enabled water monitoring system. *2015 IEEE 4th Glob. Conf. Consum. Electron. GCCE 2015*, 2016.
48. Nigussie, E., Olwal, T., Musumba, G., Tegegne, T., Lemma, A., Mekuria, F., IoT-based Irrigation Management for Smallholder Farmers in Rural Sub-Saharan Africa. *Proc. Comput. Sci.*, 177, 86–93, 2020.
49. Haque, M.A., Haque, S., Sonal, D., Kumar, K., Shakeb, E., Security Enhancement for IoT Enabled Agriculture. *Mater. Today Proc.*, 2021. https://doi.org/10.1016/j.matpr.2020.12.452 is in press
50. https://www.sciencedirect.com/science/article/pii/S0168169918301959#!, González-Buesa, J., https://www.sciencedirect.com/science/article/pii/S0168169918301959#!, Salvador, M., L., An Arduino-based low cost device for the measurement of the respiration rates of fruits and vegetables. https://www.sciencedirect.com/science/journal/01681699, *Computers and Electronics in Agriculture*, 162, 14–20, 2019.
51. Saba, D., Sahli, Y., Maouedj, R., Hadidi, A., Energy management based on internet of things, In: *Recent Advances in Technology Acceptance Models and Theories. Studies in Systems, Decision and Control*, Al-Emran M. and Shaalan K. (Eds.), vol 335, Springer Nature, Switzerland, pp. 349–372, 2021.

The Internet of Things (IoT) for Sustainable Agriculture

Sadiq, M.S.[1]*, Singh, I.P.[2], Ahmad, M.M.[3] and Karunakaran, N.[4]

[1]Department of Agricultural Economics and Extension, FUD, Dutse, Nigeria
[2]Department of Agricultural Economics, SKRAU, Bikaner, India
[3]Department of Agricultural Economics, BUK, Kano, Nigeria
[4]Department of Economics, EKNM Government College Elerithattu, Kerela, India

Abstract

Increasingly, agriculture is becoming more knowledge-intensive. The challenge of feeding the ever-rising population will not be an easy task. Most of the food consumed in developed nations is provided by half a billion small-family farmers. Small-scale farming families play a critical role in increasing food production for our future food and nutritional security. However, they often have limited access to markets, knowledge, new technology and skills, new inputs, emerging value chains, and other opportunities. The development of agricultural research and its effective applications in the agricultural sector through the transfer of extension and advisory services is critical in achieving improved and sustainable agricultural production and productivity growth. Improved access to and availability to information and communication technologies (ICTs), especially cell phones, computers, radio, Internet, and social media, has created many more opportunities for multiformat information gathering, processing, storage, retrieval, management and sharing.

Keywords: IoT, weather, sustainability, agriculture

*Corresponding author: sadiqsanusi30@gmail.com

Roheet Bhatnagar, Nitin Kumar Tripathi, Nitu Bhatnagar and Chandan Kumar Panda (eds.)
The Digital Agricultural Revolution: Innovations and Challenges in Agriculture through Technology Disruptions, (199–224) © 2022 Scrivener Publishing LLC

8.1   Introduction

Agricultural production depends on many variables, the main factor being weather. Weather varies with space and time; its forecast can also help reduce farm losses by proper agricultural operations management. It is not possible to fully prevent all farm losses due to weather conditions, but it can be reduced to some degree by making changes through timely and reliable weather forecast details. Agromet's weather forecast and weather-based advisories help increase the economic gain of farmers by recommending effective management practices in compliance with weather conditions [3].

The success or failure of the production of agricultural crops is determined primarily by weather parameters. Via its impact on soil and plant growth, the weather manifests its influence on agricultural operations and farm development. A large portion of the overall annual crop losses are because of aberrant conditions. The loss could be reduced by timely and reliable weather forecasting by making changes to the coming weather. With the aid of advanced weather forecasts, agricultural operations may be advanced or postponed for 3 to 10 days. Agricultural forecast useful not only for the efficient management of farm inputs but also contributes to reliable impact assessments [4].

Weather is one of the most significant factors deciding agricultural production's success or failure. It has an impact on any stage of plant growth and development. Any weather variability during the crop season, such as monsoon delay, excessive rains, floods, droughts, too-high or too-low temperature spells, will affect crop growth, and ultimately the yield quality and quantity. With timely and reliable weather forecasts, crop losses can be minimized by doing proper crop management in time. The weather forecast also offers guidance on the selection of crops best suited to the climatic conditions predicted.

The aim of the weather forecast is to inform farmers on the real and expected weather and its effect on the different daily farming operations, i.e., sowing, weeding, pesticide spray time, irrigation scheduling, application of fertilizer, and so on, and overall crop management. Increased agricultural output, reduced losses, reduced risks, reduced input costs, improved yield efficiency, increased productivity in the use of water, labor, and energy, and reduced contamination through judicious use of agricultural chemicals are all benefits of the meteorological forecast. Climate and weather data can be used to make better-informed policy, institutional, and community decisions that reduce risks and increase opportunities, improve the efficient use of scarce resources, and boost crop, livestock, and fisheries production [3].

In agriculture, there are several different types of weather and climate-related threats: limited water resources, drought, desertification, soil erosion, deforestation, hail, floods, early frosts, and so on. Farmers' decision-making processes will be supported by accurate weather and environmental information and advisory services, which will improve their management of relevant agricultural risks. Such services can aid in the development of sustainable and economically viable agricultural systems, as well as the improvement of productivity and quality, the reduction of losses and risks, the reduction of costs, the efficient use of water, labor, and energy, the conservation of natural resources, and the reduction of pollution caused by agricultural chemicals and other age-related pollutants.

The ability of information and communication technologies (ICTs) has opened up new ways of knowledge management over the last decade, which could play a key role in addressing the common challenges of knowledge and technology sharing, exchange, and dissemination. Information and communication technologies are now widely acknowledged as a central factor in the transformation of agricultural extension and information services [5]. Globalization, dynamic market forces, the need for value-added farming, and sustainable use of the natural resource base all necessitate a drastic transformation of agriculture in the developing world. The new agricultural paradigm requires the use of ICTs.

Traditional structures have been used to disseminate agricultural information to farmers in the past, such as literature, posters, radio, and television. In this context, there are several time delays in the transfer of information from research laboratories to farmers. Farmers may depend on extension staff for expert guidance on how to plant the crop. Weather forecasting is one of the most important aspects of farming, because it helps farmers to make the best decisions at the right time. Rather than a set of conventional crop practices, today's farmers need more knowledge of selling rates for local markets, selling intelligence, and precision farming.

Information and communication technologies are seen as a critical component in making such a transition. Information and communication technologies are the most efficient and fast partners for agricultural extension. By improving access to information and exchanging knowledge, ICT-enabled extension systems play a key role in changing the agricultural situation and the lives of farmers. Agricultural extension using ICT opens up exciting possibilities and has the potential to empower farming communities.

8.2   ICT in Agriculture

Information and communication technology is a concept that focuses on utilizing and incorporating information technology (IT) communication systems [3]. Information and communication technology applies to any system or product that allows "electronically recording, storing, transmitting and displaying data and information." This includes the Internet and all hardware and software for computers, including radio, digital television, cellular networks, mobile phones, and satellite systems [6].

Information and communication technology is the global economy's driving force (ICT). It has been recognized as a key development tool for improving citizens' economic and social well-being [1]. Information and communication technology has become a part and parcel of our daily life in this digital age. Without its integration into the knowledge age, countries or regions have no chance of evolving. In addition to opening up new opportunities for economic growth and social progress, the ICT revolution has also created problems and challenges. In the agricultural, industrial and social sectors, it can form and enhance a wide range of developmental applications and affect all sections of society.

For human development, ICT offers unique opportunities. It refers to any electronic means of information collection, retrieval, storage and dissemination. For all attempts to bring about a social shift, communication is important. The advent of ICT has allowed a rapid pace of collaboration, interaction, and data that have had a greater effect on society.

Information and communication technology is a diverse collection of technical tools and resources for knowledge creation, distribution, storage, added value, and management. In particular, advances in ICTs and the Internet have revolutionized the entire field of agriculture, creating new markets, altering the structure of the distribution systems for agriculture, and reengineering all processes [2].

During the last two decades, there has been a great deal of interest in understanding the capacity of ICTs to achieve socioeconomic growth [5]. This resulted in studies in areas, such as agriculture, health, government, financial services, education, and jobs with different ICTs and their implementations. Many of these programs clearly show the tremendous potential of ICTs to enhance the quality and effectiveness of delivering accurate information to rural communities.

In the recent past, ICTs have played an important role in promoting the management of skills and, as a result, fostering innovation in the agriculture sector [7]. Providing localized and customized advisory services, assisting in information management, enabling extension actors to collaborate on innovation, enabling farmers and others to "gain a voice" through social media, and supporting farmers, extension practitioners, and other AIS actors' capacity development are all examples of ICT-based extension advisory methods. Information and communication technologies not only encourage scientists and extension practitioners to exchange knowledge but also enable farmers to connect better returns to the market and consumers. It also provides farmers with the ability to share their farming practices and challenges. Information and communication technology needs to be harnessed by all the players for agricultural production. Technological applications can hit millions of farmers, stakeholders, and rural areas and serve as a catalyst for social change and for food security.

8.3   Internet of Things in Agriculture and Allied Sector

The global recession's revival has created ripples across both developed and emerging economies. To ensure global food security, the agricultural sector would have to be even more productive and resilient. Together, modern-day agriculture and society demand increased food production to feed the global population. New innovations and solutions are being applied in the agricultural sector to provide an effective alternative to collecting and processing data while increasing net productivity.

At the same time, the alarming effects of climate change and the escalating water crisis necessitate the creation of new and improved methodologies for food and agricultural fields in the modern age. In terms of farm size, technology, trade, government policies, and so on, farmers in underdeveloped and developing countries are significantly disadvantaged. Information and communication technologies can help farmers solve some of their problems. To accomplish this goal, automation and smart decision making are also becoming more important [7]. The Internet of Things (IoT), pervasive networking, ad-hoc wireless and sensor networks, radio frequency identifiers, cloud computing, remote sensing (RS), and so on, are becoming increasingly common in this regard [1, 4].

After the World Wide Web (of the 1990s) and the mobile Internet, we are now heading to the third and probably most "disruptive" stage of the Internet revolution, the "Internet of Things (IoT)," also known as "Ubiquitous Computing" (of the 2000s) (Figure 8.1) [8]. Agriculture, health care, retail, transportation, the environment, supply chain management, infrastructure monitoring, and other fields are all impacted by IoT implementations.

In the field of agriculture, we promote sustainable agriculture and productivity improvement through the use of IoT, and the integration of IoT in

Internet Evolution

Figure 8.1 Internet evolution. Source: [2].

agriculture pushes for smart agriculture [9, 10]. Agricultural applications include soil and plant monitoring, greenhouse environment monitoring and control systems, food supply chain monitoring, animal monitoring, and so on [10]. Precision farming equipment with wireless links to data from remote satellites and ground sensors may take crop conditions into account and adjust how each part of a field is farmed, such as by applying additional fertilizer to areas that need more nutrients [4, 10, 11].

The networking of things or physical objects must be cost-effective and useful for end users in order for IoT to be accepted and widely adopted [1, 3]. For emerging and underdeveloped economies, the Global ICT Standardization Forum has defined the following potential benefits of IoT: (i) improved efficiency, visibility, and scalability; (ii) better and more cost-effective operation; (iii) consistency of physical flows and accurate status details; and (iv) improved quality, precision, agility, and automation.

The IoT is a worldwide network of interconnected computers [12]. Pervasive networking, computation, and environmental knowledge are all part of it. Internet of Things is a vision in which "stuff," especially everyday items, such as all home appliances, furniture, clothes, vehicles, roads, and smart materials, can be read, recognized, found, addressed, and/or controlled through the Internet. This will serve as the foundation for a wide range of emerging technology, including energy management, transportation safety systems, and building security.

The Internet of Objects will connect the world's products in a sensory and intelligent way by combining technological developments in object recognition ('tagging items'), sensors and wireless sensor networks ('feeling stuff'), embedded systems ('thinking things'), and nanotechnology ('shrinking things') [8]. The following are some of the benefits of IoT applications in agriculture:

1. improved efficiency of inputs for use (soil, water, fertilizers, pesticides, etc.),
2. reduced production costs,

3. augmented profitability,
4. sustainability,
5. safety in food,
6. environmental security.

The IoT has the potential to transform how people live around the world [12]; we now have more efficient factories, connected cars, and smarter cities, all thanks to an integrated IoT system [13].

By 2050, the world's population will have risen to 9.6 billion people [14]. As a result, the agricultural industry must embrace IoT to feed this massive population. The need for more food necessitates the resolution of issues, such as increasing climate change, extreme weather, and the environmental consequences of intensive agricultural practices. Smart farming can help farmers minimize waste and increase productivity by using IoT technologies. This may be because of the amount of fertilizer used in relation to the number of trips taken by farm vehicles. The term "smart farming" refers to a high-tech food-growing system that is both clean and healthy for the general public [11]. It is also the introduction and application of modern ICTs to agriculture (Figure 8.2).

Internet of Things agriculture applications include precision farming, agriculture drones, livestock monitoring, and smart Greenhouses (Figures 8.3 and 8.4).

8.3.1 Precision Farming

Precision farming is a method or system for raising livestock and crops that makes the process more precise and supervised. The use of IT and items, such as sensors, autonomous vehicles, automated hardware, control

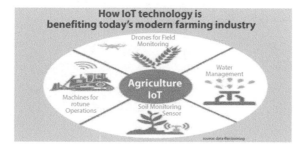

Figure 8.2 IoTs and today's innovative farming industry. Source: data-flair.training.

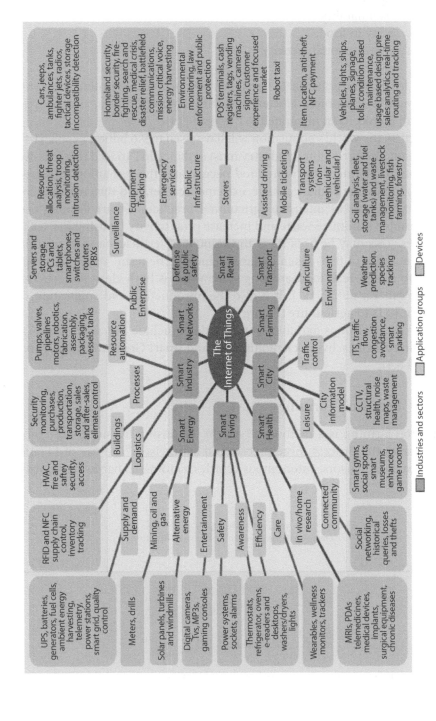

Figure 8.3 IoT proliferation. Source: [2].

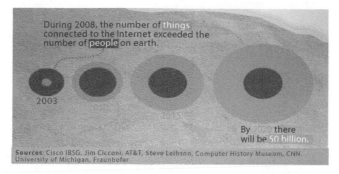

Figure 8.4 People-to-IoT ratio. Sources: Cisco IBSG, Jim Cicconi, AT&T, Steve Leibson, Computer History Museum, CNN. University of Michigan, Fraunhofer; [2].

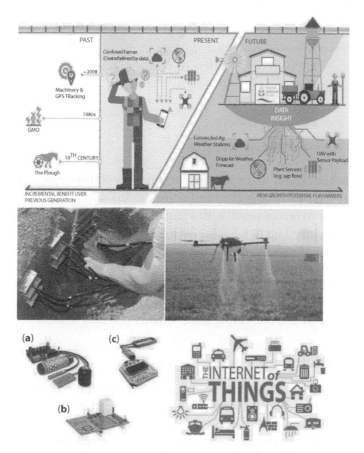

Figure 8.5 The future of agriculture with IoT and smart devices (a-c). Source: [2].

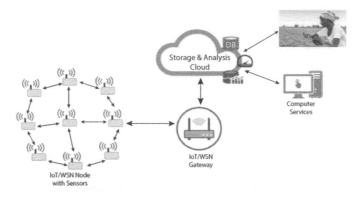

Figure 8.6 The general system architecture. Source: [2].

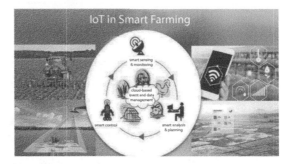

Figure 8.7 IoT in smart farming. Source: [2].

systems, robotics, and so on, are key components of this strategy. Precision agriculture has been one of the most common IoT applications in the agricultural sector in recent years, with a large number of organizations around the world using it (Figure 8.5).

Internet of Things systems offer a variety of products and services, including soil moisture probes, variable rate irrigation (VRI) optimization, virtual optimizer PRO, and more. The VRI optimization is a method for maximizing the profitability of irrigated crop fields with soil variability, increasing yields and increasing water quality (Figures 8.6 and 8.7).

8.3.2   Agriculture Drones

Agricultural drones are a great example of IoT applications in agriculture (Figure 8.8). Agriculture is one of the most important sectors in which drones can be used today. Drones, both ground-based and aerial-based, are being used in agriculture in a variety of ways, including crop health assessment, irrigation, planting, and soil and field analysis.

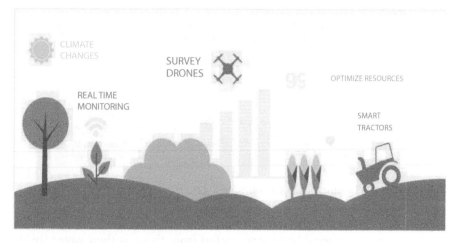

Figure 8.8 Agricultural drones. Source. [2].

Drones have many benefits, including ease of use, time savings, crop health imaging, interactive Geographic Information System (GIS) mapping, and the potential to increase yields. Drone technology will offer the farming industry a high-tech makeover by using strategy and preparation based on real-time data collection and processing. Farmers may use drones to survey specific fields by entering specific data. Choose if the field data are extracted at a higher altitude or at a lower ground resolution. The data collected by the drone can be used to make useful observations on various factors, such as plant counting and yield prediction, plant health indices, plant height estimation, canopy cover mapping, nitrogen content in wheat, drainage mapping, and so on. During the flight, the drone collects thermal, multispectral, and visual data and photographs before landing in the same location from which it took off.

8.3.3   Livestock Monitoring

Farmers may use IoT applications to collect data on their livestock's location, well-being, and health [15, 16]. They will use this information to determine the health of their livestock, such as detecting infected animals and isolating them from the rest of the herd, preventing the disease from spreading to the rest of the herd. The ability of ranchers to use IoT-based sensors to locate their cattle reduces labor costs significantly.

JMB North America, a company that provides cattle farmers with cow tracking solutions, is an example of an IoT system in use by a company (Figure 8.9). Among the many options offered, one of the solutions is to

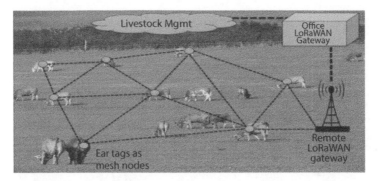

Figure 8.9 IoT in livestock management. Source: [2].

assist cattle owners in observing their pregnant and about to give birth cows. A sensor-powered battery is ejected from them as their water splits. The rancher or the herd's manager will then receive the information. As a result, the sensor aids farmers in concentrating more.

8.3.4   Smart Greenhouses

Greenhouse farming is a method of increasing grain, fruit, and vegetable yields. Greenhouses regulate environmental parameters in one of two ways: manually or through a proportional control mechanism.

Manual intervention, on the other hand, has disadvantages, such as production loss, energy loss, and labor cost, making these methods less effective. Via IoT-embedded systems, a smart greenhouse not only intelligently manages but also regulates the environment, obviating the need for human intervention (Figure 8.10) [9, 10]. Different sensors that calculate environmental parameters according to the plant requirement are used to monitor the environment in a smart greenhouse. As it uses IoT to connect, a cloud server is installed to allow remote access to the computer. The greenhouse's cloud server aids in data analysis and the implementation of a control action.

This design provides farmers with optimal to cost-effective solutions with minimal to almost no manual interference.

Illuminum Greenhouses, an Agri-Tech greenhouse company that uses technology and the Internet of Things to provide services, is one example. It creates modern and inexpensive greenhouses by using solar-powered IoT sensors. The greenhouse status and water consumption can be monitored using these sensors, which send SMS updates to the farmer through an online portal. Temperature, pressure, humidity, and light levels are all measured by sensors in the greenhouse IoT system.

automatically controlled by sensor))) or time 🕒

Figure 8.10 Smart greenhouse. Source: [2].

8.4   Geospatial Technology

Geospatial technology refers to the simulation, calculation, and study, using specialized equipment, of the characteristics of the earth or other natural phenomenon viewed from space. The RS-GIS and GPS are the fundamental components involved in this technology that enable the creation of a Decision Support System (DSS) with regard to the dissemination of data or information produced. For the visual analysis of geospatial features using satellite sensors and the interpretation of image data, space-based technology, such as RS, has been adopted for this purpose. Geospatial characteristics and their suitable locations provide a forum for companies in different fields to develop, and many organizations are interested in using this technology to improve their business or research work.

In any given geographical location, produced and stored data regarding geospatial characteristics have a strong visual impact displayed through maps, and maps play a vital role in monitoring and quantifying change over time scale over this problem. The technology of RS and GIS is directly and indirectly involved in developing geospatial information and geodatabase management. The RS-GIS has provided a single window forum for the dissemination of geospatial features relevant to farmer advisory services under the ICT mode.

8.4.1   Remote Sensing

The collection of data about an object or a phenomenon using RS requires no physical contact with the object (Figure 8.11). It's a phenomenon with a wide range of applications, including photography, surveying, geology,

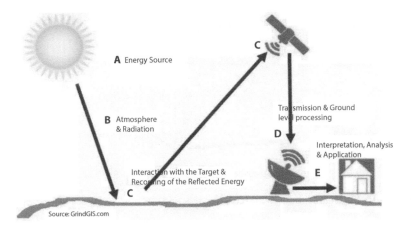

Figure 8.11 Remote sensing. Source: GrindGIS.com.

forestry, and more. So, what exactly is RS? The art and science of collecting knowledge about the surface of the earth without making any direct interaction with it is RS. This is achieved by detecting and recording energy that is reflected and released.

The agricultural sector has a wide range of RS applications. The following is a list of these applications, referred to as digital satellite image processing in this case:

a. **Crop identification:** RS has also played an important role in crop identification, especially in cases where the crop being observed is mysterious or has some mysterious characteristics. Crop data are obtained and transported to laboratories, where various aspects of the crop, including crop culture, are examined.

b. **Field acreage estimation:** RS has also proven very useful in estimating the amount of agricultural land on which a crop has been planted. This is usually a repetitive process if performed manually because of the large sizes of the lands being measured.

c. **Predictive planting and harvesting dates:** Because of the predictive nature of RS technology, farmers can now use RS to observe a range of variables, such as weather patterns and soil types, to forecast the planting and harvesting seasons of each crop.

d. **Crop condition assessment and stress detection:** RS technology plays an important role in determining each crop's health status, as well as the degree to which it has withstood stress. This knowledge is then used to determine the crop's quality.

e. **Drought monitoring:** Weather patterns in a given area, including drought patterns, are tracked using RS technology. The data can be used to forecast rainfall patterns in a given region, as well as to determine the time difference between current precipitation and the next precipitation, which aids in drought tracking.

f. **Crop yield modeling and estimation:** RS often aids farmers and experts in predicting the estimated crop yield of a given farmland by estimating crop quality and farmland extent. This information is then used to estimate the crop's average yield.

g. **Crop production forecasting:** RS is used to forecast crop production and yield over a given area, as well as to decide how much of the crop will be harvested under specific conditions. Researchers will forecast the amount of crop that will be grown in a given farmland over a given period of time.

h. **Crop damage and development assessment:** RS technology may be used to access farmland in the event of crop damage or crop growth and to determine how much of the donated crop was lost and how the remaining crop on the farm is developing.

i. **Cropping systems and horticulture research:** RS technology has also been useful in analyzing various crop planting systems. This technology has primarily been used in the horticulture industry to examine flower growth trends and make predictions based on the findings.

j. **Soil moisture estimation:** Without the aid of RS technology, soil moisture calculation can be challenging. Remote sensing provides data on soil moisture, which aids in determining the amount of moisture in the soil and, as a result, the type of crop that can be grown there.

k. **Irrigation monitoring and control:** RS offers information on the amount of soil moisture. This expertise is used to determine whether a soil is deficient in moisture and to prepare irrigation needs for that soil.

l. **Soil mapping:** One of the most popular and important applications of RS is soil mapping. Farmers may use soil mapping to determine which soils are appropriate for which crops and which soils need irrigation, as well as which soils do not. This expertise is useful in precision agriculture.

m. **Land cover and land loss mapping:** Experts have used RS to chart a particular region's land cover. Experts may now tell which areas of the land have been degraded and which parts are still intact. This also allows them to take measures to reduce soil degradation.

n. **Identification of problematic soils:** RS has also played a critical role in identifying problematic soils that have a difficult time sustaining maximum crop yield during the planting season.

o. **Detection of crop nutrient deficiency:** RS technology has also aided farmers and other agricultural experts in determining the extent of crop nutrient deficiency and developing solutions to increase the amount of nutrients in crops, thus increasing overall crop yield.

p. **Crop yield forecasting:** Using crop data, such as crop quality, soil and crop moisture levels, and soil crop coverage, RS technology can provide accurate estimates of expected crop yield during the planting season. When all of this information is combined, the crop yield can be estimated fairly accurately.

q. **Precision agriculture:** RS has played a key role in precision agriculture. Precision agriculture has resulted in the cultivation of healthy crops that ensure optimum harvests for farmers over a set period.

r. **Crop intensification:** RS may be used to collect critical crop data, such as crop patterns, crop rotation needs, and crop diversity, over a given soil for crop intensification.

s. **Flood mapping and monitoring:** Farmers and agricultural experts may use RS technology to map out flood-prone areas, as well as areas with insufficient drainage. This experience could then be put to use in the event of a flood disaster.

t. **Satellite meteorology:** RS technology is useful for the generation of various weather data products. Satellite-derived rainfall products are widely used for a variety of land and water management applications.

u. **Water resource mapping:** RS is useful for mapping water supplies through farmland that can be used for agriculture.

Farmers may use RS to determine what water sources are available for use on a specific piece of land and if the supplies are adequate.

v. **Climate change monitoring:** RS technology is critical for monitoring climate change and keeping track of climate conditions that influence where crops can be grown.

w. **Farmer compliance monitoring:** Agricultural experts and other farmers depend on RS to keep track of all farmers' farming practices and ensure compliance. This ensures that all farmers follow the proper procedures when planting and harvesting crops.

x. **Soil management practices:** RS technology is critical for determining soil management practices based on data obtained from farms.

y. **Air moisture estimation:** RS technology is used to estimate air moisture, which is used to assess the humidity of an area. The type of crops that can be grown in the area is determined by the humidity level.

z. **Land mapping:** RS aids in the mapping of land for various uses, including crop production and landscaping. The mapping technology used in precision agriculture, where unique land soils are used for specific purposes, is beneficial.

8.4.2   Geographic Information System

Is a computer system that collects, stores, modifies, evaluates, manages, and displays all types of spatial or geographical data (Figure 8.12). End users can use the GIS framework to perform spatial queries, analyze and edit spatial data, and generate hard-copy maps. Geographic Information System is simply an image that is referenced to the Earth or synchronized with x and y coordinates, and the attribute values are stored in a table. These x and y coordinates are dependent on a variety of projection systems, and there are several different types of projection systems. The majority of the time, GIS is used to build and print maps. In order to perform the basic task in GIS, layers are mixed, modified, and created. So, what exactly is GIS? "A GIS allows us to visualize, query, evaluate, and interpret data to better understand relationships, patterns, and trends."

"GIS can be used to address location-related questions like 'What is located here?' or 'Where can I find unique features?'" The GIS user can extract value from the map, such as how much forest land is shown on the land use map. This is accomplished by using the query builder function.

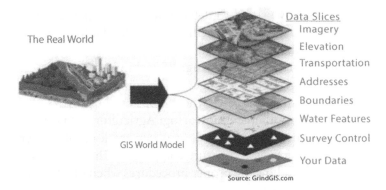

Figure 8.12 GIS and the agro-ecology. Source: GrindGIS.com.

The ability to combine different layers to display new information is the GIS's next major feature. For example, you can combine elevation data, river data, land use data, and other data to view information about the area's landscape. You can tell from the map where the highlands are or where the best spot to build a house with a view of the river is. To find new knowledge, GIS helps.

Data visualization: The GIS software can show the geographical data stored in the databases.
Combining data: Layers are combined to create a map of desire.
Query: To look for a value in the layer or to run a geographic query.

Geographic Information System is a piece of software that allows users to create interactive queries, analyze spatial data, edit data, chart, and present the results of all of these operations in a more general context. GIS technology is becoming an increasingly valuable tool for combining various maps and RS data to generate various models that can be used in real-time situations.

The geographical information system is a science that employs geographical concepts, implementations, and systems [15]. The GIS can be used for analysis, resource management, asset management, environmental impact assessment, urban planning, cartography, criminology, history, advertising, marketing, and logistics. Agricultural planners may use geographical data to decide on the best locations for location-specific crop planning by integrating soil, topography, and rainfall data to assess the size and position of biologically suitable areas. Land-ownership overlays, transportation, infrastructure, labor supply, and distance from market centers can all be factors in the final product. Geographic Information System use has the following advantages:

i.   better political decision-making by individuals,
ii.   use layered data to help you make better decisions,
iii. people are more engaged as a result of a better structure,
iv.   support to recognize neighborhoods where infrastructure is at risk or missing,
v.   helps to recognize concerns around criminology,
vi.   better natural resource management,
vii. good coordination in an emergency,
viii. because of better judgment, cost savings,
ix.   seeing various types of developments within the group,
x.   planning for shifts in demography.

8.4.3   GPS for Agriculture Resources Mapping

GPS stands for Global Positioning System. In the recent past, this technology has progressed impressively and has diverse applications throughout a range of industries (Figure 8.13). One of the main areas where GPS has found interest is in precision farming and agriculture. The GPS has become increasingly popular as a guidance receiver and navigation app that tells us where we are and how to get from point A to point B in recent years. This has also been employed in the development of digital maps. However, GPS

Figure 8.13 GPS application in the farm field. Source: GrindGIS.com.

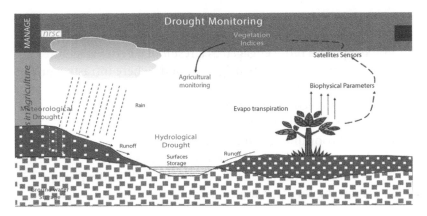

Figure 8.14 Drought monitoring. Source: [2].

applications are used by a variety of organizations, as well as people for different purposes.

Pilots, surveyors, fishermen, boat captains, military officers, and scientists, among others, will find it useful. Aside from the standard GPS on our phones, other highly advanced applications are extremely powerful and are used for specific tasks in a variety of industries.

Farmers have a specific planting, weeding, and harvesting season, and because of this, they install GPS receivers on their tractors and other farming equipment (Figure 8.14). This allows them to map their plantations and ensure that they return at the same time the following season to plant or weed. This technique is especially effective in foggy, low-visibility seasons because the device continues to operate as guided by its GPS rather than by visual reference. Furthermore, because of its high precision, it can be used to locate soil sample mapping locations, allowing farmers to classify areas with agriculturally suitable soils. We look at some of the most important agricultural GPS applications and how they have changed the way farmers operate.

    i.   **Soil profiling:** GPS provides the data needed to accurately assess soil variability and determine if a certain type of soil is appropriate for growing a specific crop. Soil sampling is often used in soil profiling to distinguish between viable and nonviable soils.

    ii. **Weed location:** Using linear sampling methods, GPS can be used to locate weed patches in vast areas of land. Weed inhibits a crop's productive growth and, as a result, reduces subsequent yields over time.

iii. **Accurate planting:** When preparing the planting of a given crop, GPS is also useful. Depending on the soil type, each seed has special spacing and depth necessary. It is easier to say what spacing a given seed needs and at what depth the seed should be planted using GPS in order to return full yields.

iv. **Determination of planting ratios:** In deciding the planting ratios of seeds, GPS may also be used. Some seeds have unique spaces between them, whereas those with other seeds may be planted. In deciding the ratio of this sort of planting, GPS helps.

v. **Yield map creation:** In the creation of yield maps for specific crop types, GPS plays an important role. For example, during harvesting, GPS can be used to map the expected yields of a given crop from a given piece of land based on the land's characteristics and the seed's characteristics.

vi. **Harvesting:** GPS plays an important role in determining when an area of a farm is ready to be harvested and how it will be harvested. The GPS will also provide an estimate of the size of the region being harvested as well as the estimated returns from the area.

vii. **Locating a yield map:** GPS can be used to locate a yield map by installing a GPS receiver on farm machinery and then collecting data.

viii. **Environmental control:** using herbicides or pesticides based on each square meter's capacity reduces the amount of pesticide used in the application. This aids the soil in absorbing all of the contaminants, lowering the risk of runoff.

ix. **Farm planning:** In the planning of ready-to-plant agricultural property, GPS plays an important role. GPS will provide the overall size of the field and assist in deciding what crop will be planted on what portion of the farmland based on a variety of elements such as soil and crop characteristics.

x. **Land mapping:** GPS provides a precise estimate of the land that will be used for agriculture. Experts will be able to tell which parts of the field will be used for agricultural purposes and which will be used for nonagricultural purposes using this method.

xi. **Soil sampling:** Soil sampling is one of the most important applications of GPS in agriculture. Knowing what kind of soil is available on a given piece of farmland is critical, as it will influence the kind of crop that will be planted there.

xii. **Crop scouting:** GPS allows for precise mapping of a region, which aids in the scouting of crops grown in that area. Experts will use this to determine the nature and type of crops that grow in a given location and help to improve the quality of that crop.

xiii. **Yield mapping:** After a crop has been planted and is ready for harvesting, GPS may be used to estimate the yield of a given farmland. This can be accomplished by aerial mapping, which allows experts to estimate the volume of a yield based on the crop area covered.

xiv. **Crop yield production technique correlation:** GPS can be used to calculate the relationship between the crop yields over time and the production technique used over a given piece of land. This knowledge can then be used to assess the effectiveness of a process.

xv. **Soil property mapping:** GPS plays an important role in evaluating the soil property of a given soil in order to assess its variability and suitability for a given crop (Figure 8.15). It also enables researchers to decide what type of soil

Figure 8.15 Crop X is a hardware and software system that measures soil moisture, temperature, and electrical conductivity and sends the information to the cloud, where it can be accessed from any mobile or fixed device. Source: [2].

is present in a given farmland region and which region is best suited for a particular crop.

xvi. **Machinery location:** GPS makes it easier to find some farm machinery on a big plot of land. The farmer does not need to physically go out and find farm equipment, particularly if the number is large. GPS may be used to pinpoint the precise position of farm equipment.

xvii. **Machinery direction:** Technology has necessitated the use of autonomous farm machinery in farming. These devices are driven by GPS to determine the direction in which the seeds are placed as well as the spacing between each seed.

xviii. **Determining which areas are suitable for cultivation:** In a given agricultural zone, GPS plays an important role in determining which areas are suitable for cultivation. Aerial mapping of the under-cultivated area and analysis of soil samples was used to determine the viability of the soil.

xix. **Geographical classification of growing areas based on various characteristics:** GPS may be used to classify different growing areas based on various characteristics such as soil types and terrain maps. Areas that are not suitable for cultivation can be identified and alienated, whereas those that are suitable can be established.

xx. **Determination of water supply in a specific area:** GPS has been used to assess the availability of water or water supplies in a specific area. Water bodies, such as rivers and canals, can be easily detected using GPS.

xxi. **Identification of irrigated and nonirrigated crops:** GPS may also be used to locate areas where irrigated and nonirrigated crops coexist. This helps create a profile between irrigated and nonirrigated crops to allow for comparisons.

xxii. **Detection of swamps and other waterlogged areas:** GPS can be used to identify swampy and waterlogged areas that aren't appropriate for certain crop types. This aids in determining if certain forms of land are ideal for certain crops but not for others.

xxiii. **River mapping:** GPS aids in the creation of a map of all rivers within a given area, resulting in a water flow profile for the region. Farmers and researchers may be able to detect the presence of rivers and assist in the selection of crops to be grown in that region.

xxiv.   **Land use in the locality:** GPS may be used to map land use in a particular region. It is easier to say what portion of the land has been cultivated and what portion has been left barren using GPS.

xxv.   **Contour mapping:** In cases where the land is irregular, GPS has become extremely useful in determining the contours within a specific locality. This is because of the fact that some crops will not thrive in contoured lands, while others will thrive.

xxvi.   **Mapping of irrigation systems such as dams and canals:** In cases where a land needs to be irrigated, GPS can assist in identifying certain irrigation systems such as dams and canals. It will be more convenient because the necessary water will be used to irrigate the land.

xxvii.   **Meteorological mapping, such as climate patterns:** GPS plays an important role in deciding the type of crop that can grow in a given region while mapping those climatic conditions. Personnel Mapping: At certain times of the day, GPS can be useful in determining the number of jobs on a given piece of farmland. If a farmer wants to quantify the productivity of farm employees, this is crucial.

xxviii.   **Plantation mapping:** GPS can assist in the development of a plantation map as well as the calculation of a plantation's crop yields.

xxix.   **Water bodies mapping:** GPS can be used to map identified water bodies within a given area in order to determine the viability of crop growth and yields in a given region.

8.5   Summary and Conclusion

Extension agents may use IT-enabled tools to help the farming community in a number of ways, allowing them to become more reliable and productive extension managers. One or more business processes are distributed to an external service provider through ICT-enabled services. The service provider owns, manages, and administers the selected processes based on defined and measurable performance measures. The core ICT-enabled facilities and instruments in our country have the ability to produce creative, efficient, and learner-centered extension services. This would have a major impact on farmers, rural residents, and the agricultural economy as a whole.

References

1. Meadthaisong, S. and Meadthaisong, T., Smart farming using Internet of Thing (IoT) in agriculture by tangible progarmming for children, in: *2020 17th International Conference on Electrical Engineering/Electronics, Computer, Telecommunications and Information Technology (ECTI-CON)*, IEEE, pp. 611–614, 2020.

2. Srikanth, S.V., *Internet of things (IoT): application in agriculture.* A microsoft power point paper for Massive Open Online Courses of National Institute of Agricultural Extension Management (MANAGE), A publication of National Institute of Agricultural Extension Management (MANAGE), Hyderabad, India, 2020.

3. Thysen, I., Agriculture in the information society. *J. Agric. Eng. Res.*, 76, 3, 297–303, 2000.

4. Ray, P.P., Internet of things for smart agriculture: Technologies, practices and future direction. *J. Ambient Intell. Smart Environ.*, 9, 4, 395–420, 2017.

5. Yan-e, D., Design of intelligent agriculture management information system based on IoT, in: *2011 Fourth International Conference on Intelligent Computation Technology and Automation*, vol. 1, pp. 1045–1049, 2011.

6. Khan, N., Siddiqui, B.N., Khan, N., Ismail, S., The Internet of thing in sustainable agriculture. *Artech J. Res. Stud. Agric. Sci.*, 2, 12–15, 2020.

7. Tanaram, C., Fujii, Y., Ongsuwan, S., Remote agriculture and automation control using Internet of thing (IoT) design and implementation. *Kasem Bundit Eng. J.*, 8, 25–37, 2018.

8. Ferrández-Pastor, F.J., García-Chamizo, J.M., Nieto-Hidalgo, M., Mora-Pascual, J., Mora-Martínez, J., Developing ubiquitous sensor network platform using Internet of things: Application in precision agriculture. *Sensors*, 16, 7, 1141, 2016.

9. Baranwal, T. and Pateriya, P.K., Development of IoT based smart security and monitoring devices for agriculture, in: *2016 6th International Conference-Cloud System and Big Data Engineering (Confluence)*, IEEE, pp. 597–602, 2016.

10. Chae, C.J. and Cho, H.J., Smart fusion agriculture based on Internet of Thing. *J. Korea Converg. Soc.*, 7, 6, 49–54, 2016.

11. Ruengittinun, S., Phongsamsuan, S., Sureeratanakorn, P., Applied Internet of thing for smart hydroponic farming ecosystem (HFE), in: *2017 10th International Conference on Ubi-media Computing and Workshops (Ubi-Media)*, IEEE, pp. 1–4, 2017.

12. Guang, O.T.W., Business model for Chinese agriculture Internet of thing enterprises: cases of long-com and linkage. *Chin. J. Manage.*, 3, 004, 204, 2013.

13. Elijah, O., Rahman, T.A., Orikumhi, I., Leow, C.Y., Hindia, M.N., An overview of Internet of Things (IoT) and data analytics in agriculture: Benefits and challenges. *IEEE Internet Things J.*, 5, 5, 3758–3773, 2018.
14. Khanna, A. and Kaur, S., Evolution of Internet of Things (IoT) and its significant impact in the field of Precision Agriculture. *Comput. Electron. Agric.*, 157, 218–231, 2019.
15. Zhao, J.C., Zhang, J.F., Feng, Y., Guo, J.X., The study and application of the IoT technology in agriculture, in: *2010 3rd International Conference on Computer Science and Information Technology*, vol. 2, pp. 462–465, 2010.
16. Khan, N., Siddiqui, B.N., Khan, N., Ismail, S., The Internet of thing in sustainable agriculture. *Artech J. Res. Stud. Agric. Sci.*, 2, 12–15, 2020.

9

Advances in Bionic Approaches for Agriculture and Forestry Development

Vipin Parkash[1]*, Anuj Chauhan[2], Akshita Gaur[1] and Nishant Rai[2]

[1]Forest Pathology Discipline, Forest Protection Division, Forest Research Institute (Indian Council Forestry Research & Education, Autonomous Council Under Ministry of Environment & Forests, Government of India), Dehradun, Uttarakhand, India
[2]Department of Life Sciences, Graphic Era (Deemed to be) University, Dehradun, Uttarakhand, India

Abstract

With the development in nanotechnology, nanosensors have emerged to be an innovative and intelligent technology that has several applications in agriculture and forestry sectors. Nanosensors are upcoming cutting edge research track for smart agriculture practices. Nanomaterial usage in agriculture may help in the reduction of cost and efforts in precision farming leading to innovative agriculture systems. In agriculture-related sector, nanosensors can be used to monitor soil conditions, soil health, soil nutrient deficiency, crop growth plant diseases, estimation of agrochemicals in soil, toxicity of chemicals to ensure the health of soil and plant. Irrigation is the most important and labor intense process for the farming in most part of the world because of the lack of proper and advance irrigation and soil system, there is loss of soil and crop health, not only this, further soil moisture and other parameters can be monitored. This nanosensor-based or automated irrigation system has great potential to prevent excess loss of water in drought-affected area and soil degradation and maximize the water efficiency leading to improvement in crop health and soil management. Modern nanosensors combine biology with nanomaterials to be more accurate and rapid when spotting crop losses. It is a new and broader outlook for a better future. Such wireless nanosensors can be used for real-time monitoring of crop and trees health in particular cultivated and natural areas. Likewise, accurate plant disease and

---

*Corresponding author: bhardwajvpnpark@rediffmail.com

Roheet Bhatnagar, Nitin Kumar Tripathi, Nitu Bhatnagar and Chandan Kumar Panda (eds.)
The Digital Agricultural Revolution: Innovations and Challenges in Agriculture through Technology Disruptions, (225–254) © 2022 Scrivener Publishing LLC

insect, pest detection can be monitored, which will help for timely application of accurate fertilizers, fungicides, insecticides, and pesticides to protect the crop or plant. Agriculture drones are next-generation solutions in the agricultural sectors that deal with a variety of issues, such as climatic conditions, precision farming, higher productivity, and crop production management. Drone with the image recognition approach nanosensors can identify the defects accurately, such innovation can enable to understand the crop stress, diseases, pest, and even soil defects. Applications of nanosensors in forestry include the uses in forest health protection, forest management wood and paper processing, and chemotaxonomy. The nanotechnology sector has best applied its technology in precision farming by developing nanobionics plants by inserting nanosensors into living plants that can be utilized to communicate as infrared devices and also for sensing objects in the plant's environment. Therefore, nanobionic approach has opened a new vista into plant nanomaterial research. In this review paper, some of nanobionic approaches for agriculture and forestry development have been discussed briefly.

Keywords: Nanosensors, precision farming, unmanned aerial vehicles, nanobionics, agroforestry

9.1 Introduction

The traditional approach to agriculture and forestry development that has been pursued since ages is marked as obsolete. Nanotechnology is the next-generation innovative technology that has proved to have an immense potential for the development of agriculture and forestry sectors. Under this approach, agriculture and forestry sector linked to the progression of the ecodevelopment, sustainability, and productivity on the basis of profit and cost-benefit analysis. Nanotechnology can be referred as to restructuring materials or building devices on the scale of atoms and molecules [1]. Nanotechnology is also considered the art and science of manipulating matter at nanoscale [2]. Nanotechnology has a great potential to advance agricultural productivity through increasing with suitable techniques, such as drug delivery to specific sites, genetic improvement of plants, delivery of genes, and nanoarray approach to study plant gene expression during stress [3, 4]. The nanosensors are being recognized for early detection of pathogens, contaminants in soil and water, precision farming, and smart delivery systems for agricultural chemicals, such as fertilizers and pesticides, as well as smart systems integration for food processing and monitoring agricultural organization [3–6]. Technology innovation and research development are prime necessity in forestry sector because it is an important element to combat worldwide challenges like climate change, maintain balance of our ecosystem. Sustainable and bionic agricultural practices are an approach aiming to increase the yield of food from the same existing agriculture land without affecting or the environment [7, 8]. Nanotechnology offers an efficient tool for sustainable agricultural growth and rapid working approach when applied to agriculture and forestry [9]. Nanotechnology, when combined with automated tools having artificial intelligence (AI), machine learning (ML), and remote sensing features, unlocks wide applications in terms of smart agriculture. For instance, use of drones to monitor agriculture fields and spraying nanofertilizers and nanofungicides can further help in reducing human errors and unnecessary labor [9–11]. India's agriculture contributes to approximately 18% of India's total GDP growth, and along with forestry and fishing, it values to around Rs 18.55 lakh crore (US \$265.51 billion) as of 2019 [12]. However, irrespective of the massive contribution that India's agriculture and forestry sector plays in the overall GDP, the efficiency and productivity stands poor. The reason being improper crop monitoring methods, inadequate water irrigation, inefficient use of pesticides resulting in imbalance of high cost/return ratio. Thus, the use of advanced and more efficient technology is a must to improve the current scenario of agriculture and forestry.

9.2   Precision Farming

Advances in agriculture and forestry can be brought about when one can accurately calculate and analyze the habitat of plants or plants. This can only be achieved with the help of technologies that can monitor the dynamics of the environment and thus reduce human effort and installation (fertilizers, pesticides, etc.). The effectiveness of the monitoring program depends on reduced calculation in local harvest conditions [13]. Direct or indirect farming is all about doing the right thing, in the right place, in the right way, at the right time. The concept of precision tillage is based on observation, measurement and response to internal, and in-field changes in plants. Using this approach, the site-specific differences between fields within a farm are identified, and the appropriate management practice is implemented [14]. In other words, "digital agriculture" includes the development of a very large farm-level map, the creation of a complete database of the necessary resources generated by the placement and field viewing and the formulation of a comprehensive plan to increase yields and reduce installation costs using decision support [15]. Precision farming is supported by technologies that include (a) remote sensing, (b) Geosynchronous Positioning System (GPS), and (c) Geographical Information System (GIS). The GPS pinpoints the precise location of field data such as boundaries, obstructions, soil type, weed invasion, pest occurrence, and water holes. The GIS are computer-based maps of field topography that provide information about the land or agriculture field, soil conditions, soil properties, soil types, soil testing groundwater resources, surface drainage, irrigation, chemical rate of application, and crop production. In addition to GPS and GIS, a variety of sensors has been used to measure physical characteristics, texture, structure, humidity, vegetation, nutrient levels, humidity and temperature, and analyze the data for precision monitoring of the crop environment [16, 17]. The precision agriculture cycle is shown in Figure 9.1. Variable rate technology (VRT) and yield monitors are key components of precision farming, which rely on a combination of GIS and GPS machinery, including the use of VRT field instruments. Variable-rate fertilizer (VRT) and grid soil sampling application require the field to be divided into multiple small and equal divisions. To accomplish this, the tractor is equipped with a dish antenna that receives satellite signals. From each sub division's soil samples are mechanically collected. Nanosensors are critical in precision farming for (a) monitoring physical and chemical changes in environment of soil and crop, (b) nutrient analysis of soils and plants, (c) crop pathogen detection and so on [9, 14]. Physical nanosensors (used to measure mass, pressure, and displacement), chemical nanosensors (for measuring gas concentrations and analyzing molecular species), and biological nanosensors are the three broad types of nanosensors (to monitor biomolecular processes). Precision farming generally requires the use of wireless nanosensor networks (WNSN) for accurate and continuous data collection [14]. A WNSN is a collection of advanced nanosensor nodes that communicate via electromagnetic waves [9]. The WNSN employs this Time Spread On–Off Keying (TS–OOK) modulation technique based on short pulses [18]. Apart from traditional communication, which relies on continuous signal transmission, nanodevices are incapable of producing high-power signals.

In addition to obtaining comprehensive and detailed data of crop and soil environments, such as moisture in the soil, status of crop nutrient, crop temperature, weed, pest and insect infestations, and plant diseases, the Internet-connected nanosensors would transmit that data in real time to adjacent locations [19]. As a result, real-time monitoring and surveillance with mobile nanodevices across farmlands provides important data on the best crop sowing period and harvesting times, the precise application exact amounts of water required for irrigation and fertilizer, pesticide needed and herbicide application, and a variety of other treatment options [20]. Precision farming's future is being shaped by the development of low-cost wireless sensors comprised of nanopolymer-coated cantilever beams microelectromechanical systems (MEMS) that detects moisture and piezo-resistive sensor for sensing temperature [9, 105]. There are some

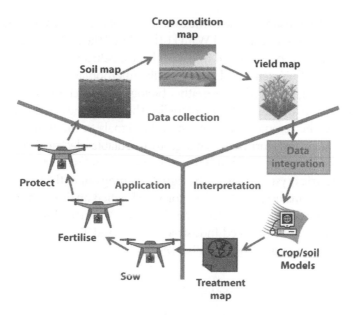

Figure 9.1 Precision agriculture cycle. Image source: Modified from Comparetti *et al.* (2011).

advanced smart agriculture concepts based on nanotechnology, such as "smart dust sensors," that is so tiny that remain in the environment like a dust to analyze the crop environment and collect the data [21] "agro informatics," a blend of information and communication for agriculture applications [22], ambient intelligence. This is a more advanced form of intelligence designed to create smart environments that use sensors comprising of artificial intelligence (AI) to anticipate individual needs and respond accordingly [23], as the agriculture industry continues to evolve, data acquisition, analysis, storage, and dissemination of accurate and consistent information about crop production environments will become increasingly important. A nanosensor "smart card" with unique characteristics to achieve high precision, capacity, and appropriateness of procedures and operations that can reform agriculture as smart can also be developed in the near future [9]. Figure 9.1 illustrates the precision agriculture cycle.

9.2.1 Nanosensors and Its Role in Agriculture

Nanosensors are analytical devices, which on receiving a specific sensation (biochemical/physical) responds through signals and can be utilized by humans. The sensors having nanoparticles have wider applications pertaining to their unique thermal, optical, and electrical properties. The presence of nanoparticles in sensors increases the overall area of reception and thus overall sensitivity increases. Kaushal and Wani [14] outlined the major components of a biosensor. Biosensor is divided into a probe, transducer, and a detector. The probe consists of bio-sensitized elements like microorganisms, nucleic acids, receptors and organelles which are either biologically developed or are created mimicking the true nature of the organelle. The probe measures the changes occurring on the receptors and forwards the signals to the transducers. The transducer then transforms the change to calculable electrical output. The transducers are characterized into thermistors, electrodes, optrodes (Optical) and piezoelectric crystals (mass). The signals coming out of the transducer are amplified and transferred to the detector which when analyzed is transferred to an output unit. In 2004, the Research Centre of Advanced Bionics of Japan's National Institute of Advanced Industrial Science and Technology developed the first biosensor to diagnose soil diseases [14].

9.2.1.1   Nanobiosensor Use for Heavy Metal Detection

There are various techniques being used in heavy metal detection. Zhylyak *et al.* [24] used conductometric biosensor based on hydrolysis of urease for heavy-metal ion determination. These biosensors consisted of gold electrodes coated with enzyme membranes. The difference in hydrolysis of urea in presence and absence of heavy metals was quantified. Because heavy metals inhibit urea hydrolysis, the decrease in hydrolysis was directly related to presence of heavy metals. An alternative method to heavy metal detected was developed by Chini *et al.* [25] who used nanodots, a novel optical sensing device based on fluorescence resonance energy transfer (FRET) for detection of heavy metal pollutants. In this case, graphene carbon dots were used as a donor, and carbon dots were used as receptors. The FRET energy transfer inhibits in the presence of heavy metals and thus helps in their detection. Similarly, Jalilzadeh *et al.* [26] used surface plasmon resonance (SPR) nanosensor for the detection of Zn (II) ions. Satapathi *et al.* [27] developed a multimodal nanosensor, which was used to not only detect but also remove mercury ions. This nanosensor used fluorescence and magnetic functionality to detect and remove mercury ion with high sensitivity. Iron oxide nanoparticles displaying super magnetic properties were used for removal of mercury ions. To avoid aggregation, citric acid was used as a surfactant.

9.2.1.2   Nanobiosensors Use for Urea Detection

Kaushik *et al.* [28] developed iron oxide-chitosan–based nanosensor for urea detection. The detection was enabled through a biochemical reaction occurring because of the decomposition of urea in the presence of urease resulting in production of hydrogen bicarbonate which on reaction with α-Ketoglutarate in the presence of Glutamate Dehydrogenase enzyme produces L-glutamate. This L-glutamate gives oxidation/reduction reaction with iron oxide-chitosan nanobio composite, which can further be transduced into an electrochemical signal.

9.2.1.3   Nanosensors for Soil Analysis

Nanosensors can be used to monitor various soil health parameters like pH, nutrient status, soil moisture, and residual pesticides. These data in turn can help in automation of agricultural systems. Vajpayee *et al.* [29] designed a nano pH sensor, which can be installed in the fields for real-time soil analysis. Nanosensors have been used in plants to detect the glucose and sucrose level based on FRET technology.

9.2.1.4   Nanosensors for Disease Assessment

Nanobiosensors can be used in disease assessment by measuring the oxygen consumption data of potential microbes in soil *in vitro*. Then comparing this data to analyses favorable conditions for growth of a particular microbe. Thus, real-time monitoring will enable us to know that favorable conditions have arisen for attack of pathogen. Yao *et al.* [30] demonstrated the use of fluorescence silica nanoprobe for detection of plant pathogens. Firrao *et al.* [31] also used nano biotransducer for detecting infectious agent in *Vitis vinifera* L. the nanochips are highly sensitive and specific in detecting single-nucleotide changes in microorganisms [32].

9.3   Powerful Role of Drones in Agriculture

Unmanned aerial vehicle (UAV) shows potential as a valuable tool for agricultural production. Farmers in this new digitalized era can use a variety of high-tech tools (sensing devices) based on GPS, remote-sensing devices, direction-finding systems, and farm management software [33]. The introduction and application of cutting-edge farm technologies results in drastic changes in farming. Thus, modern agricultural technology transforms the way farmers work. Using precise technology, farmers can maximize farm productivity and profitability based on real-time field data, which can be a game changer for the agriculture sector [34].

9.3.1   Unmanned Aerial Vehicle Providing Crop Data

The UAVs, also known as drones, are light weighted and small and light aerial vehicles that can fly at very high altitudes and carry multiple recording and navigation systems or devices, such as red, green, and blue (RGB) cameras, infrared cameras, and some other sensors, as shown in Figure 9.2. Drones are very useful in farming because of their capability for deploying several sensors and capturing high-resolution, low-cost images of conditions of the crop on the field [33, 34]. Despite their primary use for spraying chemicals, drones are also great tools for collecting aerial footage with their cameras and sensors. There are various types of images that can be captured, ranging from visible light photographs to multiple images that can assist in understanding various aspects of plant and weed & material life [33]. The drones or UAVs collects raw data and convert it into beneficial information (algorithm) shown in Figure 9.3. As a result, they can be used for a variety of agricultural applications shown in Table 9.1, such as the monitoring of the subsequent constraints [35–37].

Figure 9.2 Drones flying over the field and collecting images (source image: unmanned-aerial.com).

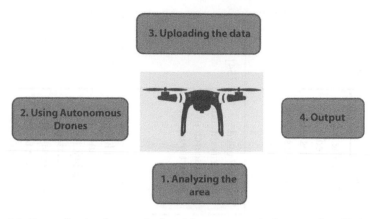

Figure 9.3 Data collection from agricultural drones occurs in the stages listed below.

(a) Crop health monitoring damage made by insects, pests, other microbial diseases [37, 38]; (b) plants indices; plant yield, detection of abnormalities in the leaf area, treatment efficacy, phenology [39]; (c) plant density and height [40]; (d) plant investigation: plant size, planter skips, field statistics, standing number, conceded fields [41]; (e) watering orchard fields that are water-stressed or that need to be watered [42]; (f) investigation and study of availability of soil nutrients, plant nutrients, plant management [43].

To summarize, drones assist farmers in making more efficient use of inputs for example water, seeds, fertilizers and pesticides. By doing so, it facilitates timely pest control, reduces crop scouting time, lowers overall farm production costs, and ensuring maximum yield and improving crops quality [10–13].

9.3.2   Using Raw Data to Produce Useful Information

With a camera mounted on top of the UAV or drone, it takes high-resolution images of the field. The dignified parameters determine which band of spectrum to use for these images; each image is captured in a different band, from visible (color) to infrared spectrum, shown in Figure 9.4. Raw data is collected in the form of images that is needed to be processed to obtain specific information or results. As the drone captures pictures, they are immediately transmitted to software, in which various prescribed maps are generated based on the task the farmer wishes to undertake on the agricultural land. This is done by uploading the maps to specific farm machines or system which modifies their input value (seeds, fertilizers, etc), which will be used in the field accordingly [34, 36, 41].

Table 9.1 List of various application of UAV in agriculture sector.

S. no	Type	Implementation details	Components	Application	Remarks	References
1	Four rotor (UAV)	Bluetooth is used to communicate between the quadcopter and the Android device	Barometer, accelerometer, gyroscope.	The android device is used for spraying pesticides and fertilizer	Reduces the risks associated with pesticides and fertilizer sprayed by farmers	[46]
2	Four rotor (RPV)	An autonomous quadcopter UAV flight	IMU, 2.4GHz telemetry, ESC.	It is a simple, quick, and effective method for conducting any type of research	The OSP quad copter is intended for research or project purposes	[54]
3	Four rotor	Modified the quadcopter and sprayer modules	BLDC, ESC, MPU 6050 sensor	To increase production, pesticide spraying mechanisms are used in agriculture	Increased lifting power and stability. In comparison to a helicopter vehicle, quadcopters are easy to control	[47]

(Continued)

Table 9.1 List of various application of UAV in agriculture sector. (*Continued*)

S. no	Type	Implementation details	Components	Application	Remarks	References
4	Four rotor	Air pollution can be tracked using GPS	Sensors include, for example, the temperature sensor, humidity sensor, MQ6 for smoke, MQ135 for CO2, LDR for light intensity, and GPS for location tracking	Used to measure CO_2, temperature, light intensity, and humidity in the air	It is a less expensive and more efficient model	[56]
5	Four rotor	A micro drone md4-1000 was used in the photogrammetric flight	Sensor α ILCE-5100L with an E 20 mm F2.8 lens, Sony	For accuracy of determining the impact of pests on the grape orchids	UAVs mounted with RGB cameras enable more accurate detection of impacted vegetation	[57]

(*Continued*)

Table 9.1 List of various application of UAV in agriculture sector. (*Continued*)

S. no	Type	Implementation details	Components	Application	Remarks	References
6	Six rotors	Hexacopter	IMU, RGB camera, CMOS sensor	Crop management monitoring tools for insect pest detection/ surveillance	By using such RGB, multispectral, and hyperspectral cameras in the air, grape phylloxera can be detected	[58]
7	Fixed wing	The NDVI of a UAS was compared to the NDVI of sensors aboard a manned aircraft and a tractor	RGB camera, GPS	Used for detecting measures of crop health and assessment of aphid stress on sorghum grain	Effective, efficient and advance technique to measure crop height	[55]

(*Continued*)

Table 9.1 List of various application of UAV in agriculture sector. (*Continued*)

S. no	Type	Implementation details	Components	Application	Remarks	References
8	Four rotor	To develop and implement a quad copter UAV for agricultural usages. Pesticides are sprayed using an agricultural sprinkler	Accelerometer Wi-Fi module GPS module servo motor	Farmers will save time by using a pesticide spraying machine.	The quad copter is beneficial to farmers and reduces their workload	[59]
9	Four rotor	This project makes use of UAVs to spray pesticides in farmlands	BLDC, ESC, ratio controller, Transmitter.	Using the basic drone mechanism, it is able to enhance crop yield range and crop surveillance	Using a drone, the farmers can spray pesticides safely from a remote location	[60]
10	Four rotor	Using a quad copter, this model sprays pesticides	BLDC, ESC, Transceiver, Infrared Camera.	Pesticides are sprayed to remove the effects of their toxins	Using PSQ, find fewer labors where there are	[61]

Figure 9.4 Image captured by a drone give NDVI field map (Source image: unmanned-aerial.com).

I. Monitoring Irrigation

Drones or UAVs with thermal, hyperspectral, or multispectral sensors detect particular areas that are too dry or areas that are needed to be improved by the farmer. Survey and inspection carried out by drone/UAV helps to improve water efficiency and detects potential congestion or leakage of irrigation by providing irrigation monitoring that generates plant index calculations, which help to understand plant health and released heat/energy [42].

The drones are outfitted with thermal imaging cameras and remote sensing capabilities, which can aid in the defeat of irrigation issues or areas receiving insufficient or excessive moisture. The RGB images' field topography assists farmers in positioning and separating crops to maximize drainage, follow natural land drainage, and avoid water-logging. Farmers will be able to easily adapt to innovative and diverse environments with this sort of technology [33, 37, 42].

II. Pesticide Spraying

More than 250 models are evaluated and summarized to select the best UAV for agriculture [44]. In the lower region off the UAV, the sprinkling system is attached to which as a jet beneath the tank contains pesticides and fertilizers as shown in Figure 9.5. Qin *et al.* [45] investigated the effect of UAVs (N-3) on the spray parameters at different altitudes, and each with a different concentration of pesticide spraying on a wheat field, as well as the occurrence of powdery mildew in the Asia-Pacific region. Kedari *et al.* [47] suggested the Quadcopter (QC) system, which is lightweight and cheaper for spraying

Figure 9.5 Drones used for spraying pesticides (source image, www. Krishigaran.com).

fertilizers and pesticides using android phones. Sadhana *et al.* [47] examined the UAV for the controlled mechanism of pesticides spray system to the agriculture field and increase in crop production. For the spraying of pesticides, a set of GPS coordinates in the underlying zone was developed based on a quadcopter aerial camera, an automatic pesticide sprayer (AAP) [48]. When using pesticides, the efficiency of the irrigation system installed on the UAV is increased using a PWM controller [39]. Yanliang *et al.* [49] introduced an electrostatic sprayer, designed on electrostatic spray technology with hexa rotor drone, to reduce the wastage of pesticides.

9.3.3   Crop Health Surveillance and Monitoring

It is important to ensure plant health and detect bacterial/fungal infections early on. Agricultural drones can detect which plants reflect various amounts of green light and near-infrared spectroscopy (NIRS) lights. This information will assist us in creating multispectral images to monitor the current state of crops. Rapid monitoring and fault detection can help to save crops. In the circumstance of crop failure, the farmer can also document the losses to file accurate insurance claims. The UAVs can cover hectares of land in a single flight [54]. Thermal and multispectral cameras were used to record the reflectance of the green vegetation during the whole observation [50, 51]. In recent decades, NASA's solar-powered pathfinder plus has been used as an image collection platform to display the 3500-ha coffee plantation in Hawaii [52]. Similarly, a low-cost UAV VIPtero performed monitoring over a vineyard [53].

III. Assessment of crop damage: The drones or UAVs equipped with multi-spectral and RGB sensors to detect weeds, diseases, and pests in field areas. The pictures or images of field are taken in five different visible bands with varying wave lengths, i.e., blue wavelength, 440 to 510 nm; green wavelength, 520 to 590 nm; red wavelength, 630 to 685 nm; red edge wavelength, 690 to 730 nm; and near-infrared wavelength, 760 to 850 nm. According to this information, it is known precisely how much chemicals are needed to tackle these infestations, which helps to reduce the farmer's investments on the crop [54, 55].

9.4   Nanobionics in Plants

Plant nanobionics is an innovative field of bioengineering that involves inserting nanoparticles into the cells of living plants, which then modify or enhance the functioning of the plant tissue and organelle [62]. According to Michael Strano, a professor of Chemical Engineering, the goal of nanobionics is to give plants superpowers. Applications of plant bionics include agriculture, biosensors, and many others [63]. The use of such technology can enhance the agriculture production, such as use of biosensors in crop protection to detect plant pathogens and diseases, genetically manipulating plants using nanodevices, and so on [64].

In today's world, there are numerous concerns about soil pollution, as a variety of adverse environmental conditions distort soil health. Plant nanobionics has the capability to collects information from the soil by altering the structure of plants using nanotubes located in them, developing plant species capable of detecting pollutants and preparing us to deal with larger problems. Bioremediation is a procedure that can clean up polluted soils by changing the environmental conditions so as to promote the growth of microorganisms in the soil that can disintegrate the pollutants. This means that sensors can be developed and incorporated into plants. Sensors like these can help us better to monitor pesticide utilization, as well as detect infections caused by microbe-produced toxins. Plant nanobionics can detect metals and metalloids in contaminated soils [65]. Biosensors can also be used to remove pollutants from the soil through the phytoremediation process. Plant leaves have been implanted with novel sensors that detect a lack of water in the plant and allow us to identify plants that are suffering from drought conditions [66]. This wonderful technology was invented by Michael Strano, Professor of Chemical engineering at MIT [65]. This ideal technology could be used to alert farmers about the drought situation as soon as it becomes apparent. Nanobionics allows the plants to sense the scarcity of the water in the soil according to the plants as some can survive in low water conditions, but for others, it may need the precise proper amount of water required for the plant. On a spinach plant, a nanobionic-plant system based on single-walled carbon nanotubes (SWCNTs) as nanoparticles was invented [67].

Researchers always have worked hard to create materials that can mimic biological systems. Abionic materials are the materials that are aimed to increase, preserve, and utilize living things for engineering purposes. However, some scientist believe that such bionic materials can perform like a natural material as a fiction [68]. On the other hand, Chiara Darayo *et al.* [69], published a paper titled "Biomimetic heat-sensitive layer of artificial leather," which utilizes the properties of synthetic wood. The pectin films were introduced into artificial skins to enhance the sensitivity of temperature detection. One of the best examples of nanobionic material can be the pectin material with combination with carbon nanoparticles that can serve as temperature sensors [69]. Researchers of MIT are working on vision that plant will function as table or desk lamps. Some research result showed that few attempts have been made in this direction to create a light emitting plant. However such plants produce very dim light and were very costly and require strong genetic engineering methodology. Light-emitting process from plants can be performed only on selected plants with studied genomes [70]. Through the use of nanotechnology, traditional agricultural practices can be reduced to produce greater output with less effort and generate less waste. Some of the major applications of nanotechnology in agriculture is to monitor the quality of soil, pesticides management, diseases detection, and various factors, such as humidity and temperature. Kris Pister of University of California, Berkley came up with the idea of circling the earth with thousands of tiny sensors, smaller than the size of rice grains [71]. He referred to them as "smart dust" particles that can sense environmental changes [72]. The smart dust consists of tiny MEMS, such as sensors, robots, and so on that can detect light, temperature, and so on. Smart dust has the ability to sense, compute, and communicate wirelessly, and because of its small size and light weight, it floats in the atmosphere like a dust particle.

9.5   Role of Nanotechnology in Forestry

For many years, the forest has played a significant role in civilization as a source of lignocellulosic materials for the development of different wood products. In fact, wood products are a part of society in the form of furniture, timbers, papers, and a variety of other materials.

Many of the current forest product manufacturing industries such as the paper and pulp industries, could be transformed by nanotechnology [73].

Table 9.2 Agricultural and forestry applications of e-noses.

Electronic nose	Applications	Chemical detected	References
Moses II	Crop production	Pesticide traces	[101]
BH-114	Environment	Cd, As, Pb, Zn (in water)	[102]
ProSAT		Diesel oils	[98]
FreshSense		CO, H2S, NH3, SO2	[98]
Aromascan A32S	Plant pathology	Disease detection, wood decay, and fungi ID	[94, 97]
Cyranose 320		Detection of post-harvest diseases	[96]
LibraNose 2.1		Wood decay & fungi ID	[95]
Aromascan A32S	Plant taxonomy	Plant identifications, chemo-taxonomy (classifications)	[97]
A-nose	Quality control/quality assurance	Identification and categorization of coffee sample/batch flaws	[99, 100]
EOS 3, 9	Waste	Gas effluent composting, alcohols, sulfur compounds	[103]
PEN 2		Monitoring of waste treatment	[104]

It is expected that nanotechnology will transform the forest industry in the production of wood-based products, fiber-based, paper, pulp-based products, and so on [74]. The forest industry could immensely be benefited by the use analytical nanotools and using nanotechnology knowledge with other industries. Throughout the forest sector, the impact of nanotechnology has become increasingly visible and realizable during the last few years. Nanotechnology has provided a platform for the development of forest materials and wood materials that can prove to be one of the foremost contributors to the forest sector economy [73]. With the advancement of nanotechnology, recent advances have been made to develop an instrument called Electronic-nose (e-nose), based on a wide variety of aroma-sensor technologies, designed for a variety of applications in a wide range of forestry applications. Electronic noses have been used in a variety of commercially used agricultural and forestry related industries listed in Table 9.2, including the agricultural sectors of botany, agronomy, horticulture, pesticide detection, plant cultivar selections, environmental monitoring. Forestry applications include chemotaxonomy, wood and paper processing, forest management, forest health protection, log tracking, and waste management.

9.5.1   Chemotaxonomy

Forestry, forest management and production, and forest science can all be enhanced by identifying wood types and characteristics. In forested ecosystem, the microenvironmental characteristics, types of flora and fauna (animal life), and types of microorganism present, relative consumption of wood as a food and habitat base, and quality of forest products made from several wood types are influenced by the type of wood present and its composition. Traditional identifications of wood samples through microscopic and chemical methods are time taking and extensive. A new method of identification of wood samples could facilitate determination of biological activities, ecological and interaction of microorganism, insects and invertebrates interacts with the wood living and dead trees. The characterization of types of wood based on distinctive mixtures of wood volatiles is also important for determining special functions of microbes and microinvertebrates in vegetated ecosystems and chemotaxonomy studies [75, 76]. In addition to providing better insight into ecosystem microclimates, these data will aid in understanding how organisms function and interact in urban and rural forest landscapes, thus leading to more effective multipurpose forest management. In woody plant parts, empty space fugitive molecules reveal useful chemotaxonomic data, which often confirms genetic information (DNA sequence-homology), and also helps to establish relatedness between plant species within and between plant families. Wilson *et al.* [76] reported in an article how wood chips determine the type of wood from just a small portion of sample present in the wood chip mixture. Garneau *et al.* [77] developed a sensor Cyranose 320 e-nose made up of carbon black composite (CBC) to distinguish the fingerprints (odor) of wood based on wood type and composition.

9.5.2   Wood and Paper Processing

More than 400 tons of paper and paperboard are produced worldwide each year [78] in this digital era, where people operate most of their functions on mobile but still the use of paper and paper products is in preference by the community. Paper is produced from lignocellulosic synthetic fibers that are obtained through a sequence of repairs, treatments, papermaking, coating, and drying processes. During the paper-making phase, all of the mixer press and accessories are added and modified to create various end products [79]. Nanotechnology is used in paper and pulp as nanoadditives or nanomaterials, for instance, forest materials or lignocellulosic equipment could be used to retrieve nanocellulose, a nanosized building block that acts as a support system to provide special mechanical properties, flexibility, and performance [79]. Nanomaterials or nanoadditives are being used in the paper industry to develop and enhance the productivity of paper products. Nanocellulose is used in papermaking to improve paper strength. Two classes of nanocellulose, i.e., nanofibrillated cellulose (NFC) and nanocrystalline cellulose (NCC) are the most widely read nanomaterials in the field and paper field for product development. Many activities have been reported as NFC is a nanoadditive study widely studied in paper making [80, 81]. It has already been reported that the use of NFC improves the oil resistance and oxygen barrier [82]. Hult *et al.* [83] attempt to depict the use of NFC on paper and paperboard to reduce oxygen transmission rate, air permeability, and water vapor transfer, making it a potential barrier packaging material. Nanofibrillated cellulose can be utilized as a substrate in electronic applications in addition to films and paper products. It was reported that by addition of NFC as filler can minimize the amount of wood pulp used, lowering production costs. The addition of 2% to 10% NFC as a polymer increases the strength by 50% to 90% [84].

Nanocoating is a process that can be used to coat wood products for protection and improved visual appearance, as well as preservatives to safeguard against fire and biological factors (bacteria, fungi, pest, and insects). A nanocoating is an applied material whose main purpose is to improve the mechanical properties, fire resistance, UV absorption, and water absorption of wood and wood products [85]. One of the purposes of nanocoatings is to inhibit the growth of different microorganisms, such as bacteria and fungi. Nanocoatings are designed to inhibit the growth of microorganisms, such as bacteria and fungi. Metal oxide nanoparticles, such as zinc oxide (ZnO) [86, 87], titanium oxide [87, 88], and cerium oxide (CeO2) [89], have been shown to have strong antibacterial characteristics. According to recent findings, treated bamboo timber with these nanocoatings had improved resistance to *Aspergillus niger V. Tiegh* (*A. niger*), and *Penicillium citrinum* Thom (*P. citrinum*), but poor resistance to *Trichoderma viride* [90]. Furthermore, polymeric nanocarriers encapsulated with pesticides are powerful nanotechnology techniques that can significantly improve pesticide impregnation in wood. Pesticides can be formulated with this technique to increase their water solubility and to slow their release [91]. By using this technology, pesticides can not only be delivered safely they can also be kept in the wood for a longer period, providing extended protection [92]. This technology is being used by researchers to create smart paper that is electrically conductive, as well as to investigate the possibility of nanocoating lignocellulose microfibers with controlled conductive coatings that can be incorporated into paper. The use of electrical paper displays, sensors, and communication devices can be enhanced by using conduction nanocoating on wood. This area of research can be revolutionary for the paper and pulp industry [93]. A few applications of nanotechnology to the paper and wood industries are shown in Figure 9.6.

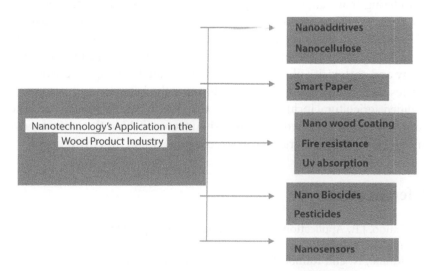

Figure 9.6 Nanotechnology's application in the wood product industry.

9.6   Conclusion

Nanotechnology offers significant potential in areas such as agriculture and forestry. Moreover, because nanotechnology displayed its competencies in several fields and continues to expand in many sectors. To date, nanotechnology has numerous opportunities to reform agriculture and forestry sector with its unique, advanced, modern gadgets. In agriculture, nanosensors have emerged as one of the most advanced technologies for determining plant nutrient, moisture, and physiological status, which aids in the implementation of appropriate and timely corrective measures. Intelligent sensors are utilized to precisely determine the plant nutrient deficiencies, detect crop pathogens and soil conditions accordingly in a manner to achieve the mission of precision farming. With the different innovations in biotechnology, plant nanobionics is one of the novel feature that we witnessed, a combination of engineering and biotechnology where nanoparticles are inserted into plant that may alter the plant behavior. The core principle behind nanobionics is to equip plants with novel capabilities such as infrared communication devices, sensors, smart dust, and so on. Similarly, UAVs or drones with camera mounted are the exceptional piece of engineering that are widely used to aimed to monitor crop and trees and wild animals in agriculture and forest respectively. Besides this, using a UAV to spray pesticides and fertilizers will save energy and reduce agricultural risk. Developing new materials and techniques for wood processing in forestry, as well as strengthening wood's resistance to insects, are feasible initiatives in the future, moisture resistance is reduced, and UV degradation occurs. Considering that nanotechnology is relatively new and has great potential, it is an exciting time for forestry research. Yet it is important to evaluate the risk associated to the humans, animals, and environment. There is a huge gap in our knowledge of the interaction of nanoparticles with plants, where the energy and ecotoxicity of various nanoparticles are taken up. Therefore, further research is urgently needed to determine the behavior and outcome of modified agricultural inclusion. Further advances in nanotechnology are a key sector that can be expected to be the driving forces behind the economy over time and for profit, farmers, producers, consumers, and the environment.

References

1. Sahoo, J.P., Application of Nanotechnology in Agriculture. *Agrobios Newsl.*, 11, 22–23, 2020.
2. Kumar, N. and Kumbhat, S., *Essentials in nanoscience and nanotechnology*, vol. 486, Wiley, Hoboken, 2016.

3. War, J.M., Fazili, M.A., Mushtaq, W., Wani, A.H., Bhat, M.Y., Role of Nanotechnology in Crop Improvement, in: *Nanobiotechnology in Agriculture. Nanotechnology in the Life Sciences*, K. Hakeem and T. Pirzadah (Eds.), Springer, Cham, 2020.

4. Abobatta, W.F., Nanotechnology application in agriculture. *Acta Sci. Agric.*, 2, 6, 99–102, 2018.

5. Vikesland, P.J., Nanosensors for water quality monitoring. *Nat. Nanotechnol.*, 13, 8, 651–660, 2018.

6. Shang, Y., Hasan, M., Ahammed, G.J., Li, M., Yin, H., Zhou, J., Applications of nanotechnology in plant growth and crop protection: a review. *Molecules*, 24, 14, 2558, 2019.

7. Baulcombe, D., Crute, I., Davies, B., Dunwell, J., Gale, M., Jones, J., Pretty, J., Sutherland, W., Toulmin, C., *Reaping the benefits: science and the sustainable intensification of global agriculture*, The Royal Society, London, 2009.

8. Turcotte, M.M., Araki, H., Karp, D.S., Poveda, K., Whitehead, S.R., The eco-evolutionary impacts of domestication and agricultural practices on wild species. *Philos. Trans. R. Soc. B: Biol. Sci.*, 372, 1712, 20160033, 2017.

9. Pramanik, P., Krishnan, P., Maity, A., Mridha, N., Mukherjee, A., Rai, V., Application of nanotechnology in agriculture, in: *Environmental Nanotechnology*, vol. 4, pp. 317–348, Springer, Cham, 2020.

10. Saxena, A., Suna, T., Saha, D., Application of Artificial Intelligence in Indian Agriculture, Souvenir: RCA Alumini Association, Udaipur, India, 2020.

11. Moulick, R.G., Das, S., Debnath, N., Bandyopadhyay, K., Potential use of nanotechnology in sustainable and 'smart'agriculture: advancements made in the last decade. *Plant Biotechnol. Rep.*, 14, 1–9, 2020.

12. Manida, M.M. and Nedumaran, G., Agriculture In India: Information About Indian Agriculture & Its Importance. *Aegaeum J.*, 8, 3, 729–736, 2020.

13. Blackmore, S., Precision farming: an introduction. *Outlook Agric.*, 23, 4, 275–280, 1994.

14. Kaushal, M. and Wani, S.P., Nanosensors: frontiers in precision agriculture, in: *Nanotechnology*, pp. 279–291, Springer, Singapore, 2017.

15. Klerkx, L., Jakku, E., Labarthe, P., A review of social science on digital agriculture, smart farming and agriculture 4.0: New contributions and a future research agenda. *NJAS-Wagening. J. Life Sci.*, 90, 100315, 2019.

16. Segarra, J., Buchaillot, M.L., Araus, J.L., Kefauver, S.C., Remote Sensing for Precision Agriculture: Sentinel-2 Improved Features and Applications. *Agronomy*, 10, 641, 2020.

17. Goswami, S.B., Matin, S., Aruna, S., Bairagi, G.D., A review: the application of remote sensing, GIS and GPS in precision agriculture. *J. Adv. Technol. Eng. Res.*, 2, 50–54, 2012.

18. Rupani, V., Kargathara, S., Sureja, J., A review on wireless nanosensor networks based on electromagnetic communication. *Int. J. Comput. Sci. Inf. Technol.*, 6, 2, 1019–1022, 2015.

19. Joseph, T. and Morrison, M., *Nanotechnology in agriculture and food*, A Nanoforum report, available for, Nanoform publishers, EU, 2006.
20. Comparetti, A., Precision agriculture: past, present and future, in: *International scientific conference agricultural engineering and environment*, pp. 216–230, 2011.
21. Mashalkar, Y. and Kazi, A., Wireless sensor network (MOTES): Smart dust. *Int. J. Comput. Electron. Res.*, 3, 4, 308–312, 2014.
22. Opara, L.U., Agricultural Engineering education and research in knowledge-based economy, in: *Proceedings of the 30th international symposium on agricultural engineering*, S. Kosutic (Ed.), Zagreb, Croatia, pp. 33–46, 2002.
23. Cook, D.J., Augusto, J.C., Vikramaditya, J.R., Ambient intelligence: technologies, applications, and opportunities. *Pervasive Mob. Comput.*, 5, 4, 277–298, 2009.
24. Zhylyak, G.A., Dzyadevich, S.V., Korpan, Y.I., Soldatkin, A.P., El'Skaya, A.V., Application of urease conductometric biosensor for heavy-metal ion determination. *Sens. Actuators B: Chem.*, 24, 1–3, 145–148, 1995.
25. Chini, M.K., Kumar, V., Javed, A., Satapathi, S., Graphene quantum dots and carbon nano dots for the FRET based detection of heavy metal ions. *Nano-Struct. Nano-Objects*, 19, 100347, 2019.
26. Jalilzadeh, M., Çimen, D., Özgür, E., Esen, C., Denizli, A., Design and preparation of imprinted surface plasmon resonance (SPR) nanosensor for detection of Zn (II) ions. *J. Macromol. Sci., Part A*, 56, 9, 877–886, 2019.
27. Satapathi, S., Kumar, V., Chini, M.K., Bera, R., Halder, K.K., Patra, A., Highly sensitive detection and removal of mercury ion using a multimodal nanosensor. *Nano-Struct. Nano-Objects*, 16, 120–126, 2018.
28. Kaushik, A., Solanki, P.R., Ansari, A.A., Sumana, G., Ahmad, S., Malhotra, B.D., Iron oxide-chitosan nanobiocomposite for urea sensor. *Sens. Actuators B: Chem.*, 138, 2, 572–580, 2009.
29. Vajpayee, S., Kumar, B., Thakur, R., Kumar, M., Design and Development of Nano pH Sensor and Interfacing with Arduino. *Int. J. Electron. Electr. Comput. Syst. IJEECS*, 8, 6, 66–75, 2017.
30. Yao, K.S., Li, S.J., Tzeng, K.C., Cheng, T.C., Chang, C.Y., Chiu, C.Y., Lin, Z.P., Fluorescence silica nanoprobe as a biomarker for rapid detection of plant pathogens, in: *Advanced materials research*, vol. 79, pp. 513–516, Trans Tech Publications Ltd, Switzerland, 2009.
31. Firrao, G., Moretti, M., Gobbi, E., Locci, R., Nanobiotransducer for detecting flavescence dorée phytoplasma [Vitis vinifera L.; grapevine]. *J. Plant Pathol. (Italy)*, 87, 2, 101–107, 2005.
32. Lopez, M.M., Llop, P., Olmos, A., Marco-Noales, E., Cambra, M., Bertolini, E., Are molecular toolssolving the challenges posed by detection of plant pathogenic bacteria and viruses? *Curr. Issues Mol. Biol.*, 11, 13, 46, 2009.
33. Mogili, U.R. and Deepak, B.B.V.L., Review on application of drone systems in precision agriculture. *Proc. Comput. Sci.*, 133, 502–509, 2018.

34. Iost Filho, F.H., Heldens, W.B., Kong, Z., de Lange, E.S., Drones: Innovative technology for use in precision pest management. *J. Econ. Entomol.*, 113, 1, 1–25, 2020.

35. Deepak, B.B.V.L. and Singh, P., A survey on design and development of an unmanned aerial vehicle (quadcopter). *Int. J. Intell. Unmanned Syst. J. Intelligent Unmanned Syst.*, 4, 2, 70–106, 2016.

36. Mallick, T.C., Bhuyan, M.A.I., Munna, M.S., Design & implementation of an UAV (Drone) with flight data record. *IEEE International Conference in Innovations in Science, Engineering and Technology (ICISET)*, pp. 1–6, 2016.

37. Devi, G., Sowmiya, N., Yasoda, K., Muthulakshmi, K., Balasubramanian, K., Review on Application of Drones for Crop Health Monitoring and Spraying Pesticides and Fertilizer. *J. Crit. Rev.*, 7, 667–672, 2020.

38. Bendig, J., Bolten, A., Bareth, G., Introducing a low-cost mini-UAV for thermal-and multispectral-imaging. *Int. Arch. Photogramm. Remote Sens. Spat. Inf. Sci.*, 39, 345–349, 2012.

39. Huang, Y., Thomson, S.J., Hoffmann, W.C., Lan, Y., Fritz, B.K., Development and prospect of unmanned aerial vehicletechnologies for agricultural production management. *Int. J. Agric. Biol. Eng.*, 6, 3, 1–10, 2013.

40. Anthony, D., Elbaum, S., Lorenz, A., Detweiler, C., On crop height estimation with UAVs. *IEEE/RSJ International Conference on Intelligent Robots and Systems*, pp. 4805–4812, 2014.

41. Ren, Q., Zhang, R., Cai, W., Sun, X., Cao, L., Application and Development of New Drones in Agriculture, in: *IOP Conference Series: Earth and Environmental Science*, vol. 440(5), IOP Publishing, p. 052041, 2020.

42. Reinecke, M. and Prinsloo, T., The influence of drone monitoring on crop health and harvest size. *International Conference on Next Generation Computing Applications*, pp. 5–10, 2017.

43. Primicerio, J., Di Gennaro, S.F., Fiorillo, E., Genesio, L., Lugato, E., Matese, A., Vaccari, F.P.A., Flexible unmanned aerial vehicle for precision agriculture. *Precis. Agric.*, 13, 4, 517–523, 2012.

44. Marinello, F., Pezzuolo, A., Chiumenti, A., Sartori, L., Technical analysis of unmanned aerial vehicles (drones) for agricultural applications. *Engineering for Rural Development*, vol. 15, 2016.

45. Qin, W., Xue, X., Zhang, S., Gu, W., Wang, B., Droplet deposition and efficiency of fungicides sprayed with small UAV against wheat powdery mildew. *Int. J. Agric. Biol. Eng.*, 11, 2, 27–32, 2018.

46. Sadhana, B., Naik, G., Mythri, R.J., Hedge, P.G., Shyama, K.S.B., Development of quad copter based pesticide spraying mechanism for agricultural applications. *Int. J. Innov. Res. Electr. Electron. Instrum. Control Eng.*, 5, 2, 121–123, 2017.

47. Kedari, S., Lohagaonkar, P., Nimbokar, M., Palve, G., Yevale, P., Quadcopter-A Smarter Way of Pesticide Spraying. *Imp. J. Interdiscip. Res.*, 2, 6, 2016.

48. Vardhan, P.H., Dheepak, S., Aditya, P.T., Arul, S., Development of Automated Aerial Pesticide Sprayer. *Int. J. Eng. Sci. Res. Technol.*, 3, 4, 458–462, 2014.

49. Yanliang, Z., Qi, L., Wei, Z., Design and test of a six-rotor unmanned aerial vehicle (UAV) electrostatic spraying system for cropprotection. *Int. J. Agric. Biol. Eng.*, 10, 6, 68–76, 2017.

50. Bendig, J., Bolten, A., Bareth, G., Introducing a low-cost mini-UAV for thermal-and multispectral-imaging. *Int. Arch. Photogramm. Remote Sens. Spat. Inf. Sci.*, 39, 345–349, 2012.

51. Simelli, I. and Tsagaris, A., The Use of Unmanned Aerial Systems (UAS) in Agriculture, in: *HAICTA*, pp. 730–736, 2015.

52. Herwitz, S.R., Johnson, L.F., Dunagan, S.E., Higgins, R.G., Sullivan, D.V., Zheng, J., Slye, R.E., Imaging from an unmannedaerial vehicle: agricultural surveillance and decision support. *Comput. Electron. Agric.*, 44, 1, 49–61, 2004.

53. Primicerio, J., Di Gennaro, S.F., Fiorillo, E., Genesio, L., Lugato, E., Matese, A., Vaccari, F.P., A flexible unmanned aerial vehicle for precision agriculture. *Precis. Agric.*, 13, 4, 517–523, 2012.

54. Sabikan, S. and Nawawi, S.W., Open-source project (OSPs) platform for outdoor quadcopter. *J. Adv. Res. Des.*, 24, 13–27, 2016.

55. Stanton, C., Starek, M.J., Elliott, N., Brewer, M., Maeda, M.M., Chu, T., Unmanned aircraft system-derived crop height and normalized difference vegetation index metrics for sorghum yield and aphid stress assessment. *J. Appl. Remote Sens.*, 11, 026035, 2017.

56. Ghosal, M., Bobade, A., Verma, P.A., Quadcopter Based Environment Health Monitoring System for Smart Cities. *Second International Conference on Trends in Electronics and Informatics (ICOEI)*, pp. 1423–1426, 2018.

57. del-Campo-Sanchez, A., Ballesteros, R., Hernandez-Lopez, D., Ortega, J.F., Moreno, M.A., on behalf of Agroforestry and Cartography Precision Research Group, Quantifying the effect of Jacobiasca lybica pest on vineyards with UAVs by combining geometric and computer vision techniques. *PLoS One*, 14, 4, 0215521, 2019.

58. Vanegas, F., Powell, D., Weiss, J., Gonzalez, F., A novel methodology for improving plant pest surveillance in vineyards and crops using UAV-based hyperspectral and spatial data. *Sensors*, 18, 260, 2018.

59. Mohane, V., Butle, V., Papadkar, S., Fulzele, A., Kadu, P., Development of Unmanned Aerial Vehicle (UAV) for agricultural spraying-Approach towards farmers' empowerment. *Int. J. Innov. Eng. Sci.*, 4, 8, 11–13, 2019.

60. Desale, R., Chougule, A., Choudhari, M., Borhade, V., Teli, S.N., Unmanned Aerial Vehicle For Pesticides Spraying. *Int. J. Sci. Adv. Res. Technol.*, 5, 4, 79–82, 2019.

61. Khamuruddeen, S., Leela, K., Sowjanya, K., Battula, B., Intelligent Pesticide Spraying System using Quad Copter. *Int. J. Recent Technol. Eng.*, 7, 5S4, 302–305, 2019.

62. Ghorbanpour, M. and Fahimirad, S., Plant nanobionics a novel approach to overcome the environmental challenges, in: *Medicinal plants and environmental challenges*, pp. 247–257, Springer, Cham, 2017.

63. Sharma, S.R. and Kar, D., An Insight into Plant Nanobionics and Its Applications, in: *Plant Nanobionics*, pp. 65–82, Springer, Cham, 2019.
64. Mansoori, G.A., An introduction to nanoscience and nanotechnology, in: *Nanoscience and plant-soil systems*, M. Ghorbanpour and et al. (Eds.), Springer International Publishing AG, Cham, 2017.
65. Jha, S. and Pudake, R.N., Molecular mechanism of plant-nanoparticle interactions, in: *Plant nanotechnology*, C. Kole, D. Kumar, M. Khodakovskaya (Eds.), Springer, Cham, 2016.
66. Saxena, R., Tomar, R.S., Kumar, M., Exploring nanobiotechnology to mitigate abiotic stress in crop plants. *J. Pharm. Sci. Res.*, 8, 9, 974, 2016.
67. Skrzypczak, T., Krela, R., Kwiatkowski, W., Wadurkar, S., Smoczyńska, A., Wojtaszek, P., Plant science view on biohybrid development. *Front. Bioeng. Biotechnol.*, 5, 1–17, 2017.
68. Tee, B.C., Wang, C., Allen, R., Bao, Z., An electrically and mechanically self-healing composite with pressure-and flexion-sensitive properties for electronic skin applications. *Nat. Nanotechnol.*, 7, 12, 825–832, 2012.
69. Mecke, A., Dittrich, C., Meier, W., Biomimetic membranes designed from amphiphilic blockcopolymers. *Soft Matter*, 2, 751–759, 2006.
70. Kwak, S.Y., Giraldo, J.P., Wong, M.H., Koman, V.B., Lew, T.T., Ell, J., Weidman, M.C., Sinclair, R.M., Landry, M.P., Tisdale, W.A., Strano, M.S., A nanobionic light-emitting plant. *Nano Lett.*, 17, 7951–7961, 2017.
71. Warneke, B., Last, M., Leibowitz, B., Pister, K.S.J., Smart dust-communicating with a cubic millimetre computer. *IEEE J. Comput.*, 34, 1, 44–51, 2001.
72. Gorder, P.F., Sizing up smart dust. *IEEE J. Comput. Sci. Eng.*, 5, 6, 6–9, 2003.
73. McCrank, J., *Nanotechnology applications in the forest sector*, Natural Resources, Ottawa, Canada, 2009.
74. Atalla, R., Beecher, J., Caron, R., Catchmark, J., Deng, Y., Glasser, W., et al., Nanotechnology for the forest products industry vision and technology roadmap. Office of Energy Efficiency and Renewable Energy (EERE), Washington, DC (United States), 2005.
75. Wilson, A.D., Diverse applications of electronic-nose technologies in agriculture and forestry. *Sensors*, 13, 2, 2295–2348, 2013.
76. Wilson, A.D., Application of a conductive polymer electronic-nose device to identify aged woody samples, in: *Proceedings of The 3rd International IARIA Conference on Sensor Device Technologies and Applications*, Rome, Italy, vol. 19(24), pp. 77–82, 2012.
77. Garneau, F.X., Riedl, B., Hobbs, S., Pichette, A., Gagnon, H., The use of sensor array technology for rapid differentiation of the sapwood and heartwood of Eastern Canadian spruce; fir and pine. *Holz Roh. Werkst.*, 62, 470–473, 2004.
78. Jasmani, L., Rusli, R., Khadiran, T., Application of Nanotechnology in Wood-Based Products Industry: A Review. *Nanoscale Res. Lett.*, 15, 207, 2020.

79. Moon, R.J., Martini, A., Nairn, J., Simonsen, J., Youngblood, J., Cellulose nanomaterials review: structure, properties and nanocomposites. *Chem. Soc. Rev.*, 40, 7, 3941–3994, 2011.
80. Bajpai, P., *Pulp and paper industry: nanotechnology in forest industry*, Elsevier, London, 2016.
81. Boufi, S., Nanofibrillated cellulose as an additive in papermaking process: a review. *Carbohydr. Polym.*, 154, 151–166, 2016.
82. Lavoine, N., Desloges, I., Khelifi, B., Bras, J., Impact of different coating processes of microfibrillated cellulose on the mechanical and barrier properties of paper. *J. Mater. Sci.*, 49, 7, 2879–2893, 2014.
83. Hult, E.L., Iotti, M., Lenes, M., Efficient approach to high barrier packaging using microfibrillar cellulose and shellac. *Cellulose*, 17, 3, 575–586, 2010.
84. Sehaqui, H., Berglund, L. A., Zhou, Q., BIOREFINERY: Nanofibrillated cellulose for enhancement of strength in high-density paper structures. *Nordic Pulp Paper Res. J.*, 28, 2, 182–189, 2013.
85. Hincapié, I., Künniger, T., Hischier, R., Cervellati, D., Nowack, B., Som, C., Nanoparticles in facade coatings: a survey of industrial experts on functional and environmental benefits and challenges. *J. Nanopart. Res.*, 17, 7, 287, 2015.
86. Okyay, T.O., Bala, R.K., Nguyen, H.N., Atalay, R., Bayam, Y., Rodrigues, D.F., Antibacterial properties and mechanisms of toxicity of sonochemically grown ZnO nanorods. *RSC Adv.*, 5, 4, 2568–2575, 2015.
87. Chakra, C., Raob, K., Rajendar, V., Nanocomposites of ZnO and TiO2 have enhanced antimicrobial and antibacterial properties than their disjoint counterparts. *Dig. J. Nanomater. Biostructures*, 12, 185–193, 2017.
88. El-Naggar, M.E., Shaheen, T.I., Zaghloul, S., El-Rafie, M.H., Hebeish, A., Antibacterial activities and UV protection of the in situ synthesized titanium oxide nanoparticles on cotton fabrics. *Ind. Eng. Chem. Res.*, 55, 10, 2661–2668, 2016.
89. Tomak, E.D., Yazici, O.A., Parmak, E.D.S., Gonultas, O., Influence of tannin containing coatings on weathering resistance of wood: combination with zinc and cerium oxide nanoparticles. *Polym. Degrad. Stab.*, 152, 289–296, 2018.
90. Li, J., Wu, Z., Bao, Y., Chen, Y., Huang, C., Li, N., Wet chemical synthesis of ZnO nanocoating on the surface of bamboo timber with improved mould-resistance. *J. Saudi Chem. Soc.*, 21, 8, 920–928, 2017.
91. Margulis-Goshen, K. and Magdassi, S., Nanotechnology: an advanced approach to the development of potent insecticides, in: *Advanced technologies for managing insect pests*, pp. 295–314, Springer, Berlin, 2013.
92. Nair, R., Varghese, S.H., Nair, B.G., Maekawa, T., Yoshida, Y., Kumar, D.S., Nanoparticulate material delivery to plants. *Plant Sci.*, 179, 3, 154–163, 2010.
93. Agarwal, M., Lvov, Y., Varahramyan, K., Conductive wood microfibres for smart paper through layer-by-layer nanocoating. *Nanotechnology*, 17, 21, 5319, 2006.

94. Wilson, A.D. and Lester, D.G., Utilization of aromascan analysis to identify host species of forestpathogens from woody samples. *Proc. Miss. Assoc. Pl. Pathol. Nematol*, vol. 17, 1999.

95. Baietto, M., Wilson, A.D., Bassi, D., Ferrini, F., Evaluation of three electronic noses for detecting incipient wood decay. *Sensors*, 10, 1062–1092, 2010.

96. Li, C., Krewer, G.W., Ji, P., Scherm, H., Kays, S.J., Gas sensor array for blueberry fruit disease detection and classification. *Postharvest Biol. Technol.*, 55, 144–149, 2010.

97. Wilson, A.D., Application of a conductive polymer electronic-nose device to identify aged woody samples. *Proceedings of The 3rd International IARIA Conference on Sensor Device Technologies and Applications*, Rome, Italy, vol. 19, pp. 77–82, 2012.

98. Olafsdottir, G., Jonsdottir, R., Lauzon, H.L., Luten, J., Kristbergsson, K., Characterization of volatile compounds in chilled cod (*Gadus morhua*) fillets by gas chromatography and detection of quality indicators by an electronic nose. *J. Agric. Food Chem.*, 53, 10140–10147, 2005.

99. Rodriguez, J., Duran, C., Reyes, A., Electronic nose for quality control of Colombian coffee through the detection of defects in "Cup Tests". *Sensors*, 10, 36–46, 2010.

100. Adak, M.F. and Yumusak, N., Classification of E-nose aroma data of four fruit types by ABC-based neural network. *Sensors*, 16, 3, 304, 2016.

101. Canhoto, O. and Magan, N., Potential for the detection of microorganisms and heavy metals in potable water using electronic nose technology. *Biosens. Bioelectron.*, 18, 751–754, 2003.

102. Bourgeois., W. and Stuetz, R.M., Use of a chemical sensor array for detecting pollutants in domestic wastewater. *Water Res.*, 36, 4505–4512, 2002.

103. Sironi, S., Capelli, L., Céntola, P., Del Rosso, R., Grande, M.I., Continuous monitoring of odours from a composting plant using electronic noses. *Waste Manage.*, 27, 389–397, 2007.

104. Littarru, P., Environmental odours assessment from waste treatment plants: Dynamic olfactometry in combination with sensorial analysers "electronic noses". *Waste Manage.*, 27, 302–309, 2007.

105. Comparetti, A., Precision agriculture: past, present and future, in: *International scientific conference agricultural engineering and environment*, pp. 216–230, 2011.

10

Simulation of Water Management Processes of Distributed Irrigation Systems

Aysulu Aydarova

Information Technologies Department, Tashkent University of Information Technologies named after Muhammad al-Khwarizmi, Tashkent, Uzbekistan

Abstract

In this study, mathematical models of the water resources management process of canals in the middle reaches of the Chirchik River were developed using simplified differential equations of Saint-Venant in partial derivatives, necessary conditions for optimality of water distribution were developed, an algorithm for solving the problem of optimal water resources management of distributed irrigation canals was developed.

Keywords: Water management, modeling, mathematic model, algorithm, irrigation system

10.1 Introduction

In this world, paramount issues in modeling water resources management processes in distributed irrigation systems with various hydraulic structures is water saving. Nowadays, a whole range of research works is being carried out aimed at improving and developing methods, selecting criteria for the distribution of water in canals, developing new and derivative from existing mathematical models of water resources management.

Email: aysulu.aydarova@gmail.com

Roheet Bhatnagar, Nitin Kumar Tripathi, Nitu Bhatnagar and Chandan Kumar Panda (eds.)
The Digital Agricultural Revolution: Innovations and Challenges in Agriculture through Technology Disruptions, (255–268) © 2022 Scrivener Publishing LLC

10.2   Modeling of Water Facilities

Currently, in a number of countries around the world, research is being carried out on the rational management and mathematical modeling of water facilities, some scientific and practical results have been obtained. These include foreign scientists: M.Levent Kavvas, James Polsinelli, Afshar A. (USA), M. Qi, L.Cao, L.Hu, J.Zhang (China), Sven-Joachim Kimmerle, R.Shoda, R.Shilling, J.Thurso, B.Stoffel (Germany), Valérie Dos Santos, Mickael Rodrigues, Mamadou Diagne (Spain), Park C.C., Kunj J.A., Holli F.M. (Great Britain).

In modern science, partial differential equations are used to describe the movement of water in open channels Saint-Venant. In their most common form, they can be written as follows:

- equation of balance of water consumption

$$\frac{\partial Q}{\partial L} + \frac{\partial \omega}{\partial t} = 0 \qquad (10.1)$$

- equation of dynamic equilibrium

$$i - \frac{\partial h}{\partial x} = \frac{Q^2}{K^2} + \frac{v}{g}\frac{\partial v}{\partial x} + \frac{1}{g}\frac{\partial v}{\partial t} \qquad (10.2)$$

where i is the bottom slope, Q, K, v are consumption, flow modulus and average cross-sectional velocity, ω, h, free area and flow depth, x, distance; t, time; g, gravity constant [1].

The integral form of the Saint-Venant equations is derived from the equations of conservation of mass and momentum (Navier-Stokes equations), which are valid in situations where the shallow water conditions are not met:

$$\int_{x_1}^{x_2}(\omega_{t_2} - \omega_{t_1})dx + \int_{t_1}^{t_2}(Q_{x_2} - Q_{x_1})dt = 0, \qquad (10.3)$$

where $Q = v\omega$;

ω, free area; x, coordinate along the length of the segment; t, time.

Without taking into account the Coriolis forces, friction, and viscosity, the differential form of the system of one-dimensional Saint-Venant equations has the form:

$$i - \frac{\partial h}{\partial x} = \frac{v}{g} \frac{\partial v}{\partial x} + \frac{1}{g} \frac{\partial v}{\partial t} + \frac{|v| v}{C^2 R} + \frac{qv}{g\omega},$$

$$\frac{\partial \omega}{\partial t} + \frac{\partial Q}{\partial x} = q;$$

(10.4)

where C is Chezy coefficient; R, hydraulic radius; q, lateral inflow [2].

In the middle course of the Chirchik River, we denote the water surface as region D in 3-dimensional Euclidean space ε^3 with the border ∂D, which we will define as s. Let the equation of this surface have the form $\gamma(x) = 0$ [3]. We introduce a generalized function $\delta(\gamma(x))$, or $\delta_s(x)$, or δ_s—simple surface layer S, for which:

$$(\delta_s, F) = \int_D \delta_s(x) F(x) dx = \int_S F(x) \, dS$$

(10.5)

So, let $f(x)$—continuous function on S.
We introduce a generalized function:

$$\frac{\partial}{\partial n} \big(f(x)\delta_s(x) \big),$$

which works by the rule below

$$\frac{\partial}{\partial n}\big(f(x)\delta_s(x), F(x)\big) = \int_D F(x) \frac{\partial}{\partial n}\big(f(x), \delta_s(x)\big) dx =$$

$$= -\int_S \frac{\partial F(x)}{\partial n} f(x) \, dS.$$

(10.6)

For equation (10.6) the standardizing function is

$$\omega(x) = f(x) - \frac{\partial}{\partial n}(g(x), \delta_s(x)).$$

(10.7)

This corresponds to the well-known solution of this problem, expressed like the Green's function G(x, "ξ):

$$Q(x) = \int_D G(x,\xi) f(\xi) d\xi - \int_S \frac{\partial G(x,\xi)}{\partial n_\xi} g(\xi) dS. \qquad (10.8)$$

The change in air temperature in space depending on the flow of water, evenly distributed along a straight line perpendicular to the xy plane and passing through a point (ξ, η) plane xy. The free surface has a given temperature (concentration) independent of y [4].

The same for a half-plane isolated on both sides, with a boundary maintained at a given temperature.

$$-\left[\frac{\partial^2 Q(r,\theta)}{\partial r^2} + \frac{1}{r}\frac{\partial Q(r,\theta)}{\partial r} + \frac{\partial^2 Q(r,\theta)}{\partial \theta^2}\right] = f(r,\theta), \qquad (10.9)$$

$$|Q(0,\theta)| < \infty, \qquad \frac{\partial Q}{\partial r}(R_1,\theta) = g_1\theta, \qquad \frac{\partial Q}{\partial r}(R_2,\theta) = g_2\theta,$$

$$Q(r,\theta+2\pi) = Q(r,\theta),$$

$$R_1 \leq r \leq R_2, 0 \leq \theta \leq 2\pi.$$

Indeed, equation (10.9) shows the flow rate of water in a plane isolated on both sides. However, this thesis explores an irrigation system that is not limited on both sides [5].

And the inclination of the bottom cannot be strictly taken as a right angle. Consequently, equation (10.9) cannot be used as the basis for this study.

To model the processes of water resources management in canals of distributed irrigation systems with distributed parameters, let us consider a simple direct wave model [6].

The water flow rate is determined using a discrete unit function q_i. Direct wave model in the channel section in the form of a differential equation:

$$\frac{\partial Q(x,t)}{\partial t} + v\frac{\partial Q(x,t)}{\partial x} = q(x,t). \qquad (10.10)$$

Here $Q(x, t)$—this is a change in water consumption at the site, v—flow speed.

Input condition:

$$Q(x, 0) = Q_0(x),$$

$Q_0(x)$—input distribution of water flow at the beginning of the canal section.

Boundary condition:

$$Q(0, t) = Q_1(t),$$

$Q_1(t)$—change in water flow in the beginning of canal section.

Variable scope

$$x \geq 0, t \geq 0, v > 0.$$

Water consumption at the points of water intake of the channel section $q(x, t)$ with discreteness of water supply has the form:

$$q(x,t) = -\sum_{i=i}^{5} q_i \delta(x - a_i)(t - T). \tag{10.11}$$

Let there be a channel of constant cross-section (Figure 10.1) with a constant slope of the bottom, extending to infinity along the x axis. Also, let an incompressible fluid flow in this channel in the gravity field [7]. It is supposed that the liquid is devoid of interior friction, friction against the walls and riverbed, and the level of the liquid above the bottom of the channel h is small in comparison with the characteristic dimensions of the flow,

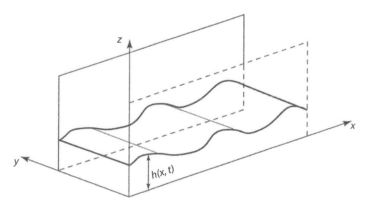

Figure 10.1 Constant cross-section channel diagram.

the dimensions of the bottom irregularities, and so on. Suppose that the water flow is distinguished by one spatial variable (x) and depends on the time (t). Consequently, it is assumed that the fluid velocity u has a nonzero component ux (which we will denote by u), and the other components can be neglected; in addition, it is assumed that the level h also hang on only on x and t [8].

Let a perturbation be given at a certain point x = x1, such that either the velocity is equal to u, or the elevation in the free surface h changes in a specific way in time. And at the same time, there is a big difference between the propagation of a disturbance, which is caused by a monotonic lowering of the free surface at the point x = x_1, and the disturbance that arises when the free surface rises at this point. In the first case (with the distribution of the decrease in standing (quiescent) water), the flow is continuous everywhere. In the second case, the water flow will be continuous only up to a certain point in time, after which jumps are formed, which can be interpreted as the development of boars and breakers in the water [9].

The available water resources of the irrigation system are characterized by the amount of water in the basin of the studied river. Climatic conditions, landscape, and atmosphere determine the hydrological cycle of the region. Economic methods are an alternative to direct water resources management. Their role is to create conditions for achieving water savings, without which water management methods will be ineffective [10].

Thus, to study the balance of water resources in the middle reaches of the Chirchik River, as a unit of research, we will consider an irrigation canal with two sections connected by a hydraulic structure.

Considering a section of an irrigation canal with 4 water intakes (Figure 10.2), we define the problem of water management as ensuring the delivery of each water intake at the moment of time t water consumption q_i.

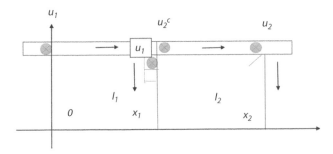

Figure 10.2 Irrigation canal diagram.

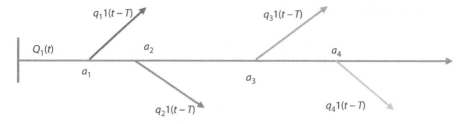

Figure 10.3 Irrigation canal section diagram.

The main goal of the labor is to minimize water consumption during its delivery to side water intakes using water management at the beginning of the canal section [11] (Figure 10.3):

$$I = \int_0^t [Q(x,t) - Q^*]^2\, dxdt + \int_l^T [Q(l,t) - Q^*]^2\, dt \qquad (10.12)$$

Under the following conditions:

$$\begin{cases} \dfrac{\partial Q(x,t)}{dt} + v\dfrac{\partial Q(x,t)}{dt} = q(x,t), \\[2mm] q(x,t) = -\sum_{i=1}^n q_i \delta(x - a_i)l(t - T), \\[1mm] Q(x,0) = Q_0(x) \\[1mm] Q(0,t) = u(t) \\[1mm] x \geq 0, t \geq 0, \\[1mm] v > 0 \end{cases} \qquad (10.13)$$

The variational equation has the form:

$$\frac{\partial \delta Q}{dt} + v\frac{\partial \delta Q}{dt} - \delta q = 0 \qquad (10.14)$$

We calculate the variation of the functional:

$$\delta I = \int_0^t 2[Q(x,T) - Q^*]\delta Q(x,T)dx \qquad (10.15)$$

Let's introduce a variable λ:

$$\iint_{\infty}^{T_h}\left[\frac{\partial \delta Q}{\partial t}+v\frac{\partial \delta Q}{\partial t}-\delta q\right]\lambda\,dx\,dt \qquad (10.16)$$

Subtracting (10.12) from (10.13) we obtain

$$\delta I=\int_0^l 2(Q(x,T)-Q^*)\delta Q(x,T)\,dx-$$

$$\int_0^T\int_0^h\left[\frac{\partial \delta Q}{\partial t}+v\frac{\partial \delta Q}{\partial t}-\delta q\right]\lambda\,dx\,dt, \qquad (10.17)$$

$$\iint_{0^0}^{T_l}\left[\lambda\frac{\partial \delta Q}{\partial x}\right]dx\,dt=\int_0^l[\lambda\,\delta Q]_0^T-\int_0^T\left[\frac{\partial \lambda}{\partial x}\delta Q\right]dt=$$

$$\int_0^l\left[\lambda(x,T)\delta Q(x,T)-\lambda(x,0)\delta Q(x,0)-\int_0^T\left[\frac{\partial \lambda}{\partial x}\delta Q\right]dt\right]dx \qquad (10.18)$$

$$\iint_{0^0}^{T_l}\left[\lambda\frac{\partial \delta Q}{\partial x}\right]dx\,dt=\int_0^T[\lambda\,\delta Q]_0^l-\int_0^l\left[\frac{\partial \lambda}{\partial t}\delta Q\right]dt=$$

$$\int_0^T\left[\lambda(l,T)\delta Q(l,T)-\lambda(0,t)\delta Q(0,t)-\int_0^l\left[\frac{\partial \lambda}{\partial x}\delta Q\right]dt\right]dx \qquad (10.19)$$

Taking into account expressions (10.18) and (10.19), we write down the variation of the functional as:

$$\delta I=\int_0^e[2[Q(x,T)-Q^*]\delta Q(x,T)]dx$$

$$-\int_0^T v\left[\lambda(l,t)\delta(l,t)-\lambda(0,t)\delta Q(0,t)+\int_0^l\left[\frac{\partial \lambda}{\partial x}\delta Q\right]dx\right]dt+$$

$$+\int_0^l\lambda(x,T)\delta Q(x,T)-\lambda(x,0)\delta Q(x,0)+\int_0^T\left[\frac{\partial \lambda}{\partial t}\delta Q\right]dt\,dx \qquad (10.20)$$

Let us calculate the variations of the initial and boundary conditions:

$$\delta Q(x,\, 0) = 0,$$

$$\delta Q(0,\, t) = \delta u(t) \qquad\qquad (10.21)$$

Let us rewrite the variation of the functional taking into account the variation of the initial and boundary conditions:

$$\delta I = \int_0^l \int_0^T \left(\frac{\partial \lambda}{\partial t} - v \frac{\partial \lambda}{\partial x} \right) \delta Q\, dx\, dt +$$

$$\int_0^l [2[Q(x,T) - Q^*] + \lambda(x,T)] \delta Q(x,t)\, dx +$$

$$+ \int_0^T v[\lambda(l,t) \delta Q(l,t) - [\lambda(0,t-1)] \delta Q(0,t) - \lambda(0,t) \delta u(t)]\, dt$$

$$(10.22)$$

Choosing a variable λ, so that it satisfies the following equation with initial and boundary conditions [12]:

$$\frac{\partial \lambda}{\partial t} - v \frac{\partial \lambda}{\partial x} = 0$$

$$\lambda(x,t) = 2[Q(x,T) - Q^*]$$

$$\lambda(0,t) = 1, \lambda(l,t) = 0, \qquad\qquad (10.23)$$

Then the variation of the functional has the form:

$$\delta I = \int_0^T [v\lambda\,(l,t) \delta Q(l,t) - \lambda(0,t) \delta u(t)]\, dt \qquad\qquad (10.24)$$

Thus, the necessary condition for the optimality of water management is in the case of a direct wave model, it is formulated as follows: in order for the control to be optimal, the following condition must be fulfilled [13]:

$$\lambda(l,\, t) \delta Q(l,\, t) - \lambda(0,\, t) \delta u(t) = 0 \qquad\qquad (10.25)$$

inside the area of limitation.

10.3 Processing and Conducting Experiments

For processing and conducting experiments in this study, three channels were selected in the middle course of the Chirchik River: Karasu, Parkent, Khandam. Karasu has three concrete layers.

To solve the issue of modeling the management of water resources of the irrigation system within the framework of this dissertation work in the middle reaches of the Chirchik River, the daily water discharge from 2010 till 2020 (over 10 years) was studied in three canals: Parkent, Karasu, and Khandam. Information on water expending was obtained up to the day of the concluding calculation of the program developed within the frame-work of this dissertation work. Also, in the materials studied, there is a monthly flow rate of each channel in million m^3/s. For example, in the Karasu canal, the water discharge in 2020 varied from 56.8944 to 329.4432 million m^3/s, in the Parkent canal from 5.7888 to 52.0128 million m^3/s, and in the Handam canal—from 4.4928 up to 34, 8192 million m^3/s.

To compile long-term statistics in the middle reaches of the Chirchik River, the following canals were adopted: Karasu, Parkent, and Khandam. The Karasu Canal is 89.9 km long, the Parkent Canal is 87.94 km long, and the Khandam is 73.3 km long. Karasu was built in 1900. Parkent Canal was built in 1983, reconstructed twice in 1998 and in 2012. The Handam Canal was built in 1971. Karasu's carrying capacity is 260 m^3/s, the tied area is 40359 hectares, of which cotton is grown on 10,530 hectares, grain crops on 11,726 hectares, and other crops on 18,102 hectares. Karasu has four large waterworks. In total, it has 42 hydraulic structures, 17 of which are intended for water distribution, 2 water intakes, 17 gauging stations, 5 siphons.

The carrying capacity of the Parkent canal is 57 m^3/s, the associated area is 26871 hectares, 124 hectares of which are grown cotton, 4211 hectares—grain crops, 22,536 hectares—other crops. Parkent has 1 large waterworks. In total, it has 281 hydraulic structures, 99 of which are intended for water distribution, 10 water intakes, 90 gauging stations, 13 siphons, 13 bridges.

The carrying capacity of the Khandam canal is 30 m^3/s, the associated area is 7376 hectares, 443 hectares of which are grown cotton, 1723 hect-ares—grain crops, 5209 hectares—other crops. Int total Khandam has 197 hydraulic structures, 81 of which are intended for water distribution, 1 water intakes, 81 gauging station, and 16 siphons.

Table 10.1 shows information on the average annual water discharge in the Karasu, Parkent, Handam canals for the last 10 years.

Figure 10.4 shows the dynamics of water discharge in the Parkent, Karasu and Khandam canals from 2011 to 2020.

Table 10.1 Average annual water consumption in Karasu, Parkent, Handam in 2011–2020.

Years	Average temperature	Karasu Average water consumption, mln m³/s	Parkent Average water consumption, mln m³/s	Khandam Average water consumption, mln m³/s
2011	16,375	134,76235	30,42	13,466
2012	16,5416	112,415045	34,81	22,92
2013	17,666	134,66155	37,35	20,742
2014	15,4166	153,57744	27,835	18,558
2015	17,666	129,517	28,7834	21,3228
2016	18,5833	163,73	34,077	21,8124
2017	13,333	149,49	40,95	22,3056
2018	16,9166	156,73	32,326	20,78
2019	17,2916	91,55	133,329	63,864
2020	19,25	144,35	24,3	22,21

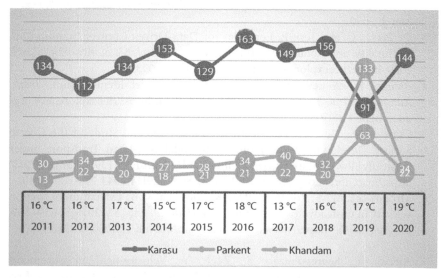

Figure 10.4 Dynamics of water consumption.

The dynamics of water flow in Figure 10.4 shows that the water flow in the Karasu canal is the highest. Average flow rates are shown on the Parkent Canal. The Handam canal has the lowest water flow rate.

10.4 Conclusion

This chapter presents the necessary conditions for optimal management of water resources in distributed irrigation systems. For optimal control, the values on the left side of equality (15) must be nonpositive if the control reaches the lower bounds and non-negative if the control reaches the upper bounds. This is a necessary condition for optimal control [14]. The following shows a model for managing information processing in a network of distributed irrigation systems. A verbal algorithm for working out problems of modeling water management processes in distributed irrigation systems is developed in this article.

References

1. Ikeda, T., Nagahara, M., Ono, S., Discrete-Valued Control of Linear Time-Invariant Systems by Sum-of-Absolute-Values Optimization, *Trans. Autom. Control*, 62, 6, 2750–2763, June 2017.
2. Vu, D.T. and Pham, T.C., Solving two-dimensional Saint venant equation by using cellular neural network, *Trans. Autom. Control*, 65, 3, 909–924, March 2020.
3. De Persis, C. and Tesi, P., Formulas for Data-Driven Control: Stabilization, Optimality, and Robustness, *Trans. Autom. Control*, 65, 3, 909–924, March 2020. https://ieeexplore.ieee.org/document/8933093.
4. Akaike, H., A new look at the statistical model identification, *Trans. Autom. Control*, 19, 6, pp. 716–723, Dec 1974. https://ieeexplore.ieee.org/document/1100705.
5. Guney, M.S., Bombar, G., Aksoy, A.O., Experimental Study of the Coarse Surface Development Effect on the Bimodal Bed-Load Transport under Unsteady Flow Conditions, ASCE Library, *J. Hydraul. Eng.*, 139, 1, January 2013. https://ascelibrary.org/doi/10.1061/%28ASCE%29HY.1943-7900.0000640.
6. Mrokowska, M.M., Rowiński, P.M., Kalinowska, M.B., Evaluation of friction velocity in unsteady flow experiments, *J. Hydraul. Eng.*, 53, 2015, 5, 659–669, 21 Aug 2015. https://www.tandfonline.com/doi/full/10.1080/00221686.2015.1072853.
7. Aleixo, R., Soares-Frazão, S., Zech, Y., Velocity-field measurements in a dam-break flow using a PTV Voronoï imaging technique, *Exp.*

Fluids, 50, 1633–1649, 2011. https://link.springer.com/article/10.1007/s00348-010-1021-y.

8. Cheng, N.-S., Resistance Coefficients for Artificial and Natural Coarse-Bed Channels: Alternative Approach for Large-Scale Roughness, ASCE Library. *J. Hydraul. Eng.*, 141, 2 - February 2015. https://ascelibrary.org/doi/10.1061/%28ASCE%29HY.1943-7900.0000966.

9. Yan, B.W., Li, Q.S., He, Y.C., Chan, P.W., RANS simulation of neutral atmospheric boundary layer flows over complex terrain by proper imposition of boundary conditions and modification on the k-ε model, *Environ. Fluid Mech.*, Springer Link, USA, 16, pp. 1–23, 2016, https://link.springer.com/article/10.1007/s10652-015-9408-1.

10. Worm, G.I.M., Mesman, G.A.M., van Schagen, K.M., Borger, K.J., Rietveld, L.C., Hydraulic modelling of drinking watertreatment plant operations, *Drink. Water Eng. Sci.*, pp. 15–20, 2009, https://www.researchgate.net/publication/40742084_Hydraulic_modelling_of_drinking_water_treatment_plant_operations.

11. Urbanowicz, K. and Firkowski, M., Modelling Water Hammer with Quasi-Steady and Unsteady Friction in Viscoelastic Pipelines, SpringerLink, USA, 2017. https://link.springer.com/chapter/10.1007/978-3-319-96601-4_35.

12. Chiang, P.-K. and Willems, P., Combine Evolutionary Optimization with Model Predictive Control in Real-time Flood Control of a River System, *Water Res. Manag.*, SpringerLink, USA, 29, pp. 2527–2542, 2015, https://link.springer.com/article/10.1007/s11269-015-0955-5.

13. Szemis, J.M., Maier, H.R., Dandy, G.C., A framework for using ant colony optimization to schedule environmental flow management alternatives for rivers, wetlands, and floodplains, AGU Advancing Earth and Space Science, *Water Resour. Res.*, 48, 8, August 2012. https://agupubs.onlinelibrary.wiley.com/doi/full/10.1029/2011WR011276.

14. Ooi, S.K., Weyer, E., Campi, M., Control Applications, CCA 2003. *Proceedings of 2003 IEEE Conference, IEEE*, USA, 2, 2003. https://www.researchgate.net/publication/4029372_Finite_sample_quality_assessment_of_system_identification_models_of_irrigation_channels.

11

Conceptual Principles of Reengineering of Agricultural Resources: Open Problems, Challenges and Future Trends

Zamlynskyi Viktor[1]*, Livinskyi Anatolii[2], Zamlynska Olha[2] and Minakova Svetlana[3]

[1]Department of Management, Odessa National Polytechnic University, Odessa, Ukraine
[2]Odessa State Agrarian University, Odessa, Ukraine
[3]Ivano-Frankivsk National Technical University of Oil and Gas, Ivano-Frankivsk, Ukraine

Abstract

One of the most pressing issues is the sustainable development of the agricultural complex system at the macroeconomic level. Synthesis of the concepts of scientists from all over the world should become priorities for building a global strategy for the future and take into account a large number of different factors and motivational components, located in a priority sequence. However, the agricultural revolution today is being carried out both in the interests of structures operating on the principles of initial capital accumulation, and respectable and law-abiding, socially oriented business structures. An ineffective confrontation can lead to the loss of stability of the world economic system, which will certainly entail an environmental and food disaster. The introduction of innovations in agriculture should be aimed at economic stimulation of the environmental activities of enterprises in a global market governance environment, as well as changes in the reputational preferences of business and the motivational principles of the existence of each person in the context of his participation in the formation of a better life for future generations.

*Corresponding author: zam.agrariy@gmail.com; smmnkv@gmail.com

Roheet Bhatnagar, Nitin Kumar Tripathi, Nitu Bhatnagar and Chandan Kumar Panda (eds.)
The Digital Agricultural Revolution: Innovations and Challenges in Agriculture through Technology Disruptions, (269–288) © 2022 Scrivener Publishing LLC

Keywords: Agricultural outlook, modernization, ecological compatibility, organic products, agrarian sector, ecological and economic principles, tools for protecting economic interests, the reproduction process

11.1   Introduction

Economy—a necessary condition and means of human life, but not its purpose, not the highest value and not the determining cause. The true meaning of human life is how a person understands, appreciates and uses it. The erroneous basis of the fact that man allegedly controls the life of nature, rather than coexisting with it for a very short period.

Agriculture is a complex system that operates simultaneously in both the natural and social environments. The first place belongs to nature, in the second place—a person who consumes food and gradually depletes the natural resource potential. The global agricultural resource is exhaustive, but can be renewed. Also, the state of ecological balance of the environment and human existence depends on how this system takes into account natural conditions and the impact of human existence on them. Along with successes in productivity of land and people, the problem of human existence directly in the agricultural region is ignored. Large corporations are lobbying for laws to maximize their profits. This is usually the adoption of laws on trade in land resources, easing tax conditions, improving logistics. Working for young people in agriculture is not prestigious, many families who have nurtured their own agricultural business and gained experience for centuries are forced to sell their business because their children are not interested in it and do not want to continue the family business. The lack of a human factor and thousands of hectares of agricultural land removes many problems for "big money." It is much easier to administer and control, so the zoning of processing, storage and consumption centers, livestock complexes, and large urban settlements will gradually take place.

The management system of each enterprise must be environmentally and socially justified, environmental. This applies to all industries without exception—agriculture, animal breeding. Specialization of the economy, organization of land use, location of production, including crops, livestock farms, and other production facilities, used machinery and technology must be environmentally friendly. If, along with the increase in agricultural production in a particular region, we begin to see an increase in rural population, the number of small- and medium-sized farms, a variety of products and an increase in the share of organic production, then there is hope that our concept is heard and implemented.

Each of such system is an agrobiogeocenosis that includes humans, plants, soil, animals, microorganisms, and other components. The task of science—on the basis of in-depth research to establish how the system combining natural and anthropogenic factors, the specific participation of each structural element, their relationship, compatibility and impact on the environment, crops, human, and animal health.

Farmers in the process of work (tillage, sowing, plant care, fertilizers, chemical plant protection products, drainage, and irrigation of lands) constantly and actively influence the agrobiogeocenosis, especially the soil and plants. Unfortunately, such exposure is often environmentally hazardous. Numerous facts of destruction and pollution of soils testify to the advantage of profits over the preservation of the environment, which presents a low point of moral and environmental responsibility of specialists, the lack of relevant regulations (permits) for the use of equipment, chemicals, and land reclamation. As a result, some areas have reached a state of ecological catastrophe.

Agriculture is a complex system that functions in a natural environment. And the state of the ecological balance of the environment depends on how this system takes into account natural conditions, how it "fits" into them. Therefore, the management system of each enterprise should be not only profitable but also environmentally sound, environmentally friendly, and socially responsible.

The world's population is expected to grow to almost 10 billion by 2050, boosting agricultural demand—in a scenario of modest economic growth—by some 50% compared with 2013. Income growth in low- and middle-income countries would hasten a dietary transition toward higher consumption of meat, fruits, and vegetables, relative to that of cereals, requiring commensurate shifts in output and adding pressure on natural resources [1].

Each such system is an agrobiogeocenosis, including humans, plants, soil, animals, microorganisms, and other components. The task of science is to establish, on the basis of in-depth research, how a system that combines natural and anthropogenic factors functions, the direct participation of each structural element in it, their relationship, compatibility and impact on the environment, crops, human and animal health on a global and regional scale. It will also ensure the restoration and preservation of existing natural habitats, finding a set of factors to maintain their integrity and life support functions to improve the quality of life of living organisms, improve the demographic situation, which will ensure sustainable development of the anthropogenic factor along with its habitat. Agricultural resources are the basis of human life support, the reproduction of which is based on the use of solar energy, water, soil fertility. The dynamics of these biospheric processes, based on a resource-depleting strategy, is increasing, accelerating the degradation of the habitat.

11.2   Modern Agronomy and Approaches for Environment Sustenance

Numerous facts of destruction and pollution of soils indicate a low level of ecological culture, the absence of socially responsible communication skills of specialists, the absence of appropriate regulations for the use of technology, chemical treatments, land reclamation. As a result, some territories have reached the state of ecological disaster.

In these conditions, the global economic system, together with modern agronomy, must radically revise the approaches and methods of developing zonal farming systems. The ecological and economic rationale for modern farming systems must become the immutable rule. Livestock management should also be carried out in accordance with environmental standards. On the one hand, to ensure the health of animals and get the maximum high-quality products from them, it is necessary to create appropriate conditions for keeping and feeding them, and on the other, to make sure that the livestock complex, farm, herd in the pasture do not cause pollution of the land and water sources.

We are talking about a balanced organization of farming and animal husbandry, taking into account natural conditions, ensuring their harmonious unity. The land must feed the animals, and the farm must feed the field. All manure must be returned to the soil. Ignoring the law of the unity of agriculture and animal husbandry, the law of return is unacceptable, because it will lead to the loosening and destruction of the ecosystem, and ultimately to a decrease in productivity of both land and animals.

Environmental requirements for agricultural machinery are constantly growing. The fact is that with the help of machines, their working organs, people constantly interfere with the life of the soil. This often leads to a deterioration in the physical condition of the soil (spraying, compaction, deterioration of water, and air regimes), a decrease in its microbiological activity, the development of accelerated erosion, salinization and other negative consequences. To prevent this, it is necessary to create new machines and working attachments for them, which could carry out highly qualified operations to preserve moisture, apply fertilizers, and prepare the soil for intensive technologies.

Moreover, this technique must be differentiated according to the natural zones of the country, taking into account the size of the fields, the relief, the mechanical composition of the soil, the set of crops, and the technology of their processing. The design of the machines must correspond to the natural functioning of the ecological and economic system.

It is generally recognized that mankind is faced with the task of creating an environmentally and economically efficient production capable of solving the problem of increasing production while preserving and improving the sur-rounding nature. In this regard, a new concept of balanced integrated planning of the development of regions on a modern ecological and economic basis is needed. The sectoral approach has not justified itself, as evidenced by the sad experience of creating large industrial facilities, livestock complexes, during the construction of which the environmental factor was ignored.

An important direction in the development of environmentally friendly and economically efficient production is the development and application of resource-saving and waste-free technologies, the implementation of which significantly reduces the amount of waste generated, polluting nature, or they are practically eliminated. Thus, in the food industry, more than two-thirds of the waste is plant residues that can be used for livestock feed.

Trying to avoid economic risks some farmers have reduced the cost of purchasing high-quality pesticides and fertilizers, as well as other means of production. As per one position, this qualifies as a sustainable agricul-tural production. For instance, in the United States, sustainable agricultural production is considered to be one that uses fewer industrial fertilizers, herbicides, and pesticides. In some systems, such as growing wheat in arid areas without steam treated with herbicides, pesticides and fertilizers have always been important. However, estimates show that this system is not stable. This system would be close to defining organic by the standards of some organizations in the United States (but not by the norms worked out by International Federation of Organic Agriculture Movements [IFOAM]), because certification programs usually state what should not be done, and only secondarily, what should be done. In addition, this system is not the best possible in terms of environment and resources. Other systems would be more effective in increasing soil productivity, reducing erosion, pre-serving wildlife habitats and increasing farmers' incomes without the use of materials that are considered undesirable. And this system of mono-culture, of course, does not meet the definition of "ecological," because it barely represents the complex ecological structure that it has replaced.

11.2.1 Sustainable Agriculture

Sustainable agricultural production is a synthesis of concepts that are a priority for most countries in the world, developed through various fac-tors and motivational components. It is constantly being modified and improved in response to the existing economic pressure on farmers and the growing concern for the environment in connection with agricultural activities. Although its roots go much deeper, sustainable agricultural pro-duction as a well-defined concept has diverse, alternative, and inconsistent trends, it is still young compared with the time it will take to study the potential of all industries and fully understand its basic principles.

Only a harmonious combination of nature and agricultural production provides conditions for a normal human life. This will also be facilitated by the economic stimulation of environmental protection activities of enterprises in the global conditions of market management.

Normal functioning of human-created ecological and economic systems is impossible without the introduction of strict monitoring of the biosphere and its components. At the same time, its consistency should be considered a qualitatively new level of monitoring, it allows providing a comprehensive assessment of various components of the biosphere.

It is important that the systems are adaptive, designed for flexible maneuvering in accordance with difficult weather conditions, economic conditions, and other factors that change.

Sustainable economic development depends on a number of indicators: subindicators are infrastructure, macroeconomic stability, product market, labor market, financial system, innovation capability, economic globalization, economic decline, uneven development, business environment, and economic quality. As for the social component, only the influence of the number of refugees and IDPs is weak, and that of employment is less than the average. Among the indicators that have a significant influence, there are health/life expectancy, education, social capital, social globalization, demographic tension, human flight and brain drain, health, environment, and income inequality [2].

The term "sustainable agricultural production" is used to refer to a strategy aimed at solving a number of problems that arise in agriculture and are of increasing concern around the world. The main ones are pollution of the environment with pesticides, fertilizers, and precipitation; loss of soil and deterioration of its quality; lack of nonrenewable resources, such as fossil energy; decrease in income of agricultural enterprises and farms.

This concept is based on several general principles:

- a variety of types of agricultural crops, allowing to increase the biological and economic stability of the economy, for example, due to crop rotations, processing of catch crops;
- selection of varieties of agricultural crops and livestock breeds, adapted to the soil and climatic conditions of the economy and resistant to diseases and pests;
- preference for the resources produced on the farm in comparison with purchased and local production of the necessary materials (if possible) in comparison with those imported from remote regions;

- strengthening the circulation of nutrients to minimize their losses outside the farm due to composting manure and the use of crop rotations with the inclusion of legumes for nitrogen fixation;
- placement and maintenance of livestock on pastures at a low density, the inclusion of more roughage in the diets of ruminants instead of concentrated ones, determining the size of the herd by the ability of the farm to produce fodder and effectively use manure;
- increasing the ability of the soil to absorb the introduced nutrients for subsequent release as needed by the cultivated crops, as opposed to the direct absorption by the crop during their application;
- maintenance of the protective soil cover throughout the year through cultivation, in which plant residues are preserved on the surface, as well as through cover crops and live mulch;
- the introduction of crop rotations with the inclusion of crops with a root system, deeply buried, to extract reserves of nutrients from the lower layers of the soil, allows you to control the spread of weeds by alternating crops grown in cool and warm seasons;
- the applying of resolvable mineral enrichment, if necessary, only in such quantities that the agricultural crop can effectively use, and only if the nutritive deficiency cannot be filled with pus and legumes;
- the use of synthetic insecticides and herbicides to suppress weeds, insect pests and diseases only as a last resort and only with a clear threat to the cultivated crop.

The principles of sustainable development of agricultural enterprises were formed from many sources—both modern and past experience, which originates from organic agriculture. In the beginning, organic farming was about reusing the sources of nutrients produced by the farm; the introduction of nutrients in the form of animal feed or chemical fertilizers was not encouraged. At this time, the rejection of the use of synthetic pesticides is especially emphasized.

The depression in the agrarian economy has led to shifts in priorities from "maximum production" to "optimal," which is based on the idea that the system should be assessed not by how much it made but by the comparative meaning of output versus cost.

Frequent reduction in the consumption of means of production by farmers for the sake of saving money turns out to be harmful to the environment and human health. The trend for low-cost farming can help address another significant challenge that have come to the fore in last years, such as avoiding farther groundwater pollution by pesticides and meeting the raising requires for water and organic food. These issues have generated considerable interest in sustainable agricultural production, although even its basic ideas have not yet been fully developed. The concept of "sustainable (balanced) agricultural production" is used in the singular, in fact, it is multidimensional, and so far, none of the definitions has received general acceptance.

Over the past decades, all of these concepts have come into use as definitions for rural systems that share common purposes: to reduce the use of purchased inlet, especially poisonous or nonrenewable inputs; reduce environmental loss and improve the soil, water, and wildlife defense.

"Sustainable" agricultural production has a temporal size and means the power to persist extremely, possibly evolving in accordance with it; "alternative" means something various from the predominant or "traditional" context; "Low cost" refers to reducing the use of external materials; "environmental"—the rules and methods that govern the surroundings; "restorative" refers to the capacity to create the means the system needs.

These concepts in relation to agricultural production have not yet acquired additional features. Thus, "alternative" is not only another type of agricultural production, it must also differ in a certain way, be more stable. So far, this has not been clarified, and the definition of "stable" has begun to be used in such different situations that there is a danger of losing its true meaning.

Low-cost agricultural production is identified with sustainable, the question arises, does sustainable agricultural production primarily reduce some costs or costs in general, or, before the introduction of good practices, makes some costs unnecessary? Organic farming, a precursor to stable, eschewal or significantly reduces the use of two important categories of purchased inputs, synthetic pesticides and highly soluble inorganic fertilizers. The reasons for this are related to the productivity of the soil, the surrounding, and other biological and chemical factors. For farmers engaged in organic farming, operating costs are reduced.

Sustainable agricultural production must be based on affirmative interventions to improve land richness, pest control, and other functions. This concept emphasizes the importance of nutritive cycling, natural pest control, species variety, permanent soil protection with live crops or plant residues, and healthy livestock management (Figure 11.1).

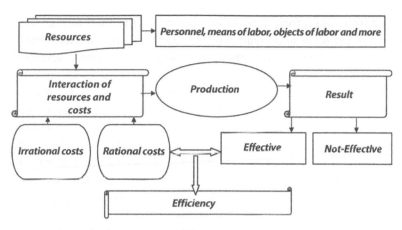

Figure 11.1 Scheme for the formation of the rational use of resources.*
* Own development of the authors.

Large fattening enterprises are potential sources of concentrated pollution. Farmers must receive compensation from the state for destroying the infrastructure of rural areas, which has led to a lack of jobs and environmental pollution. Innovative agricultural productivity is the functioning of intensive livestock systems leads to a decrease in the content of vitamins and trace elements and the accumulation of harmful substances (hormones, antibiotics, nitrates, pesticides), reduction of genetic diversity in livestock systems. Therefore, it is necessary to encourage entrepreneurs to breed rare nontraditional animals at the state level. For example, snails, grape snails, pheasants, pigeons, turtles, ostriches, earthworms, mussels, oysters. Animal biodiversity expansion programs will provide biologically complete food, animal feed, the demand for which is not limited today. In recent years, there has been a trend toward the development of highly profitable large agroindustrial associations with a closed production cycle (from the formation of the feed base to the processing of meat). They are gradually absorbing their direct competitors in small- and medium-sized businesses, devastating entire villages, catastrophic aging of labor resources, and the outflow of young people from rural areas to large cities. From the beginning of the 20th century about 75% of plant genetic diversity has been lost because of the fact that all over the world farmers have abandoned different local varieties and breeds in favor of genetically identical high-yielding varieties. Modern genetically modified animals cannot exist and reproduce on their own in the wild. By regular selection, the number of animals is constantly decreasing, there are farm animals, which give the maximum increase in live weight in the shortest possible time. Therefore, it is promising for a Ukrainian farmer to start a business to preserve and create wildlife reserves (horses, sheep, buffaloes, pigs, etc.). Countries, such as the United Kingdom, France, New Zealand, and Australia, have public and community programs to create new and conserve existing wildlife. From such keeping of animals for the sake of the future genetic resource, it is possible to plan profit in the form of its combination with "green tourism." Today, there are many crowdfunding startups—platforms, venture, and environmental funds that are offering interesting business projects, it is possible to get funding from international organizations for the protection of animals and the environment. In addition, animal biodiversity reduction processes can stop government subsidies on a permanent basis for small livestock complexes. For example, in the EU, there is a system of subsidies of 20% to 80% of the cost of production. The epicenter of state support needs to be modified in favor of maintaining the profitability and efficiency of small-scale and organic production, rural infrastructure development, and green tourism. The loss of biodiversity and knowledge systems for multicultural agriculture increases the risks to farming systems in the context of global natural and economic change, including climate change [3].

11.3   International Federation of Organic Agriculture Movements (IFOAM) and Significance

The International Federation of Organic Agriculture Movements, which is the only institution with bountiful status to speak with authority on issues, such as technical norms for organic agricultural products, states eight positive targets, ranking from high-quality products to support genetic variety and income provision for agricultural workers; a current, innovative method that has positive effects on global surrounding and social challenges. It is the title of a vision and overall strategic plan of the global organic movement for further growth and sustainability to increase the positive influence on the whole world.

Organic farmers do not just automatically attempt to decrease their use altogether. In fact, they can compensate for the decrease by increasing the use of other means of production. For example, mechanical methods of weed control vice using herbicides require extra machinery and fuel, as does the use of dung instead of concentrated manuring. Some farmers purchase organic fertilizers, which usually cost more than the same nutrients in inorganic form. If professional workers need to be hired to control nonchemical pests, then one type of expense (material) is replaced by another (maintenance).

According to the environmental criteria, the use of professionals is undoubtedly preferable, but economically, it can be disadvantageous.

Other systems would be effective in increasing soil productivity, reducing erosion, conserving wildlife, and increasing farmers' income without using materials regarded undesirable. And this monoculture structure certainly does not fit the definition of "ecological" because it hardly represents the compound ecological structure it has replaced.

Sometimes, at agricultural enterprises, the fertilizer system changes only because, by chance, there is a source of organic waste in the neighborhood that can replace purchased inorganic fertilizers. Such production fulfills one requirement of stability: it does not use substance that is nonrenewable and potentially hazardous to the surroundings. Naturally, the waste must be used in an environmentally sound style, otherwise another problem arises. However, this is not a low-cost system, only the kind of the production factor has varied, so it is also attackable to external destruction, just like the system, depending on the production factors from nonrenewable resources. It is just that one source of vulnerability is replaced by another because the source of waste can be closed.

There is an opinion that in sustainable agricultural production, agrarians themselves can transfer some production systems to others without any significant changes in the economical, political, and social situation. In other discussions, socioeconomic change is given more weight than the technical distinction between sustainable and traditional agricultural practices. These transformations include the link between agricultural production and industry; more direct links between manufacturers and consumers; greater regional food security; the advantage of family farms over agricultural enterprises and cooperatives; a policy of rewarding resource conservation; higher employment in agriculture; equitable distribution of income among various groups of producers and between present and future generations, as well as social and economic revitalization of farmers.

The connection between such reorganizations and changes in specific practices can be carried out in any direction, that is, each socioeconomic environment can become both a reason for the adoption of ways of sustainable agricultural production on a large scale, and a consequence of such a decision. For example, the extensive employ of chemical insect control methods, as sometimes argued by advocates of disjunctive farming, is the result of the dominance of the agrochemical industry community, which is believed to influence producer solutions and investigate priorities. Therefore, this dominance must be decreased before manufacturers become receptive to alternative solutions. On the other hand, if manufacturers resolve to use methods with less of chemicals because they anticipate that the use of certain agrochemicals will cause problems (for example, high cost, fear of loans or health risks), then this transition will reduce the impact of the agrochemical industry.

The next important question, which still remains open, concerns the scale of sustainable agricultural production. Its proponents generally find it more suitable for small to medium sized production. However, empirical evidence for such an opinion is usually lacking, and theoretical arguments are dubious. Of course, the trend toward the enlargement of agricultural production has historically been associated with specialization, while sustainable agricultural production prefers diversification over specialization. In addition, sustainable agricultural production may require more management attention. On the one hand, in a small production, the farmer can take more care of each field or each animal, on the other hand, large farms can rather afford to recruit specialists or have better equipment and machinery.

The relationship between the production method and the farmer's personal assessments is also unclear. Some writers do not see any communication here. Modern growers can, if they wish, use sustainable agricultural production practices without thinking about motives, valuations, or broader categories if an alternative solution is more attractive in terms of economic, health, or safety benefits. According to another point of view, agrarians are worried not only with short-term incomes, but also with the well-being of future generations, the rural societies in which they live and work, the natural surroundings, landscape aesthetics, and the resources that are spent in agriculture, which would be a hallmark of sustainable agricultural production.

11.4   Low Cost versus Sustainable Agricultural Production

If renters could be persuaded to care more about surrounding values, they would choose environmentally healthier ways. And if they can be assured to assume these practices, whatever the causes (eg, economic or stricter surrounding legislation), the result will be a system that better protects environmental values. A possible objection to the last point is that changes due to purely economic grounds can be short-lived if economic conditions are variable. If production uses less pesticides because the prices of the crops grown were too low to justify the costs, this surrounding friendly modification may not be implemented the next time the prices of crops rise. The growing interest in low-cost agricultural production is closely aligned with the decline in production. This points to a major inequality between "low-cost" and "sustainable" treatments: even though both can have long-term effects from decreasing pesticide use, the latter does so for more ephemeral reasons than the temporary wastefulness of high-dose pesticide use when agricultural prices cultures are at a low level. The distinction between the two concepts can perhaps be eliminated by merging them into one term "lower cost/sustainable agricultural production."

It seems necessary to make a distinction between the two concepts ("sustainable" and "low-cost" agricultural production). Although the authors of sustainable agricultural production may give preference to an emphasis on long-term factors, short-term economic factors cannot be overlooked: if the system does not provide sufficient income, allows the agrarian to run his business, then it is unstable. Ideally, with suitable crop revolution, crop varieties and tillage techniques, an agrarian who, for ecological reasons, does not want to apply pesticides, will not be tempted to use them, even if crop values rise again.

In the literature on sustainable agricultural production, there are different opinions about the qualitative inequalities between the main processes underlying stable and traditional production chains. According to one point of view, both types of systems can be described and analyzed using the same concepts. They differ only in the specific conditions that are created with unequal farming practices. Another point of view is that complex interactions between the components of a sustainable agricultural production system give rise to new phenomena that were not overseen with the simpler structure of the traditional scheme. Each of these views has a right to exist, and they often differ in what is emphasized.

It is wrong to say that sustainable and traditional agricultural production is guided by opposite principles and mechanisms—"natural" against to "chemical"—despite the different role of these mechanisms in the two accesses.

This issue has significant implications for explore policy on the renovation of agricultural enterprises. It is possible that the methods approved in them are suitable for sustainable agricultural production, but new approaches and ways are needed with significant inequalities in the main theories and concepts. Agroecology, which is gaining increasing attention in relation to sustainable agricultural production, is an effort to introduce new theoretical fundamentals for the analysis of agricultural systems. However, this area is not yet fully formed and main agroecological research does not yet receive hard support from most agricultural producers.

The question of whether strategic economic changes and a different scientific point of view require recognition of sustainable agricultural production, alternately, raises the question - can existing scientific and educational foundations properly process this system. Long before the concept of "sustainable agricultural production" came into use, methods with similar purposes were already gaining attention. Samples include integrated pest management to decrease pesticide application, improved storage and application of manure to maximize nutrient utilization, and minimum tillage schemes to prevent soil erosion. At one time, many agricultural institutions began to implement programs in the direction of "sustainable agricultural production." Such programs explicitly recognize the impact of the sustainable agricultural production movement and point out the interest of the mainstream agricultural production in the application of its ideas.

Promoting sustainable agricultural production ideas means challenging certain strategic economic, social and political restraints that mainstream agricultural foundations cannot accept (Figure 11.2).

Since several concepts were formed under the name "ecological agricultural production," agricultural production, which is oriented towards the traditional direction, was able to choose the most "safe" option, process it, making it acceptable for bureaucratic bodies, and appropriate it for itself.

Global surrounding problems associated with climate variation, loss of biological variety, desertification and other negative acts for the surrounding, increasing environmental loss from natural disasters and man-made disasters, contamination of atmosphere, surface and ground waters, as well as the marine environment, affect the interests of each state.

The strategic goal of the state environmental policy is the conservation of natural systems, maintaining their continuity and life-supporting functions for the stable development of community, integration of environmental policy of underdeveloped countries to the socioeconomic global

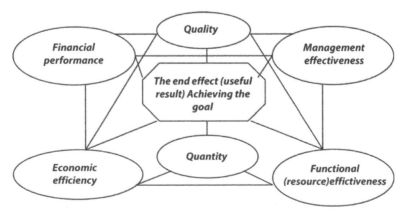

Figure 11.2 The system of internal interdependence and subordination of economic categories of research of the renovation of the economic mechanisms of the activity of animal husbandry enterprises.

development of the system, refining the quality of life, refining the health of the population and the demographic context, ensuring surrounding safety.

The relationship between institutions is traditional, and supporters of sustainable agricultural production will no doubt be clarified later. The saddest result will be the transformation of the concept of "sustainable agricultural production" into some other, official one, used in those cases when it is necessary to show an imitation of innovations. But perhaps the trunk will be receptive to the new ideas behind the title "Alternative" agricultural production. In such a case, it is necessary to proceed to challenge the foundations and force them to move further than their usual momentum can allow. On the other hand, if the spirit of sustainable agricultural production is achieved as an overall strategy, rather than just specific details of the system, the distinction between the terms "alternative" and "traditional" agricultural production can eventually be neglected as unnecessary.

Sustainable agricultural production requires more organization than traditional, since in the conduct of sustainable agricultural production, technological control of the conditions for growing crops replaces knowledge. For example, in traditional agricultural production, animal disease can be fully controlled by trivial prophylactic antibiotic management, while in sustainable agricultural production, the aim is to prevent disease by decreasing the stresses that make animals more sensitive to disease and keeping them in conditions, which are less friendly to the spread of disease. In this case, the manufacturer must carefully observe the animals in order to start treatment on time, if necessary.

Sustainable agricultural production is often described as the adaptation of general principles to the specific conditions of a particular enterprise, that is, it is characterized by the need for flexibility in approaches.

If sustainable agricultural production poses great challenges to management at the present time, this problem may become less acute after farmers gain the appropriate experience, as well as government bodies and consulting services pay more attention to them. Complaints about the lack of reliable information sources are constantly heard from farmers engaged in organic agricultural production, and there is no doubt that this also applies to other approaches to sustainable agricultural production. Ultimately, the perception of the complexity of management in sustainable agricultural production may disappear and what now seems incredibly difficult will become more achievable.

Sustainable agricultural production is a synthesis of concepts that have arisen from different origins based on different motivations. It is constantly being modified and improved in response to the existing economic pressures on agricultural producers and the growing environmental concerns associated with agricultural activities. Although its roots go deep into the depths, sustainable agricultural production as a clearly articulated concept is still young compared to what would be required to study all its branches and fully understand its basic principles.

Of course, a lot of investigations and development is needed to use the concept of stable agricultural production to specific situations. To reach its full potential, sustainable agriculture needs more intellectual courage. Fundamental principles need to be evolved and improved [4].

Global surrounding problems associated with climate varieties, loss of biological variety, desertification, and other negative acts for the surrounding, increasing environmental damage from natural disasters and man-made disasters, pollution of atmosphere, surface and ground waters, as well as the marine environment, indicate the need for reengineering agrarian economy. The environment in cities and in the adjacent territories is subject to great negative effects, the origin of which are industrial, energy and transport plant, as well as capital construction facilities. In the event that food production lags behind the growing demand, the shortage will give an impetus to irreversible geopolitical, social and economic events. The increase in agricultural productivity in various regions will be a significant factor in the revitalization and diversification of global agricultural production, reducing regional poverty and increasing food security [5].

11.5   Change of Trends in Agriculture

This is a period of change in the agricultural sector. The Internet and satellite communications will give an impetus to the development of agricultural drones for full control over agro-reclamation methods of agriculture, fast and accurate spraying of crops, mapping of lands, identification, and fixation of all kinds of problems, thanks to sophisticated outfit. Facts collection will also be integrated with satellite crop control systems to constantly maintain the situation under control and collect comprehensive information for quick action when necessary. Genetic engineering will also play a very significant role. By using genome editing techniques to transfigure specific parts of plant genes, new plant modifications that are more productive and more resistant can be produced much faster than traditional crossing and hybridization methods permit.

Demographic problems, especially a sharp increase in the elderly, and the growing need for food and water, leading to a shortage of resources, require finding a way to unite, coordinate, account, compromise, planning for the long term for the heterogeneous interests of social strata, government structures, and business, moreover in the face of dynamic risks and pandemics.

The paradigm for obtaining maximum profit should be replaced by a global concept of environmental and food responsibility to minimize the risk of an unfavorable future for all mankind and develop a global strategy to increase the chances of positive developments.

Rural areas suffering from a lack of services and infrastructure are represented mainly by the elderly population, whose demands are fundamentally opposite to innovative and ambitious projects, youth start-ups. These disadvantages, among other things, are the reason for the unattractiveness of these regions and serve as a barrier to job creation.

Given the growing globalization of the economy and the massive demand for remote work and the dispersal of people, new model of agrarian valley—"Silicon" villages will be in great demand.

Modern information technologies will be concentrated there, which will make it possible to effectively establish remote work, implement projects on energy efficiency, and the use of renewable energy sources. Progress is carried out through the accumulation of business proposals, start-ups, projects, their research and transformation into business strategies, which, after being tested and confirmed by the market, are entitled to life, growth and development. Diverse foundations, centers and other financially and intellectually secured structures provide potential innovative businessmen with their skills, one-to-one business coaching, industry connections and funding to identify and connect with key customers, test the market and transform an idea, dream or MVP or a service from a commercial offer to a highly profitable business.

The agrarian market today has a shortage of young, independent, creative and market-aware entrepreneurs with the necessary multidisciplinary skills to address not only key challenges in the agrifood sector, but also to make an important contribution to the safety and security of the global food system. The main factor of sustainable agrarian economic development can only be the growth of a person's intellectual potential, including his moral and cultural properties in conjunction with scientific and technological innovations, the use of which significantly changes the volume and quality of production and consumption. Modern transformational processes in the socioeconomic and political spheres of development cause an overestimation of the human factor, actualizing the problem of preventive human resource management. The active direction of individual intelligence, the potential of employees for the development of a particular object or socioeconomic system with which a person interacts, forms the basis for the processes of intellectualization of their operational and management activities in market conditions. That is, the process of transition to a new management model is traced, the main elements of which are personal and team intelligence, the transfer of knowledge and intellectual capital, and most importantly, the development of intellectual activity, the content of which is to create the necessary conditions for team members to realize their natural and professional potential.

Corporate Social Responsibility in a contemporary understanding is a pillar of Corporate Sustainability. It could regard as the corporate response to sustainable development represented by strategies and practices that address the key issues for the world's sustainable development [6]. Today, the most important element of cooperation is social capital, which combines trust, team spirit and willingness to cooperate in the implementation of innovations. Another potential innovation could be the development of a strategy for retirement migration to rural areas and "green" tourism, social agriculture (provision of services for educational or therapeutic purposes). These innovations are modern trends and will be able to improve the investment climate, together with political, socioeconomic, innovative, legal and territorial-climatic factors, to prove the effectiveness of investment and the attractiveness of the agricultural region.

A strategy for the production, distribution, and consumption of food for the entire population of the world is required, which must have the potential to create productive, nutritious, safe, sustainable, and transparent food systems that promote to the success of the global sustainable evolution goals. In particular, technological innovation, opening up land markets in developing countries, investment, and tax incentives projects are projected to play a significant role in transforming our feed strategy and reaching global food security for hereafter generations.

State structures should act as a guarantor of food, social, economic, and environmental security, and promote sustainability and coordination between participants in the agricultural market. Key concepts should always be pretested during a pilot project, which will allow to find new opportunities for the development of agricultural areas and the agrifood sector, taking into account the risks associated with climate, ecology, lack of land, water and energy for food production.

Relatively, with the growth of world food prices, we will receive large-scale investment income, which will be selectively distributed and associated with institutional changes in regional and global food markets, a significant redistribution of markets for imports and exports of certain products. For each agrarian country, the priority is to develop and implement urgently a full chain of changes in public policy and in the policy of all agricultural companies to form its own concept of production of genetically modified and organic products, to update the means of production in conformity with current environmental trends, growing influence of producers and consumers on the formation of renovation mechanisms of the agrinutrition segment. The development of a system of risk insurance and tax benefits for ecologically oriented farms, which pay attention to the continuous improvement of the surrounding biosystem, use of alternative energy sources and production of food suitable for children, can improve the situation. Thus, promising areas for intensification of agricultural enterprises are to build their own strategy of the national producer in the context of the global resource-innovative model of environmental and social responsibility.

References

1. *The future of food and agriculture. Trends and challenges*, FAO. 2017. The future of food and agriculture – Trends and challenges. Rome, p. 11, http://www.fao.org/3/i6583e/i6583e.pdf.
2. Gryshova, I., Kyzym, M., Hubarieva, I., Khaustova, V., Livinskyi, A., Koroshenko, M., Assessment of the EU and Ukraine Economic Security and Its Influence on Their Sustainable Economic Development. *Sustainability*, 12, 7692, 2020, https://doi.org/10.3390/su12187692.
3. Zamlynskyi, V., Structural transformations of the livestock industry in the context of global food security. Ekonomika APK "The Economy of Agro-Industrial Complex". *International Scientific and Production Journal*, 4, 22–28, 2019. https://doi.org/10.32317/2221-1055.201904022
4. Zamlynskyi, V., Renovation mechanisms of intensification of enterprises of the agro industrial sector / Problems and prospects of economics and management. *Sci. J.*, 1, 17, 50–59, 2019, Retrieved from https://ppcu.stu.cn.ua/articles/1561385745302.pdf.
5. Zamlynskyi, V.A., Implementation of economic security of Ukraine in the context of application of indicators of institutional provision of agricultural sector / V.A. Zamlynskyi, S.O. Kushnir // Economics: time realities. *Sci. J.*, 1, 41, 25–34, 2019, Retrieved from https://economics.opu.ua/files/archive/2019/N about 1 / 25.pdf. DOI: 10.5281 / zenodo.3387288.
6. Yevdokimova, M., Zamlynskyi, V., Minakova, S., Biriuk, O., Ilina, O., Evolution of corporate social responsibility applied to the concept of sustainable development. *J. Secur. Sustain. Issues*, 8, 3, 473–480, 2019, https://doi.org/10.9770/jssi.2019.8.3(14).

12

Role of Agritech Start-Ups in Supply Chain—An Organizational Approach of Ninjacart

D. Rafi[1*] and Md. Mubeena[2]

[1]*Department of Agricultural and Rural Management, TNAU,
Coimbatore, India*
[2]*Department of Agricultural Extension, Business Manager,
ABI, ICAR–NRCM, Hyderabad, India*

Abstract

Supply Chain Management is the method of strategic maintenance of procurement, storage of products, material movement through the organization, and its distribution channel that directs in getting maximum profits through cost-reductive fulfilment of orders. In simple, supply chain acts as a bridge between demand and supply. Start-ups are bringing new shape to an agrisupply chain by using new-age technologies like artificial intelligence, machine learning, IOT, and block-chain management where they directly procure from farm gates and supply retailers. Ninjacart's supply network runs with its own inbuilt enterprise resource planning. Data are the spinal cord to their system for forecasting real-time data over the supply chain. It is made more readable and accessible for a whole organization through do-it-yourself (DIY) query systems. Ninjacart entered into the market and altered the existing supply chain by means of their approach at the farm level. Ninjacart's approach of dealing with farmers directly has reduced the middlemen involvement number in the marketing channel. Ninjacart procurement made farmers benefit in getting the remunerative price, reducing the cost of handling of the product, and so on. During pandemic situations, this type of supply chain mechanism made farmers get a sustained price for their produce. Furthermore, Ninjacart can concentrate on adding other features like the end-to-end food footprint traceability, live price-demand forecasting, and so on. Like Ninjacart, many other start-ups are

---

Corresponding author: rafilucky34@gmail.com

Roheet Bhatnagar, Nitin Kumar Tripathi, Nitu Bhatnagar and Chandan Kumar Panda (eds.)
The Digital Agricultural Revolution: Innovations and Challenges in Agriculture through Technology Disruptions, (289–300) © 2022 Scrivener Publishing LLC

successful in their own way but yet there exist many gaps and opportunities, which are to be the focus. It is essential for supply chain network pioneers to comprehend the difficulties and position themselves well to defeat them.

Keywords: Supply chain, procurement, traceability, machine learning, agritechs, start-ups

12.1   Introduction

Supply Chain Management is the method of strategic maintenance of procurement, storage of products, material movement through the organization and its distribution channel that directs in getting maximum profits through cost reductive fulfilment of orders. In simple supply chain acts as a bridge between demand and supply [1].

With the advent of new technologies in agriculture, all traditional techniques and methods are replaced with modern methods. Supply chain is not an exception for this change in adopting new methods during flow of materials in market.

Agrisupply chain management (ASCM) of India is one of the most fragmented ones in the world. This fragmented supply chain results in 25-30 % wastage of food grains, vegetables & fruits before they reach to the market, where end consumers should bear the wastage costs [9, 10].

The Indian Agriculture Output supply chain (AOSCM) is facing with challenges stemming from the inherent issues like the inefficient price signals, limited reach of mandis, too many intermediaries, information asymmetry, lack of effective distribution channel and high wastage of fruits & vegetables [7, 8].

E-commerce involvement, operational efficiency and emergence of lean supply chain concept have some positive trend in Indian supply chain, however India's economy is entering a time of vulnerability. It is essential for supply chain network pioneers to comprehend the difficulties and position themselves well to defeat them [1].

Start-ups are bringing new shape to agrisupply chain by using new-age technologies like artificial intelligence, machine learning, IoT and blockchain management where they directly procure from farm gates and supplying to retailers. By means of this business to business (B2B) model some start-ups are trying to enter into the market for reducing or eliminating middlemen's compare to the traditional model [2].

To understand the supply chain management with the entry of start-ups, Ninjacart is taken as an example to analyse how it operates in the market.

NINJACART is India's largest application based Business 2 Business fresh produce network platform as shown in Figure 12.1 founded in 2015 [15, 16].

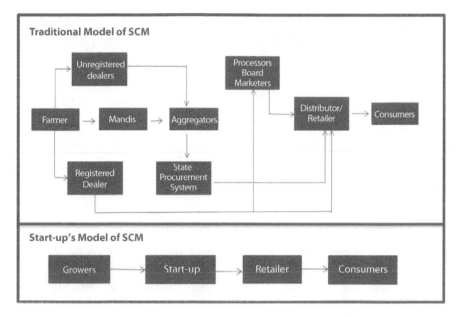

Figure 12.1 Traditional model of SCM vs Start-up model of SCM.

The platform leverages new techniques and innovations to settle the store related issues in supply chain by linking farmers directly with retailers in eliminating middlemen & offering a remunerative price for both farmers and retailers compare to mandi price with consistent demand to supply within 12 hours, reducing postharvest wastage by 20% to 30% [3, 4, 11, 12, 19].

12.2   How Does the Chain Work?

Here, the supply chain is very simple and is directly linked to the farmers and is thereby linked to retailers in reaching the product to consumer as shown in Figure 12.2. The entire chain is divided into two parts. They are

    1. Preprocurement stage
       a. Forecasting
       b. Pricing
    3. Postprocurement stage
       a. Collection center
       b. Fulfilment center
       c. Distribution center

Source: www.ninjacart.in/blog
Figure 12.2 Flow chart showing SCM of Ninjacart.

Source:/www.ninjacart.in/blog
Figure 12.3 Flowchart showing operations involved in preprocurement stage.

The detail operations of these two chains are as follows

1. **Preprocurement stage:** This stage of supply chain deals with forecasting of demand, planning about purchase of material and analysing the price (Figure 12.3).

Forecasting
Ninjacart inventory network begins with week by week determining, where the outreach group distributes the client development plan for the week. With help of historic demand data, market conditions adding analytics to it help them to draft weekly sales and procurement forecast at stock keeping unit level [6, 13, 14, 17].

Once the forecast is done, the procurement group provides week to week indent to the farmers based on the farm harvest calendar. With leveraged deep machine learning, they forecast at 97% accuracy, helping them to reduce overall wastage by 4% as compared with 25% in the traditional supply chain.

"**Forecasting** is very crucial in the agriculture sector where it depends on a lot of external factors. But its unique value-adding factor for Ninjacart compared with others helps them to draft purchase plan and help to reduce wastage by making supply chain much more efficiently"

Pricing

Before 2 days of actual delivery date based on current market conditions and price fluctuations, the procurement team again revises before issuing final indent to farmers to reconfirm it once again.

Based on the indent, the farmers harvest the produce and bring it to collection centers. Here, the produce goes to quality checking in front of a producer to maintain transparency. Immediately, the farmer gets a receipt, and the amount gets credited to the farmer's account within 24 hours of time compared with 6 to 10 days in a traditional model.

"**Market Intelligence** and **Machine Learning** algorithms are being used to predict market prices. The farmer knows the price before harvesting which helps them to harvest & sell their produce"

2. **Postprocurement stage:** This stage of supply chain deals with storage of collected produce procured from farmers and distribution of same produce to retailers at their respective outlets in Figure 12.4. The functioning mechanism of this stage is as follows

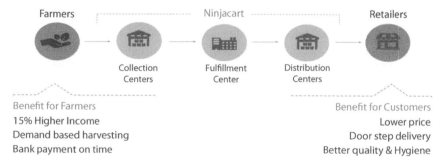

Source:/www.ninjacart.in/blog

Figure 12.4 Flowchart showing operations involved in postprocurement stage.

Collection centres (CC) to Fulfilment centres (FC)

It's the centre where produce is procured from farmers which are located near to their respective villages. Here items are graded, weighed, batched and dispatched to their fulfilment centres (FC).

Optimization:

Depending on how much quantity of produce should procure from Collection Centre (CC), the type of vehicle, dispatch and arrivals slots are fixed by their **optimal route plan** using their algorithms.

Fulfilment centres (FC) to Distribution Centre (DC)

FC's delivers the products from fulfilment centre to distribution centres. Here an arbitrary examination of the nature of produce in every vehicle will be done and accordingly bunching the things and afterward dispatching activities goes on to DC's.

Optimization:

They take the **distance between the FC's and DC's** into account to plan out each route with maximum capacity at a minimal cost.

Distribution centres (DC's) to Retailer

Once items reach DC's, sorting the products & batching will be done according to customers' requirements.

Optimization:

Using extremely **sophisticated software tools** they set up everyday route map, based on the maximum capacity of each vehicle, the locations to delivery, and the cost that incurs to service each customer will be added to run their optimized route plan every day.

Retailers to Distribution centres (DC)

Mobile phones are issued to drivers for live tracking and managing the delivery system. Drivers drop the item at the shops in transit back they collect empty containers and money from the clients and then they deposit the same in distribution centres.

Optimization: Operations were **orchestrated by pre-set conditions** which minimizing them on need & dependency from other team members. And helping them to complete the receiving & dispatch process **<15 min.**

Ninjacart technological innovation wheel contains:

> ➤ Ninjacart's supply network runs with its own inbuilt enterprise resource planning. Data are the spinal cord to their system for forecasting real-time data over the supply chain. It is made more readable and accessible for whole organisation through DIY query systems [5].
> ➤ They highly invested in machine learning to improve forecasting, pricing, and crop recommendations and also to bring traceability into the chain, which helps consumers to trace fresh produce back to its origin.
> ➤ The platform leverages radio frequency identification (RFID) technology to track deliveries and their app provides the shortest routes to the truck drivers transporting the crates.
> ➤ There is no manual convention for segregation; everything is backed by an application and technology is foolproof. *For example*, tamper-proof tags are used to crates so there is will be no pilferage. The retailer gets access to open crates once he types OTP given by the app.
> ➤ Dolly carts are being used to unload and load the containers faster than the traditional lift-and-place.

Impact of Ninjacart in market:

100% traceable food	• **RFID** powered supply chain, providing complete transparency
Tomorrow ready ERP	• Delivers with undisrupted supply chain by ensuring **zero paper**
Demand forecasting	• Use of **deep machine learning** by forecasting to 97% and reducing wastage by 4%
Price intelligence	• Farmer knows the price and demand **before harvesting**
Connected logistics	• **Route optimization** helps keeping **load factor at 92%** and delivers fresh produce at cost almost **1/3rd of the traditional supply chain**
Social Security	• **Cashless and instant payments** helping both farmers and retailers to put money in their hands on same day

Ninjacart vs Others

Ninjacart	Other players
Quick delivery of digitalised money to farmers without commission	They provide loans for buyers and working capital for producers
Several agriculture-related teaching schemes for farmers	Networks more cities and towns than Ninjacart.
100% traceability and 99% fulfilment rate	Provisions like electronic book-keeping, advance payments, and individual rating system
New technology adopted during supply chain	Still dependent on traditional models

Ninajacart Mind Map

The details regarding mind map of Ninjacart is shown in Figure 12.5.

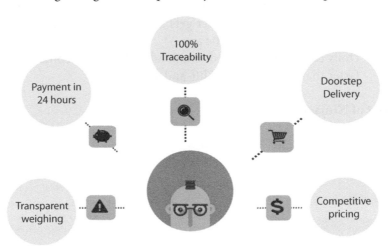

Source://www.ninjacart.in/blog/

Figure 12.5 Mind map of Ninjacart.

Unique Selling Propositions of Ninjacart:

➢ Always-connected logistics network
➢ Changing how retailers manage fruits and vegetables
➢ Changing how farmers look at selling their harvest
➢ Hygiene and quality by adopting a "one-touch" method

12.3   Undisrupted Chain of Ninjacart During Pandemic-19

Indian Agrisupply chain most fragmented type and pandemic hit chain worse. Where the mandis are been closed. As the Ninjacart model is sustainable they ran the cycle even country went shutdown [18, 20, 21]. They take an initiative of

"Harvest the Farms (HTF) of Ninjacart"

Ninjacart's initiative of harvest the farm identifies the excess and unharvested produce in their farmer network. Customers can purchase the items from **Ninjacart-Powered stores** that have access in Zomato, Swiggy, and Dunzo applications (Figure 12.6).

Figure 12.6 Harvest the Farms model of Ninjacart.

Future goal of sustainability
Future goal of sustainabile strategy of Ninjacart is shown in Figure 12.7.

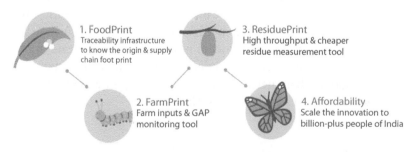

Figure 12.7 Flowchart showing future goal of sustainability of Ninjacart.

FoodPrint	by end-to-end food traceability
FarmPrint	by best practices monitoring tool to follow Good Agricultural Practice (GAP) and Lower maximum residue limit (MRL)

298 The Digital Agricultural Revolution

ResiduePrint	to check the residues of products procured by Ninjacart to ensure quality by residue measurement tool
Affordability	To make the chain more sustainable, reliable and affordable

12.4 Conclusion

There is a clear change in agrisupply chain after the introduction of tech-enabled farm to fork model in India. Taking the advantage of changes in supply chain, many players entered and changed the structure of market. Number of start-ups working and investments made by them became high in agrisupply chain. Recent agricultural reforms also added benefit to agritech players where the government has taken steps on eliminating the middlemen and increasing supply efficiency in the nation through one national-one market. With all these positive hope, Ninjacart entered into market and altered existing supply chain by means of their approach at farm level. Ninjacart approach of dealing farmers directly has reduced the middlemen involvement number in marketing channel. Ninjacart procurement made farmers benefited in getting the remunerative price, reducing cost of handling of product, and so on. During pandemic situations, this type of supply chain mechanism made farmers to get sustained price for their produce. Further Ninjacart can concentrate on adding other features like the end-to-end food footprint traceability, live price-demand forecasting, and so on. Like Ninjacart, many other start-ups are successful in their own way but yet there exist many gaps and opportunities, which are to be the focus. E-commerce involvement, operational efficiency, and emergence of lean supply chain concept have some positive trend in Indian supply chain, yet India's economy is entering a year of uncertainty. It is essential for supply chain network pioneers to comprehend the difficulties and position themselves well to defeat them.

References

1. Carter, C.R. and Washispack, S., Mapping the Path Forward for Sustainable Supply Chain Management: A Review of Reviews. *J. Bus. Logist.*, 39, 242–247, 2018.
2. Tebaldi, L., Bigliardi, B., Bottani, E., Sustainable Supply Chain and Innovation: A Review of the Recent Literature. *Sustainability*, 10, 3946, 2018.

3. Roy, V., Silvestre, B.S., Singh, S., Reactive and proactive pathways to sustainable apparel supply chains: Manufacturer's perspective on stakeholder salience and organizational learning toward responsible management. *Int. J. Prod. Econ.*, *227*, 107672, 2020.

4. Marshall, D., McCarthy, L., Heavey, C., McGrath, P., Environmental and social supply chain management sustainability practices: Construct development and measurement. *Prod. Plan. Control*, *26*, 673–690, 2015.

5. Mani, V., Gunasekaran, A., Papadopoulos, T., Hazen, B., Dubey, R., Supply chain social sustainability for developing nations: Evidence from India. *Resour. Conserv. Recycl.*, *111*, 42–52, 2016.

6. Ali, S.S., Kaur, R., Ersöz, F., Altaf, B., Basu, A., Weber, G.-W., Measuring carbon performance for sustainable green supply chain practices: A developing country scenario. *Cent. Eur. J. Oper. Res.*, *28*, 4, 1389–1416, 2020.

7. Tonelli, F., Evans, S., Taticchi, P., Industrial Sustainability: Challenges, perspectives, actions. *Int. J. Bus. Innov. Res.*, *7*, 143–163, 2013.

8. Roy, V., Schoenherr, T., Charan, P., The thematic landscape of literature in sustainable supply chain management (SSCM): A review of the principal facets in SSCM development. *Int. J. Oper. Prod. Manage.*, *38*, 1091–1124, 2018.

9. Kashmanian, R.M., Building a Sustainable Supply Chain: Key Elements. *Environ. Qual. Manage.*, *24*, 17–41, 2015.

10. Tseng, M.-L., Islam, M.S., Karia, N., Fauzi, F.A., Afrin, S., A literature review on green supply chain management: Trends and future challenges. *Resour. Conserv. Recycl.*, *141*, 145–162, 2019.

11. http://www.businessworld.in/article/NinjaCart-A-Disruptor-In-The-Food-Supply Chain/08-03-2019-167962/

12. http://www.berojgarengineers.com/ninjacart-case-study/

13. https://www.whizsky.com/2018/12/ninjacart-founder-funding-business-model-and-competitor/

14. https://medium.com/ninjacart/how-ninjacart-logistics-works-a16d3e4191b4

15. https://yourstory.com/2019/03/start-up-ninjacart-tech-enabled-supply-chain-farmers-yrlcfr3a40

16. https://www.quora.com/What-is-the-business-model-for-ninjacart

17. https://legalease.in/blog/ninjacart—revolutionizing-the-fresh-produce-supply-chain

18. https://medium.com/accel-india-insights/when-product-meets-market-how-ninjacart-reimagined-the-complex-sabzi-mandi-supply-chain-from-73a46f572147

19. https://corporatebytes.in/see-vegetables-saw-problem-sharath-loganathan-iim-grad-found-ninjacart-disprupt-wastage-vegetables-sabbzi-mandis/

20. https://www.thehindubusinessline.com/info-tech/were-investing-heavily-in-machine-learning-ninjacart-ceo/article33423097.ece

21. https://www.ninjacart.in/blog/harvest-the-farms-htf-initiative-by-ninjacart/

13

Institutional Model of Integrating Agricultural Production Technologies with Accounting and Information Systems

Nataliya Kantsedal[1]* and Oksana Ponomarenko[2]†

Department of Accounting and Economic Control, Poltava State Agrarian University, Poltava, Ukraine

Abstract

Institutional nature of using digital techniques in modern agrarian production was studied in this article. As a result, the approach illustrating the synergy of economic, ecological, and social effectiveness as a progressive direction of global economic system's development was worked out. The general model of a new informational paradigm of agricultural activities' organization based on the agility of knowledge and analytical data transferring into value information was determined.

The model of institutional interaction of information agents in agricultural production was constructed. The model's aim is based on the principle "lose less and feed more" and presupposes multiagent interaction of primary information sources (agricultural enterprises) with data bases of public unions (their activities are directed at solving the problems of agriculture and the environment) and government bodies, which make strategic managerial decisions based on macroeconomic indicators.

At the empirical stage, the design of the process of solving individual accounting problems or their complexes can be used in multiagent information systems (artificial intelligence and the Internet of Things) to obtain relevant information about specific objects of agricultural production.

*Corresponding author: nataliia.kantsedal@pdaa.edu.ua
†Corresponding author: oksana.ponomarenko@pdaa.edu.ua

Roheet Bhatnagar, Nitin Kumar Tripathi, Nitu Bhatnagar and Chandan Kumar Panda (eds.)
The Digital Agricultural Revolution: Innovations and Challenges in Agriculture through Technology Disruptions, (301–310) © 2022 Scrivener Publishing LLC

In particular, the accounting tasks of GMO objects were decided on the basis of open data, design documents and standard design solutions, which can be the basis for further development of functional application packages.

Keywords: Agricultural technology, information systems, databases, accounting, biosafety

13.1   Introduction

Globalization processes, institutional changes, and other social transformations stimulate the development of innovations and their introduction in all spheres of human activities.

Under increasing potential threats, connected with limited resources, using digital techniques is a key factor in solving social problems. Innovative character of the economy and agrarian production makes urgent the necessity of searching rational correlations of using resources based on the principles of careful attitude to the environment and at the same time, achieving the maximum economic effect from agricultural activities.

In the near future, science and scientists will play a decisive role in solving the issue of "digitalization of agriculture," which can significantly change agricultural business models; that is, farm structures, the value chain and stakeholder roles, networks and power relations, and governance [1].

Large-scale introduction of the Internet of things allows to create interconnections of computer networks with production capacities, which gives the chance of remote control of technological process, its visualization, and achievement of obvious economic effect [2]. Along with this, the negative aspects of excessive automation in agriculture should be mentioned, which result in distorting objective data that may contain information about real threats, negligent attitude to the environment, deliberately or unconsciously violating ethical standards of sustainable nature use.

The problem of the destructive impact of mechanization, electrification and computerization of production processes has become the subject of active scientific discussions around Industry 4.0 [3], and at the present stage, the search for ways to solve it is vital.

13.2   Research Methodology

The research methodology envisages: (1) profound analysis of informational systems' ability to aggregated using data about agricultural activities and their latest objects (the objects of synthetic biology, genetically modified organisms, ecological image of farm products); (2) revealing chains of responsibility, ways of interpreting and analyzing informational streams both at the level of agricultural subject and nationwide level; (3) the diagnostics of possibilities to overcome "the electronic information gap" of communicative connections of separate systems, generating financial and nonfinancial information about agricultural activities.

13.3 The General Model of a New Informational Paradigm of Agricultural Activities' Organization

In modern conditions, the activities of agricultural enterprises are increasingly reoriented to the economy of a new technological system—bioeconomy. At the same time, there is a strong emphasis on its main components, which are as follows: biopower, biotechnologies, organic farming, and organic production.

The state, households, and enterprises are the main subjects of bioeconomy. At the same time, the activity of enterprises has to be focused on receiving profit, taking into account the transformation of social consciousness, which involves the use of new production technologies based on biosecurity and economical resources using.

Therefore, the management values of agrarian production must be based not only on revolutionary introduction of innovations to increase production volumes but also the integration of technologies with accounting and information systems, which allow to determine the real parameters of economic operations and assess their consequences both locally and globally.

The managerial concept must be aimed at "digital leadership"—leadership in the area of digital economy, which envisages the ability to import and interpret strategically important indicators [4].

Developing countries are rapidly implementing innovative technological solutions combining modern ICTs with knowledge management skills and the ability to bridge the gap between research and the practical application of scientific knowledge. An example of this idea's implementation is Plantwise project, launched by CABI nonprofit organization. The goal of the project is to reduce crop losses by focusing on improving plant health information services throughout the developing world, where up to 80% of the world's food is produced [5].

"Society 5.0" strategy involves the careful regulation of information about socially important processes through high-tech developments, which provide a high degree of fusion between cyberspace and physical space [6].

Thus, the general model of the new informational paradigm of organizing agricultural activities must be based on the dexterity of transferring knowledge and analytical data into value information (Figure 13.1).

Information field in which the core "Big Data Databases of agricultural activities" is formed, is marked with dotted line ellipse in Figure 13.1, which should be understood as an integrated approach to the formation of digital information. Conditional values illustrating the synergy of economic, environmental and social efficiency of the presented model are marked separately: (A.1, investment; A.2, financial; B.1, operational; B.2, managerial).

At the stage of introducing innovative technologies of agricultural production, the investment effect (A.1) is more pronounced, which is stipulated by the desire to reduce costs and increase volumes of production. The financial effect (A.2) is achieved by taking into account the investment recoupment period. The operational effect (B.1) is determined as a result of systematizing and analyzing economic information about the operational activities of separate agricultural enterprises. Operational and managerial effects (B.1 and B.2) are presented in the left part of the model, as we emphasize on the prevalence of the environmental component of agricultural production (biosafety and economical use of resources).

Therefore, to achieve the maximum synergetic effect of ecological and economic systems, it is necessary to bridge the "digital gap" between automated production technologies and accounting information technologies.

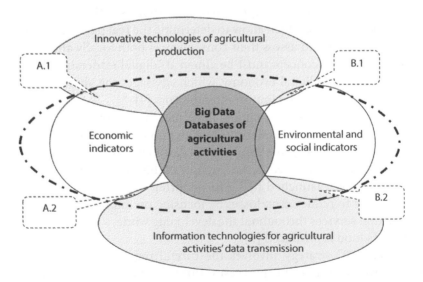

Figure 13.1 General model of the informational paradigm of organizing agricultural activities (ORIGINAL FIGURES).

The necessity of integrated approach to creating Big Data Databases of agricultural activities is connected with the growing human needs in food products, as well as solving the key problem of achieving food security in the XXI century—soil and water preservation [7].

Integrated digital innovations will require simultaneous institutional innovations [8] to communicate effectively with the key institutes involved in the creating, accumulating, transmitting, storing, and analyzing of information for decision making.

13.4 The Model of Institutional Interaction of Information Agents in Agricultural Production

In the agricultural sector of "Society 5.0," it is necessary to focus on controlling the negative effects of the activity guided by the principle "lose less and feed more". This requires coordinated interaction of objects-institutes to create relevant data on the real parameters of agricultural activities. For example, in 2011, the Organization for Economic Cooperation and Development (OECD) presented a methodological approach to monitoring indicators—Green Growth Indicators, which envisages combining the main characteristics of green growth with the basic principles of accounting and "pressure-state-response" sustainable development model [9].

According to the OECD measurement methodology, green growth indicators are divided into four groups:

1) indicators of ecological and resource efficiency;
2) indicators of economic and natural assets;
3) indicators of ecological quality of life;
4) economic opportunities and political instruments.

To improve the abovementioned indicators, the OECD member countries, as well as other countries, which support the conceptual bases of green growth policy, are synchronizing efforts to implement the system of environmental accounts in national statistical databases.

Scientific search for the rational ways of assessing and systematizing ecological indicators of agricultural activities is conducted proceeding from the motives of preserving the natural biodiversity and resumable ability of the corresponding landscape, and visualization of such indicators is achieved by using cartographic methods [10, 11]. This enables to obtain context-specific data, which can be integrated into Google Maps system aimed at identifying causal-consequence connections in agroecosystems. At the same time, researchers in this area pay attention to the fact that to promote organic farming the application of ecological markers on maps is insufficient [10]. Therefore, with the aim of further promoting the ideas of public visualization of local agroecosystems, it is necessary to take into account additional indicators, connected with using information technologies of accounting.

The necessity to strengthen the role of accounting is emphasized by some researchers in the field of agricultural sciences, in particular, those who deal with the problems of separate components' interaction in agroecosystems. For example, I. Keren in the study of pests' impact on crop yields stresses on the need of statistical accounting of direct and indirect interactions between many pests in the agroecosystem and further integration of this information into the model used for managerial decision making [12]. Thus, primary nonfinancial information can be further analyzed according to several scenarios to make the optimal decision, as well as to calculate the forecasted financial losses due to crop yields loss according to this or that scenario.

The creation of institutional space for generating data about agricultural entities' activities "is key to realizing the full potential of the emerging digital innovation agenda" [8].

Modern science already describes the positive experience of improving the accounting methodology to prove the value of innovations [13], so the conceptual basis of the model developed by us is the accounting system of an agrarian enterprise.

The model of institutional interaction of information agents in agricultural production is presented in Figure 13.2.

The model is directed toward achieving maximum synergic effect of ecological and economic systems. Practical value of the developed model consists in its ability to assess critically interconnected objects-institutes (analogues of real phenomena, processes, subjects), and on this basis, to set tasks to developers of specialized software products and digital information platforms.

The key to successful implementation of this model is synchronizing the capabilities of separate institutional units with the institutional enquiries of others. The ultimate goal of this model is to apply a multipurpose statistical methodology, which describes the interaction between the economy and environment. This will make it easy to import accounting data to new types of information systems, for example, such as the OECD, as the OECD uses accounting concepts, classifications, and principles.

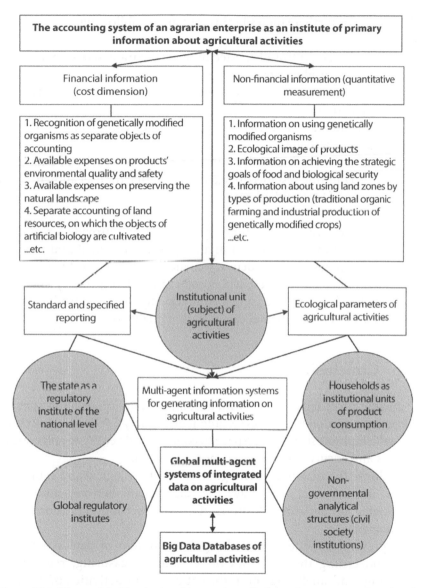

Figure 13.2 The model of institutional interaction of information agents in agricultural production (ORIGINAL FIGURES).

The practical implementation of this model requires in-depth multi-disciplinary researches, which means the cooperation of various scientific fields (accounting, economics, management, law, agronomy, ecology, IoT, and AI). This will allow to identify and solve the problems of the corresponding institutional subjects' interaction.

Prospects for further studies in this area are the following:

1) multilevel control of the technological parameters of agricultural production;
2) construction of self-optimizing chains of commodity circulation;
3) implementation of data "openness" policy concerning agricultural activities;
4) use of tools, which will ensure information security of data in accounting systems (for example, multifactor user authentication [14]), and others.

Thus, the convergence of technologies, which will provide a real connection between the physical and digital spheres in agricultural production, must be focused on in-depth analytical analysis. To do this, each agricultural entity has to present a certain amount of primary data, the use of which will enable to ensure a complex approach to introducing the methodology of environmental dimension of quality of life.

13.5   Conclusions

The integration of technologies with accounting and information systems is a priority direction for the development of "Society 5.0" strategy, according to which physical and cyberspace become a single entity to solve social problems and ensure sustainable economic growth.

To achieve the maximum synergetic effect of ecological and economic systems, it is necessary to bridge the "digital gap" between automated technologies of agricultural production and accounting information technologies.

The presented model is a well-regulated system of data synchronization concerning the processes of revealing, measuring, registering, accounting, and analyzing the information about activities of agricultural enterprise.

The practical implementation of the proposed model will facilitate the identification of new objects of accounting observation and the development of multi-disciplinary teams for complex multiagent systems of a new type, which meet the criteria of "Society 5.0."

References

1. Shepherd, M., Turner, J., Small, B., Wheeler, D., Priorities for science to overcome hurdles thwarting the full promise of the "digital agriculture" revolution. *J. Sci. Food Agric.*, 100, 14, 5083–5092, 2020, https://doi.org/10.1002/jsfa.9346.

2. Ershov, M., Ershov, A., Votinov, M., Selyakov, I., Industrial Internet of Things concept and energy efficient technologies implementation at a fish drying unit, in: *2019 IOP Conf. Series: Earth and Environmental Science*, vol. 403, 2019, https://doi.org/10.1088/1755-1315/403/1/012017.

3. Olsen, T. and Tomlin, B., Industry 4.0: Opportunities and Challenges for Operations Management. *Manuf. Serv. Oper. Manage.*, 22, 1, 113–122, 2019, https://doi.org/10.1287/msom.2019.0796.

4. Kankaew, K., The evolution of agribusiness management values from labor to brain mechanism that shape leadership style, in: *XIII International Scientific and Practical Conference "State and Prospects for the Development of Agribusiness – INTERAGROMASH 2020"*, vol. 175, 2020, https://doi.org/10.1051/e3sconf/202017513033.

5. Powell, A., CABI's innovative use of technology, data, and knowledge transfer to reduce crop losses in the developing world. *Food Energy Secur.*, 6, 3, 94–97, 2017, https://doi.org/10.1002/fes3.113.

6. *Society 5.0. Hitachi and The University of Tokyo Joint Research Laboratory*, Springer, Singapore, 2018, https://doi.org/10.1007/978-981-15-2989-4_9.

7. Delgado, J.A., Short, N.M., Roberts, D.P., Vandenberg, B., Big Data Analysis for Sustainable Agriculture on a Geospatial Cloud Framework. *Front. Sustain. Food Syst.*, 3, 54, 1–13, 2019, https://doi.org/10.3389/fsufs.2019.00054.

8. Steinke, J., Etten, J., Müller, A., Ortiz-Crespo, B., Gevel, J., Silvestri, S., Priebe, J., Tapping the full potential of the digital revolution for agricultural extension: an emerging innovation agenda. *Int. J. Agric. Sustain.*, 19, 5–6, 549–565, 2020, https://doi.org/10.1080/14735903.2020.1738754.

9. Green Growth Indicators 2014, in: *The OECD green growth measurement framework and indicators*, OECD Publishing, Paris, 2014, http://dx.doi.org/10.1787/9789264202030-4-en.

10. Petway, J., Lin, Y., Wunderlich, R., A place-based approach to agricultural nonmaterial intangible cultural ecosystem service values. *Sustainability*, 12, 2, 669, 2020, https://doi.org/10.3390/su12020699.

11. Nahuelhual, L., Carmona, A., Laterra, P., Barrena, J., Aguayo, M., A mapping approach to assess intangible cultural ecosystem services: The case of agriculture heritage in Southern Chile. *Ecol. Indic.*, 40, 90–101, 2014, May, http://dx.doi.org/10.1016/j.ecolind.2014.01.005.

12. Keren, I., Menalled, F., Weaver, D., Robison-Cox, J., Interacting Agricultural Pests and Their Effect on Crop Yield: Application of a Bayesian Decision

Theory Approach to the Joint Management of Bromus tectorum and Cephus cinctus. *PloS One*, 10, 2, 1–15, 2015, February, https://doi.org/10.1371/journal.pone.0118111.

13. Barman, E., Hall, M., Millo, Y., Demonstrating Value: How Entrepreneurs Design New Accounting Methods to Justify Innovations. *Eur. Accounting Rev.*, 30, 4, 675–704, 2020, https://doi.org/10.1080/09638180.2020.1770113.

14. Pysarenko, V., Dorohan-Pysarenko, L., Kantsedal, N., Application of new data formats for electronic document management in government bodies, in: *IOP Conference Series: Materials Science and Engineering*, vol. 568, pp. 1–6, 2019, https://doi.org/10.1088/1757-899X/568/1/012102.

14

Relevance of Artificial Intelligence in Wastewater Management

Poornima Ramesh[1], Kathirvel Suganya[1]*, T. Uma Maheswari[2],
S. Paul Sebastian[3] and K. Sara Parwin Banu[1]

[1]Department of Environmental Sciences, Tamil Nadu Agricultural University,
Coimbatore, India
[2]Department of Food Science and Nutrition, Community Science College
and Research Institute, Madurai, India
[3]Department of Soil Science and Agricultural Chemistry, Anbil Dharmalingam
Agricultural College and Research Institute, Trichy, India

Abstract

Increasing water demand for utilization in various sectors throughout the world poses rapid technological interventions in recycling and reuse of wastewater for ensuring environmental quality. As regulations for the water treatment process are tightening up, water uses must constantly look for new technologies that enhance process control for the reduction of chemical, biological, and other pollutants. Every process is controlled by a complex nonlinear relationship among various physical, chemical, and operating parameters in the water processing industry. Historically, these relationships were attempted by fitting databases into mathematical formulas. Simultaneous adjustments in over one or two main process parameters were not commonly taken into account and often fail if they are extended to full-scale systems. The current process control in the water treatment sector is not based on a model—it relies on the expertise of plant operators—but rather on a collection of loosely defined heuristics on combination with the expert. Plant operators need instruments to select suitable operating conditions to achieve the ideal effluent quality based on instantaneous influential water quality to improve treatment procedures.

Artificial intelligence (AI) techniques have recently exhibited promising results in monitoring through the latest advancement of computer systems. In the water

*Corresponding author: suganya.k@tnau.ac.in; ksuganyaphd@gmail.com

Roheet Bhatnagar, Nitin Kumar Tripathi, Nitu Bhatnagar and Chandan Kumar Panda (eds.)
The Digital Agricultural Revolution: Innovations and Challenges in Agriculture through
Technology Disruptions, (311–332) © 2022 Scrivener Publishing LLC

sector, a range of problems associated to the structuring of data and intelligent water services are present, by which AI has tremendous potential if these problems were tackled. The AI tools, artificial neural networks (ANNs), and genetic algorithms (GA) in particular, have been used extensively in water treatment for multipurpose applications. There are few applications in which water treatment procedures and operational condition optimization are modeled. The ANN approach focuses on the discovery, among process input and output, of repeatable, identifiable, and predictable patterns. Models of ANN learn from previous operational data and override the models of real contacts of the microphone. The ANN modeling approach does not need to explain how processes take place in micro or macro settings, only awareness of important process-controllable variables. This function is a valuable process choice in the ANN modeling approach. The ANN modeling method represents an important alternative for process modeling in the drinking water production industry. This paper provides a comprehensive analysis of four aspects of artificial intelligence implementation in treatment of wastewater: management, technology, reuse, and economics of wastewater. Lastly, we would provide an insight into the future prospects of the use of artificial intelligence in the treatment of wastewater, which, in complex practical applications, simultaneously address pollutants removal, water reuse and management, and cost-efficient challenges.

Keywords: Artificial intelligence (AI), artificial neural network (ANN), wastewater treatment, pollutant removal

14.1   Introduction

A number of effective and realistic tools have been evolved by artificial intelligence, to unravel complex glitches in real-world applications in diverse fields. Owing to its easy use, high operation speed and reasonable precision, many scientists have been using AI without the need to consider physical problems [1]. Artificial intelligence technology is employed in medicinal illness prevention, diagnosis, and treatment [2, 3]. Artificial intelligence is becoming increasingly important in the financial sector, and AI is also implemented for predicting financial flow [4]. It is used for risk control in the supply chain to measure risks and establish contingency measures to fortify against large changes in the supply chain and to prevent major loss [5]. The use of AI in various technical disciplines is because of its ability to resolve practical challenges, including wastewater treatment [6, 7], improving water quality [1, 8], modeling the quality of river water [9], and recycling the water resources [10]. The most significant step in reducing aqueous pollutants and promoting the safety of water is the disposal of wastewater. The characteristics of wastewater is extremely complex, whereas the quantity of contaminant and wastewater treatment plants vary significantly [11]. Wastewater treatment has many chemical, physical, and microbiological influences affecting a dynamic treatment mechanism. Stochastic disturbances and influential fluctuations often enable operators to perform effective system operational controls [12, 13]. In wastewater treatment facilities, the complexity of natural events, anthropogenic behaviors, and processes leads to several uneasiness. Furthermore, the volume, consistency, and efficiency of wastewater disposal fluctuates predictably [11]. More limits on emissions and new energy conservation and resource recovery rules face modern wastewater treatment plants [14, 15]. To solve these challenges, scientists have sought to use AI technologies to WWTPs. This chapter, in brief, describes the application of AI in treatment of wastewater and future research directions.

14.2   Digital Technologies and Industrial Sustainability

Digital systems will radically increase the productivity of non-working resources in an unreached way. It can increase the utilization of resources by benchmarking analytics, where vast amounts of data from a plant can be utilized to find "golden moments" where a single product can be produced in a different period for nearly half of the CO_2 emissions or the energy or of the same product produced, or to use the same data to compare it anonymously between plants. The implementation of artificial intelligence (AI), IIoT, augmented reality (AR), and data analysis will achieve increased resource efficiency. To promote efficiency, AR is necessary because it allows engineers to see in the factory in real-time power, water, and waste flows. This encourages them to increase their conventional efficiency abilities to an expense that has only historically been seen in tables. Augmented reality technologies will ultimately lead to better tools for plant design. A major decrease in overall production costs, including grid benefits and the development of new businesses that export these brilliant innovations is the scope of the benefits of the use of emerging technology to make previously unknown or complicated circumstances clear [16].

The forecast is for supply chains, from material availability because of geopolitics to flooding, droughts, and power shortages, to be more widespread and seriously disrupted. One approach to reduce such disturbances is to demand fewer resources per unit of production value added, and this is achieved by a push toward resource efficiency. In another technique, many industries use sensors to detect short-term grid strains and employ IIoT technologies to adapt energy consumption to short-runs by manufacturing machinery (like heating systemsor refrigerators). This has negligible or no impact on the operating process yet serve the grid to manage supply and demand of electricity. The utility is a sort of demand flexibility [17], which is a part of the transformation into an intelligent energy grid. The next step in the development of sustainability in modern technology is to integrate a number of plants, or even clusters of local factory into the grid to supply grid resources, such as peak demand shifts and frequency response services [18]. This is referred to as Factory-to-Grid (F_2G) as the useful analog of the V2G, but it offers far more power than V2G. Material efficiency with the use of emerging technology can also be improved. Many plants utilizes the waste generated from other factories as the substrate; but the origin, condition, and time of supply hinders the simple integration into a carefully designed scheme where the manufacturing factory does not want to wait until the arrival of raw materials [16]. Digital technology can help forecast the availability of potential waste and its accuracy values. Because of the increased scale of such individual waste exchanges, maps and analyses of resource flows are also possible, which have been considered a powerful but not usable method for government and business planning.

The overarching objective of the modern system must be the potential of the world to sell oil, water, and material as raw materials. It is impossible to sustain the alternative. This ambition is evidently taken increasingly seriously by both large and small producers. A "foraging factory" employs technology analogous to the waste exchange plants. You should find out which raw materials are probably available at home and in the near future. This is possible only because new systems, robotics, and process control technologies are very flexible. Often businesses use the capacity to find and remanufacture components and materials by increasing data availability. Some of the original producers depend on sensors to know how poor their goods are on the ground to get them to the new plant. Moreover, innovation business models and the circular economy will advise world industries about how to modernize their value exchange systems and how to start their path to become a circular enterprise. Even if the benefits of this move toward sustainability can very early be predicted, emerging solutions would probably reduce downtime and add value (since less resources are being used in the system), as well as cleaner air and energy systems. Reproduction is relatively labour intensive and would raise jobs directly, even coupled with sophisticated and modular automation [16].

14.3   Artificial Neural Networks and Its Categories

Single and hybrid approaches are the two types of AI technologies used in wastewater treatment science (Figure 14.1). An AI approach that is modeled on biological neurons is a big AI approach [19]. Artificial neural networks can solve nonlinear multivariate problems by providing proper data and training algorithm [20]. Artificial neural networks are often mostly used to eliminate pollutants during water/wastewater treatment in experimental designs [7]. Artificial neural networks use extremely simplistic models consisting of numerous processing elements—artificial neurons—connected to black box representations of systems via links of variable weight. Per neuron receives, processes, and transmits input signals from other neurons, which in turn are transferred as inputs from the following neuron [21]. The ANN acquires details from the training data and identifies the underlying link among the data points that can be utilized to simulate, forecast, and optimize. Artificial neural network is like the human brain [22]—they differ from those with either one or two single-way logical layers to dynamic multi-input networks with multiple directions and layers. Models can be utilized in building and simulate the process involved in wastewater treatment with various ANNs, such as the MLP, RBF, WNN, FNN, SOM, RNN, ENN. Typical single AI technologies include ANN, FL, GA, and ES. In modeling complex and inaccurate structures, FL has been created, which consists of four components: FIS, flush, defluency and flouted law [23]. It consists of four parts: fuzzifier, deference motor, base of information, and defluent. FIS is the most commonly used

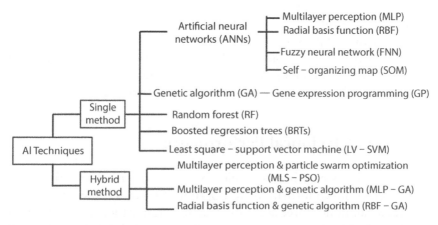

Figure 14.1 Various AI techniques used in wastewater treatment (original diagram).

one [24]. GA, the evolutionary algorithm, uses the principle of Darwin to model the evolutionary mechanismand obtains the optimum objective functions. Selection, crossover, and heterogeneity are the main rules for adding genetic transmitters to chromosome populations. In GA, the solution set consists of a group of discrete variables, which contain multiple issues [25]. ES can model the decision-making method to crack difficult problems using the skills and knowledge of several experts in a specific field [26].

The AI technology also contains several atypical approaches, including MT, DM, algorithm of clustering, SVM, BN, and PSO. MT model is applied by dividing the input into several subdomains and harnessing a linear multivariate regression to the subdomains to resolve continuous class problems. This can also achieve a structural depiction of the data set with a linear model in pieces to analyse a nonlinear connection [27, 28]. In DM, problems are resolved by splitting into many subdomains and by integrating the result. Clustering is an uncontrolled data grouping process using a certain similarity measure [23]. The cluster algorithm organizes unclassified function vectors into a set of clusters conferring to the aggregation theorem, a quantitative, multivariant statistical analysis. BN, an acyclic model that incorporates nodes and edges of linked nodes, is a Bayesian faith network [29]. Each node is a random variable with a conditional probability distribution of the node combination [30]. The PSO, a meta-heuristic evolutionary algorithm, unravels optimization problems from a random result and searches the ideal solutions using iteration [31]. SVM is a widespread linear classifier used to resolves the problem of binary classification using the optimal class separation principle [32]. SVMs and algorithms specific to the pattern recognition have been rapidly developed [33]. The aim is to improve further the performance of ANNs with the ANFIS (hybrid neural and fuzzy method) [34–36]. In adjusting prerequisite and conclusion parameters, ANFIS practices a least square algorithms with combined backpropagation and can automatically produce rules for "if/then." ANN-GAs employs a GA to enhance and increase the issue solving capacity of the neural network parameter on an iterative basis.

14.4   AI in Technical Performance

Most AI strategies have been modeled on laboratory results for the simulation, prediction, confirmation, and optimization of wastewater contaminant removal. Either three sections (teaching, ratification, and testing) or any two parts have been separated into experimental data (teaching and testing). The trainings were utilized to build and refine the model using the data set and to validate the designed model during the prevision phase. The results of the test include the comparing of experimental information to the forecast data are model accuracy.

(i) Chemical Oxygen Demand (COD): In WWTP's bio-chemical and physicochemical processes there are several models for forecasting, simulating, and maximizing COD retrieval. Moral *et al.* [37] have also analyzed ASP at a Wastewater Treatment plant, in Iskenderun, utilising an ANN model, which has a COD (R^2) of 0.632. An oxic or anoxic process with least MAPE of 1% and R2 value of 0.982 were designed to forecast the removal of COD in a full-scale Papermill treatment plant [15]. Aimed at multi-objective optimization of anaerobic method of digestion, a nondominant GA II and GA-ANN sorting are suggested. The GA-ANN model had less MSE, a lower RMSE, and a greater correlation coefficient than the ANN model [14]. BP-ANN exhibited better performances, with strong positive R^2 value, an average error of 2% to 4% and an RMSE of 1.45 to 1.86, relative to RSM and the modeling approaches used in other studies to evaluate the Fenton process' results [38]. In general, single ANN model is commonly used to understand the biochemical treatment, and combined modeling (GA-ANN and ANFIS) has shown better performance. In predicting the COD load present in sewage treatment plant in urban region, a hybrid AI model using ARMA and VAR has been implemented. Its accuracy of prediction was almost 99% higher than in BPANN and GA-BP-ANN [39]. The concentration of COD in treated wastewater in commercial treatment plants was correctly predicted via the hybrid model of mixing GM and GAs. In comparison to the results of the ANN and Monte Carlo analyses, this model was tested and provided good predictive efficiency (R^2, 0.85; RMSE, 68.9; MAPE, 20.2%) [40]. The application of AI in pollutant removal is presented in Table 14.1.

(ii) Biological Oxygen Demand (BOD_5): In biochemical wastewater treatment processes, NNE, ANN, FL, and SCFL are applied to simulate, predict, and optimize the removal of BOD5. In aeration diffusion plant, the ANN

Table 14.1 AI application in pollutant removal during wastewater treatment.

Pollutant	Treatment process	AI model	Reference
COD	Aeration, nitrification and denitrification	ANN	Moral *et al.* [37]
	Anoxic oxic biological	ANFIS	Wan *et al.* [15]
	Anaerobic digestion	ANN-GA	Huang *et al.* [14]
	Fenton oxidation	MLP-ANN	Sabour and Amiri [38]
	Aeration diffusion	ARMA-VAR, BP-ANN, GA-BP-ANN	Man *et al.* [39]
BOD_5	Biological	NNE	Nourani *et al.* [42]
	Activated sludge bioreactor	ARIMA-ORELM	Lotfi *et al.* [43]
NH_4^+, NO_3^-	Contact aeration	BP-ANN	Chen *et al.* [44]
NO_3^-	Biochemical	MOPSO	Han *et al.* [46]
PO_4^{3-}	Aerobic and anaerobic	Q-learning	Pang *et al.* [47]
NH_4^+, TN	Anammox and Partial nitritation	FFBP-ANN	Antwi *et al.* [6]
Cd^{2+}	Adsorption	ANFS	Fawzy *et al.* [49]
Pb^{2+}	Adsorption	MLP-ANN, RSM	Zaferani *et al.* [52]
Methylene blue	Photocatalytic	RBF-ANN	Ranjbar – Mohammadi *et al.* [54]

(Continued)

Table 14.1 AI application in pollutant removal during wastewater treatment. (*Continued*)

Pollutant	Treatment process	AI model	Reference
Bisphenol A, Carbamazepine, Ketoprogen, Tonalide	Adsorption	ANN, RSM	Vakili *et al.* [56]
Boron	Electrocoagulation	ANN	Silva Ribeiro *et al.* [63]

model was successful in the prediction of BOD5 removal [41]. The performance prediction of the BOD_{eff} removal method was carried out with a traditional MLR and three related nonlinear AI models—FFNN, ANFIS, and SVM. By estimating the performance efficiency in AI modeling at the verification level, the ensemble models have increased 14%, 20% and 24% by easy averaging, weighted average assemblies and NNE, respectively [42]. The combined ARIMA and ORLM model were implemented for the prediction of wastewater effluents, such as dissolved solids, COD, BOD_5, and gross suspended solids [43].

(iii) Nutrients: In physicochemical and biochemical wastewater treatment, there are several models for simulation, prediction, and optimization of nutrient removal. Using the touch aeration technique, ANN model was employed for the nitrogen load for treated effluent. The model will achieve 90% of its prediction precision [44]. For improved biological phosphorus removal an ABM was developed. For polyphosphate accumulating species with conventional population simulation, the calibrated maximal acetate absorption rate is 38% lower than for ABM with a randomization parameter [45]. In the framework of the enhanced mixed objective PSO algorithm, Han *et al.* [46] suggested an enhanced MOOC technique to achieve the optimum nitrate performance in the treatment of wastewater. MOOC had a 0.0344 squared error and a 0.1012 absolute integral error. This optimized Q-learning algorithm is an outstanding and stable control strategy for the biological phosphorus removal in aerobic and anaerobic system [47]. A network of SDAE deep learning systems was developed on a conventional aerobic/anaerobic process to forecast the efficiency of biofilm that deal with domestic wastewaters. The HMMs and MNLRs were designed for the accuracy of 84% mixed model for the prediction of total inorganic nitrogen in treated wastewater [48]. To assess the effluent efficacy of the wastewater treatment facilities, BN is used to estimate wastewater SBRs. The TP_{out} and TN_{out} accuracy were 95.2% and 93.1% on comparing the forecast outcomes with monitoring data [30]. In conjunction with ANN and GA, nanocomposite absorbents were able to strip phosphate from the wastewater [19]. In one word, in biochemical treatment procedures, For the removal of nutrients, a combination of GA and ANN model was used. Higher and less precise errors were found in single models—ANNs, ABMs, BNs, and SDAEs. In the course of the Partial nitritation and Anammox processes with R^2 values of 0.989 to 0.997 and an agreement index of 0.993 to 0.998, two novel feed forward BP-ANN models for the removal of TN and NH_4^+ in wastewater have been developed [6].

(iv)   Heavy metals: to predict the copper removal efficiency, the RBF-ANN has been used in the membrane emulsion technique. RBF-ANN can be trained faster than other neural networks. The forecast values fit the experimental values with a value of R^2 of 0.997. The efficacy of Cd^{2+} ions adsorption from the aqueous solution to *Typha domingensis* using ANFIS indicated that Cd^{2+} ion adsorption has a major influence on pH [49]. To estimate the efficacy of As^{3+} and As^{5+} wastewater algae remediation, ANNs have been used. The correspondence level of As^{5+} and As^{3+} respectively was 88% and 85%, respectively. The experimental data and simulation data have R^2 values of 0.9998 (for As^{3+} and As^{5+}) and can evaluate the removal of As^{3+} and As^{5+} in different conditions using the proven ANN model [50, 51]. While simulating the consequence of Thiosemicarbazide modified chitosan in Pb^{2+} elimination, MLP-ANN has greater prediction accuracy (R^2, 0.990) than the RSM [52].

(v)   Organic pollutants: The degradation of mediated polycyclic aromatic hydrocal carbon in seawater can be correctly predicted by ANN [53]. Using MLP-ANN model, better estimates than other, the MLP-ANN and the RBF-ANN approaches could simultaneously maximize methylene blue and malt green water reduction and performance [54]. The adsorbing activity of triamid on multi- and single-walled carbon nanotubes was simulated with MLR and ANN-GA and shown that the ANN had highly precise adsorption performance compared to MLR model. The ANNGA was 0.986 for R^2 and 0.0005 for MSE. The MLR was 0.751 for R^2 and 0.011 for MSE [55]. The ANN can also well improve micropollutant removal in water using fixed columns of chitosan/zeolite (bisphenol A, carbamazepines, ketoprofen, tonalides) [56]. The results of $K_2S_2O_8$ and H_2O_2 on the photo degradation of 2-nitrophenol in water have been studied based on RSM and ANN. Furthermore, ANN had better predictions compared to RSM [57]. CNN was applied to identify the occurrence of microbeads in wastewater with microscopic picture and with 89% classification accuracy to assess the emerging contaminant of microplastics in water [58].

(vi) Mixed pollutants: SBR model was simulated using RBF-ANN and MLP-ANN, with an efficiency of 86%, 79%, and 93%, respectively, of COD, overall phosphate (TP) and NH_4^+-N. [23]. R2 values rangingbetween 0.90 and 0.99 and RMSE was close to zero for both MLP-ANN and RBF-ANN variants. Simulation findings demonstrate that the R^2 and RMSE value of the MLP-ANN are higher than the RBF-ANN. The best comparison with 5 other models (BP-ANN, help vector reversal, intense learning equipment, gradient improvement decision tree, and stacking automotive encoder) are the predictions of the SDAE deep learning network RMSA (COD), 1.26 (TN)), and 1.27 (NH_4-N) [59]. BP-ANN model was educated and validated with 3.3% testing error and 0.95 R^2 value to estimate NH_4-N and COD elimination. Both BRT and BPANN will forecast and simulate Cd^{2+} and methylene blue adsorption on walnut carbon [60]. Both BP-ANNGA and MLP-ANN will simulate and maximize removal from aqueous solution of malachite green and Pb^{2+} with a removal rate of nearly 98.7% and an R^2 value of over 0.999 ($R^2 = 0.99970$ and 0.9994, respectively) [61]. The random forest has been found to be highly precise and predictable (R^2 = 0.973) in biochar adsorption of heavy metals (Cu^{2+}, Zn^{2+}, Cd^{2+}, Pb^{2+}, As^{3+}, Ni^{2+}) [62]. Generally, the heavy metal removal from wastewater is largely based on physical and chemical methods; the models of these processes are commonly used in both ANN and its combinations, with close to R^2 values equivalent to 1.

14.5   AI in Economic Performance

Han *et al.* [46] suggested a better approach for the MOOC and created an adaptive kernel function model to explain complicated dynamic water quality and power consumption processes. The MOOC reduces the power consumption values by 1.6%, 1.2%, and 2.2%, respectively in sunny, snowy, and stormy weather conditions, as compared with PI controller technique and multitarget differential evolution algorithm. To maximize ASP, a DM system was used to monitor DO in wastewater. Airflow can be lowered by 15% if energy saving is given priority over effluent quality [64]. A model for optimizing the aeration process was implemented by [65], which reduces aeration oxygen by 31.4% while retaining the same efficiency (greater than the standard) of the effluent. During wastewater treatment, the pump system is a critical factor of energy use. Through ANN models, the fluid flow rate and pump energy significantly reduced the energy consumption. Innovative predictive controls combined statistical and deep RL learning to minimize energy use have reduced by 16.7% relative to standard operating condition [66]. Data-driven neural networks designed to increase the efficiency of the sewage pump systems have been able to sustain energy-conserving pumping performance with an estimated energy savings of around 10% [67]. The FL control was extended to decrease WWTP energy use, showing that the aeration fuzzy control could save more than 10% of energy while retaining a reasonable removal level [68]. The flushing neural was used in a series of computer models to illustrate the performance of ANFIS controllers to achieve economic goals. This model could save almost 33% of running costs as a powerful and reliable DO control tool [13]. To meet business cost targets, wastewater efficiency and energy use were considered, a two-tier hierarchical management strategy with FF and MPC was created. The total costs of this technique were decreased by 0.7% and aerating capacity by approximately 6% [69].

14.6   AI in Management Performance

(i) Biological process: Biological wastewater treatment also has problems because the information obtained by one WWTP is not readily transferred to another. The aerobic method of biological wastewater processes was designed to test ANFIS and ANN. This study shows that ANFIS induced aeration efficiency is higher than ANN performance. The ANFIS model's R^2 value was 0.99 and its R^2 value 0.95 [13]. Sattar et al. [28] assessed and forecasted stepped helium aeration performance in three flow plans that were higher than current regression-oriented equations focused on adaptive learning networks (EPRs). Furthermore, the EPR was greater than the MT by including equation each for every regime, and the MT by a number [28]. The NF model was used to estimate the efficiency of the anaerobic filter, AFBR, and anaerobic reactor sludge upflow to various disturbances. Studies have shown the good device efficiency of neurofuzzy simulation. For AFBR the RMSE rates were 0.146, 6.67, and 6.55, for VMP, influential TOC, and R^2 0.99, 0.83, and 0.72. AFBR was used for RMSEs. RMSEs were 0.154, 39.92, 50.62, and R^2 were 0.93, 0.97 and 0.88, and used in anaerobic filters were 0.93, TOC and VFA. To develop a model evaluating the efficiency of the wastewater treatment plant, a self-organizing function map neural network has been developed [70]. Anaerobic wastewater treatment schemes are diagnosed using BNs. The methane production and COD removal rate improved to 25 L d^{-1} and 98%, respectively, in mixed-liquor with volatile suspended solid content up to 25,000 mg L^{-1} [71]. The major disruption of the wastewater management process was due to the unexpected organic excess resulting from collisions or washing in treatment plants. A fluid-based ES was created for the analysis, analysis of its operational patterns and accurate knowledge and advice to operations of the pilot wastewater treatment plant [72]. Artificial neural network (RBF-ANN and MLP-ANN) models to forecast sludge growth in wastewater plants were built to track SVI. In addition, the forecast outcome of the R^2, 0.99 MLP-ANN, and the lowest of the 4 mL g^{-1} RMSE values, for denormalized results, was more reliable than that of the RBF-ANN [73]. An advanced framework was developed to enhance the predictive precision of SVI in the biological wastewater treatment by means of an informative algorithm and an updated LM algorithm. The error variable was detected 100% and the intelligent detection system suggested was successful. A new fault diagnostic system based on the Granger causal Mard-RCP was developed and implemented in the Benchmerk simulation model and the full-scope WWTP to identify the initial fault diagnoses during wastewater treatment.

Initial sensor failure, sludge bulking, and influence shock could be reliably detected in this model. The simulation and optimization of membrane bioreactor efficiency was based on ANN, gene expression programs, and the minimum squares SVM. The least squares of SVM are among the most optimizing (MSE = 0.0002; R^2 = 0.99) [74]. In diagnosing process failures in the sludge process enabled, the PFA was enhanced based on a technique of variable frequency mutation. The algorithm provided good accuracy of estimation and error diagnosis for active sludge. To model the influential flow rate from short term to long term, the hybrid ANFIS and GFO model was created. This hybrid model has been more predictable and more efficient than ANFIS [75].

(ii) Physical processes: AI was also utilized to reduce membrane fouling during filtration in water and wastewater treatment. In crossflow microfiltration, the flux decrease was simulated with an FFNN model that delivers exact forecasts and an R^2 of 0.99 [76]. The development of total hydraulic resistances in the microfiltration and membrane bioreactor of wastewater treatments is well used by MLP-ANN and ANN [77, 78]. Artificial neural networks were used as pollution predictions for large-scale membrane bioreactors and found to have high predictive capacity for membrane pollution along with standard ANN models RNNs, SVMs, SOMs, ENNs, and WNNs [23]. The forecast for the WNN was more accurate than the model for the BPANN. By defining the non-linear relationship between five main factors and energy, RBF-ANN may measure the interface energy of membrane fouling in membrane bioreactors. Technical ANFIS, BP-ANN, SVM, and RBF-ANN models have been used to estimate the influential flow rate in WWTP that significantly impacts the success of the procedure. The 5-year results showed a more precise forecast for SVM and feed forward BP-ANN than ANFIS and RBF-ANN flow rate [79].

14.7 AI in Wastewater Reuse

A number of researchers are focusing on water/water management sustainable for WWTPs [10, 80]. The clean water, electricity, and diverse materials could be recovered during wastewater treatment by AI technology. Reuse of wastewater will increase environmental sustainability and produce economic benefits while increasing water efficiency [81]. To estimate wastewater reusability capacity produced by groundwater recharge, an existing neural network model was used. The precipitation index has been regarded as a valuable reference to the model for improving the cost efficiency of wastewater reuse and decisions varied from the conditions of the atmosphere. Wastewater reuse was primarily aimed at rural drainage, artificial groundwater recharge, and industrial uses. A coordinated, rigorous methodology was used to determine the viability of wastewater reuse by the evidence basis justification process.

14.8 Conclusion

Tech, economy, maintenance, and reuse are the four aspects of wastewater treatment using AI technologies. The FL and ANN models are the most common approaches in single models, while the ANN-GA and NF are found in hybrid models even more commonly. Models, such as FL, ANN, ANFIS, ANN-GA, and ABM, were mostly used for traditional contaminants (BOD, COD, NH_4, TN, TP, NO_3^-, and PO_4^{3-}). The predominant use of ANN was the elimination of chemical compounds and mixed contaminants. The use of AI technologies could further minimize operating costs by up to 30%, by reducing the use of ANN, DM, ANFIS, RL, FL, NF, and ES models for electrical, chemical, and labor consumption. AI technology will minimize overall energy use by up to 15% by regulating aeration. To analyze, forecast, assess, and diagnose wastewater treatment activities, AI technology utilizes primarily models, such as ANN-GA, ANN, MT, DM, NF, SMV, and ANFIS. The AI technology has helped improve aeration performance, pumping efficiency, and solve sludge expansion issues in the biological treatment of wastewater. Increasing workflow performance and lower costs, through the management of everyday traffic, flow influences, measurement systems, and WWTP automation, AI technologies (ANFIS, ANN, MOOC, NW, and RL). In future AI study, (i) further hybridization of single AI models is necessary, especially in complicated operational circumstances. This means greater capacity for optimum operation, higher reduction of the pollutant, and lower operating costs; (ii) for the operators to be able to handle parameter shocks and to maintain wastewater release consistency levels the predictability of IA technology should be enhanced by the variety of critical parameters of wastewater processing; (iii) we propose that future experiments include a wide number of field or online data to help the AI model to become more user oriented and work more reliably in realistic implementation for wastewater management. The smaller sizes and narrower variety of experimental data restrict the practical application of AI models and (iv) a model that integrates holistic and comprehensive facets of wastewater treatment including technical, economic, management, and recycled wastewater connections should be developed. Such a model should help to deal effectively with pollutant elimination, avoidance of costs, conservation of water, and concurrent management problems.

References

1. Rajaee, T., Ebrahimi, H., Nourani, V., A review of the artificial intelligence methods in groundwater level modeling. *J. Hydrol.*, *572*, 336–351, 2019.
2. Basile, A.O., Yahi, A., Tatonetti, N.P., Artificial intelligence for drug toxicity and safety. *Trends Pharmacol. Sci.*, *40*, 9, 624–635, 2019.
3. Gilvary, C., Madhukar, N., Elkhader, J., Elemento, O., The missing pieces of artificial intelligence in medicine. *Trends Pharmacol. Sci.*, *40*, 8, 555–564, 2019.
4. Yang, Q., Liu, Y., Chen, T., Tong, Y., Federated machine learning: Concept and applications. *ACM Trans. Intell. Syst. Technol. (TIST)*, *10*, 2, 1–19, 2019.
5. Baryannis, G., Validi, S., Dani, S., Antoniou, G., Supply chain risk management and artificial intelligence: state of the art and future research directions. *Int. J. Prod. Res.*, *57*, 7, 2179–2202, 2019.
6. Antwi, P., Zhang, D., Xiao, L., Kabutey, F.T., Quashie, F.K., Luo, W., Li, J., Modeling the performance of Single-stage Nitrogen removal using Anammox and Partial nitritation (SNAP) process with backpropagation neural network and response surface methodology. *Sci. Total Environ.*, *690*, 108–120, 2019.
7. Fan, M., Hu, J., Cao, R., Ruan, W., Wei, X., A review on experimental design for pollutants removal in water treatment with the aid of artificial intelligence. *Chemosphere*, *200*, 330–343, 2018.
8. Ahmed, A., Elkatatny, S., Ali, A., Abdulraheem, A., Comparative analysis of artificial intelligence techniques for formation pressure prediction while drilling. *Arab. J. Geosci.*, *12*, 18, 1–13, 2019.
9. Elkiran, G., Nourani, V., Abba, S., II, Multi-step ahead modelling of river water quality parameters using ensemble artificial intelligence-based approach. *J. Hydrol.*, *577*, 123962, 2019.
10. Xu, J., Yang, P., Xue, S., Sharma, B., Sanchez-Martin, M., Wang, F., Parikh, B., Translating cancer genomics into precision medicine with artificial intelligence: applications, challenges and future perspectives. *Hum. Genet.*, *138*, 2, 109–124, 2019.
11. Long, S., Zhao, L., Liu, H., Li, J., Zhou, X., Liu, Y., Yang, Y., A Monte Carlo-based integrated model to optimize the cost and pollution reduction in wastewater treatment processes in a typical comprehensive industrial park in China. *Sci. Total Environ.*, *647*, 1–10, 2019.
12. Loos, R., Carvalho, R., António, D.C., Comero, S., Locoro, G., Tavazzi, S., Gawlik, B.M., EU-wide monitoring survey on emerging polar organic contaminants in wastewater treatment plant effluents. *Water Res.*, *47*, 17, 6475–6487, 2013.

13. Mingzhi, H., Jinquan, W., Yongwen, M., Yan, W., Weijiang, L., Xiaofei, S., Control rules of aeration in a submerged biofilm wastewater treatment process using fuzzy neural networks. *Expert Systems with Applications. 36*, 7, 10428–10437, 2009.

14. Huang, M., Ma, Y., Wan, J., Chen, X., A sensor-software based on a genetic algorithm-based neural fuzzy system for modeling and simulating a wastewater treatment process. *App. Soft Comput., 27*, 1–10, 2015.

15. Wan, C., Pan, R., Li, J., Bi-weighting domain adaptation for cross-language text classification, in: *Twenty-Second International Joint Conference on Artificial Intelligence*, 2011, June.

16. Demartini, M., Tonelli, F., Bertani, F., Approaching industrial symbiosis through agent-based modeling and system dynamics, in: *Service orientation in holonic and multi-agent manufacturing*, pp. 171–185, Springer, Cham, 2018.

17. Burger, N., Demartini, M., Tonelli, F., Bodendorf, F., Testa, C., Investigating flexibility as a performance dimension of a Manufacturing Value Modeling Methodology (MVMM): a framework for identifying flexibility types in manufacturing systems. *Proc. CIRP, 63*, 33–38, 2017.

18. Lonardo, P., Anghinolfi, D., Paolucci, M., Tonelli, F., A stochastic linear programming approach for service parts optimization. *CIRP Ann., 57*, 1, 441–444, 2008.

19. Zhang, Y. and Pan, B., Modeling batch and column phosphate removal by hydrated ferric oxide-based nanocomposite using response surface methodology and artificial neural network. *Chem. Eng. J., 249*, 111–120, 2014.

20. Wang, J. and Deng, Z., Modeling and prediction of oyster norovirus outbreaks along Gulf of Mexico coast. *Environ. Health Perspect., 124*, 5, 627–633, 2016.

21. Chakraborty, T., Chakraborty, A.K., Chattopadhyay, S., A novel distribution-free hybrid regression model for manufacturing process efficiency improvement. *J. Comput. Appl. Mathematics, 362*, 130–142, 2019.

22. Zhang, Y., Gao, X., Smith, K., Inial, G., Liu, S., Conil, L.B., Pan, B., Integrating water quality and operation into prediction of water production in drinking water treatment plants by genetic algorithm enhanced artificial neural network. *Water Res., 164*, 114888, 2019.

23. Bagheri, M., Akbari, A., Ahmad, S., Advanced control of membrane fouling in filtration systems using artificial intelligence and machine learning techniques : A critical review. *Process Saf. Environ. Prot., 123*, 229–252, 2019.

24. Chanapathi, T. and Thatikonda, S., Fuzzy-based regional water quality index for surface water quality assessment. *J. Hazard., Toxic, Radioact. Waste, 23*, 4, 04019010, 2019.

25. Adeloye, A.J. and Dau, Q.V., Hedging as an adaptive measure for climate change induced water shortage at the Pong reservoir in the Indus Basin Beas River, India. *Sci. Total Environ., 687*, 554–566, 2019.

26. Wagner, W.P., Trends in expert system development: A longitudinal content analysis of over thirty years of expert system case studies. *Expert Syst. Appl.,* 76, 85–96, 2017.

27. Rahimikhoob, A., Comparison between M5 model tree and neural networks for estimating reference evapotranspiration in an arid environment. *Water Resour. Manage.,* 28, 3, 657–669, 2014.

28. Sattar, A.A., Elhakeem, M., Rezaie-Balf, M., Gharabaghi, B., Bonakdari, H., Artificial intelligence models for prediction of the aeration efficiency of the stepped weir. *Flow Meas. Instrum.,* 65, 78–89, 2019.

29. Graham, S.E., Chariton, A.A., Landis, W.G., Using Bayesian networks to predict risk to estuary water quality and patterns of benthic environmental DNA in Queensland. *Integr. Environ. Assess. Manage,* 15, 1, 93–111, 2019.

30. Li, D., Yang, H.Z., Liang, X.F., Prediction analysis of a wastewater treatment system using a Bayesian network. *Environ. Model. Software,* 40, 140–150, 2013.

31. Qiao, Y., Zhang, S., Wu, N., Wang, X., Li, Z., Zhou, M., Qu, T., Data-driven approach to optimal control of ACC systems and layout design in large rooms with thermal comfort consideration by using PSO. *J. Clean. Prod.,* 236, 117578, 2019.

32. Sousa, V., Matos, J.P., Matias, N., Evaluation of artificial intelligence tool performance and uncertainty for predicting sewer structural condition. *Autom. Constr.,* 44, 84–91, 2014.

33. Lu, H., Li, H., Liu, T., Fan, Y., Yuan, Y., Xie, M., Qian, X., Simulating heavy metal concentrations in an aquatic environment using artificial intelligence models and physicochemical indexes. *Sci. Total Environ.,* 694, 133591, 2019.

34. Mohandes, M., Rehman, S., Rahman, S.M., Estimation of wind speed profile using adaptive neuro-fuzzy inference system (ANFIS). *Appl. Energy,* 88, 11, 4024–4032, 2011.

35. Potter, C.W. and S. Member, M., Negnevitsky, Very Short-Term Wind Forecasting for Tasmanian Power Generation, 2014, https://doi.org/10.1109/TPWRS.2006.873421.

36. Yang, Z., Liu, Y., Li, C., Interpolation of missing wind data based on ANFIS. *Renew. Energy,* 36, 3, 993–998, 2011.

37. Moral, H., Aksoy, A., Gokcay, C.F., Modeling of the activated sludge process by using artificial neural networks with automated architecture screening. *Comput. Chem. Eng,* 32, 10, 2471–2478, 2008.

38. Sabour, M.R. and Amiri, A., Comparative study of ANN and RSM for simultaneous optimization of multiple targets in Fenton treatment of landfill leachate. *J. Waste Manage.,* 65, 54–62, 2017.

39. Man, Y., Hu, Y., Ren, J., Forecasting COD load in municipal sewage based on ARMA and VAR algorithms. *Resour. Conserv. Recycl.,* 144, 56–64, 2019.

40. Chen, Y., Yu, G., Long, Y., Teng, J., You, X., Liao, B.Q., Lin, H., Application of radial basis function artificial neural network to quantify interfacial energies

related to membrane fouling in a membrane bioreactor. *Bioresour. Technol.*, *293*, 122103, 2019.

41. Hamed, M.M., Khalafallah, M.G., Hassanien, E.A., Prediction of wastewater treatment plant performance using artificial neural networks. *Environ. Model. Software*, *19*, 10, 919–928, 2004.

42. Nourani, V., Elkiran, G., Abba, S., II, Wastewater treatment plant performance analysis using artificial intelligence–an ensemble approach. *Water Sci. Technol.*, *78*, 10, 2064–2076, 2018.

43. Lotfi, K., Bonakdari, H., Ebtehaj, I., Mjalli, F.S., Zeynoddin, M., Delatolla, R., Gharabaghi, B., Predicting wastewater treatment plant quality parameters using a novel hybrid linear-nonlinear methodology. *J. Environ. Manage.*, *240*, 463–474, 2019.

44. Chen, J.C., Chang, N.B., Shieh, W.K., Assessing wastewater reclamation potential by neural network model. *Eng. Appl. Artif. Intell.*, *16*, 2, 149–157, 2003.

45. Bucci, V., Majed, N., Hellweger, F.L., Gu, A.Z., Heterogeneity of intracellular polymer storage states in enhanced biological phosphorus removal (EBPR)–observation and modeling. *Environ. Sci. Technol.*, *46*, 6, 3244–3252, 2012.

46. Han, H.G., Zhang, L., Liu, H.X., Qiao, J.F., Multiobjective design of fuzzy neural network controller for wastewater treatment process. *Appl. Soft Comput.*, *67*, 467–478, 2018.

47. Pang, J.W., Yang, S.S., He, L., Chen, Y.D., Cao, G.L., Zhao, L., Ren, N.Q., An influent responsive control strategy with machine learning: Q-learning based optimization method for a biological phosphorus removal system. *Chemosphere*, *234*, 893–901, 2019.

48. Suchetana, B., Rajagopalan, B., Silverstein, J., Investigating regime shifts and the factors controlling Total Inorganic Nitrogen concentrations in treated wastewater using non-homogeneous Hidden Markov and multinomial logistic regression model. *Sci. Total Environ.*, *646*, 625–633, 2019.

49. Fawzy, M., Nasr, M., Adel, S., Nagy, H., Helmi, S., Environmental approach and artificial intelligence for Ni (II) and Cd (II) biosorption from aqueous solution using Typha domingensis biomass. *Ecol. Eng.*, *95*, 743–752, 2016.

50. Mandal, S., Mahapatra, S.S., Sahu, M.K., Patel, R.K., Artificial neural network modelling of As (III) removal from water by novel hybrid material. *Process Saf. Environ. Prot.*, *93*, 249–264, 2015.

51. Podder, M.S. and Majumder, C.B., The use of artificial neural network for modelling of phycoremediation of toxic elements As (III) and As (V) from wastewater using Botryococcusbraunii. *Spectrochim. Acta A: Mol. Biomol. Spectrosc.*, *155*, 130–145, 2016.

52. Zaferani, S.P.G., Emami, M.R.S., Amiri, M.K., Binaeian, E., Optimization of the removal Pb (II) and its Gibbs free energy by thiosemicarbazide modified chitosan using RSM and ANN modeling. *Int. J. Biol. Macromol.*, *139*, 307–319, 2019.

53. Jing, L., Chen, B., Zhang, B., Zheng, J., Liu, B., Naphthalene degradation in seawater by UV irradiation: the effects of fluence rate, salinity, temperature and initial concentration. *Mar. Pollut. Bull.*, *81*, 1, 149–156, 2014.

54. Ranjbar-Mohammadi, M., Rahimdokht, M., Pajootan, E., Low cost hydrogels based on gum Tragacanth and TiO2 nanoparticles: characterization and RBFNN modelling of methylene blue dye removal. *Int. J. Biol. Macromol.*, *134*, 967–975, 2019.

55. Ghaedi, A.M., Ghaedi, M., Pouranfard, A.R., Ansari, A., Avazzadeh, Z., Vafaei, A., Gupta, V.K., Adsorption of Triamterene on multi-walled and single-walled carbon nanotubes: Artificial neural network modeling and genetic algorithm optimization. *J. Mol. Liq.*, *216*, 654–665, 2016.

56. Vakili, M., Mojiri, A., Kindaichi, T., Cagnetta, G., Yuan, J., Wang, B., Giwa, A.S., Cross-linked chitosan/zeolite as a fixed-bed column for organic micro-pollutants removal from aqueous solution, optimization with RSM and artificial neural network. *J. Environ. Manage.*, *250*, 109434, 2019.

57. Bararpour, S.T., Feylizadeh, M.R., Delparish, A., Qanbarzadeh, M., Raeiszadeh, M., Feilizadeh, M., Investigation of 2-nitrophenol solar degradation in the simultaneous presence of K2S2O8 and H2O2: Using experimental design and artificial neural network. *J. Clean. Prod.*, *176*, 1154–1162, 2018.

58. Yurtsever, M. and Yurtsever, U., Use of a convolutional neural network for the classification of microbeads in urban wastewater. *Chemosphere*, *216*, 271–280, 2019.

59. Shi, S. and Xu, G., Novel performance prediction model of a biofilm system treating domestic wastewater based on stacked denoising auto-encoders deep learning network. *Chem. Eng. J.*, *347*, 280–290, 2018.

60. Mazaheri, H., Ghaedi, M., Azqhandi, M.A., Asfaram, A. J. P. C. C. P., Application of machine/statistical learning, artificial intelligence and statistical experimental design for the modeling and optimization of methylene blue and Cd (II) removal from a binary aqueous solution by natural walnut carbon. *Phys. Chem. Chem. Phys.*, *19*, 18, 11299–11317, 2017.

61. Dil, E.A., Ghaedi, M., Asfaram, A., Mehrabi, F., Bazrafshan, A.A., Ghaedi, A.M., Trace determination of safranin O dye using ultrasound assisted dispersive solid-phase micro extraction: Artificial neural network-genetic algorithm and response surface methodology. *Ultrason. Sonochem.*, *33*, 129–140, 2016.

62. Zhu, X., Wang, X., Ok, Y.S., The application of machine learning methods for prediction of metal sorption onto biochars. *J. Hazard. Mater.*, *378*, 120727, 2019.

63. da Silva Ribeiro, T., Grossi, C.D., Merma, A.G., dos Santos, B.F., Torem, M.L., Removal of boron from mining wastewaters by electrocoagulation method: Modelling experimental data using artificial neural networks. *Miner. Eng.*, *131*, 8–13, 2019.

64. Kusiak, A. and Wei, X., Optimization of the activated sludge process. *J. Energy Eng.*, *139*, 1, 12–17, 2013.

65. Asadi, A., Verma, A., Yang, K., Mejabi, B., Wastewater treatment aeration process optimization: A data mining approach. *J. Environ. Manage.*, 203, 630–639, 2017.
66. Filipe, J., Bessa, R.J., Reis, M., Alves, R., Data-driven Predictive Energy, Optimization in a Wastewater Pumping Station. *Preprints*, 1–46, 2019.
67. Zhang, Z., Kusiak, A., Zeng, Y., Wei, X., Modeling and optimization of a wastewater pumping system with data-mining methods. *Appl. Energy*, 164, 303–311, 2016.
68. Fiter, M., Güell, D., Comas, J., Colprim, J., Poch, M., Rodríguez-Roda, I., Energy saving in a wastewater treatment process: an application of fuzzy logic control. *Environ. Technol.*, 26, 11, 1263–1270, 2005.
69. Santín, I., Pedret, C., Vilanova, R., Applying variable dissolved oxygen set point in a two level hierarchical control structure to a wastewater treatment process. *J. Process Control*, 28, 40–55, 2015.
70. Çinar, Ö., New tool for evaluation of performance of wastewater treatment plant: artificial neural network. *Process Biochem.*, 40, 9, 2980–2984, 2005.
71. Bagley, D.M., Diagnosing Upsets in Anaerobic Wastewater Treatment Using Bayesian Belief. *J. Envi. Eng.*, 13, 302–310, 2014. https://doi.org/10.1061/(ASCE)0733-9372(2001)127
72. Carrasco, E.F., Rodriguez, J., Punal, A., Roca, E., Lema, J.M., Rule-based diagnosis and supervision of a pilot-scale wastewater treatment plant using fuzzy logic techniques. *Expert Syst. Appl.*, 22, 1, 11–20, 2002.
73. Bagheri, M., Mirbagheri, S.A., Ehteshami, M., Bagheri, Z., Modeling of a sequencing batch reactor treating municipal wastewater using multi-layer perceptron and radial basis function artificial neural networks. *Process Saf. Environ. Prot.*, 93, 111–123, 2015.
74. Hamedi, H., Ehteshami, M., Mirbagheri, S.A., Zendehboudi, S., New deterministic tools to systematically investigate fouling occurrence in membrane bioreactors. *Chem. Eng. Res. Des.*, 144, 334–353, 2019.
75. Dehghani, M., Seifi, A., Riahi-Madvar, H., Novel forecasting models for immediate-short-term to long-term influent flow prediction by combining ANFIS and grey wolf optimization. *J. Hydrol.*, 576, 698–725, 2019.
76. Aydiner, C., Demir, I., Yildiz, E., Modeling of flux decline in crossflow microfiltration using neural networks: the case of phosphate removal. *J. Membrane Sci.*, 248, 1-2, 53–62, 2005.
77. Dornier, M., Decloux, M., Trystram, G., Lebert, A., Dynamic modeling of crossflow microfiltration using neural networks. *J. Membrane Sci.*, 98, 3, 263–273, 1995.
78. Schmitt, F. and Do, K.U., Prediction of membrane fouling using artificial neural networks for wastewater treated by membrane bioreactor technologies: bottlenecks and possibilities. *Environ. Sci. Pollut. Res.*, 24, 29, 22885–22913, 2017.

79. Najafzadeh, M. and Zeinolabedini, M., Prognostication of wastewater treatment plant performance using efficient soft computing models: an environmental evaluation. *Measurement*, *138*, 690–701, 2019.
80. López-Morales, C.A. and Rodríguez-Tapia, L., On the economic analysis of wastewater treatment and reuse for designing strategies for water sustainability: Lessons from the Mexico Valley Basin. *Resour., Conserv. Recycl.*, *140*, 1–12, 2019.
81. Bozkurt, H., van Loosdrecht, M.C., Gernaey, K.V., Sin, G., Optimal WWTP process selection for treatment of domestic wastewater–A realistic full-scale retrofitting study. *Chem. Eng. J.*, *286*, 447–458, 2016.

15

Risks of Agrobusiness Digital Transformation

Inna Riepina[1], Anastasiia Koval[1*], Olexandr Starikov[1] and Volodymyr Tokar[2]

[1]Department of Business Economics and Entrepreneurship, Kyiv National Economic University named after Vadym Hetman, Kyiv, Ukraine
[2]Department of Software Engineering and Cybersecurity, Kyiv National University of Trade and Economics, Kyiv, Ukraine

Abstract

The aim of the study is to discover methods for assessing the impact of digital transformation risks on the business model of agricultural enterprises. Industry 4.0 is accompanied by the rapid transformation of a number of sectors under the influence of "breakthrough" digital innovations such as blockchain, the Internet of Things, artificial intelligence and augmented reality.

In agrobusiness, the development of mobile technologies, remote sensing services and distributed data processing are already expanding small farmers' access to information, production resources, finance and training. Digital technologies open up new opportunities for the integration of small farms into digital agro-food systems. On the other hand, digital transformation of agrobusiness and the food supply chain is accompanied by a number of issues that cannot be ignored.

Transition countries, as well as rural areas with underdeveloped technical infrastructure face such problems as the high cost of technology, low level of computer literacy, digital skills and limited access to digital services. Therefore, it is important for agrobusiness to have a system in place for studying these risks that would promptly respond to changes in the external environment and identify potential threats that could affect the company's performance. The use of economic and mathematical methods makes it possible to apply the risk management system in relation to the digital business model of the agricultural enterprise.

*Corresponding author: a.rykunich@gmail.com

Roheet Bhatnagar, Nitin Kumar Tripathi, Nitu Bhatnagar and Chandan Kumar Panda (eds.)
The Digital Agricultural Revolution: Innovations and Challenges in Agriculture through Technology Disruptions, (333–358) © 2022 Scrivener Publishing LLC

If managed properly, digital transformation can change all parts of the agro-food chain. Resource management of any element of that system has to be built on the principles of optimization, individual approach, reasonableness and predictability. The operation of the system in real time can be ensured by hyper connection based on the actual data. With the application of the appropriate risk management system it will be possible to create optimal and adaptable business models for the management of agricultural land, crops and animals throughout production and distribution chains. That in turn will allow the digital transformation of agribusinesses to create systems that are characterized by the high productivity, predictability and the ability to adapt to changes, including those aggravated by the altering climate. Consequently, it will help increase food security, profitability and sustainability throughout the globe. Creating digital agrobusiness ecosystem requires favourable conditions and costs associated with the formation of the IT infrastructure. The digital transformation will change the structure of the agricultural labour market and the nature of the work itself.

Keywords: Risks, digital transformation, agrobusiness, entrepreneurship, digital ecosystem of agrobusiness, business model

15.1   Modern Global Trends in Agriculture

Modern global trends in agriculture determine the need for transformation of business models used by farmers and agricultural holdings. Different authors disclose various aspects of the new era of agricultural production. For example, some researchers include the following factors affecting the food industry and agriculture [16]:

- population growth in the world, which causes the opposite changes in different countries depending on their ability for transformation—growth or decline in the level of welfare; globalization of demand and rapid spread of global trends;
- food embargo, trade wars resulting in development of trade alliances and simplification of customs procedures;
- environmental disasters, coronavirus pandemic, climate change;
- development of tourism (growth of tourist flow, transport and logistics, and others infrastructures);
- increasing government involvement in the form of imposing different types of regulation, including the implementation

of traceability programs, digital marking, and disseminating international standards;
- changes in consumer preferences shifting towards healthy, functional, and organic food;
- trend on noncontact;
- growing popularity of the comfort food segment;
- growth in demand for individual products, for instance, avocado, mango, Brussels sprouts, tea, and so on.
- growing popularity of contrasting flavours (new and unusual combinations—sweet and salty, bitter and spicy, sour and spicy);
- growing demand for food, produced using sophisticated technologies, or from unique products;
- growing demand for ready-to-eat food delivery and ordering products 24/7.

Other researchers insist on distinguishing the most important ten global trends, some repeating certain ideas of the previous approach [12]:

- a growing population (by 2050, there will be 10 billion people on Earth);
- the globalization of trade, when crops are grown in the most fertile lands, and processed and sold around the world;
- urbanization (already more than 50% of people live in cities);
- biotechnology and nanotechnology (genomics will improve existing varieties);
- agricultural technologies (new technologies allow you to get more crops at lower costs);
- integrated production and distribution chain large holdings are starting to use vertical integration to optimize the value chain;
- social change (consumption of resource-intensive foods (meat, organic food) is increasing);
- regulation and standards (quality checks and new export laws);
- climate change (changing weather conditions trigger soil change);
- moving from a grocery to a service model (agricultural material producers are starting to provide more and more services in addition to traditional products).

All of these peculiarities stimulate the rise of agrobusiness with the emphasis on data and analytics as the main functionality (digitalization and integration of vertical and horizontal value chains; digitalization of the offered goods and services; digital business models and solutions that provide customers with access to the manufacturer's systems). The related digital technologies include [12]: mobile devices, cloud computing, IoT platforms, intelligent sensors, 3D-printing, augmented reality/wearable technology, location technologies, big data analysis and advanced algorithms, authentication and fraud detection, multilevel customer interaction and collection of customer information, as well as advanced interfaces for human-machine interaction.

The industry is still at the beginning of a digital evolution. The world in general is still at level of partial process automation, but the prospects look more optimistic. For example, in 5 to 10 years, the digitalization will result in maximum automation of production and management business processes in agricultural. The perspective of nearest 10 to 15 years is partial or full implementation of ERP systems in enterprises, primarily in management business processes. The first attempts to implement individual digital services in production, including services based on Internet of Things technologies (GPS trackers, fuel sensors, personal identifiers, parallel driving systems, differential application systems, UAVs/drones, smart meteorological stations, soil analysers, IP cameras, animal activity sensors, animal milking systems, etc.), self-learning and robotization of routine processes (elements of a "smart" enterprise) and other "end-to-end" and world-leading digital technologies [1].

The perspective of several decades is combining all digital services of an agricultural enterprise into a single digital platform for managing all typical processes at an enterprise, the use by agricultural enterprises of high-tech digital technologies in the field of big data, genetic materials, artificial intelligence, the Internet of things, robotics and sensorics in the field of the agro-industrial complex, including the implementation of complex digital technologies "Smart Farm," "Smart Land Management," "Smart Garden," and so on. In the internal business processes of an enterprise, a person is left with only creative, including strategic functionality.

The tasks of national governments will be in the sphere of creating and introducing an open "metasystems" as an integrated system of state. digital platforms for agriculture, including [1]:

- a geographic information platform;
- a platform containing information about all agricultural plants in the regions;

- a platform containing information about all agricultural animals in the regions;
- a platform for managing the export and import of agricultural products;
- a platform for bidding and procurement of agricultural products;
- a platform for objective monitoring and management of transport and logistics infrastructure in agriculture;
- an electronic atlas of agricultural land;
- a platform for digital and "precision farming" for differential positioning signals;
- a platform that allows digital analysis of the structure, composition and condition of soils, monitoring crops to increase yields and predictive analysis of yield, pests, and so on.

The most dramatic changes are expected to occur by 2050 to 2060, when the industry will transform into a constituent of a multi-cluster, and then into a single digital environment that unites the economy of neighbouring countries [1].

15.2   The Global Innovative Differentiation

The current stage of development of the world economic system is characterized by an increasing role of innovation and investment in ensuring national competitiveness, the formation of the foundations of sustainable economic development in the context of global financial and economic instability.

Today, because of the differentiation of countries according to the possibilities of technological development, they are divided into three groups [10]: 1) technological innovators or countries of the "golden billion" (able to generate high technology, intelligently exploit the world, have high technological competitiveness); 2) technological followers (to some extent can use high technology and at least hypothetically set development goals that have targets of the first group of countries); 3) technological outsiders or "third world" (not capable of competitive self-development in a globalized environment).

Peripheral and semi-peripheral countries (which include Ukraine) are trying to bridge the gap with the leaders (USA, EU countries, Japan), accelerating the stages of competitive development of the country (Figure 15.1).

At the first stage, the economy is based on factors available to the country: relatively cheap labor and natural resources.

Figure 15.1 Evolution of competitive development of the national economy at the present stage of development of the global economic system [11].

The second stage requires significant domestic and foreign investments, so the transition to this stage requires appropriate institutional prerequisites (regulation, guarantee of property rights, macroeconomic stability, a harmonious combination of fiscal, monetary, and customs policies).

The third stage requires the stable functioning of the institutions of infrastructure for innovative development and the formation of an appropriate culture and level of knowledge of the population. Thus, the evolution of the national economy is not possible solely through the self-development of existing conditions but requires an effective combination of efforts of public and private sectors of the economy, the purposeful formation of institutional foundations.

The effective development of a market economy is based on 12 main pillars: four should be created in the first stage, six in the second and two in the third one (Figure 15.2).

The innovation-investment model of economic development provides an increase in the efficiency of social production through the growth of

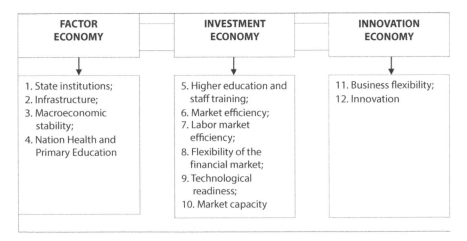

Figure 15.2 Competitiveness of the national economy based on innovation and investment activities [11].

knowledge, while innovation is closely linked with investment. Innovative activity is in fact in this context one of the forms of investment activity, which consists in making investments to implement the achievements of scientific and technological progress in production and social sphere.

The economic growth of a market economy is explained by the following factors [2]: 1) increase in labor costs (32.0%); 2) increase in labor productivity (68.0%), including due to: innovation (28.0%), capital (19.0%). Thus, the combination of innovation and investment provides approximately 47.0% of GDP growth. Directly related to the combination of innovation and investment is the gradual evolution of the prevailing technological systems, which are characterized by the specifics of social production (Table 15.1).

There is the sixth technological mode in the world leading countries: biotechnology (including cell biology), aerospace, nanotechnology, new materials, optoelectronics, artificial intelligence systems, microelectronics, microsystems mechanics, software and information, personnel management systems; industries of the fifth technological mode: pharmaceutical, automobile, chemical, tool industry. In Ukraine, the main share of industrial production, namely 95.2%, is produced by the branches of the third and fourth technological modes [11].

The technological leaders are able to transform their agricultural systems into totally digitalized and innovative, while the rest of the world need to solve several problems at the same time, including simultaneous reforming of their technological systems and introducing methods and special institutions, which are way ahead of the general real sector of economy.

In turn, the main problems of the scientific and technical sector of Ukraine are [4]: 1) the aging of scientific personnel; 2) moral and physical aging of the research and production base; 3) inadequate system of formation of priorities of works; 4) detachment from the next stages of the innovation cycle (introduction into serial production, market research and ensuring effective demand). In the complex, the situation is characterized by the following negative trends [3]: 1) degradation of the education system; 2) intellectual degradation of society; 3) "outflow of intelligence" from Ukraine; 4) internal "outflow of intelligence" from the field of education and science; 5) the lack of an established system of lifelong learning.

In 1990s, Ukraine lost 15.0% to 20.0% of its intellectual potential due to emigration and the transition of specialists to jobs that did not require professional work and professional knowledge. These losses are not offset by the return of migrants. First, migrants lose their qualifications by doing mostly unskilled work abroad. Second, return is often associated with the end of a working career: a significant proportion of migrants returning to Ukraine are not economically active. Third, knowledge and skills acquired

Table 15.1 The main features of technological systems [20].

Technological system	Period	Features
First	1770–1830	the increased role of labor mechanization; use of biological energy; development of the textile industry
Second	1831–1880	strengthening the processes of concentration of production and capital; priority use of the steam engine
Third	1881–1930	domination of monopolies and trusts; use of electric motors; rapid development of mechanical engineering; use of coal as the main source of energy
Fourth	1931–1980	formation of transnational corporations; growth of vertical integration of production; development of chemistry of macromolecular compounds, polymeric materials; automation of basic technological processes; transition from coal to oil
Fifth	1981–2025	integration of production and sales; development of microelectronics, information and communication technologies; flexible automation; use of composite materials; use of natural gas as the main energy source
Sixth	After 2025	use of artificial intelligence, bio- and space technologies, genetic engineering, nuclear and renewable energy

abroad are often impossible to use due to the difficulty of recognizing foreign diplomas [15].

From Ukraine, which inherited from the former Soviet Union 6.5% of world scientific and technological potential with a population of 0.1% of the world's population, at the beginning of the third millennium, when the world is moving to a postindustrial, information society using various methods to stimulate innovation, 7.0 million of the most highly skilled workers and specialists, including Candidates and Doctors of Sciences [13].

For example, the Silicon Valley in the United States employs approximately 15.0 thousand specialists from Ukraine, the value of the products they generate annually exceeds 2.5 billion dollars. USA. According to experts, Ukraine lost more than 12.0 billion dollars on the education of all emigrants who left the country in the period of 1990 to 2010. USA, which indicates the inefficiency of personnel policy in Ukraine [24].

Expenditures on financing science in Ukraine from the state budget for many years do not exceed 0.4%, which is less than in developed countries (Japan, 0.8%; USA, 0.5%; Sweden, 0.8%) [9].

The declining role of science in the country's economy leads to a reduction of employees in public administration of science and technology, whereas the state structures of science management in the United States, Germany, and France are transformed in the direction of increase. In the United States, more than 25.0% of all federal employees (about 850.0 thousand) are employed directly in the public administration of STP, in Ukraine, 2.0% [5].

If in the late 1970s to early 1980s in the former USSR for basic research was allocated 10.0% to 12.0% of total R&D expenditures (in the US at that time 14.0–16.0%), then today in Ukraine this figure has decreased to about 5.0% [5].

The material and technical base of science is in a difficult situation. Much obsolete part of the instruments and equipment is obsolete: only less than a fifth of the instruments and equipment are used for up to 2 years, and the fourth part up to 5. Because of the lack of funds, the purchase of instruments and equipment for scientific laboratories is virtually stopped, capital stock of specialists and scientists in Ukrainian science is two to three times lower than in industry (provision of research devices at the level of 10.0–25.0%, the coefficient of their use 0.1–0.3%), is slightly more 1.0% of the US level [5].

Despite serious socioeconomic problems in Ukraine, according to expert assessments obtained under the State Program for Forecasting Scientific, Technological and Innovative Development of Ukraine, domestic science has retained the ability under certain conditions to conduct research and obtain world-class results in the following areas [22]: 1) development of the latest sections of mathematics and theoretical physics; 2) development of nanotechnologies; 3) radio physics of millimetre and submillimetre range; 5) plant biotechnology and biophysics; biodegradation; 6) cryobiology and cryomedicine; 7) neuroscience, in particular neurophysiology; 8) computer science; 9) micro- and optoelectronics; 10) aerospace technologies. All of these technologies could be used to boost the digitalization of agriculture in Ukraine and neighbouring countries.

15.3   National Indicative Planning of Innovative Transformations

Any innovative changes require the combination of market economic tools and governmental indicative planning. The obvious disadvantages of Soviet-style rigid policy-making have led some economists in the post-Soviet space to conclude that any form of planning is incompatible with the market mechanism, but effective international practice denies such simplification. Leading countries of the world (for example, China, USA, France, Japan, etc.) successfully use national indicative planning systems (in turn, the EU applies certain elements, such as 7-year development plans—financial regulations).

Technological progress and the information economy stimulate the development of new management approaches. One of the reasons for the fall of the USSR was the inefficiency of the management system due to the lack of reliable calculation, but today this obstacle is actually overcome due to the development of information technology. In China, innovations are built into the system of the plan. The United States also has a clearly planned economy, where 95% of scientific and technological products are distributed through the public procurement system. All initial purchases of the military-industrial complex—the NTP locomotive in America—are carried out thanks to scientific approaches. The United States has development plans for 5, 10, and 50 years [17]. It is not necessary for the establishment of new technologies and the development of the R&D programs by the state to have 1.5 to 2.0 million contracts in the amount of $5,000 up to $2.0 billion. The founders of such a system in the United States have a lot of power, they do not disrupt the mechanism of the functioning of the market economy [23].

It is necessary to increase the power of 1.5 to 2.0 million contracts for the implementation of new technologies and the development of R&D programs from 5 thousand up to $ 2.0 billion each [6]. The founders of such a system in the United States have a lot of power, they do not disrupt the mechanism of the functioning of the market economy, in addition to the development of the market.

To mobilize internal resources and effectively use external opportunities and prevent threats, China uses a special model of indicative planning, which is characterized by the predominance of state (centralized) planning of macroeconomic processes and key strategic directions at the meso and macro levels. Development plans of industries and regions are the main elements of the state plan; long-term planning plays a leading role.

The Chinese model of indicative planning involves the following stages: preparatory work; development of specific figures; drawing up and submission for approval of the draft plan; consideration, approval and transfer of the plan for implementation to the relevant authorities [7]. Planning is used to mitigate possible reform imbalances. Indicative planning is complemented by other elements of mobilization development, which ensure the accelerated development of the Chinese economy.

Peculiarities of the culture of this country: an unsettled link between national self-awareness and traditional values; homogeneous population; broad acceptance of the idea of the strong China; the manifestation of the possibility of Chinese diaspora,—the PRC allowed the concept of "socialism with Chinese specificity" as a way to move the mobile model to develop, as on the way to the accelerated remaking of the country. By the head of the social and economic revision of the outsider countries, the national competitiveness is being protected on the basis of innovations, which is an important change in the mind of the step change in the presentation of the golden provincial powers. The flexibility of the field in the need for a high rate of growth of the economy and good structural changes, so as to meet the needs of an innovative hole [18, 19]. Some of the regions of the periphery should be able to reach the short-line accelerated growth, which is negatively perceived on the social and economic systems through those that are based on the outdated technology.

There is a need to introduce scientifically sound forecasting of technological and socioeconomic trends in the strategic horizon of 25 to 30 years, this period is explained by the approximate duration of waves of technological innovation. Timely forecasting of the emergence and spread of fundamentally new technologies, equipment and industrial designs allows the national socioeconomic system to gradually adapt to new challenges, reducing fluctuations for domestic producers and consumers.

Long-term research proves the effectiveness of the use of 5-year indicative plans for innovation and investment activities of industrial enterprises, which is because of the sufficiency of this period to achieve the following results: 1) construction of large enterprises, 2) development of natural deposits, 3) creation of production and special infrastructure, 4) completion of the training cycle. In Ukrainian conditions, there are additional reasons in favour of such a time horizon.

"Economic miracles" (one of which Ukraine will have to perform for the sake of basic survival) are always based on broad public support and a willingness to temporarily worsen living standards to achieve positive reform results in the future. The ambiguity (rather the actual absence) of the ultimate strategic goals, which are expressed in concrete and achievable indicators, leads to the spread of alimony and neglect of national priorities for the sake of their own interests by all segments of the population. Thus, in the long-term development strategy of Ukraine it is necessary to clearly indicate the "picture of the future," i.e., what specific goals are set for the national socioeconomic system as a whole and by what means they will be achieved (Figure 15.3).

An important element of the institutional block of indicative planning is the relationship between indicative plans and medium-term development budgets, which should be drawn up for a period of 5 years. Given the specifics of Ukraine, it is advisable to propose the introduction of common financial and economic "rules of the game" for the entire period of the indicative plan—the development budget (moratorium for 5 years). We are talking, first of all, the abolition of the annual adjustment of tax legislation, which is changed each time to implement the current budget with complete disregard for the interests of the private sector (strategic investor expects investment projects for a period significantly exceeding 1 year).

The choice of 5 years as a planning period is explained, in particular: 1) the sufficiency of this period for the construction of most facilities, 2) completion of the training cycle in the required areas of qualification, 3) the period of office of the executive and legislative branches of government,

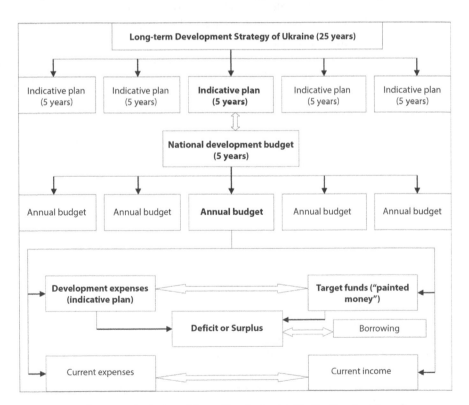

Figure 15.3 Conceptual scheme of the national system of indicative planning of innovation and investment activity original figure.

4) the period of implementation of most investment projects. Based on 5-year development budgets, the functioning of the national financial system should take place, with an emphasis on priority preferential lending to priority areas and segments of the economy.

In turn, the National Development Budget should be detailed in annual budgets, which should be clearly divided into two parts: 1) revenues (trust funds) and development expenditures (implementation of the indicative plan); 2) current expenses with indication of sources of financing. The highest priority in funding should be given to the costs associated with the implementation of activities under the 5-year indicative plan. The rest of the costs (current costs) (unfortunately, at the initial stage, even of a social nature) must be made in proportion to the residual principle.

This approach is usually not in line with current populist rhetoric, but practice shows that in the race to raise prices and wages and pensions always win first. Even unplanned income is simply "eaten up," the country is confidently moving towards a catastrophe when there are no assets left for privatization and the excessive tax burden will no longer be able to ensure the fulfilment of social obligations by the state (already social funds, such as pensions) are in short supply.

Development costs (costs associated with the implementation of the indicative plan) should be financed by trust funds, which should be financed according to the proven principle of "painted funds." This principle means that a certain share (or completely) of certain revenues (taxes, special fees, and charges) are directed to specialized funds and can be used only for predetermined purposes according to the approved budget.

The use of the budget deficit should be limited only to the financing of development expenditures. This powerful tool for stimulating socioeconomic development should be used only for the purpose of implementing infrastructure projects that are of strategic importance for the national economy.

Chronologically, the recent global financial crisis has identified the weaknesses and strengths of the concept of national competitiveness of different socioeconomic development countries: from outsiders to leading representatives of the "golden billion." A developed financial sector is not always an indicator of a country's strength and security.

Insufficient public control over the financial sector leads to the fact that, breaking away from the real economy, the virtual speculative superstructure instead of serving the needs of simple and expanded reproduction of integration and national socioeconomic systems, develops under its own laws and causes devastating consequences at the national, regional and global levels.

The alternation of periods of strengthening and weakening the state's presence in the economy is explained by the logic of social development, which requires different stages of change in the structure of the socioeconomic system in general and the national financial system.

The primary element of the conceptual scheme of optimization of the national financial system is the formation of an interconnected institutional block "indicative planning—financial and credit system." As a primary optimization of the structure of the national financial system of Ukraine, it is advisable to introduce the triad "Single regulator of the financial sector— the National Bank for Reconstruction and Development—the National Bank of Ukraine" (Figure 15.4). Concentration and combination of efforts of these institutions should facilitate the implementation of priority investment projects, which are formed based on indicative development plans.

Lending to businesses (public and private sectors of the economy) and the academic sector should take place on preferential terms (below market rates) and exclusively for the national currency of Ukraine—the hryvnia. The socioeconomic system of Ukraine (national financial system in particular) should gradually reduce the level of dollarization of transactions and

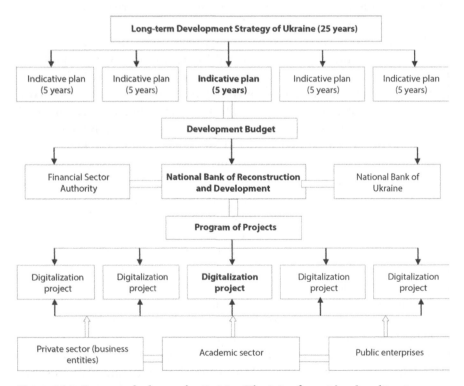

Figure 15.4 Conceptual scheme of optimizing Ukrainian financial and credit system within agricultural digitalization original figure.

meet the requirements of the Constitution and other regulations regarding the hryvnia as the only legal tender in Ukraine.

Lending to businesses (public and private sectors of the economy) and the academic sector should take place on preferential terms (below market rates) and exclusively for the national currency of Ukraine—the hryvnia. The socioeconomic system of Ukraine (national financial system in particular) should gradually reduce the level of dollarization of transactions and actually meet the requirements of the constitution and other regulations regarding the hryvnia as the only legal tender in Ukraine.

If we consider the methods of project-operational management of investment potential of innovation activities of enterprises, their interaction is to integrate a set of targeted, systematic methods of establishing relationships between the main factors influencing innovation and investment activities of the enterprise, determining its innovation potential on the basis of proj ect-operative portfolio analysis of investments of multichannel financing of innovations and strategic management of scenario modeling of competitiveness for a choice of optimum administrative decisions in the course of realization of innovation and investment activity of the enterprise.

The effective implementation of innovative transformations at the regional and national levels depends on the functioning of institutional blocks, which should be developed taking into account the national socioeconomic specifics of Ukraine. First, we are talking about the budget and tax sphere and the algorithm for implementing innovative transformations, starting with limited experiments at the regional level and ending with national practice. The primary task is to move from the preparation of annual development budgets to strategic scientific and technical forecasting and medium-term indicative planning with priority given to innovative segments of the economy (Figure 15.5).

Quite often innovative transformations are socially neutral in nature, sometimes with unpredictable consequences for the national socioeconomic system, so it is absolutely justified to introduce an algorithm for gradual implementation of innovative projects from local experiments to national practice to minimize possible negative effects.

The national development budget should be based on regional budgets, which should be formed in accordance with national priorities for the current 5-year planning period. The expenditure part of regional development budgets should be based on the budget of the target regional innovation program (Figure 15.6).

The distribution of budget funds should be based on tenders and competitions in clearly defined areas of the innovation segment of the economy (for example, solving problems of providing alternative energy sources for a

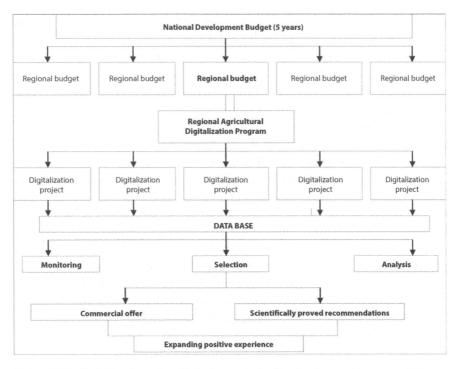

Figure 15.5 Algorithm for using "limited experiments" to implement measures within the indicative planning of digitalization of agrobusiness Original figure.

Figure 15.6 Institutional Block "Indicative planning – innovative projecting" Original figure.

particular region, settlement, production area). The private sector can also participate in the financing of innovative projects on a commercial basis. As you know, to attract real foreign direct investment, it is necessary to gradually provide phased financing for the development of the territory: first, at the expense of budget funds; secondly, to stimulate the presence of domestic investors, which will serve as a positive criterion for foreign strategic investors.

Based on individual innovative projects, it is quite logical to create a Database with free access to it by the private sector, the main functions of which are monitoring, analysis and selection of the most commercially attractive results for resale on the free market and development of a scheme to spread the positive effect to the next level. and eventually implementation as a national practice.

15.4   Key Myths and Risks of Digitalization of Agrobusiness

Stereotypes are the main hazards for innovative changes in agrobusiness in general, and digitalization. There is a common feeling that digitalization is long, expensive, and difficult process, but in practice it is a short-term (usually up to 7 days), one-time investment in an understandable user-friendly environment.

The main risks and hazards for digitalization in post-Soviet countries are [21]:

- lack of staff, outflow of young specialists;
- lack of confidence in the justification of such expenses;
- low awareness of opportunities;
- illiteracy and conservatism;
- sabotaging the implementation of automation systems, ensuring the transparency of processes, theft;
- legal barriers in the field of certification and operation;
- different data formats
- lack of appropriate financial resources.

The significance of the human factor in digitalization is hard to underestimate. At first glance, the Internet of Things is a purely technological story, but factors, such as culture, organization, and leadership, play a huge role in it. Three of the four main factors that have determined the success of IoT projects have to do with people and their interactions [21]:

- collaboration between IT and business units;
- a technology-oriented production culture based on the principles of top-down leadership and management support.
- Internet of things experience gained internally or as a result of cooperation with external partners.

15.5   Examples of Use of Digital Technologies in Agriculture

Digital technologies introduced in crop production aim at the development of precision farming and monitoring the health of agricultural crops. For example, the use of drones for fertilization. The use of drones when sowing and processing plants, irrigating the soil, photographing hard-to-reach areas. The introduction of these technologies allows you to spray chemicals 30 times faster than a person.

For data processing, special labor-intensive models are required, the spatial structure of which allows the use of modern technologies computer vision, in particular convolutional neural networks.

The use of drones allows you to create electronic maps of fields in real time, promptly monitor the state of crops, monitor the performance of work in the field, predict crop yields and conduct environmental monitoring of land. Land cover maps can be used to assess the state of the environment and monitor land use. The result of the introduction of innovations is to increase yields, improve the agrochemical properties of the soil, save financial costs due to the optimal use of seed material, fertilizers, plant protection products and fuel.

The Global Food and Agriculture Information and Early Warning System monitors the status of major food crops around the world. The information system uses remote sensing data to provide information on the availability of water and vegetation during the harvest seasons. Finally, automatic irrigation systems aimed at providing plants with the strictly necessary amount of water, taking into account the actual precipitation.

Digital technologies introduced in animal husbandry are aimed at recording livestock and characteristics of livestock and forming a diet, including machine vision for accounting livestock; livestock face recognition systems, shaping animal diet [1].

Today, along with traditional isolated solutions in different segments, most large manufacturers are following the path of creating and developing their own digital ecosystems, entering partnerships both with specialized development companies and with each other.

An example is a digital solution that automatically exchanges data between equipment and an office system based on accounting system (1C) in a two-way format. The system allows not only to control the technical characteristics of the machine, but also performs the functions of a Monitor with the implemented functionality of work according to instructions. This solution allows the integration of equipment from different manufacturers in one system, and also makes it possible to use different cartographic data.

The digitalization of veterinary activities is aimed primarily at the robotization of a part of veterinary services, animal counting and their remote health [1].

15.6 Imperatives of Transforming the Region into a Cost-Effective Ecosystem of Digital Highly Productive and Risk-Free Agriculture

Transformation of the region into a cost-effective ecosystem of digital highly productive and risk-free agriculture of the world level is possible only via technical modernization of the agro-industrial complex through the introduction of revolutionary digital models and technologies in the fields of crop production, animal husbandry, and industrial aquaculture, as well as complexes of intellectual autonomous agricultural machines.

If we take into consideration, the approach of the Russian Federation, we should admit the existence of the following challenges, both objective and subjective caused by the modern Russian socioeconomic system [1]:

- preserving national interests and ensuring food security in the agro-industrial complex and agricultural machinery;
- ensuring the leadership of national business entities of the agro-industrial complex and agricultural machinery in world market;
- creation and implementation of technologies for risk-free autonomous agriculture;
- implementation of innovations in the most conservative sector of the Russian economy—agriculture;
- resource saving, recycling water supply systems, reducing the negative impact on the environment and the health of citizens.

Considering the set of competitive advantages of the Rostov region, the main of them are [1]: favourable climatic conditions and a rich raw material base; developed transport infrastructure; highly developed industry, primarily the machine-building complex.

The modern strategy for self-sufficient production caused the transformation of scientific state services, which include four dimensions, namely [1]:

1) R&D for business (improvement of existing products/technologies; creation of new products/technologies; import substitution);

2) digital transformation of the enterprise (increased speed and flexibility of production; cost reduction; improving product quality);

3) personnel of a new generation (training of specialists for enterprises; increased labor productivity; work safety);

4) state support for business (federal project status; government funding; intangible support).

The deficit of professionals and population aging calls for the early identification, selection and training of children who have shown outstanding abilities in studies, science, and creativity; creating conditions to support the research trajectory and personal and professional development of students. The mission of the government in the Russian Federation is to form the integrated macro-regional system for identifying, selecting, training, and psychological and pedagogical support for gifted children and talented youth, which meets the principles of the national technological initiative and based on the mechanisms of social partnership and networking of educational organizations of all levels of education and other participants in the system of innovative development of the South of Russia.

The agro-industrial complex is still at the stage of vertically integrated holdings as the dominant business model, there is an increase in the consolidation of players, someone goes to the upstream, someone to the downstream. It is the modern idea to rebuild the existing business models resulting in adding the new layer of producers—module manufacturers. Figure 15.1 shows the interconnection between three different layers of suppliers, which form a unified system aimed at reducing risks and implement the digital transformation at local, national, and global levels.

The transformation of production systems and implementing digitalization in agriculture relies on active farmers of particular type. Farming for her or him is a way of living—the farm is passed down from generations to generations, working with children with plans to inherit the farm. Such farmers know everything about the production process, have special education, but not business education. These people have an established production process and main distribution channels and are at the stage of searching for growth points (there is generally money for growth). The average portrait includes the feature of understanding modern technologies with the active use of the Internet.

The key challenges in modern post-Soviet countries are [14]: finding reliable suppliers with quality goods to build partnerships supplier relationships that affect product quality; finding specialists as there is a deficit of professional, which can be trusted in terms of product quality, therefore, the way out is to hire young people, train and develop; poor logistics—even though there are available networks open for cooperation, but delivery still stays a problem. The only solutions are to find young and promising, quality raw materials and reliable suppliers, equipment and sophisticated technique, buying services aimed at improving the production process.

The ideal digital ecosystem for agrobusiness entities must have the following features [14]. All goods, services, and services of the agricultural sector should be collected here, which enable the automation of agricultural processes, save time, resources and bring out the agribusiness of small farms to a new level. Digitalization, which has affected all sectors of the economy, has not bypassed the agriculture. However, the introduction of IT technologies is not easy for many farms. Being busy with numerous current tasks they have there is simply not enough time and resources for implementation, even already existing technological solutions. Farming is worth telling about complex agricultural technologies in simple language, help farmers farms and enterprises of the agro-industrial complex to automate work and receive in a convenient digital format the necessary for these services. Form chains that ensure the movement of goods, and so by the most to fulfil one of the tasks facing the state within digital agriculture. Provide agricultural producers with access to standardized information about new advanced technologies in agriculture; increase the level of knowledge of agricultural producers through placement in the ecosystem of distance online courses created in partnership with specialized educational institutions; to ensure the growth of exports of agricultural products by creating special services for potential exporters; facilitate access to financial resources by creating dedicated consulting services to help farmers to find their way and prepare the required information.

Industry 4.0 forms the technological framework for adoption of cyber-physical integration principles in manufacturing, supply chains, and logistics. The online nature of data, the use of offline decision-making tools is limited to real needs in decision-making support in SC disruption risk management [8].

The data analytics methodology is new for this field, therefore, a lot of aspects could be predicted and evaluated, for example, the geospatial spread of diseases, emerging trends in consumer behavior during pandemic and other disasters, and so on. There are several basic principles to underline the new approaches in decision-making process concerning agriculture.

First, decision-making support is considered a viable system model consisting of predisruption, disruption, and postdisruption elements. Decisions in risk management are in correspondence with disruption profiles, containing periods of preparedness, response, and recovery and stabilization. Optimization models, as well as simulation ones assist in resilience analysis, stress-testing and simulation of contingent policies of recovery.

Second, there is the unification of cyber and physical information applying online modeling. Decision making support models use physical sources data (ERP, RFID, sensors), as well as cyber sources (blockchain, supplier collaboration portals, and risk data).

Third, the supply chain models integrate both cyber and physical networks.

Fourth, risk analytics systems of data-driven supply chain rely on the data usage for disruption pattern recognition and learning.

15.7   Conclusion

Modern global trends in agriculture determine the need for transformation of business models used by farmers and agricultural holdings. The key global trends are rapid population growth; increasing government involvement; changes in consumer preferences shifting towards healthy, functional, and organic food; growing demand for food, produced using sophisticated technologies, or from unique products; biotechnology and nanotechnology; integrated production and distribution chains; moving from a grocery to a service model.

The related digital technologies used in agrobusiness include mobile devices, cloud computing, IoT platforms, intelligent sensors, 3D-printing, augmented reality/wearable technology, location technologies, big data analysis and advanced algorithms, authentication and fraud detection, multilevel customer interaction and collection of customer information, as well as advanced interfaces for human-machine interaction.

The efficiency of digitalization of agriculture depends on the type of countries providing it. There are three basic groups with the descending efficiency: technological innovators or countries of the "golden billion" (able to generate high technology, intelligently exploit the world, have high technological competitiveness); technological followers (to some extent can use high technology and at least hypothetically set development goals that have targets of the first group of countries); technological outsiders or "third world" (not capable of competitive self-development in a globalized environment).

The technological leaders can transform their agricultural systems into totally digitalized and innovative, while the rest of the world need to solve several problems at the same time, including simultaneous reforming of their technological systems and introducing methods and special institutions, which are way ahead of the general real sector of economy.

In turn, the main problems of the scientific and technical sector of Ukraine also creating risks of digitalization failure in agriculture are the aging of scientific personnel; moral and physical aging of the research and production base; inadequate system of formation of priorities of works; detachment from the next stages of the innovation cycle (introduction into serial production, market research and ensuring effective demand). In the complex, the situation is characterized by the following negative trends: degradation of the education system; intellectual degradation of society; "outflow of intelligence" from Ukraine; internal "outflow of intelligence" from the field of education and science; the lack of an established system of lifelong learning.

Any innovative changes require the combination of market economic tools and governmental indicative planning. Leading countries of the world (for example, China, USA, France, Japan, etc.) successfully use national indicative planning systems (in turn, the EU applies certain elements, such as 7-year development plans—financial regulations). Technological progress and the information economy stimulate the development of new management approaches. There is a need to introduce scientifically sound forecasting of technological and socioeconomic trends in the strategic horizon of 25 to 30 years, this period is explained by the approximate duration of waves of technological innovation. Timely forecasting of the emergence and spread of fundamentally new technologies, equipment and industrial designs allows the national socioeconomic system to gradually adapt to new challenges, reducing fluctuations for domestic producers and consumers.

Long-term research proves the effectiveness of the use of 5-year indicative plans for innovation and investment activities of industrial enterprises, which is due to the sufficiency of this period to achieve the following results: construction of large enterprises; development of natural deposits; creation of production and special infrastructure; completion of the training cycle.

Stereotypes are the main hazards for innovative changes in agrobusiness in general, and digitalization in particular. There is a common feeling that digitalization is long, expensive, and difficult process, but in practice it is a short-term (usually up to 7 days), one-time investment in an understandable user-friendly environment. The main risks and hazards for digitalization in post-Soviet countries are lack of staff, outflow of young specialists; lack of confidence in the justification of such expenses; low awareness of opportunities; illiteracy and conservatism; sabotaging the implementation of automation systems, ensuring the transparency of processes, theft; legal barriers in the field of certification and operation; different data formats; lack of appropriate financial resources.

Transformation of the region into a cost-effective ecosystem of digital highly productive and risk-free agriculture of the world level is possible only via technical modernization of the agroindustrial complex through the introduction of revolutionary digital models and technologies in the fields of crop production, animal husbandry, and industrial aquaculture, as well as complexes of intellectual autonomous agricultural machines.

The modern strategy for self-sufficient production caused the transformation of scientific state services, which include four dimension, namely R&D for business (improvement of existing products/technologies, creation of new products/technologies, import substitution); digital transformation of the enterprise (increased speed and flexibility of production, cost reduction, improving product quality); personnel of a new generation (training of specialists for enterprises, increased labor productivity, work safety); state support for business (federal project status, government funding, intangible support).

References

1. Alekseev, A., The role of scientific and educational centres in solving the problem of digital transformation of priority sectors of the regional economy. Experience of the Rostov region in the field of agro-industrial complex, in: *Series of online broadcasts "Digital transformation of regions". Session 4. Digitalization of the agro-industrial complex: opportunities and risks*, 2020, October, https://events.vedomosti.ru/events/spb_%D1%81ifrovaya_transformaciya_4/materials.
2. Antoniuk, L., Poruchnyk, A., Savchuk, V., Innovations: theory, in: *mechanism of development and commercialization*, Kyiv National Economic University named after Vadym Hetman, Kyiv, 2003.
3. Arhiereev, S., *Innovative potential of Ukraine: Predictive and Analytical Estimations*, Golden Pages, Kharkiv, 2008.
4. Drozdenko, V., Innovations in the era of globalization, in: *Collection of scientific publications of IWEIR of NAS of Ukraine*, vol. 49, pp. 58–62, 2006.
5. *Economic security*, Knowledge, Kyiv, 2009.
6. *Global competitive space*, Kyiv National Economic University named after Vadym Hetman, Kyiv, 2007.
7. Demidova, L.G., Klimov, S.M., Sherbakovskiy, G.Z., Ananov, N.G. *Indicative planning: theory and ways of improvement*. Znaniye, Saint Petersburg, 2000.

8. Ivanov, D. and Dolgui, A., A digital supply chain twin for managing the disruption risks and resilience in the era of Industry. *Prod. Plan. Control.*, 32, 9, 775–788, 2021. https://doi.org/10.1080/09537287.2020.1768450.

9. Khvesyk, M., Development of productive forces of Ukraine: status quo and prospects, in: *Formation of market economy. Special issue*, 2009.

10. Kirdina, O., Improving methods and principles of organization of investment and innovation activities in railway transport. *Bull. Transp. Econ. Ind.*, 32, 262–269, 2010.

11. Kosenko, A., Innovation and investment component of the formation of the competitiveness of the national economy. *Actual problems Public administration*, 1, 358–365, 2010.

12. Kosogor, S., Digital transformation of the agro-industrial complex: tasks and prospects for digitalization of agriculture. Expert opinion. *Ser. Online broadcasts "Digital transformation regions". Session 4. Digitalization agro-industrial complex: opportunities risks*, 4, 2020, October. https://events.vedomosti.ru/events/spb_%D1%81ifrovaya_transformaciya_4/materials.

13. Kukurudza, I., Innovative component of economic security of Ukraine. *Bull. Econ. Sci. Ukr.*, 2, 14, 93–97, 2008.

14. Lyubaeva, I., Digital Ecosystem for Agro-Industrial Complex Enterprises. *Ser. Online broadcasts "Digital transformation regions". Session 4. Digitalization agro-industrial complex: opportunities risks*, 4, 2020, October. https://events.vedomosti.ru/events/spb_%D1%81ifrovaya_transformaciya_4/materials.

15. Malinovska, O., *Labour migration: social consequences and ways of reaction*, National Institute of Strategic Research, Kyiv, 2011.

16. Nikitchenko, A., Digitalization of the agro-industrial complex in Russia and the world: trends, technologies, best practices and barriers. *Series of online broadcasts. Digital transformation regions". Session 4. Digitalization agro-industrial complex: opportunities risks*, 4, 2020, October. https://events.vedomosti.ru/events/spb_%D1%81ifrovaya_transformaciya_4/materials.

17. Pakhomov, Yu. N., The main tasks of forming a post-crisis model of economic development in Ukraine. *Economic Annals-XXI*, 1–2, 3, 2010.

18. Sednev, V., Far Eastern alternative. Chinese phenomenon, in: *Civilization models of our time and their historical roots*, Naukova Dumka, Kyiv, 2002.

19. Sednev, V., Asian reforms: a formula for success, in: *Civilizational models of our time and their historical roots*, Naukova Dumka, Kyiv, 2002.

20. Shvydanenko, H., Kuziomko, V., Noritsyna, N., and others, *Economic security of business*, Kyiv, Kyiv National Economic University named after Vadym Hetman, 2011.

21. Skrytnikova, I., Risks of digitalization: myths and reality, concerns of industry participants. *Ser. Online broadcasts "Digital transformation regions". Session 4. Digitalization agro-industrial complex: opportunities risks*, 4, 2020, October. https://events.vedomosti.ru/events/spb_%D1%81ifrovaya_transformaciya_4/materials.

22. *Strategy of innovative development of Ukraine for 2010-2020 in the conditions of globalization challenges,* Parliamentary edition, Kyiv, 2009.

23. Volynsky, G., About the quality of corporate governance. *Econ. Ukr.,* 1, 43–44, 2009.

24. Yevdokimov, F. and Gubska, M., Social potential as a function of the innovative model of economic development of the enterprise. *Mark.: Theor. Pract.,* 14, 15, 2008. http://www.nbuv.gov.ua/Portal/Soc_Gum/Mtip/2008_14/evdokimov.pdf.

16

Water Resource Management in Distributed Irrigation Systems

Varlamova Lyudmila P.[1]*, Yakubov Maqsadhon S.[2] and Elmurodova Barno E.[3]

[1]Department Computational Mathematics and Information Systems, National University of Uzbekistan, Tashkent, Uzbekistan
[2]Department Information Technologies, Tashkent University of Information Technologies named after Muhammad Al-Kwarazmi, Tashkent, Uzbekistan
[3]Department Information Technologies, Karshi Branch of Tashkent University of Information Technologies named after Muhammad Al-Kwarazmi, Karshi, Uzbekistan

Abstract

The important waterways of the Amu Darya and the Syr Darya run in Central Asia, which have their own tributaries and provide fresh water to the regions of several countries. One of the problems of farming is water supply. Here, an important role is played by special climatic and tectonic conditions, different spatiotemporal levels, the filling capacity, and dependence of water bodies on rainfall, snow melting, the presence of erosion-accumulative processes, and the formation of a micro-stream network.

Since water management systems and facilities have large spatial dimensions, as well as many technological parameters, it is possible to obtain quantitative and qualitative changes in their characteristics only on the basis of mathematical modeling methods. To date, there is no unified systematic approach to the issue of modeling the dynamics of water management facilities, there is only a wide class of mathematical models of individual objects of different complexity. That is why the choice of mathematical models that will describe the complex processes of water distribution in water management systems with the required degree of accuracy is a very problematic task.

---

*Corresponding author: vlp@bk.ru

Roheet Bhatnagar, Nitin Kumar Tripathi, Nitu Bhatnagar and Chandan Kumar Panda (eds.)
The Digital Agricultural Revolution: Innovations and Challenges in Agriculture through Technology Disruptions, (359–378) © 2022 Scrivener Publishing LLC

Keywords: Mathematical modeling, water resources, waterways, agriculture, irrigation channels, static and dynamic model, lumped parameter

16.1   Introduction

Today, the development of computer technologies makes it possible to use them for modeling and managing water resources of water management systems and objects, which include sections of rivers, reservoirs and canals of irrigation systems. Computer modeling makes it possible to simulate the behavior of individual water facilities in conditions close to real ones, taking into account all influencing factors.

The important waterways of the Amu Darya and the Syr Darya run in Central Asia, which have their own tributaries and provide fresh water to the regions of several countries. Since the climate in Central Asia is sharply continental, there is practically no precipitation in summer, and agriculture requires water supply. Here, an important role is played by special climatic and tectonic conditions, different spatiotemporal levels, the filling capacity and dependence of water bodies on rainfall, snow melting, the presence of erosion-accumulative processes and the formation of a micro-stream network.

Quantitative and qualitative changes in the characteristics of the water management system objects, which has a large spatial extent, many technological parameters, can be investigated on the basis mathematical modeling methods. To date, modeling the dynamics of complex processes of water management objects is carried out using mathematical models of individual objects. A complex water management system is divided into separate parts, then modeling problems of varying complexity are solved. There is no unified systematic approach. The task of choosing a mathematical model for the processes of distribution water resources in water management systems, with the required degree of accuracy, is difficult.

16.2   Types of Mathematical Models for Modeling the Process of Managing Irrigation Channels

For solving problems modeling the process of managing irrigation channels, mathematical models are divided into three groups:

- models describing the static state of the system;
- models describing the system in dynamics consider processes with lumped parameters;
- dynamic models of systems with distributed parameters.

These models differ from each other in the initial parameters, the amount and type of input information, the degree of results detail of obtained, and the degree of calculation accuracy.

In static models, algebraic dependencies between the required and known parameters are determined. This includes various modifications of regression models, hydrological series models, and so on. Indicators of these models are calculated based on observational data and field experiments using identification methods (least square methods, maximum likelihood method, etc.).

The advantages of static models include their simplicity, a small amount of input information, the possibility of using a computer, and the speed of obtaining information. With their help, it is possible to determine the characteristics of the watercourse in the sections where the observations were carried out, with a certain degree of probability. The disadvantages of static models include the limited possibilities of using them for the designed objects. Static models do not provide a sufficient amount of information about the process and are of little use outside the water facilities, sections, which are being monitored.

Lumped dynamic models explore small stretches of a river by comparing its wavelength. The characteristics of these models are concentrated at a single point, and the size of the plot is ignored. These models are used to calculate water flow characteristics only in individual sections of the site. Lumped-parameter models also include hydrological models, such as linear and nonlinear reservoir models, black box models, and so on.

When exploring dynamical systems, their dimensions are often neglected, considering that we are talking about material points that do not have geometric dimensions. The study of objects with distributed parameters should take into account their spatial extent. There are a number of ways to mathematically model distributed objects:

1. using partial differential equations;
2. with the help of linear integral equations, the kernel of which reflect the intrinsic properties of the object;
3. based on the structural theory of distributed systems, which allows transfer functions of typical objects of distributed systems to obtain the structure of a complex object;

4. modal representation in the form of expansion of the state function in an infinite series;
5. approximate modeling by simplified representation of the original differential equations of the object.

16.3   Building a River Model

A river basin can be viewed as a dynamic system with lumped parameters that transform the input factors $p(t)$—liquid precipitation and snowmelt—into a basin flow hydrograph $Q(t)$. The same applies for the river section.

Here, $p(t)$—input, a $Q(t)$—output, which are functions of time t. The general expression for the ratio between the input and output of a linear dynamic system with concentrated parameters can be written as:

$$a_n(t)\frac{d^n Q}{dt^n}+a_{n-1}(t)\frac{d^{n-1}Q}{dt^{n-1}}+\cdots+a_1(t)\frac{dQ}{dt}+a_0(t)Q=$$
$$b_n(t)\frac{d^n P}{dt^n}+b_{n-1}(t)\frac{d^{n-1}P}{dt^{n-1}}+\cdots+b_1(t)\frac{dP}{dt}+b_0(t)P, \qquad (16.1)$$

where coefficients a_i and b_i are the parameters that characterize the system properties. Solving this equation under zero initial conditions leads to the following expression:

$$Q(t)=\int_0^1 h(t,\tau)P(\tau)d\tau, \qquad (16.2)$$

function $h(t, \tau)$ shows reaction of system during the time t per unit input pulse per time τ. There are numerous approximations for representing hydrological systems as equations that include the influence function $h(t, \tau)$.

If coefficients a_i and b_i are constant in time, that the system is time invariant and equation (16.2) turns into the Duhamel integral:

$$Q(t)=\int_0^1 h(t-\tau)P(\tau)d\tau. \qquad (16.3)$$

To solve the problem of modeling the processes of water resources management in irrigation systems, in this paper, a simplified form of Saint-Venant equations is used.

It should be noted that the considered types of water flow are realized in channels, the cross-sections of which can have different shapes and change along the axis. The integral form of the Saint-Venant equations is derived from the equations of conservation of mass and momentum (Navier–Stokes equations), which are valid in situations where shallow water conditions are not met:

$$\int_{x_1}^{x_2}(\omega_{t_2}-\omega_{t_1})dx+\int_{t_1}^{t_2}(Q_{x_2}-Q_{x_1})dt=0, \qquad (16.4)$$

where $Q = v\omega$;

ω, the area of the live section; x, coordinate along the length of the section; t, time.

Without taking into account the Coriolis forces, friction, and viscosity, the differential form of the system of one-dimensional Saint-Venant equations has the form:

$$i-\frac{\partial h}{\partial x}=\frac{v}{g}\frac{\partial v}{\partial x}+\frac{1}{g}\frac{\partial v}{\partial t}+\frac{|v|v}{C^2R}+\frac{qv}{g\omega}, \qquad (16.5)$$

$$\frac{\partial \omega}{\partial t}+\frac{\partial Q}{\partial x}=q;$$

where C, Shezi coefficient; R, hydraulic radius; q, lateral inflow.

The advantage of the above models is the use of a small number of proven initial positions, clear and strict mathematical formulation of problems.

A significant advantage of hydraulic models is their versatility. They are applicable both in the design and in the operation of sections of rivers and canals, suitable for long-term intensive use in difficult conditions. With their help, it is possible to obtain characteristics of processes with the required detail and an acceptable error. Therefore, despite the high cost of development, they have become widespread. This primarily applies to one-dimensional mathematical models.

The disadvantages of hydraulic models are mainly related to processes in riverbeds, where there is an occurrence of thickened or other sections of the river where the water almost does not move. Nontransit zones serve as storage tanks, so such zones should not be taken into account in the flow cross-section. In channels with proper maintenance, the appearance of nontransit zones is almost not observed, so these disadvantages of hydraulic models can be ignored.

Thus, it is hydraulic models that are of the greatest interest for the study of dynamic processes in water management facilities and systems.

16.3.1   Classification of Models by Solution Methods

The abovementioned models can be classified by their solution methods. Methods for solving shallow water equations (Saint-Venant) are divided into three groups. The first group includes solutions obtained as a result of attempts to find the General integral of the Saint-Venant equations using the method of differential characteristics followed by the use of equations in finite differences.

The second group consists of solutions using mathematical analysis in the theory of small-amplitude waves.

The third group includes solutions obtained as a result of approximate integration of the Saint-Venant equations with their preliminary replacement by equations in finite differences. The mathematical modeling of unsteady water movement in streams was led by the research of Saint-Venant, Navier-Stokes, L. A. Rastigin, J. Stoker, and others.

16.3.2   Method of Characteristics

In the method of characteristics of Khristianovich, the system of Saint-Venant equations is replaced by an equivalent system of four ordinary differential equations, which are two equations of the characteristics (forward and reverse) and two equations that connect the flow elements along these characteristics. The system of four equations is solved in finite differences and allows calculating the coordinates t and s of the nodes of the characteristic grid in the wave plane. Then the calculated coordinates are used to determine the values of the flow parameters: $Q(s, t)$, $z(s, t)$. In addition, equations in characteristic form are used in grid methods for calculating regime elements in boundary gates. When deterministic methods do not allow us to solve problems with the required accuracy, we have to intentionally introduce an element of randomness into the search algorithm. Then randomness will serve to collect information about the behavior of the object of study and management goals. For the first time, the idea of the benefits of random behavior in search was formulated By W. R. Ashby in his book "the construction of the brain", one of the first in Russia to solve this problem was L. A. Rastrigin. The main idea of the random search method is to find a random point on the water surface and integrate the study function from the initial (base) point to it. Despite the randomness of the sample point selection, the random search algorithm provides a consistent approximation to the extreme region.

16.3.3   Hydrological Analogy Method

The method of hydrological analogy [3] is based on the construction of a graphical relationship between the flow of two rivers. Let us say that for river Y there is a hydrological series of observations for n years. In this case, the coefficient of variation is determined, and the standard error is calculated based on it (<10%):

$$C_v = \sqrt{\frac{\Sigma(k_i - 1)^2}{n-1}} \qquad (16.6)$$

$$\delta q = \frac{C_y}{\sqrt{n}} \cdot 100\% \qquad (16.7)$$

Average annual expenditure:

$$Q_{cp.i} = \frac{\Sigma Q_{cp.Mec}}{12} \qquad (16.8)$$

The rate of flow:

$$Q_0 = \frac{\Sigma Q_{cp.i}}{n} \qquad (16.9)$$

If the error exceeds 10%, the hydrographic characteristics are used to determine an analog river with a large number of flow measurements (Figure 16.1):

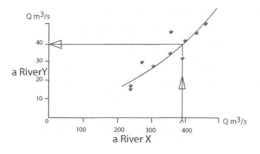

Figure 16.1 Graphical relationship between strings.

The correlation coefficient between the series values is calculated for a time section where there are readings for both rivers:

$$R = \frac{((Q_{cp.A_i} - Q_{o.A}) \cdot (Q_{cp.ИСЛ.i} - Q_{0.ИСЛ}))}{\sqrt{\Sigma \Delta Q^2_{ИСЛ.i} \cdot \Sigma \Delta Q^2_{A.i}}} \quad , R \geq 0.7 \qquad (16.10)$$

Determining the regression coefficient:

$$k_{Qa/Qисл} = R \cdot \frac{\delta_{Qa}}{\sigma_{Qисл}} \qquad (16.11)$$

Standard deviation of the series:

$$\sigma_{Qисл} = \sqrt{\frac{\Sigma(Q_{cp.ИСЛi} - Q_{0исл})^2}{n-1}} \qquad (16.12)$$

$$\sigma_{Qa} = \sqrt{\frac{\Sigma(Q_{cp.ai} - Q_{0a})^2}{n-1}} \qquad (16.13)$$

Direct regression equation: a

$$Q_{cp.ИСЛi} - Q_{0исл} = K \frac{Q_a}{Q_{исл}} * (Q_{cpai} - Q_{0a}) \qquad (16.14)$$

direct link between rivers can be constructed analytically (based on the regression equation) Figure 16.2.

The method of straight lines is considered as a limiting case of the grid method, when using a rectangular grid, one of its linear dimensions tends to zero, and the set of nodes in the limit fills a certain system of rectilinear parallel segments. In this case, partial differential equations are reduced to a system of ordinary differential equations by replacing the derivatives of the corresponding unknown with difference relations.

In the study of Semyonchin and Vandina [4], a mathematical model of unsteady water movement in the riverbed was studied, which is a system of Saint-Venant equations. Semyonchin and Vandina led the system to the

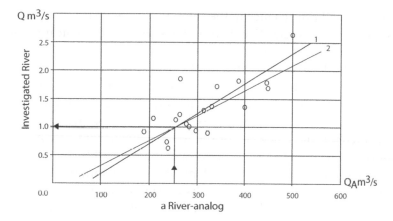

Figure 16.2 Graphical links between the flow of two rivers.

convection-diffusion equation, which, under certain restrictions on the flow depth, allows an analytical solution.

In the study of Grushevsky [5], studies of the propagation of waves of releases and floods in rivers are summarized, and the influence of factors of natural channels on waves of releases and floods is considered. The author investigates the possibility, accuracy, and limits of applying a one-dimensional model—the classical Saint-Venant equations for unsteady water movement in flood-free open channels.

16.3.4   Analysis of Works on the Formulation of Boundary Value Problems

Most of the works are devoted to the mathematical formulation of boundary problems, the creation of numerical methods for solving them using explicit difference schemes, the development of methods for determining morphometric and hydraulic characteristics, their approximation, identification and determination by solving inverse problems. Kartvelishvili [6] constructed distribution functions of multidimensional probabilities that control the process of river flow. He also derived equations in finite differences of this process to set out the basic principles of probabilistic forecasting of river flow. The main advantage of the explicit scheme is the relative ease of constructing the solution algorithm and software implementation. In addition, the solution of an explicit (difference) scheme can be written out explicitly using recurrent relations.

The stability of the difference scheme means that small perturbations in the initial data and the right side of the difference scheme lead to a uniformly small time change in the solution. The finite element method is considered the most effective method for solving hydrological problems, but it is poorly understood.

The method of combined use of water resources was studied by Shtengelov and Filimonova [7]. The essence of the method is to combine in time mutually protective surface and underground water intakes. Combined water intake systems (CVS) are environmentally friendly, as they increase the efficiency of the water management system without building new reservoirs. And groundwater is a renewable resource.

The HBV (Hydrologiska Byråns Vattenbalansavdelning) [8] model was developed by Bergstrom at the Swedish meteorological and hydrological Institute. It is a conceptual model of a catchment area that consists of precipitation, air temperature, and potential total evaporation – snowmelt, runoff, or inflow to a reservoir. The HBV model describes the overall water balance as follows:

$$P - E - Q = d/dt \, (SP + SM + UZ + LZ + VL), \qquad (16.15)$$

where P is the precipitation intensity; E, total evaporation (i.e., evaporation rate); Q, runoff (replenishment rate); SP, snow cover; SM, soil moisture; UZ, upper zone; LZ, lower zone; VL, volume of lakes.

However, in fact, equation (16.15) shows only the moisture balance.

In 1961, a monograph by Ladyynezhskaya was published, devoted to the problems of stationary fluid flow. The substance of this work is described by Ames (1965). Based on a comparison of the fluid flow problem described by the Navier-Stokes equations with other problems, Ames assumed that the only solution exists below a certain limit value of the Reynolds number. However, the question arises: are the Navier-Stokes equations themselves valid for Reynolds numbers that exceed the turbulence value? In the case of a finite-difference solution of a boundary value problem, the situation may become even more complicated because of the ambiguity of the boundary conditions.

In the work of Künge et al. [8], the possibility of using the system of Saint-Venant equations in a simplified form in the study and prediction of flood situations is shown. However, the authors do not take into account the time dependence of the flow depth and do not describe methods and algorithms for solving the resulting equation.

Levent Kavvas et al. [9] presented the results of studying water flow in a multifactional space, that is, they developed consistent equations for water management taking into account the continuity of its movement in time, space, and for the transition flow of water into the soil. Kiyoaki et al. [10] investigated the flow of two-phase media in channels; Kaganovich

[11] analyzed river processes on the basis of network theory, which allows estimating parameters in steady-state modes using generalized indicators; Lyapichev Yu [12] presented methods for calculating and designing hydraulic structures of complex and power hydroelectric facilities; Deskelesku [13] developed a system for automated water distribution by direct selection of costs; Takuya *et al.* [14] developed a method for designing discrete control for linear-invariant systems with continuous time, based on optimization of the sum of absolute values (SOAV); Duc Thai and Thuong [15] used CNN cellular neural network technology and CNN-UM universal machines with physical parallel computing architecture to solve the Saint-Venant 2D equations; Magdalena *et al.* [16] presented estimates of the friction velocity in a nonstationary flow using two formulas derived from two-dimensional Reynolds equations and one-dimensional Saint-Venant equations.

16.4 Spatial Hierarchy of River Terrain

In distributed irrigation systems solved, the problem of the reliability of the control is not processing the data, and dispersed, diverse network objects (rivers, channels, water sites, water intakes, etc.), ensuring the mode of operation of interrelated material flows system equipment, monitoring and technical analysis facilities, dispersed over large distances and control the means of processing, transmission and reception of data of distributed objects by hierarchical levels of management (Table 16.1) [1].

A small catchment basin is a complex geomorphological system in which the system-forming factor is the activity of surface waters [1]. To represent the scale of hierarchy of flow channels, we assume that rivers can be called objects with an area of at least 50 square kilometers, this corresponds to the length of a water flow of about 10 km. In other words, small rivers are in the same order of magnitude. Based on these considerations, we will build a hierarchical table of fluvial landforms.

In addition to spatial parameters, it is necessary to consider the timeframe of water bodies. Shumm [2] suggests that there are three main time intervals for calculating the water balance:

1. cyclic time—a large geological time interval, millions of years;
2. stadium time—the time during which individual landforms can reach equilibrium due to the negative feedback mechanism;

Table 16.1 Spatial hierarchy of river terrain.

No.	Interval, km	Fluvial forms
1	<0.0001	Individual irregularities, aggregates and particles
2	0.0001–0.001	Microrelief on slopes and bottom
3	0.001–0.01	Brook network
4	0.01–0.1	Slopes and bottoms
5	0.1–1	Elementary catchment areas
6	1–10	Small catchment areas
7	10–100	small river basins
8	100–1000	Middle river basins
9	>1000	Major river basins

3. sustainable development time—short periods for small areas where only a small flow of water and sediment affects the course of processes.

Modern time intervals include intervals ranging from seasonal to annual events. Modern time intervals refer to elementary river basins, slopes, and bottoms of small basins. Modern processes that occur within small catchment areas are represented by the formation and reformation of a stream network, ravine formation, and slope processes that occur before the eyes of the researcher.

Surface water in channels flows under the influence of different forces. Gravity is crucial here—it causes the movement of water and sediment, the precipitation of debris on the slopes in the channels and bottoms of small catchments. The tectonic uplift forms a hydrographic network pattern. Therefore, an adequate choice of the space-time level is of great importance for research. Heavy precipitation and snowmelt affect areas of slopes, in the formation of a micro-stream network, and in riverbeds—at the level of local deformations. The change of seasons changes the vegetation cover in the water, which affects the erosion-accumulative processes. It follows from the above that factors of high hierarchical space-time levels are conditions at lower levels. Small catchment basins are usually studied using morphometric analysis, analysis of aerial photographs, where you can examine in detail the structure of slopes, lengths, areas, and vegetation cover features.

16.4.1   Small Drainage Basin Study Scheme

Small drainage basin study scheme:

1. determination of spatial-temporal hierarchical level,
2. analysis of morphological elements, and morphological structure,
3. elucidation of characteristic features of dynamics and functioning,
4. application development—prognosis and recommendations on management.

The above diagram may vary depending on the depth of the study, but it describes the main steps in the study of small catchment areas.

16.4.2   Modeling Water Management in Uzbekistan

Modeling of water resources management processes in distributed irrigation systems is convenient to conduct from the standpoint of a formal-logical approach based on elements of the relationship theory. In this case, the description of geographically distributed systems is limited to relations, each of which is based on a pair of sets of elements of this system. Different sets of system elements can act as a pair of sets. For a formal description, the system is mathematically represented as a tuple:

$$M = <Z_B; R1, \ldots, Rm>,$$ (16.16)

where Z_B is the set of distributed elements on territory B, R_1, R_2, ..., R_m, relationships in this set.

Area B covers the territories of districts B_h (h = 1, H). In our case, these are three districts: upper, lower, and middle Chirchik. Multiple Z_B consist from:

$$Z_B = Z_1 \cup Z_2 \cup Z_3$$ (16.17)

16.4.3   Stages of Developing a Water Resources Management Model

As elements of Z_B, there may be functional subsystems, distributed objects, management tasks, performance objectives, technical means, and so on. The elements of relationships can be relations of similarity, equivalence, necessity, transitivity, subordination, and so on. Development of a water management model for irrigation systems includes:

1. Building a model of the objects and distributed in the district:

$$M_{Q_h} = <I_{hT}(Q); R_1, \ldots, R_m >$$ (16.18)

where $I_{hT}(Q)$ – set of objects with set of states $Q = \{q_1, q_2, \ldots, q_h\}$.

2. Determination of compliance of objects and the set of possible States at time T:

$$\Psi_{Q_{ht}} : I_{hT} \rightarrow Q_{hT},$$ (16.19)

where $I_{hT}(Q)$ and Q_{hT} – lots of objects and lots of their States.

3. Building a model of current management, which consists in defining

$$M_T = \langle I_{hT}(Q_T) \cdot J_{hT}(E_{hT}), E_{hT}, A_{hT}; R_1, \ldots, R_m \rangle,$$ (16.20)

where M_T is the model of this state; $I_{hT}(Q_T)$, set of objects, state of which on time T characterized by Q_T; $J_{hT}(E_{hT})$, set of works, caused by the presence of many defects E_{hT}, A_{hT}, set of material, money, work resources.

The conformity of the works and defects

$$\Psi_{E_{ht}} : E_{hT} \rightarrow J_{hT}(E_{hT}),$$ (16.21)

The conformity of the defects and object states

$$\Psi_{Q_{ht}} : E_{hT} \rightarrow Q_{hT},$$ (16.22)

The conformity of the works and objects

$$\Psi_{J_{ht}} : J_{hT}(E_{hT}) - I_{hT}(Q_T),$$ (16.23)

Recourses distribution to works

$$\Psi_{A_{ht}} : A_{hT} \rightarrow I_{hT}(Q_T), \cdot A_{hT} \subset A_{hT}^0,$$ (16.24)

where A_{hT}^{0} – the specified set of resources for the area.

4. Development of a model of operational management, which consists in determining:

Model of transmission system nodes

$$Y_i = q_i X_i + r_i, i = \overline{1,h}, \tag{16.25}$$

where q_i is the node transfer function; X_i signal on input i-th node; Y_i output signal; r_i, probability of transmitting a false signal; models of connection systems for operators serving dispersed objects; number of operators.

5. Development of a management reliability model, which includes: building a model for data transmission from distributed objects, determining the performance of distributed irrigation systems, structural methods for improving the reliability of dispersed objects, operational methods for improving reliability, determining the radius of action of distributed objects, taking into account reliability.

Unlike other methods of forming models, the formal-logical method takes into account the features of geographically distributed systems. The problems of reliability of the hierarchical level control line are considered mainly for technical systems, but for the class of geographically distributed water resources system, it has not yet been practically solved [17].

There are two groups of management structures: organizational and functional. Elements of the organizational structure are service points for distributed objects, departments, services, performers, district management, technical facilities, and so on, and functional subsystems for performing target functions, tasks of functional subsystems, task indicators, management functions, and so on.

The methodology for studying the organizational structure of management is system analysis, which assumes that the management system is divided into subsystems until the main indicators of the system are reached. The analysis is based on mathematical models

$$M_{sy} = < S_Y; R_1, \ldots, R_m >; M_{I_h} = < I_h; R_1, \ldots, R_m >;$$

$$M_L = < L_1; R_1, \ldots, R_m >; \tag{16.26}$$

$$\Psi_{S_y} : S_Y \rightarrow L; \Psi_{I_h} : I_h \rightarrow L \tag{16.27}$$

where M_{sy}, M_{I_h}, M_L are the mathematical models of subsystem S_Y set of objects I_h, management levels L; Ψ_{S_y}; Ψ_{I_h}, showing elements of set S_Y in elements of L and I_h in L.

As a result of the analysis, elements of the control subsystems $s_Y \in S_Y$, levels of the control hierarchy l∈L and object relationships are determined.

The characteristics of each type of object in conventional units are determined from the same positions using the formula

$$e_i = \frac{X_i}{x_i}, \tag{16.28}$$

where e_i is the characteristics of the i-th object; x_i, a reference unit for the i-th object type; X_i, the value of the i-th object, which is determined by the reference unit (the length of the channel portion, the wave velocity of discharge, etc.).

There are various options (r) placement of points on the surface of the water, which affect the costs of time and money to study the irrigation system. Consider these influences. Let us take the conditional value $\frac{1}{p}$ for the area of a circle with a diameter d, then the average distance between the nodes of the studied grid on the river section is

$$l_{\Pi}^h = \gamma \sqrt{\frac{4h}{\pi I_h}};$$

where γ is the path lengthening coefficient and l_{Π}^h, the average distance between network nodes.

The s_Y control subsystems are distributed across hierarchical control levels. Let us denote by S_Y^l the number of control elements of the organizational system distributed at the l-th hierarchical level.

16.5   Organizations in the Structure of Water Resources Management

In the regional structure of water resources management, in the most general terms, at the highest level of the hierarchy are the organization "Central Asian Cooperation" (CAC) and the international Fund for saving the Aral sea (IFAS), which includes water resources management in the CAR as one of the aspects of political management of the region [18].

The official structure of water resources management in Central Asia includes the following vertical hierarchy levels and corresponding water management organizations:

1. Interstate level by ICWC (interstate Commission for Water Coordination) of Central Asia. ICWC was established on February 18, 1992, by Kazakhstan, Kyrgyzstan, Tajikistan, Uzbekistan and Turkmenistan.
2. Regional basin level—basin water management Association "Amudarya", BVI "Syrdarya." Part of Audarins-basin management who include Chardzhou, Kurgan-Tyube, Urgench, Nukusskaya BU. And the Syrdarya Department includes Gulistan, Uchkurgan, Chardara, Chirchik BU [19].
3. National Level, where water resources are managed by the main Water agencies. In Uzbekistan—the ministry of water management.
4. Management of the main channels (systems).
5. Management of irrigation systems.
6. Divisions of irrigation districts.

The ministry of water management are also included On the state water inspection, Gupy "Suwayeh," "Biometrik Markaz," "Usawebsite," "Submarinechannel," Scientific Research Institute of irrigation and water problems, educational institutions [20].

16.6   Conclusion

Thus, water resources management in the Republic of Uzbekistan is carried out at three levels: main, basin and district.

It is almost impossible or difficult to carry out field experiments, therefore, the use of modeling methods in difficult irrigation conditions is simply necessary.

References

1. Bondarev, V.P., Hierarchy of small catchment areas, in: *Geomorphology*, 2, pp. 10–18, 2010. https://www.researchgate.net/publication/338409549_Ierarhia_malyh_bassejnov_Geomorfologia
2. Shumm, S.A., *The Fluvial System*, p. 243, Wiley Interscience, New York, 1977.

3. Rozhdestvensky, A.V. (Ed.), *Methodological recommendations for determining the calculated hydrological characteristics in the absence of hydrometric observations*, p. 194, Nestor-istoriya, Saint Petersburg, 2009.

4. E. A. Semenchin, N. V. Vandina The Analisis of Saint-Venant Equation System analytical and numerical Methods. Scientific Journal of KubGAU, 64, 10, 1–14, 2010. http://ej.kubagro.ru/2010/10/pdf/05.pdf

5. Grushevskiy M. S., *Waves of releases and floods in rivers.*, Leningrad: Hydrometeorological Publishing House, pp. 340, 1969. http://www.cawater-info.net/library/rus/hist/grushevskiy.pdf

6. Kartvelishvili N. A., *Stochastic hydrology.*, Leningrad: Hydrometeorological Publishing House, pp. 163, 1975.

7. Shtengelov R. S., Filimonova E. A., UDC 556.182 Combined water intake systems as a method of optimal water resources management, ResearchGate, 11, 1-8, 2019. https://www.researchgate.net/publication/337548069

8. Kyunzh, Zh. A., Holley, F.M., Vervey, A., *Numerical methods in problems of river hydraulics*, M. Energoatomizdat (Ed.), p. 256, 1985.

9. Levent Kavvas, M., Ercan, A., Polsinelli, J., Governing equations of transient soil water flow and soil water flux in multidimensional fractional anisotropic media and fractional time. Special Issue: Modeling hydrological processes and changes. *Hydrol. Earth Syst. Sci.*, 21, 1547–1557, March 2017. 10.5194/hess-21-1547-2017.

10. Kiyoaki, D., Niroyuki, T., Tomosada, J., Sudden expansion of gas-solid two-phase flow. *Bull. JSME*, 25, 200, 190–195, 1982.

11. Kaganovich, B.M., Aganovich, B.M.K., Kelko, A.V., Shamanskiy, V.A., Shirkalin, I.A., On the area of equilibrium thermodynamics application. *Proc. Of ASME 2044 International Mech. Eng. Congress*, Anaheim, California, USA, November, 13-19, pp. 197–203, 2004, 10.1115/IMECE2004-60775.

12. Lyapichev Yu. P., *Hydrotechnical structures: Textbook manual*, Moscow.: RUDN (publishing house of the Peoples' Friendship University of Russia), p. 302, 2008.

13. Deskelescu, N., Rational distribution of water in the irrigation network, translation from Romanian and ed. VC. Stefan. -Moscow.: Kolos, p. 158, 1982.

14. Ikeda, T., Nagahara, M., Ono, S., "Discrete-Valued Control of Linear Time-Invariant Systems by Sum-of-Absolute-Values Optimization". https://ieeexplore.ieee.org/document/7740936/authors#authors.

15. Vu, D.T. and Pham, T.C., "*Solving two-dimensional Saint venant equation by using cellular neural network*", https://ieeexplore.ieee.org/document/5276317/authors#authors.

16. Mrokowska, M.M., Rowiński, P.M., Kalinowska, M.B., Evaluation of friction velocity in unsteady flow experiments. https://www.tandfonline.com/doi/full/10.1080/00221686.2015.1072853.

17. Varlamova, L.P., *Multilevel distributed control system*, vol. 13, pp. 347–352, Bulletin of KazNU, Almaty, 2008.
18. Aydarova, A.B. and Yakubov, M.S., Development of a model of rational distribution of water Resources in the Chirchik river basin. *Int. Sci. J., "Science time"*, Society of science and creativity, Kazan, Russia, 3, pp. 44–49, 2017.
19. Aydarova, A.B. and Yakubov, M.S., *Rational distribution of water resources*, Lambert Academic Publishing, Germany, pp. 176, 2015.
20. Aydarova, A.B., Review of mathematical models of water resources management in irrigation systems. Technical Sciences, ISSN 2181-96. *Dog J.*, 5, vol. 3, Issue 5, pp. 63–69, 2020, 10.26739/2181-96. https://www.tadqiqot.uz/index.php/technical/article/view/2695/2549

17

Digital Transformation via Blockchain in the Agricultural Commodity Value Chain

Necla İ. Küçükçolak*† and Ali Sabri Taylan*‡

Turkish Mercantile Exchange, Ankara, Turkey

Abstract

It becomes a necessity to benefit from technological innovations for ensuring food supply security and continuity, increasing productivity and staying competitive. In the Agriculture 4.0 and digitalization era, the Internet of Things, artificial intelligence, satellite technologies, cloud computing, big data management, business intelligence, and data analytics can provide solutions from farm to fork. With limited resources because of increasing population, demographic developments, change in diet, insufficiency of food supply, and climate change, there is a need to change the way of doing business, thus utilizing the developments in technology.

Blockchain technology has become a phenomenal in recent years and is evolving into a form that institutionalized organizations can benefit from. The Internet of Things integrates blockchain technology into the agricultural sector and provide the automation of the control mechanisms in the agricultural food supply chain. In this study, utilization of technology in various forms from farm to fork is evaluated. Furthermore, a FINTECH solution framework via blockchain is made for digitalization of agricultural commodity value chain that secures contract creation, transfer, and redemption (burn) process.

Keywords: Agriculture 4.0, digital agriculture, food supply security, precision agriculture

---

(*) The ideas expressed in this study are the authors' own and do not reflect nor represent those of the Company they work for.
†*Corresponding author*: necla.kucukcolak@turib.com.tr; ORCID:0000-0002-7097-5423
‡*Corresponding author*: sabri.taylan@turib.com.tr; ORCID:0000-0001-9514-934X

Roheet Bhatnagar, Nitin Kumar Tripathi, Nitu Bhatnagar and Chandan Kumar Panda (eds.)
The Digital Agricultural Revolution: Innovations and Challenges in Agriculture through Technology Disruptions, (379–398) © 2022 Scrivener Publishing LLC

17.1   Introduction

Food insecurity has turned out to be a major issue for all countries, especially after global stresses are realized, such as the recent COVID-19 pandemic and the global food supply crisis in 2008. Researches show that the production efficiency in agriculture increased by an average of 4% every year in the 1980s and 1990s but has remained only 1% in recent years. For this reason, it becomes a necessity to utilize technological innovations in the process of assuring food supply security and continuity, making agriculture attractive as a profession and increasing its productivity [1].

Before transforming the sector in order for establishing adaptability in a digital era, it is significant to identify core problems and to define strategic objectives in food trading value chain. Accordingly, a digital ecosystem that addresses these problems and provides standardization and integration of food trading value chain can be framed. Digitalization and standardization will accelerate the vertical integration among industry, trade and agriculture, which helps development of the securitization opportunities. Thanks to vertical integration of the ecosystem, it will also be easier to access finance and funding of the ecosystem. For the efficient transformational management and adaptation, the design should be made with the collaboration of the whole system stakeholders [2–4].

In this framework, the first section of this study reviews precision agriculture in practice from farm to fork. Literature review, as well as practices on blockchain in agribusiness, is made in the second section. The third part discusses a framework for digitalization in trading chain of agricultural ecosystem. The last part makes general evaluation for the digitalization framework and recommendations for further research.

17.2   Precision Agriculture for Food Supply Security

Precision agriculture envisages to provide the effective use of inputs and thus to reduce its effects on the environment. This can also contribute to ensuring uniformity in product quality. It targets to reduce the costs of chemicals, such as fertilizers and pesticides, to reduce environmental pollution, to provide high-quantity and high-quality products, to provide a more effective information flow for business and agriculture decisions, and to establish data accumulation in agriculture, which helps to prevent the informal economy. By gathering and analyzing spatial and nonspatial agriculture-related data, precision agriculture stimulates financing, production, trading, distribution, and all other related processes. Widespread data are gathered and processed from global positioning and geographic information vehicles for precision agriculture solutions. The establishment of the data management framework, creation of ethical standards while sharing the data produced, formation of the framework for artificial intelligence are some of the points that should be addressed to establish an healthy ecosystem for precision agriculture solutions.

Technologies for determining and measuring soil moisture, plant nutrients, soil texture, crop condition, and other characteristics of soil and plant are those precision agriculture application methods at the farm level. With the widespread use of precision agricultural solutions instead of conventional use of methods, it is not only possible to improve production, literacy, income, and living standards but also to have environmentally friendly and sustainable agricultural production.

The precision agriculture has the following components [5, 6]:

i.   Internet of Things (IoT),
ii.   Sensors and remote sensing for plant, soil and weed,
iii.   Product monitoring devices,
iv.   Unmanned aerial and ground vehicles,
v.   Variable Rate Applications (VRA),
vi.   Digital image processing,
vii.   Geographic Information Systems (GIS),
viii.   Global Positioning Systems (GPS),
ix.   Big data analytics,
x.   Digital twin,
xi.   Block-chain based solutions.

The followings are some of the practices also used in Turkish agriculture sector.

17.2.1   Smart Agriculture Business

Smart agriculture business refers to managing agricultural business using technologies. Thanks to developments in imaging and remote sensing systems in recent years, unmanned aerial vehicles (UAV) are also effectively used in agriculture sector. These applications combine information and communication, as well as Internet of things (IoT), robots, artificial intelligence and big data to detect disease, water stress and weed flora; to estimate yield/maturity; to control water resources and; to monitor workers.

The agricultural UAV market is growing and a domestic solution named ZIHA has recently developed in-house jointly by TARNET and TAGEM,

Table 17.1 Comparison of ZIHA with alternative methods.

Manual	Tractor	ZIHA
Product loss 1%	*Product loss* 3–5%	*Product loss* none
Workers' health Serious health problems	*Workers' health* Health problems	*Workers' health* None
Water use 10–15 lt.	*Water use* 20–30 lt.	*Water use* 6–8 lt.

Source: [7].

respectively, the Agricultural Credit Cooperatives of Turkey participation and the General Directorate of Agricultural Research and Policies in the Ministry of Agriculture and Forestry of Turkey. The aim of the ZIHA project is to develop national agricultural technologies for proper drug distribution, examining the amount of medicine reaching the target, depending on weather conditions and spraying characteristics. ZIHA, which is expected to increase productivity in agriculture, is important in gathering agricultural data, focusing on national agricultural technology and competing with other markets (Table 17.1).

The IoT devices monitor and analyze and control the physical properties of a farm (e.g., weather conditions, humidity sensor, wind and pressure sensor, soil temperature, animal and machine tracking systems, irrigation sensor) with the data it gathers by connecting and exchanging to other devices and systems.

In the intellectual agriculture business, Doktar, a local solution provider, which collects agricultural data from the farmland, makes use of satellites, IoT remote sensing devices, drones, results of laboratory analyzes, and other tools; produces digital and precision agriculture applications assisted by farm management platforms, big data processing, machine learning, and statistical analysis on account of turn these solutions into agrarian productivity-enhancing and innovation move (Figure 17.1). Digital agricultural products provided are as follows [8]:

i.   Agricultural information services facilitates easy access to information on agricultural techniques.

ii. Agricultural sensor station to describe the best strategy about sprinkler or spraying irrigation with the field data.

Figure 17.1 Doktar: Agricultural information services, Source: [8].

   iii. Digital soil analysis to perform fast and profitable outcomes by specifying the chemistry of fertilizer, water, and soil

   iv. Variable rate fertilizer application to reach yield potential by taking differences within the field into account

   v. Crop health monitoring to track farmland's health via daily satellite images to recognize problematical zones in the field

   vi. Farm management system to trace profitability by recording every operational and financial activities

   vii. Digital pheromone trap for real-time tracking of pets

Another private sector solution ImeceMobil not only exchanges agricultural sector information but also integrates banking system for agricultural loan, agricultural insurance and relevant services without going to the branch. Furthermore, it added "request an offer" feature as a bidding

Figure 17.2 ImeceMobil: Solutions for herbal production and livestock-related problems, Source: [9].

platform (Figure 17.2). The vision of the application is the use of more than 50% of farmers in Turkey [9].

17.2.2   Trading Venues for Contract Farming, Crowdfunding and E-Trades

Organized trading platforms facilitate a ready market for parties for sale and purchase defined contracts within the framework of defined rules and regulations. They provide maximum safety for everyone's investments, transparency, and efficient price formation. In addition to trading environment, organized platforms generally provide post trade solution that enables fund transfers.

Contract farming is considered as an important approach in terms of a solution for agricultural financing as an agreement between the producer and the contractor/buyer, within the specified plan, including the commitment (Figure 17.3). Within the scope of digitalization and technological transformation in the agricultural sector, it is seen that contract farming is also realized through digital platforms.

Easy to use mobile platforms for traders of every kind are also changing marketing and trading habits in all sectors. From open outcry to e-trades, the nature of commodity markets is also changing. DITAP, the Digital Agricultural Market, is another step taken for digitalization of the contract farming in Turkey by the Ministry of Agriculture and Forestry. DITAP is an advertisement board where sellers and buyers in the agrifood nosiness meet. Contractors, buyers, sellers and producers are registered on a voluntary basis

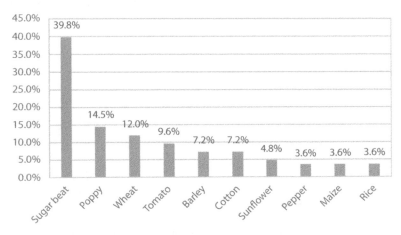

Figure 17.3 Top 10 in Contract Farming in Turkey, Source: [10].

and digital onboarding them is done through e-government digital gateway, a website offering access to all public services from a single point. The Ministry of Trade is verifying the DITAP system registered contractor's or buyer's credibility. The Agricultural Information System of the Ministry of Agriculture and Forestry will verify the existence of the producer (Table 17.2).

Table 17.2 DITAP phases.

First phase of the DITAP	Second phase of the DITAP
• Registration of producers and producers ask prices to the system on a voluntary basis, • Buyer and producer access to the system, • Verification of the buyer's creditability by the Ministry of Trade, • Inquiry of the existence of the producer with the Agriculture Information System, • Planning the production and delivery dates in accordance with the buyer and producer agreement, • Orientation to organic and agricultural practices at the request stage, • Delivery of offers to the parties via short message service-SMS, • The buyer can offer all product requested, • Making separate advance planning for payments, • Establishment of goods acceptance criteria, packaging and shipping conditions, • To be able to make cash or in-kind advances, • Signing and archiving the contract electronically, • Providing self-control based on scoring by the evaluation of each of the parties, and consequently, all stakeholders meeting.	• Including animal products in the scope, • Providing easy access to finance through banks, • Conversion of the contracts into negotiable instruments, • Integration with the state registry system, • Establishment of surveillance and third-party control mechanisms, • Processing satellite image with geographic information system, • Establishing an insurance structure that includes financial risks, • Registration of the contract through the central securities depository, • Subjecting the trading transactions made through the system to the mercantile exchange registration, • Integration with foreign markets • Coordination of the Ministries, the Turkish Union of Chambers and Commodity Exchanges to ensure its operation.

Source: [11].

DITAP also functions as crowdfunding platform in the agrifood sector via bringing together producers/sellers and contractors/buyers on an online platform without intermediaries within the scope of digitalization of agriculture to serve this purpose in terms of increasing production, productivity and trade. In this system, planned production is carried out with contracted production. In the Digital Agriculture Market, it is aimed that all stakeholders (producers, consumers, and sectors) who take an active role in the agriculture sector will gain commercially.

Regarding organized commodity market, Turkish Mercantile Exchange (TMEX) is the first national mercantile exchange and a distinct trading platform that serves for digitalization and securitization of agrifood sector commodities. The TMEX's spot Electronic Warehouse Receipt (EWR) Market was launched in the middle of grain harvest season in 2019. Turkish Mercantile Exchange was established to run markets on agrifood electronic warehouse receipts and derivative contracts with agricultural sector products' underlyings.

One of the major participants of the TMEX Trading Platform is the Turkish Grain Board, established in 1938 as a state enterprise to stabilize grain market. Thanks to its netting solution of advance payment made by the buyer in contract farming framework, major contract farming buyers, Turkey Sugar Factories Inc. and Agricultural Credit Cooperatives are other two important participants integrated to the TMEX Trading Platform. Turkey Sugar Factories Inc. is the largest company in the sugar sector. The establishment of Agricultural Credit Cooperatives of Turkey dates back to 1863 and has a Central Union and 17 Regional Unions, 1622 Cooperatives, 197 Service Bureaus, 15 Companies, approximately 9 thousand employees and 850 thousand members.

17.3   Blockchain Technology Practices and Literature Reviews on Food Supply Chain

Blockchain digital technology, with its distributed, decentralized and secure database of any transaction linking transfer of value without the need of intermediaries, is stimulating various areas in a drastic way. Its success in cryptocurrencies has attracted attention on blockchain and its use in other areas was evaluated. This technology can grant untrusted participants to communicate and send transactions between each other even though there is lack of trust between the parties involved in the collaboration. In this regard, main reasons for its preferences can be listed as efficiency and security as well as lower costs.

Among its diverse applications, banking and financial sector is dominant in utilizing this technology (Figure 17.4). It is becoming promising technology for the next generation of IoT [12] and smart contracts [13].

Blockchain helps improving significant concerns in relation to the safety and privacy protection in IoT industry. Because of transparency and fault tolerance in solving problems among untrusted parties get involved in distribution of resources; blockchain is harnessed by different entities [14, 15]. Because of its feature in ensuring identification of product origin and simplifying tracking of processes; there are various project on the integration of blockchain technology into the food supply chain around the world, most of them are projects aimed at facilitating companies' control of food safety and transparency.

Regarding use of blockchain technology in trading value chain, there are various examples at the international level for funding of small-scale farmers, whereas common practice in the agricultural sector in Turkey is the use of conventional technologies. At the trading platform level, latency is an important criterion in choosing the technology. There are still performance issues discussed due to low number of transactions processed per second in the blockchain. Another issue is that, the regulatory framework for the use of blockchain technology has not been well addressed yet by the regulatory authorities. Among the international practices, finance and finance-related sectors are utilizing blockchain technology as depicted in the Figure 17.4. For commodity market, Binkabi is an example where farmers in developing countries can sell their products, while at the same time, can be funded or mutually funded, and different commodities can be bought and sold through a common cryptocurrency [16].

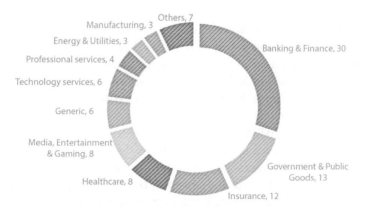

Figure 17.4 Sector-based blockchain technology usage, Source: [17].

Among various projects and researches on the integration of blockchain technology into the supply chain of the agrifood business around the world, the IBM Food Trust project provides food safety, tracking function and automation of supply chain of companies using blockchain and IoT technology. The IBM Food Trust project is also used in the product named Mousseline purée, which is launched in partnership with Nestle and Carrefour. In addition, Fairfood, Albert Heijn, and Starbucks are other examples working on blockchain projects to increase the transparency and security of the agrifood supply chain [16–18].

Considering the blockchain applications discussed above, blockchain provides communications between smart objects and smart objects are connected with Internet technology via IoTs, global networks [19]. Autonomous work can be executed by smart objects. They help removing the centralized authority or human control requirement [20]. Blockchain technology is a promising model, and it is still required further analysis to understand capabilities and limitations of this disruptive technology [21]. In the following subsections, food supply chain and smart contracts based on blockchain technology have been addressed.

17.3.1   Food Supply Chain

Blockchain technology's successful functionality in cryptocurrencies attracted other areas to address security, trust, accuracy, and cost efficiency issues. One of these areas is agriculture food supply chain. This technology is evaluated by agricultural food supply chain stakeholders to harness its features to solve problems of the chain where numerous untrusted actors get involved. It facilitates secure tracking process from farm to fork to prevent counterfeits and ensures the reliability among supply chain partners [22, 23].

According to examples in practice on utilizing blockchain in the food supply chain show that most of initiatives use blockchain to trace, locate and allow direct exchange of foods and goods without a monetary systems [24]. Based on studies of Kshetri [25], the six main categories among 49 initiatives based on blockchain technology in agrifood supply chain are as follows in Table 17.3.

Together with the IoT, it is promising that blockchain will provide smart solutions and safe means of communication that brings an efficient solution which removes centralized authority or human control necessities [19, 20]. It is more efficient and cheaper, because it enables faster cross border trade with no time zone limitations removing central authority or human control and no transfer fees [26].

Table 17.3 Food supply chain initiatives based on blockchain.

Project/initiative category	No. of projects/ initiatives	Share (%)
Food integrity	24	49.5
Small farmers' support	8	16.0
Supply chain supervision & management improvement	7	14.5
Waste reduction & environmental awareness	5	10.0
Food safety	3	6.0
Food security	2	4.0
Total	**49**	**100.0**

Source: [25].

Although major added value of the technology is on the traceability in value chain of agricultural sector, with its small and medium-sized enterprise structure, adopting to the technology is also a challenge and major barrier to spread its use in the agrifood business.

17.3.2 Smart Contracts

Smart contract is the computational object and digital illustration of an agreement between two or more parties. The concept of digital smart contracts dates back more than 20 years [27]. A smart contract created as a digital twin of a real-life legal contract is a computer-based transaction protocol, which is intended to automatically execute, control, or document the relevant events, actions and terms of agreement, such as termination method, promise object set or exercise of the right. Smart contract references the contract's subject in a dynamic form with much better observation and authentication [28–31].

Regarding the implementation of the smart contracts, blockchain technology is proposed. In this way, the trust environment is provided by blockchain technology without an authority overseeing the agreement like a real-life e-commerce transaction [32]. Smart contracts created on the blockchain with computer programs are consist of the program's code and memory files. Any user can create a contract by sending a transaction via blockchain. When the program code in the contract is created, the contract becomes fixed and cannot be changed [33] and the memory file of the smart contract is stored in the blockchain [34]. The system flow is depicted in Figure 17.5.

In developing smart contract; Ethereum is the first system. After Ethereum's introduction, numerous smart contract applications have been built either on Ethereum or by splitting Ethereum in supply chain origin crowdfunding, security, and derivatives trading. Another blockchain based program emerged was Hawk [13]. Bitcoin and NXT are other blockchain platforms that smart contracts can be developed [35]. Code analysis and performance evaluation of a smart contract creation platform are very vital since a bug can cause catastrophic damages (e.g. steal of smart contracts) [30].

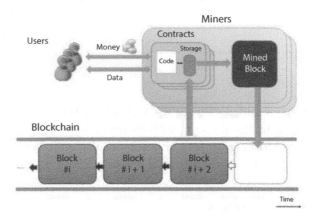

Figure 17.5 Smart contract system, Source: [33].

Figure 17.6 Agricultural sector value chain digitalization phases, Source: Drawn by the authors.

17.4   Agricultural Sector Value Chain Digitalization

The three-phased digitalization proposal (Figure 17.6) is depicted in the following section. The proposal is addressing the challenges in digitalizing commodity trading value chain, based on the existing agribusiness juristical and technical restrictions in Turkey.

17.4.1   Digital Solution for Contract Farming

Contract farming (CF) is a forward agreement between farmers and buyers, frequently at predetermined prices. Contract farming provides solutions for buyers in providing production support to manage shortcomings with respect to inputs. With CF, the producers enjoy easy access to advance payments and production services, as well as knowledge of new technology. It can reduce uncertainty and risk.

Trading venues (e.g., TMEX and DITAP in Turkey) may develop a smart contract farming technology implementation, which will leverage blockchain technology. This technology will allow buyers to purchase smart agrifood contracts which provide transparency to the steps in the process because every step is being followed up via blockchain ledger. This will be a solution for agrifood business participants to access funding for their projects.

The blockchain technology will comfort management of the contractual liabilities between the buyer and producer. This technology might also help management of utility tokens for the circulation of inputs. The inputs can be fertilizer, seeds, machinery and equipment, transportation, labor, rent, and so on. The utility-based smart contracts will hold records of buyer, producer, balance for each party, status of the deal, project, parties' performance and other data including realizations for forward agreements. The agrifood commodity-backed token will be utilized to pay farming inputs provided by the suppliers. Each transaction becomes a blockchain contract that the technological architecture assures a transparent environment where parties can track the transactions.

The smart contract, with its peer-to-peer structure, will facilitate access to various pools of fund that were never reachable to farmers. Those who provide finance to the projects will be able to get the advantageous benefits.

Delivery of the harvested product is the second step in the digitalization process after the contract farming. In this regard, agrifood and its supply chain will be subject to tokenization. This will be realized by the trading venues' tokenization protocol.

In this model, physical equivalent of agrifood commodity digitalized by the tokenization and smart contract, which is stored in authorized/licensed warehouses, will be listed in the trading venues' order book. Physical delivery principles should be defined to diminish volatility in prices for every digital agrifood commodity in the agricultural sector.

17.4.2   Commodity Funding

Farmers' access to fund is essential for sustainable agrifood business. The value chain is very fragmented that is why it is important to find collaboration areas for agrifood financing. We propose a marketplace that connects supply chain and finance providers. Tokenized structure and big data analytics will connect relevant parties, improve efficiency, and valorize (forward delivery) utility-based tokenization.

Tokens will be exchanged among crowdfunders in the trading venues. The crowdfunders will obtain profit or interest in addition to their initial capital invested. The platform might also act as a facilitator like cooperatives in organizing agreements with buyers for harvested agrifood commodities to assure the crowdfunders' gain.

17.4.2.1   Smart Contracts

Check is a type of bills of exchange that is used to meet the needs of commercial life and to resolve the problems of carrying cash [36]. Thanks to the smart contract system in the blockchain of a product, it will be possible to perform contractual production or transactions similar to postdated checks.

Although it is seen that similar cryptocurrencies meet financial transfer needs on a global scale, it is also used as an investment tool by a large part. Postdated checks, on the other hand, can be thought of as a kind of blockchain currency, for example, 6 months later, tied to TRY 10,000, unlike crypto currencies. In this way, it turns into an asset that allows the payment of today's debt rather than an investment tool [37].

In contract farming, it is aimed to have a transparent structure and to be clearly monitored by the public by the coinage of agricultural product production contracts with block chain technology, so that it can be used as a financialized instrument similar to a deferred check. All transactions carried out, depending on a certain commitment, can be shared with a certain number or all users in the system, and can be easily followed via smart contracts. While the system checks whether the amount of money to be paid to the farmer is in the wallet of the investor who will buy the product

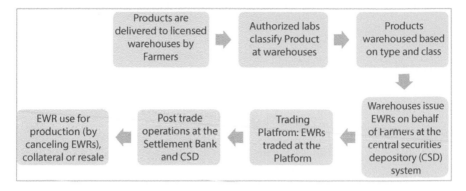

Figure 17.7 Smart contract: electronic warehouse receipts (EWR) trading ecosystem, Source: Prepared by the authors.

on the platform, it will be possible to check through the public authorities whether the farmer produces the promised product or how it produces it. In the futures sale of a product that is currently in the warehouse, a risk-free and low-cost transaction will be performed, largely thanks to the blockchain system and licensed warehousing (Figure 17.7).

17.4.2.2   Crowdfunding Token Trading

Within the framework of the tokenized commodity and smart contract trading, the Token Trading System (TTS) will allow trading of the tokens with agricommodity underlying which is stored in licensed warehouses. The TTS provides creation, redemption and transfer of commodity backed tokens services. In addition, it will also register and reconcile transactions. Furthermore, the system enables peer-to-peer trading of commodity backed digital tokens/receipts. The TTS will also allow crowdfunding tokens' trade deriving from contract farming deals.

17.4.3   Digital Transfer System

The Contract Farming Transferring System (CFTS) is the second leg of agrifood commodity and smart contract which are tokenized (Figure 17.8). The CFTS registers the smart contract farming participants, farmer and contract buyers. Once the participants agree, the buyer will provide finance via assigning a blockchain address with a digital money balance after buying the smart contract, based on utility token. Possession of the contract and title to the contract will be transferrable at the CFTS.

There are various systems for the transfer of financial instruments. One of them is Ripple, a digital network that hosts cryptocurrency and financial

Figure 17.8 Digital Commodity Ecosystem, Source: Prepared by the authors.

transactions. SWIFT, on the other hand, is an organization that ensures the reliable transfer of information arising from financial transactions carried out by member organizations. Turkish Akbank used Ripple chain block in cooperation with SWIFT began operations to international studies and Santander/UK sterling has started to transfer money [38]. EFT is a technology that empowers financial institutions over the investor's account through devices such as computers and phones that we frequently use in daily life. BIGA is a system for making tokens with block chain technology to facilitate the transfer of gold from one bank to another bank account. Gold subject to transfer is dematerialized, and physical provision is blocked. BIGA blockchain network requires permission and is designed with Hyperledger [39]. Similar tokenization examples are also seen in the energy sector. SolarCoin, established as a start-up for people generating electricity from solar energy, verifies the energy generated from solar panels in a distributed manner with other users (nodes) connected to the system and rewards the producer with SolarCoin for the energy produced in return. This coin is traded on some exchanges and can be converted into other assets such as Dollars and Bitcoin [40].

A centralized blockchain system will be very useful for the tokenization and tracking of transfer transactions. In this way, the information required to keep confidential information can be shared with the market, but should be under the supervision of the authorities, so it can be monitored. In addition, through smart contracts, all information of the agreement can be viewed by the authorities and the parties if desired. In case of disagreement between the parties, the audit will be easier thanks to the smart contracts.

17.5   Conclusion

Currently, the use of blockchain focuses on cryptocurrencies, payment methods and international financial transactions. It is thought that the use of blockchain will be quite wide in areas where supply chain management interlink with the financial sector. It is expected that IoT and blockchain will find a wide area, especially in supply chain control.

The projects and researches aim to provide solutions to inefficient supply chains in the agricultural commodity market and to the loss of value created by intermediaries in the ecosystem due to lack of trust in these supply chains. Blockchain technology might provide innovative solutions to the agrifood market. With the blockchain system, farmers access easily financing sources and trading venues to market their products at fair prices. This ecosystem will improve the income of the farmers.

In this study, digitalization of agricultural commodity trading is discussed within the framework of blockchain technology use. Beginning from warehoused agrifood commodities in the value chain, blockchain technology can be used to monitor the system at a cost efficient and reliable structure. In the digitalized agricultural product value chain, utility tokens will be utilized as a means of payment/exchange.

Necessary regulatory framework for the proposed digitalization in the agrifood commodity trading should be further addressed. It should also cover regulations that secure pretoken and posttoken issuance on agriproduct. Further research is also required in selecting the best blockchain protocols or whether there is a need to create new blockchain protocol.

References

1. General Electric Turkey, "GE Turkey Blog," General Electric Turkey, 1 May 2017. [Online]. Available: https://geturkiyeblog.com/wp-content/uploads/2017/05/ge_turkiye_blog_gida_sanayinde_dijitallesme_firsatlar_raporu.pdf. [Accessed 14 June 2020].

2. Aljamal, S., The Practice of Transformational Management and its Role in Achieving Institutional Excellence from the Point of View of Workers in the Directorates of Education in Hebron. *Int. J. Bus. Ethics Gov.*, 1, 1, 64–90, 2018.

3. Hessian, M., The Impact of Managerial Ability on the Relation between Real Earnings Management and Future Firm's Performance: Applied Study. *Int. J. Bus. Ethics Gov.*, 1, 3, 43–80, 2018.

4. OECD-FAO, in: *OECD-FAO Agricultural Outlook 2019-2028*, OECD Publishing, Paris, France, 2019.
5. Newman, D., Forbes. *Top. Six Digital Transformation Trends Agric.* 2018, [Online]. Available: https://www.forbes.com/sites/danielnewman/2018/05/14/top-six-digital-transformation-trends-in-agriculture/?sh=375d-74b7ed2e. [Accessed 7 August 2020].
6. Tarlasera, Tarlasera. *Hassas Tarım Üretiminde Devrimin Diğer Adı Olacak*, 4 April 2018. [Online]. Available: https://www.tarlasera.com/haber-11475-hassas-tarim-uretimde-devrimin-diger-adi-olacak. [Accessed 13 August 2020].
7. TARNET, ZIHA: Zirai İnsansız Hava Aracı Agricultural Unmanned Aerial Vehicle, TARNET, July 2020. [Online]. Available: http://ziha.tarnet.com.tr/. [Accessed 13 August 2020].
8. DOKTAR, DOKTAR: Digital Agriculture, DOKTAR, 2020. [Online]. Available: https://www.doktar.com/. [Accessed 11 November 2020].
9. ImeceMobil, Softtech Ventures Teknoloji. *ImeceMobil: Solution herbal production livestock related problems*, 2020. [Online]. Available: https://imece-mobil.com.tr/. [Accessed 4 August 2020].
10. Credit Registration Office of Turkey, in: *Turkey Agricultural Outlook Field Research Report (Türkiye Tarımsal Görünüm Saha Araştırma Raporu)*, KKB - Credit Registration Office of Turkey, Istanbul, Turkey, 2019.
11. Pakdemirli, B., Sözleşmeli Tarımsal Üretim: DİTAP Modeli, *Tarım Ekonomisi Dergisi*, 26, 1, 81–88, 2020.
12. Zhang, Y. and Wen, J., An IoT Electric Business Model Based on the Protocol of Bitcoin, in: *Proceedings of 18th International Conference on Intelligence in Next Generation Networks (ICIN)*, 2015.
13. Kosba, A., Miller, A., Shi, E., Wen, Z., Papamanthou, C., Hawk: The blockchain model of cryptography and privacy-preserving smart contracts, in: *Proceedings of IEEE Symposium on Security and Privacy (SP), San Jose, CA, USA*, 2016.
14. Manski, S., Building the blockchain world: Technological commonwealth or just more of the same? *Strategic Change*, 26, 5, 511–522, 2017.
15. Sharma, S., Climate Change and Blockchain, 16 December 2017. [Online]. Available: https://ssrn.com/abstract=3088990. [Accessed 12 December 2020].
16. Binkabi, Binkabi Whitepaper, 2018. [Online]. Available: https://files.binkabi.io/binkabi-whitepaper.pdf. [Accessed 4 July 2020].
17. Hileman, G., Rauchs, M., Global Blockchain Benchmarking Study, 22 September 2017. [Online]. Available at SSRN: https://ssrn.com/abstract=3040224.
18. Loosbroek, V., 10 Blockchain projects in the agri-food industry that you should keep an eye on. *Cegeka*, 2019. [Online]. Available: https://www.cegeka.com/en/be/blog/10-blockchain-projects-in-the-agri-food-industry-that-you-should-keep-an-eye-on. [Accessed 4 August 2020].

19. Miorandi, D., Sicari, S., De Pellegrini, F., Chlamtac, I., Internet of things: Vision, applications and research challenges. *Ad. Hoc. Networks*, 10, 7, 1497–1516, 2012.

20. Panarello, A., Tapas, N., Merlino, G., Longo, F., Puliafito, A., Blockchain and IoT Integration: A Systematic Survey. *Sensors*, 18, 8, 2575–2612, 2018.

21. Konstantinidis, I., Siaminos, G., Timplalexis, C., Zervas, P., Peristeras, V., Decker, S., Blockchain for Business Applications: A Systematic Literature Review, in: *BIS 2018: Business Information Systems, vol. Lecture Notes in Business Information Processing*, vol. 320, W. Abramowicz and A. Paschke (Eds.), pp. 384–399, Springer, Berlin, Germany, 2018.

22. Toyoda, K., Mathiopoulos, P., Sasase, I., Ohtsuki, T., A Novel Blockchain-Based Product Ownership Management System (POMS) for Anti-Counterfeits in the Post Supply Chain. *IEEE Access*, 5, 17465–17477, 2017.

23. Kshetri, N., Blockchain's roles in strengthening cybersecurity and protecting privacy. *Telecomm. Policy*, 41, 10, 1027–1038, 2017.

24. Gatteschi, V., Lamberti, F., Demartini, C., Pranteda, C., Santamaria, V., To Blockchain or Not to Blockchain: That Is the Question. *IT Prof.*, 20, 2, 62–74, 2018.

25. Kamilaris, A., Fonts, A., Prenafeta-Baldu, F., The rise of blockchain technology in agriculture and food supply chains. *Trends Food Sci. Technol.*, 91, 640–652, 2019.

26. Fanning, K. and Centers, D.P., Blockchain and its coming impact on financial services. *J. Corp. Account. Finance*, 27, 5, 53–57, 2016.

27. Szabo, N., Formalizing and Securing Relationships on Public Networks. *First Monday*, 2, 9, 1997. [Online]. Available: https://firstmonday.org/ojs/index.php/fm/article/view/548/469 [Accessed 3 January 2022].

28. Szabo, N., Satoshi Nakamoto Institute, in: *The Idea of Smart Contracts*, 1997, [Online]. Available: https://nakamotoinstitute.org/the-idea-of-smart-contracts/. [Accessed 4 August 2020].

29. Röscheisen, M., Baldonado, M., Chang, K., Gravano, L., Ketchpel, S., Paepcke, A., The Stanford InfoBus and its service layers: Augmenting the internet with higher-level information management protocols, in: *Digital Libraries in Computer Science: The MeDoc Approach*, vol. Vols. Lecture Notes in Computer Science, Vol. 1392, A. Barth, M. Breu, A. Endres, A. de Kemp (Eds.), pp. 213–230, Springer, Berlin, Germany, 1998.

30. Zheng, Z., Xie, S., Dai, H., Chen, X., Wang, H., Blockchain challenges and opportunities: a survey. *Int. J. Web Grid Serv.*, 14, 4, 352–375, 2018.

31. Fries, M. and Paal, B., *Smart Contracts*, Mohr Siebeck, Germany, 2019.

32. Deloitte, CFO Insights - Getting smart about smart contracts, June 2016. [Online]. Available: https://www2.deloitte.com/content/dam/Deloitte/tr/Documents/finance/cfo-insights-getting-smart-contracts.pdf. [Accessed 13 August 2020.

33. Delmolino, K., Arnett, M., Kosba, A., Miller, A., Shi, E., Step by Step Towards Creating a Safe Smart Contract: Lessons and Insights from a Cryptocurrency

Lab, in: *Financial Cryptography and Data Security, Vols. Lecture Notes in Computer Science*, J. Clark, S. Meiklejohn, P. Ryan, D. Wallach, M. Brenner, K. Rohloff (Eds.), Springer, vol. 9604, pp. 79–94, 2016.

34. Tian, F., A supply chain traceability system for food safety based on HACCP, blockchain & Internet of things, in: *International Conference on Service Systems and Service Management*, 2017.

35. Alharby, M. and Moorsel, A., Blockchain Based Smart Contracts : A Systematic Mapping Study. *Comput. Sci. Informat. Technol.*, 7, 10, 125–140, 2017.

36. Köle, M. and Görgülü, F., Formal Requirement Of Cheques In The Light Of Recent Legislation And Enforcement Procedures Peculiar To Bill Of Exchange Based On Cheques. *Dicle Üniversitesi Hukuk Fakültesi Dergisi*, 21, 35, 79–157, 2017.

37. Türün, C., Tokenization of postdated check (Vadeli çeklerin tokenizasyonu), 29 January 2019. [Online]. Available: https://cemilturun.medium.com/vadeli-%C3%A7eklerin-tokenizasyonu-f82285f6db69. [Accessed 12 December 2020].

38. Akbank, Akbank Lab, Akbank, 2020. [Online]. Available: https://www.akbanklab.com/en/homepage. [Accessed 18 August 2020].

39. Takasbank, BiGA Project WhitePaper, 2019. [Online]. Available: https://biga.takasbank.com.tr/biga_whitepaper_en.pdf. [Accessed 4 August 2020].

40. Solar Coin, SolarCoin Policy Paper, 2014. [Online]. Available: https://solarcoin.org/wp-content/uploads/SolarCoin_Policy_Paper_EN-1.pdf. [Accessed 13 August 2020].

18

Role of Start-Ups in Altering Agrimarket Channel (Input-Output)

D. Rafi[1*] and Md. Mubeena[2]

[1]Department of Agricultural and Rural Management, TNAU, Coimbatore, India
[2]Department of Agricultural Extension, Business Manager, ABI, ICAR–NRCM, Hyderabad, India

Abstract

Indian agriculture is dynamic and tends to many changes from the period of green revolution in 1960s to later economic reforms in 1990 and present market linkage through e-Nam. Supply chain also changed from traditional view to modern view with respect to change in market conditions. Start-ups created new employment opportunities in agriculture sectors, and it all defined supply chain in a new way by reducing the marketing channels. Start-ups also influenced farmers positively with their activities by providing remunerative price to their price and also involved in eliminating middlemen to some extent. New-age entrepreneurs are bringing technological innovation to address challenges in supply chain and to unlock value across the supply chain. Indian Agri start-up ecosystem is mushrooming with 450 above start-ups that are currently operational, and over 50% focused on making the supply chain more efficient by improving market linkages. Inputs play a crucial role in extracting higher yields. Existing delivery system is not appropriate because of poor supply, lack of subsidies, improper infrastructure, lack of farm credit, and poor delivery systems.

Keywords: Remunerative price, farm credit, innovation, market linkage, start-up

*Corresponding author: rafilucky34@gmail.com

Roheet Bhatnagar, Nitin Kumar Tripathi, Nitu Bhatnagar and Chandan Kumar Panda (eds.)
The Digital Agricultural Revolution: Innovations and Challenges in Agriculture through Technology Disruptions, (399–410) © 2022 Scrivener Publishing LLC

18.1   Introduction

Indian agriculture is dynamic and tends to many changes from the period of green revolution in 1960s to later economic reforms in 1990 and present market linkage through e-Nam. Supply chain also changed from traditional view to modern view, with respect to change in market conditions. Technology improvement in the field of agriculture and well-structured agribusiness in India made the entry of start-ups in agriculture field [6]. Startups created new employment opportunities in agriculture sectors, and it all defined supply chain in a new way by reducing the marketing channels [1]. Start-ups also influenced farmers positively with their activities by providing remunerative price to their price and also involved in eliminating middlemen to some extent. Ninjacart, Farm-fresh, Go-fresh, Agrostar, Agri-Bazaar, Crofarm, and Big-basket are some of the agritech start-ups, which are operating successfully by redefining supply chain [9, 10]. Most of those are focused on attaining self-sufficiency, production, and protecting the farmers and consumers [11].

Now the scenario is changing by the transformation in agrifood supply chain (AFSC) with improved coordination between players. New-age entrepreneurs are bringing technological innovation to address challenges in supply chain and to unlock value across the supply chain. Indian Agri start-up ecosystem is mushrooming with 450 above start-ups that are currently operational, and over 50% focused on making the supply chain more efficient by improving market linkages [2].

18.2   Agriculture Supply Chain Management

Agriculture Supply Chain Management is the method of strategic maintenance of procurement, storage of products, material movement through the organization and its distribution channel that directs in getting maximum profits through cost reductive fulfilment of orders. Simply, supply chain acts as a bridge between demand and supply at input level, as well as output level. The detailed profile of agriculture supply chain is mentioned in Figure 18.1.

At:

    i.   **Pre-harvest stage** (i.e., by creating access to quality fertilizers, seeds, equipment, etc.)

   ii.   **Post-harvest stage** (by establishing seamless connections with marketplaces, retailers, etc.)

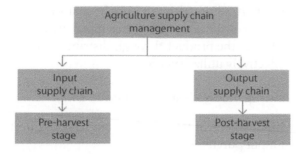

Figure 18.1 Flowchart of agrisupply chain.

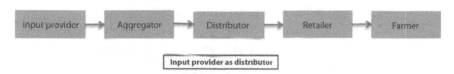

Figure 18.2 Traditional input supply chain.

Input Supply Chain

Inputs play a crucial role in extracting higher yields. Existing delivery system is not appropriate due to poor supply, lack of subsidies, improper infrastructure, lack of farm credit, and poor delivery systems.

Existing Input Models of SCM:

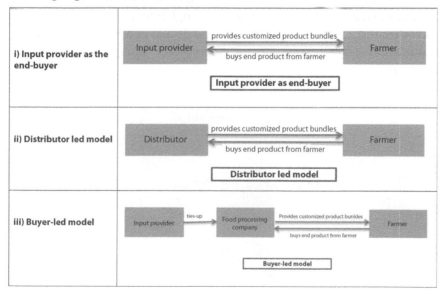

Figure 18.3 Existing models of supply chain.

In typical existing/traditional input supply chain as shown in Figure 18.2, input provider collaborates with other input providers to aggregate the supply and deliver the product through distributor and retailer. Here, all players can effectively utilize synergies.

Concerns in existing models (shown in Figure 18.3):

- More middlemen's in the supply chain resulting in the high cost of input purchase;
- Uncertainty of price, quality and availability;
- Misguiding about the right variety and type of input;
- No accountability reliable channel for crop advisory.

18.3 How Start-Ups Fill the Concerns and Gaps in Agri Input Supply Chain?

Start-ups are acting as digital aggregators by building m-commerce platforms (mobile-led Agri market place) where farmers can place orders and deliver it to the farmers' doorsteps, eliminating the middlemen and gaining cost-benefit in its markets place (Figure 18.4). By building intelligent platform, leveraging technologies like data analytics, artificial intelligence, image recognition, geo-mapping, and other social media platforms provide customized agroadvisory, soil-based crop and fertilizers recommendations and tracking farmer crop cycle through interactions via call centers and other social media platforms [3]. The details pertaining to agri-input manufacturers before and after of e-commerce emergence is shown in Figure 18.5.

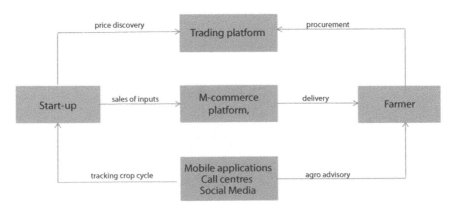

Figure 18.4 Start-up input supply chain model.

Agri-Input Manufacturers before e-Commerce

Integrated			Modularized		
Agri-Input Product formulations	Agri-Input Production	Warehousing and Distribution	Crop Advisory Services	Input Recommendations (Retailing)	Credit Management

Agri-Input Manufacturers after e-Commerce

Modularized	Integrated		
Multi-Brand Agri-Input Products (Rent and sell)	Crop Advisory Services	Input Recommendations	Credit Management

Figure 18.5 e-commerce entry in agri-input sector. Source:/*news.agropages.com/News/ NewsDetail---27418.*

In existing Agri input supply as shown in Figure 18.6, most of the players follow Go-to-Market approach, but with the rise of digitalization start-ups, it provided a wide variety of services beyond traditional ones and moved toward the customer-centric approach [4].

Coming to the revenue model, the transaction-based margin is followed for utilizing the m-commerce platform and subscription model is followed for advisory and other miscellaneous services. Few start-ups are concentrated on building a hybrid model for providing preharvest and postharvest services and other companies outsourcing the m-commerce platform for traders and merchants for providing superior services to their customers.

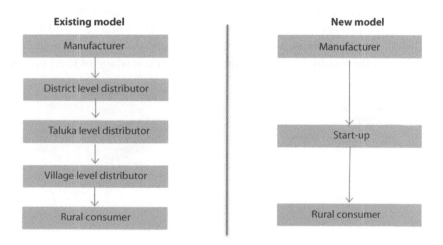

Figure 18.6 Start-up input model in eliminating middlemen.

Agri-Input manufacturers before and after emergence of e-commerce:
e-Commerce entry into the agriculture input sector made supply chain more effective by means of integrated and modularized services. The multibrand agri-input products make the supply chain at ease in providing services, as well as credit supply.

Elimination of middlemen with new Input model:
It states how startup entry restricted the middle men entry into the supply chain by providing direct services to farmers.

Start-up's working in input supply chain

18.4   Output Supply Chain

The output supply chain (OSCM) in India is looking with difficulty, coming from the characteristic issues like the strength of little/peripheral farmers, divided stockpile chains, nonappearance of scale economies, low degree of handling the products, the improper infrastructure of markets, and so on.

India's supply chain is quite possibly the most divided and inefficient ones across the world, bringing about 25% to 30% wastage of food grains,

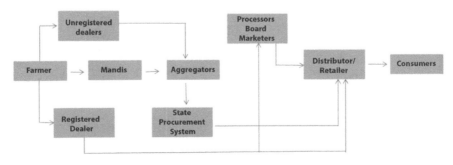

Figure 18.7 Traditional output supply chain.

vegetables and natural products before they go to the market. This implies that the ranchers and shoppers bear the expenses of the wastage [2, 7, 8].

Existing output supply chain models:
Traditional Model:
Traditional Agri Supply Chain, with much non–value-adding intermediaries, who add cost to the goods in the form of profit margins, inventory and logistics. Inefficiencies lead to lower price realization for farmers and high pricing for the customers (shown in Figure 18.7).

APMC model:
Here, the number of intermediates involved in the supply chain will be reduced compared with the traditional system and in every state Agriculture Produce Market Committee) will be there, where all aggregators and farmers meet and whole supply chain transactions will happen within the premises (shown in Figure 18.8).

New Age Models
i. Hub & Spoke Model:
Most of the established retailers like Future retail, More retail, and Spencer's retail are adopting "Hub-Spoke model." Only a few players are engaged in this model like farmers, organized retailers, wholesalers and customers. It states buying centers (hub) and stores (spoke) are operational units (shown in Figure 18.9).

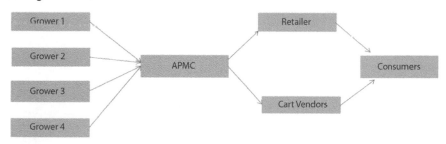

Figure 18.8 APMC model of output supply chain.

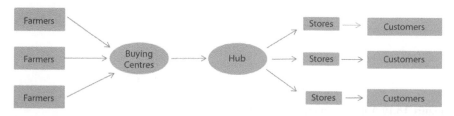

Figure 18.9 Hub & spoke model of supply chain.

ii. Value Chain Model:
Right now, a couple of coordinated retail players like Reliance Fresh and others following this model. Acquirement of F&V will be done straight-forwardly from ranchers either through agreement or by taking the home-stead on rent and offer to customers with no mediators (shown in Figure 18.10).

Concerns in existing models:

- Unorganized fragmented supply chain
- Ill-equipped and mismanagement and low access to market yards
- More number of intermediaries resulting in pushing up prices through commissions
- Lack of warehouses and cold chain
- No proper standardization, packing and labelling
- Food safety is a major concern: Hygiene and pesticide MRL not monitored
- Improper supply-demand and price information

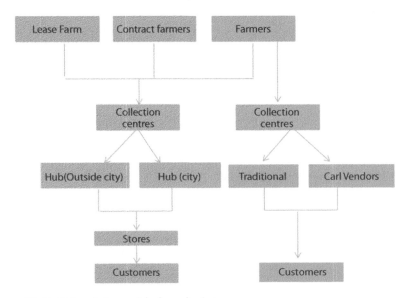

Figure 18.10 Value chain model of supply chain.

18.5   How Start-Ups are Filling the Concerns and Gaps in Agri Output Supply Chain

Using new-age technologies like machine learning, artificial intelligence, internet on things and block chain management, start-ups are bringing new shape to Agri supply chain. Start-ups directly procuring from farm gates by directly contracting the farmers produce and supplying to retailers and distributers. Through this B2B, model start-ups are eliminating 4 middlemen's compare to the traditional model and able to supply within 12hrs, reducing postharvest wastage by 20% to 30% and able to offer a fair price for both retailer and consumers [5].

At every node of chain firms using different technologies,

- For determining the best route: proprietary algorithms
- Supply and demand: price prediction engine and data intelligence
- Product quality and decreasing wastage: end-to-end traceability & radio frequency identification
- Farmer and customer relationships: customer relationship management tools

Elimination of middlemen (shown in Figure 18.11):

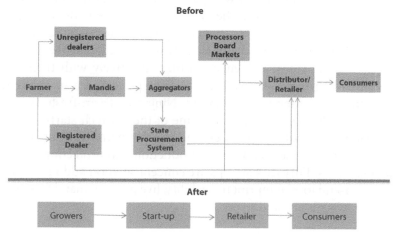

Figure 18.11 Start-up output model in eliminating middlemen.

Start-ups working in the output supply chain:

18.6   Conclusion

There is a clear change in Agri supply chain after the introduction of tech-enabled farm to fork model by start-ups. Both in the number of start-ups working and investments made are high in Agri supply chain out of which output supply chain share a higher percentage than the input supply chain. Recent agricultural reforms also added benefit to agritech players where the government has taken steps on eliminating the middlemen and increasing supply efficiency in the nation through one national-one market. Start-ups created new employment opportunities in agriculture sectors and it all defined supply chain in a new way by reducing the marketing channels. Start-ups also influenced farmers positively with their activities by providing remunerative price to their price and also involved in eliminating middlemen to some extent. Ninjacart, Farm-fresh, Go-fresh, Agrostar, Agri-Bazaar, Crofarm are some of the agritech start-ups which are operating successfully by redefining supply chain. Most of those are focused on attaining self-sufficiency, production and protecting the farmers & consumers. Further start-ups are concentrated on adding other features end-to-end food footprint traceability, live price-demand forecasting, warehouse availability, and so on.

References

1. Roy, V., Silvestre, B.S., Singh, S., Reactive and proactive pathways to sustainable apparel supply chains: Manufacturer's perspective on stakeholder salience and organizational learning toward responsible management. *Int. J. Prod. Econ.*, 227, 1072–76, 2020.

2. Mani, V., Gunasekaran, A., Papadopoulos, T., Hazen, B., Dubey, R., Supply chain social sustainability for developing nations: Evidence from India. *Resour. Conserv. Recy.*, 111, 42–52, 2016.

3. Marshall, D., McCarthy, L., Heavey, C., McGrath, P., Environmental and social supply chain management sustainability practices: Construct development and measurement. *Prod. Plan. Control*, 26, 673–690, 2015.

4. Ali, S.S., Kaur, R., Ersöz, F., Altaf, B., Basu, A., Weber, G.-W., Measuring carbon performance for sustainable green supply chain practices: A developing country scenario. *Cent. Eur. J. Oper. Res.*, 28, 1389–1416, 2020.

5. *Indian Agri-Business – Cultivating future opportunities, BCG report*, http://media-publications.bcg.com/Indian-Agribusiness.pdf.

6. *Agritech - towards transforming Indian agriculture-EY*, https://assets.ey.com/content/dam/ey-sites/ey-com/en_in/topics/start-ups/2020/09/ey-agritech-towards-transforming-indian-agriculture.pdf?download.

7. Tseng, M.-L., Islam, M.S., Karia, N., Fauzi, F.A., Afrin, S., A literature review on green supply chain management: Trends and future challenges. *Resour. Conserv. Recy.*, 141, 145–162, 2019.

8. http://news.agropages.com/News/NewsDetail—27418.htm

9. https://agribusinessmatters.substack.com/p/when-bayer-met-agrostar

10. https://indifoodbev.com/agriculture/agri-tech-startups-bridge-the-agri-retail-supply-chain

11. https://yourstory.com/2018/04/startup-market-agriculture-profit-business-farmers

19

Development of Blockchain Agriculture Supply Chain Framework Using Social Network Theory: An Empirical Evidence Based on Malaysian Agriculture Firms

Muhammad Shabir Shaharudin[1*], Yudi Fernando[2],
Yuvaraj Ganesan[3] and Faizah Shahudin[4]

[1]School of Management, Universiti Sains Malaysia, Penang, Malaysia
[2]Faculty of Industrial Management, Universiti Malaysia Pahang, Gambang, Malaysia
[3]Graduate School of Business, Universiti Sains Malaysia, Penang, Malaysia
[4]School of Economics and Management, Xiamen Universiti, Sepang, Malaysia

Abstract

Emerging technology to assist the agriculture firms in managing the complexity in the supply chain through Blockchain technology adoption has been discussed in the literature. Because the adoption of Blockchain technology is immature in the Malaysian agriculture sector, this study aims to propose a framework of Blockchain agriculture supply chain management. As the Blockchain supply chain framework in the agriculture sector is still limited, this tends to develop the framework uses Social Network theory. This study collected quantitative survey and social network data from firms registered in the Federation of Malaysian Manufacturing that operate in the agriculture sector. The demographic profiles were analyzed through IBM SPSS version 26. The social network data were analyzed through Social Network Visualizer. The outcome of the study helps aligned Blockchain with supply chain management. Theoretically, this study provides the initial framework of Blockchain agriculture supply chain management. From a practical perspective, it contributes to the adoption guideline to adopt Blockchain technology for agriculture firms. The outcome will benefit the regulatory body to design a proper mechanism that can enhance industry competitiveness. The study shows that organizational theory can support the development framework and

*Corresponding author: shabir.shaharudin@gmail.com

Roheet Bhatnagar, Nitin Kumar Tripathi, Nitu Bhatnagar and Chandan Kumar Panda (eds.)
The Digital Agricultural Revolution: Innovations and Challenges in Agriculture through
Technology Disruptions, (411–446) © 2022 Scrivener Publishing LLC

validate it through social network theory, but the result shows that intermediary is essential in the agriculture industry. Blockchain features of traceability, transparency, safety and verification were critical for agriculture supply chain firms. Thus, Blockchain adoption is recommended for this industry.

Keywords: Blockchain, agriculture supply chain management, supply chain management, agriculture sector, social network theory, social network analysis

19.1   Introduction

Blockchain is a cutting-edge technology that has been adopted in a variety of academic disciplines, business, science, and government areas, such as finance, medical, and agriculture [1]. Blockchain allows traceability, transparency, and integration of the actors in the trusted network. The benefits of Blockchain are essential for the supply chain as information sharing, product movement, and financial transaction are the critical drivers of a successful supply chain [2]. The successful supply chain is more important in the agriculture sector as it manages fresh produce, vegetables and fruits, livestock, and poultry.

Today, Blockchain technology is one of the most exciting and impressive innovations. It is a distributed database supported by several machines that can record all transactions on an ongoing basis. In a Blockchain, each block stores a list of transactions, which can be variable in size. The technology that Satoshi Nakamoto developed was publicly available in 2009 due to his creation of Bitcoin in 2008 [3]. It was quickly seen that a popular and effective implementation of Blockchain technology in the financial sector would allow digital money transactions without a third party's involvement (i.e. a central bank). Additionally, Blockchain technology is currently being used in healthcare, smart cities, electricity, and government [4]. Reliability and immutability are essential to the technology's performance.

Farming, distribution, manufacturing, and marketing all features an agricultural supply chain (ASC), "from farm to table". Food traceability is a pressing issue in recent years, and previous frameworks have been discussed to stop food controversies of the past [5]. Although it is still in its infancy, the Blockchain food traceability system investigation has not yet been sufficiently pursued. Regulatory food tracing requirements vary from one geographical location to another. A plurality of poor practices and issues arising in the agricultural sector led to the need for a traceability scheme in the first place [6]. The systematic use of pesticides and fertilizers in fruits and vegetables may have contaminants in the finished product that poses a severe threat to human health. Hormones are used in the growth process to minimize maturation duration and result in increased yield. Mineral oil is often used to make waffles and rice look pretty. Any of these activities degrade the food product and represent significant risks for the customers.

In Malaysia, Halal compliance in the supply chain has a challenging task to manage. Any of the significant challenges posed by food manufacturers mentioned in the media (where the product was contaminated with non-Halal products/materials) can be addressed using Blockchain technology. Since food products are vulnerable, and Blockchain technology can handle the visibility aspect used in the agricultural sector. It can be used to include information on the product's origins, the product supply chain, and much of the logistical, operation, and production details, including warehousing information. Additionally, information regarding the use of pesticides, determination of expiry date, and originality of the products can ensure that agriculture products are safe and quality. Nevertheless, studies in Malaysia regarding agriculture are divided into two fundamental areas; i) technology to improve the product [7] and ii) management of the behavior or practice of sustainable agriculture [2]. The research area shows a need to integrate both areas by investigating the technology management of agriculture firms in Malaysia.

This paper aims to provide a platform for agricultural firms to use Blockchain technology to monitor their ASC. The development of the framework is based on Social Network theory. The theory helps design the supply chain of agriculture firms and determine which supply chain practices can be improved using Blockchain technology. This paper contributes to the alignment of Blockchain technology and supply chain management. Additionally, the integration of Social Network theory for framework development helps agriculture firms adopt Blockchain technology in their supply chain to achieve performance.

19.2   Literature Review

19.2.1   Agriculture Malaysia

10% of the labor is in the livestock, fisheries, and forestry sectors. These sectors are responsible for 10% of the country's GDP [8]. An approximately similar proportion is made up of palm oil, rubber, chocolate, and tropical fruits to the total harvest. Second to Indonesia in the worldwide production and palm oil sale, Malaysia is also the second export figure. In 2019, Malaysia will have nearly 28% of the world's palm oil and 33% of its export value [8]. A working colony can compensate for yield or productivity improvements. The palm oil firms likewise have significant investments in other markets like Indonesia, Europe, China, and the USA. Many of Malaysia's most important and most lucrative businesses are palm oil plantations, as the state has a large stake in them. The USA has had significant Malaysian interests and policies for many years, but the palm oil sector could be much more critical than previously thought. It worries them that soybeans would hurt the USA economy. Due to the EPA's ranking, it is not an environmentally friendly fuel, but it is currently open for debate, as other scholars found it to promote sustainability [9]. Poultry is the primary source of protein all around the world. The poultry sector keeps doing well in international trade. The Malaysian federal government sought to render Malaysia a center of commerce where trade was conducted in a strictly Halal manner [10]. There is no primary beef market in Malaysia at the moment [8]. Malaysia has excellent research capability in the palm oil sector. In particular, rice is supported by market aid, input subsidies, and customer subsidies [11]. Often brand-new financial initiatives are used in the palm oil plantation regardless of the ministry's goal elsewhere.

In 2013, the Malaysian government adopted new legislation to secure and educate the primary population regarding food development [12]. In 2013, the Malaysian Ministry of Health made assurances to guarantee sector and consumer safety concerning dietary identifiers [13]. However, this statute was passed but yet to be enforced. On the other side, the Import and Export Procedures of Malaysia's Food Act was enacted to control food imports and exports. The Malaysian health and other divisions (including the Food Safety and Quality Division) are responsible for overseeing and enforcing these rules, including routine inspections, testing, and imports [14]. Halal credentials and certification or registry standards are required when distributing food and agriculture products [15]. Halal certification is needed for specific food items (such as beef or poultry) to enter Malaysia. Clearly, concerning federal services, there is a necessary prerequisite. Currently, only the Islamic Development Department of Malaysia may offer halal certification (JAKIM). Malaysia's approach was acknowledged in March 2018, allowing global dairy manufacturers and importers to sign contracts with the federal government [8]. Malaysia officially offered this scheme to boost traceability and make sure all imports from elsewhere become halal authorized. Until that stage, the application process will be speeding up for programs that had previously shipped to Malaysia. Acceptance applications would be evaluated in three to six months.

The Malaysian trade in agriculture is projected to be $43.5 billion in 2019, with $25 billion in exports and $18.3 billion in imports [8]. Over the previous decade, palm oil has been the top export and leading markets in India, the European Union, China, Pakistan, and the USA [16]. Exports from Indonesia, China, Thailand, and the USA are the primary agricultural exports to Malaysia in 2019. Malaysia exports $6.7 billion in agricultural goods, such as maise, corn, dairy products, and citrus fruits [8]. In 2019, the USA had a $128 million trade surplus with Malaysia, a $1.18 billion boost in agricultural exports 2019. Several critical items have recently been introduced to the unprecedented record-breaking produce streak, consisting of soybeans, dry fruits, nuts, and canned goods [8]. Foodservice represented about half of overall sales volume because of growing consumer demand and the competition from the market.

19.2.2   Agriculture Supply Chain

One-third of food production gets wasted along the food supply chain. Estimated food losses in established nations total $680 billion, while estimated food waste in new nations amounts to $310 billion [17]. As a result of population growth, the global population is projected to hit nine billion people by the middle of the century, necessitating a rise in the global food production of 70% [18]. Because of the population's growth and the food supply chains, fresh and organic waste have become more challenging to handle. This can be accomplished by removing intermediaries, uniting farmers and food producers, and directly connecting farmers to the market; the following becomes easier to manage [19].

A defined supply chain comprises manufacturers, vendors, outlets, dealerships, and clients and processors. Because a more significant number of people are affected, it gets complex and challenging to manage. An added obstacle to long-term agricultural targets is keeping clear of the environmental stresses. It is not easy to track the flow back to where it began raises concern about the entire ASC [20]. Counterfeit products may be manufactured in the supply chain; both federal governments and stakeholders (customers) may be affected. The ASC begins with incoming agriculture-related goods and services customers, which incorporates commodity sales to agriculture firms and then channels them to the outgoing products and services (various circulation channels are being embraced). There is a supply chain process for agriculture products, consisting of dairy products, feed, animal products, and produce. In the literature, scholars found the catalysts and offered assistance in coming up with other management approaches to use [21]. Scholars discovered some significant drawbacks to ASC development, including inadequate sorting and grading creativity, disconnected networks, and freezers' absence [22]. 30 to 35% of food production loss happens in food due to inefficient food manufacturing and transportation [23]. The severity of the questions and doubts about nutritional integrity [24], openness and responsibility in the food supply chain [25] in marketing and shipment [26], and issues concerning food stability and accountability [27] have called scholars to put more attention to in the field of ASC research.

19.2.3   Blockchain Technology

Cryptocurrencies are now emerging technology that attracts industry to adopt it into other sectors. Distributed ledger technology (DLT) has been widely researched typical recently. Decentralized DLT might be referred to as follows: the logging, processing, and verifying deals are performed in a dispersed way on an immutable journal. DLT generally includes several kinds of innovations, consisting of Blockchain [28]. A decentralized, shared value system, where deals are performed, and securities and currency are supported together with other sorts of agreements, is likewise described as the network. Simultaneously, it is the innovation that fuels alternative cryptocurrencies, such as Bitcoin and Ethereum [29]. The banking sector will benefit most from Blockchain technologies, followed by commercial products and building and construction, followed by facilities and the health care sector [30]. Nevertheless, the most crucial deterrent to extensive blockchain approval was regulative confusion [31].

One of the critical elements of Blockchain is the block. The agreement algorithm carries out essential functions in creating brand-new blocks and including them into the Blockchain. Amongst the most discussed algorithms are still proof-of-work (PoW), proof-of-stake (PoS), and proof-authority (PoA). A PoW agreement paradigm is utilized in which a node gets the right to release the next block by fixing a complex computational puzzle. Calculation outcomes are simple to examine, and other nodes can confirm and enhance the Blockchain information. Of all, getting access to the node that resolves the cryptographic riddle is to get the reward. In subsequent variations, PoW spinouts and brand-new methods have been presented to verify blocks that do not need much energy and time [32]. Whereas in PoS, the evidence strips out the work and keeps the overhead [33]. There is a time requirement besides constructing a brand-new block. One drawback of PoS is that those with "abundant" nodes will get more digital currency and claim rights to develop the next PoS [34]. Delegated PoS (DPoS), developed on the PoS design, takes various techniques because the nodes vote to choose delegates to verify on their behalf. Each algorithm has its qualities relating to incentive/reward, requirements in addition to energy expenditure.

Three common kinds of Blockchain networks can be determined: a mix of public, private, and consortium Blockchain. A consortium is where a collection of individuals runs a Blockchain [35]. Picked nodes predefine the agreement procedure utilized for Blockchain records confirmation and entry. There is a central controller for private Blockchain [36]. Only members with authentication and permission can sign up with the Blockchain network. The Blockchain will be made easily readily available. A utilized term for a Blockchain is a permissioned journal, which needs a group of entities to accept or record deals on a shared network [4]. For example, permissioned journals are used between banks for the inter-business supply chain to monitor funds and transactions. All processes are viewable to the general public in a public Blockchain, and new members might be included and removed accordingly. A public Blockchain is decentralized and merged [37]. For this kind of Blockchain, users who do not know each other are accommodated by individuals' complex finding. Stringent procedures need to be imposed to form a contract in this structure.

Smart contacts are self-executing contracts that are activated based on predefined and concurred occasions. When predefined conditions are reached, smart contracts will execute without any interventions [38]. This might be compared to what automated debit merchants do to debit a client's account. The oracle is a crucial connection between real-life and the Blockchain [39]. It is a credible third party that becomes part of the smart contract community, making it possible for relied on information feeds to be sent out to the Blockchain. Blockchain cannot access information from outside the facilities, so information needs to be supplied by a single entry point outside the system (oracle). An oracle might be physical, digital, or decentralized. An agreement oracle develops agreement amongst predefined nodes to attend to a specific concern [40].

Numerous industries are thinking about Blockchain transfers, like the federal government, banking, and production [2]. Furthermore, they are used in ASC, land registries, and digital IDs [20]. Initially established to support a more open monetary structure (in addition to cryptocurrencies), this innovation finds many developments. When a Blockchain is being established, its architecture needs to be scalable and cryptographically safe, reputable, and valuable (the material is not always encrypted). In this stage, it is a read-only, dispersed, and unmodified system. It is indicated to develop trust, cut expenses, and accelerate deals. However, it is not entirely true. Blockchain-based tasks likewise deal with innovation scarcities, incompatibility, and performance concerns even after appropriate release. There is currently a movement towards embracing blockchain-based procedures [41]; nevertheless, these are typically meaningless. At this time, firms pursue Blockchain for transparent, decentralized, and possibly minimized processing expense.

The smart contract also is being used in the agriculture industry. Agricultural insurance coverage and traceability might play a vital function in executing smart contracts [42]. Agricultural insurance coverage with information stemmed from in the field sensing units (through sensor or IoT) will benefit farmers in the instant application of floods and dry spells [43]. Information needed to promote development, such as premium legislation, should be established to guarantee smart contract agreements. While establishing, incorporating, and carrying out the smart contract in agriculture, many applications have been introduced in the ASC [44].

19.2.4   Blockchain Agriculture Supply Chain Management

The primary use of artificial intelligence (AI) in agriculture is to forecast environmental effects on crop yields, affecting their decisions about when to harvest. These applications help to uncover data that can be made useable for farmers. Furthermore, agriculture firms are designing predictive technologies that can anticipate spoiling stored foods. Several devices have been designed to help farmers decrease post-harvest losses for crops. The use of the Blockchain in the ASC would ensure that production never exceeds its storage, so it will be easier to trace the food from the field to the grocery store [45]. Scanning a QR code can reveal information about the organic material that is contained inside [46]. Furthermore, it is far more difficult for fake and counterfeit products to reach shopping outlets, where unsuspecting customers are more susceptible [47]. This additionally allows it to be more certain to establish and market genuine, premium-quality, environmentally-friendly products, such as natural and organically produced products, to hold their ground.

The Blockchain has the potential to deliver a practical and trustworthy approach to product traceability and supply chain accountability. A Blockchain is used for logging commodity movements across the ASC, maintaining quality management, and track stockpiling [48]. Agricultural firms now track crops with smart sensors, and the deployment of distributed ledger systems will amplify that initiative. Tracking enables firms to trace the natural, fiscal, health, and social effects of agricultural processes and allows businesses to quantify the "real cost of food" [42]. It helps satisfy the rising customer appetite for openness and profits, sales, and market access to resources. Farm-to-to-shelf trackability is imperative when determining an ingredient's origin and is viewed by the end-consumers as a sign of consistency and food safety [49]. As a need in the ASC, government procurement agencies should use state-in-the-art tools to monitor agricultural commodities cultivation processes and increase trust with their customers. Farming, past purchases, financial documents, and agricultural agreements will benefit from Blockchain technology. Smaller producers would have access to raw materials and equipment, as well as contracts that ensure market prices. As a result, the need for a solid long-term strategy has become particularly important because agriculture is likely to face a challenging future due to rising food demand, climate change and an ever-diminishing supply of capital. Troubling conditions, such as the ongoing crisis, have reinforced the need for a more reliable and less vulnerable supply chain [50].

19.2.5   Social Network Theory

Global trends have emerged from the system's constituents in most social networks [51]. These forms of social networks contain self-reproducing, self-evolving, and highly dynamic components. As the number of connections increases, the above patterns will become more apparent. Social network theory is used to obtain a more thorough understanding of how important it is to assess the local network's capacities [52] accurately. Studies might reveal how ineffective the networks are since then. Although analysis levels are not universally exclusive, micro and meso-levels of analysis are most commonly subdivided into sub-networks that can be broken down into three classes: micro-work, middle-work, and macro-work [53].

Expanding on the definition of "duo" and add another actor, you have a group of three. Proportionality and transitivity are crucial problems; however, the former is much more important because they can affect the network [54]. Other concepts that apply to social interactions can be derived from the study of their structure, including triads, which have been identified and described in the literature [55]. One should concentrate on network characteristics, such as depth, connectivity, and dispersion, but be aware of local properties, including concentration and separation [56].

On the other hand, micro-level and macro-level analysis is often referred to as "middle-level analysis." Unlike interpersonal networks, the meso-level mechanisms are not necessarily linked, which means each level's specific mechanisms may be distinct [52]. In more general organizations, there may be multiple layers of study. Some research organizations within the organization may, for example, place their efforts within franchise groups or semi-autonomous divisions. In this type of situation, both department and workgroup level research are performed an inter-organizational exploration of research. In particular, in scale-free networks, various vertices are characteristic of almost all connectedness, diverse sets [57]. Although the design is very stable at the hubs of a network, the capability and use of specific components can vary according to the environment in which they are implemented. When it comes to cluster count, another general feature of the scale-free property is that complexity tends to lower the Clustering Coefficient, which is expressed as node count per node [58]. This also has an inverse-exponential scale property: the more details, the more infinitesimal outputs.

Comprehensive social characteristics evident in biological and technological systems and within Euclid-like networks can be seen in the generalized to any set of relationships. Also, there are strong tails in the degree distribution and assortativity between vertices; the network is said to have a hierarchical structure [3]. There is a reciprocal significance for the networks with an agency guideline, triadic significance, and other characteristics [52]. This network representation is more complex since it includes information about features previously unknown to such network models, such as structure and hierarchy.

19.2.6   Social Network Analysis

Social network analysis (SNA) offers a view of the group's social organization and engagement processes from an overhead perspective and can help long-term analysis and monitor substantial change in the network. The two different approaches to SNA are visualization and bibliometric analysis [55].

The SNA visualization makes relationships between actors as networks, with nodes representing points (actors) that originate a flow of events and pointing to one another. In contrast, relationships derive from edges (arcs) and signify target interaction [59]. Social network analysis can be used to expose the relationships among actors and the importance of strong ties. Similarly, it can reveal the network interactions, which connects to whom and the relationship between actors and their participation degree.

Social network analysis bibliometric criteria cover several layers. It utilizes graph theory to compute nodes' metrics, or relations, for bibliometric analysis, such as the connection(s) to other actors or involvement in networking with other actors. A centrality score is calculated for each actor to decide how important the actor is to the criteria. Each score reflects the degree of centrality of the value within the social network. Other than centrality, betweenness to find the bridge or gap or linkage between two groups or strong actors can also be performed. The weightage or strength of the ties will be calculated and shown in the network. There are other methods, but centrality is used in this study and the degree of importance.

Given the many possible contexts and the likelihood of multiple approaches to be applied, there are different centrality scores for the function [52]. First, this study looks at social actors (as one aspect of an evaluation) and the second, connections between these actors (as another part of the analysis). after the application code has been mapped to SNA, a Social Network Visualizer software can be used to develop Blockchain-based ASC.

19.3   Methodology

19.3.1   Blockchain Agriculture Supply Chain Management Framework

Formulating ASC processes is the first step in developing a framework, as shown in Figure 19.1. Understanding ASC processes or activities, the network of connected relationship, actor interaction, and bridges are visible. Basic ASC includes the interaction between farmers or suppliers, or sellers

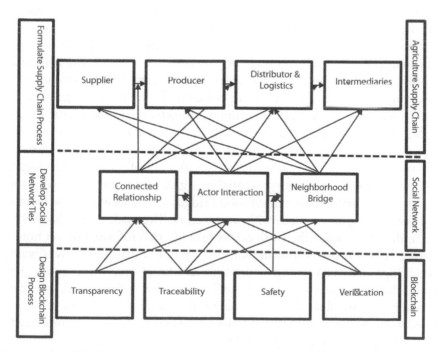

Figure 19.1 Blockchain agriculture supply chain management framework. Source: Original figure.

with firms. The transaction or interaction of supplies of fresh products or agriculture products with firms is taking place at this stage. The use of pesticides, the origin of materials, the ethical transactions, the originality of the supplies are all issue of the procurement process in the ASC. After the procurement process, the materials are processed or manufactured by the producer. This stage concerns the processing method, the environmental and social aspects of the process, and the design of products that customers accept. Issues related to the usage of Halal and non-Halal products being made together, the handling of materials, the harmful process or chemicals should be eliminated at this stage. Once the products have been made, the way firms store, handle the inventory and transportation methods concerns distribution and logistics processes. Agriculture products require delicate and careful handling of the products because they are perishable in nature and mainly commodity products. Issues, such as the temperature for perishable produces, the cold logistics transportation method, the inventory cycle, and sustainable packaging, are the main concerns in the ASC. Intermediaries connect firms with customers and agencies. While these intermediaries' removable will provide a leaner and linear supply chain process, the practice in developing countries, such as Malaysia, needs to be considered. The issues related to intermediaries are the actor's efficiency and the price factor with or without them.

Once ASC framework has been established, using Social Network theory to uncover the relationship between actors (in this case, the ASC processes), the interaction between actors (who depending on who and who is an important actor), and the bridges that make the ties stronger are critical to enabling Blockchain adoption. Connectedness shows which actor (ASC process) is significant to the ASC to the point that it needs technology (such as Blockchain) to manage. Interactions in the network can be interpreted as an important actor or the influence of the actor. The bigger the interactions, the more substantial or significant the role of that actor. On the other hand, the neighborhood bridges can be viewed as the linkage between strong actors made with weak actors. The weak actors should not be undermined since the weak actors provide rich information on how a strong actor transmits information flow. When a researcher investigates the bridges between strong actors that consist of their weak actors, the researcher can understand which ASC process has a "bottleneck" and can be supported by Blockchain technology. The entire network can be developed using SNA software Social Network Visualizer to see the connectedness, interactions, and bridges in ASC.

After SNA has analyzed the ASC model, components of Blockchain can be introduced. Blockchain is used to enable transparency of the process.

In this case, the complete information and process of ASC can be viewed by every stakeholder. The stakeholder can also trace the entire ASC origins to ensure that they can make a sound decision. Blockchain also provides safety or avoid the information being tampered. Thus, it improves the integrity of the ASC process and making the process more reliable. Lastly, stakeholders can verify the information, and the verification can avoid firms with fraudulent activities or be fined for any misleading information and improve consumers' trust.

19.3.2   Research Design

This study population is agriculture firms operating in Malaysia and registered in Federal Manufacturing Malaysia (FMM). Other databases provide information regarding agriculture firms, but FMM is more resourceful in detailing firms' information. As Social Network requires information, such as the actors, the activities, the documents or interactions between actors, FMM provides information on the respondent profile and contact information. Additionally, information regarding the product, the process, and the firms' website is listed in the directory, which helps this study. The sample frame is agriculture firms that operate in Malaysia, has exposed or interested to adopt Blockchain technology, and provide complete supply chain information. The unit of analysis is the organization represented by top management, middle management, and operational level management representatives. This study requires only one highest position available in the firm to answer the survey questions. Therefore, the sampling technique uses disproportionate stratified random sampling, where as long as respondents are coming from the managerial positions stated, they are qualified to represent their firms. The total samples in the frame are 124 firms, but only 18 firms have disclosed valuable information to develop Social Network after the 1-month data collection cutoff period.

Data collection was through an online Google form platform, where firms receive the survey questions on the first week of July 2020. Firms were reminded two times to ensure that this study can increase the response rate. At the end of July 2020, 36 responses were received, a 29% response rate. Upon cleaning and processing the data, only 18 responses providing ASC information for SNA. Therefore, the final response rate is 15% of the total population.

Demographic information consisting of firm and respondent profiles were analyzed through IBM SPSS version 26 software while the ASC was developed using Social Network Visualizer software. Social Network Visualizer was used to analyse the centrality, betweenness, and closeness of the network. The method is adopted and improved from Shaharudin *et al.* [55] on the SNA method while combining with [59] on developing a Social Network framework for its supply chain.

19.4   Results and Discussion

19.4.1   Demographic Profiles

Table 19.1 shows the 18 firms profile where most of the firms are located in Malaysia's central and northern regions. The data shows that the industrial zone in both regions has more firms willing to adopt Blockchain technology. Although these firms are still new in the agriculture sector and have a small medium enterprises (SMEs) status, these firms are already establishing their effort to adopt Blockchain and designing their supply chain network. Designing a supply chain network is critical to improving the firms' overall performances. Any new technology or external organizational pressures can be overcome by aligning all network supply chain partners. This finding is critical because it shows the capability of Malaysian agriculture firms to sustain in the business and adopting Industrial 4.0 technologies, such as Blockchain.

Table 19.2 shows the respondent profile of the 18 participated firms. Based on the result, it shows that there are considerable respondents with high-ranking position and with high academic and experience levels. However, the age and service years show that many of these respondents can be interpreted as a trendsetter. As found in previous Table 19.1 that there are many SMEs. The trend could be showing that these respondents are creating a new sector and thus willing to adopt Blockchain. The agriculture sector in Malaysia will be more relevant if the Malaysian government policies and incentives can support these firms effort. Although these firms are considering a few and small sizes, these firms can be the sector's backbone.

19.4.2   Social Network Analysis Results

SNA is the most critical parts of this study. Before proceeding with the results, there is a need to understand that the survey questions ask on a single firm's supply chain and rate the performance, the interactions, the relationships, and the process involved in their respective supply chain. This information is vital because the firm's weightage or edge (arc) is measured by the firm instead of that firm's supply chain partner. When every supply chain partner measures each of their partners' performances, the weightage

Table 19.1 Firm profile (n=18).

Detail	Count	Percentage
Location of firm		
Northern region states	6	33.33%
Central region states	8	44.44%
Southern region states	1	5.56%
East coast states	1	5.56%
Sabah and Sarawak	2	11.11%
	18	100.00%
Age of firm		
Less than 10 years	5	27.78%
10-15 years	6	33.33%
16-20 years	3	75.00%
More than 20 years	4	22.22%
	18	100.00%
Number of employees		
Less than 100	11	61.11%
100-250	3	16.67%
251-500	0	0.00%
More than 500	4	22.22%
	18	100.00%
Type of firm		
SME	14	77.78%
Medium-sized	3	16.67%
MNCs	1	5.56%
	18	100.00%

Table 19.2 Respondent profile (n=18).

Detail	Count	Percentage
Academic qualification		
SPM/O-Level	0	0.00%
STPM/Certificate/A-Level	0	0.00%
Diploma	0	0.00%
Degree	2	11.11%
Master/PhD/Professional certificate	16	88.89%
	18	100.00%
Age		
21–30 years	0	0.00%
31–40 years	3	16.67%
41–50 years	9	50.00%
More than 50 years	6	33.33%
	18	100.00%
Service year		
Less than 2 years	1	5.56%
2–5 years	6	33.33%
6–9 years	5	27.78%
More than 9 years	6	33.33%
	18	100.00%
Position		
Top Management position	6	33.33%
Middle management position	10	55.56%
Operations management position	2	11.11%
	18	100.00%

is more reliable and valid. At the same time, a single measurement from a single firm is still reliable and valid. However, it is subjective and biased to that firm's interpretation of the relationship. Nevertheless, this study's finding is still reliable and valid because the main objective is to understand the firms' ASC and integrate Blockchain technology to improve performance.

Respected figures, such as Figures 19.2–19.6 show, 18 firms' ASC network. This study used every 18 firms answer regarding their step-by-step supply chain process, the supplier relationship, the customer relationship, whether their suppliers produce to other firms, whether they produce for other firms, whether they use dedicated intermediaries or third party logistics and warehousing and provide the Blockchain features that they think will benefit their ASC. These figures show that the nodes represented by a circle icon are the supplier process. The diamond icon shows the production process. The triangle icon is the distribution and logistics processes, and the box icon is the intermediary processes. On the other hand, the edges (arcs) show the direction of interactions between nodes (firms).

Critically, Figure 19.3 shows that the supply process is the most crucial in the ASC. The degree of centrality (DC) shows that all 18 firms believed that their supplier is the center of the process. The DC shows a standardized index (DC divided by N-1 (non-valued nets) or by sumDC (valued nets). In short, DC is showing important nodes in ASC. This finding is aligned with [60] study. Table 19.3 summarizes and supports the evidence in Figure 19.3, where each individual centrality score for each supply chain network of the 18 firms is identified. The table shows that the minimum centrality point is node 74 (0.000000), whereas the highest centrality point is node 11 (0.066667). The sum of all centrality is 3.066667 with a mean of 0.040351 and a variance of 0.000173.

Figure 19.4 shows the betweenness centrality (BC) of ASC among Malaysian firms. BC shows a standardized index (BC divided by (N-1) (N-2)/2 in symmetric nets or (N-1)(N-2) otherwise. In short, BC shows that a node must go through another node to reach another node in the path. The sum of all BC is 7969.000000, with minimum betweenness of 0.000000 (node 73) and a maximum betweenness of 0.104629 (node 21). Figure 19.4 shows that supplier 21, supplier 25, and 58 are critical in the ASC. Many supply chain firms were connected through these suppliers. Table 19.3 shows the individual betweenness point for each node.

Furthermore, identifying the centrality and betweenness are vital because, in Figure 19.5, the study has included the Blockchain elements that firms believe would improve their ASC performance. The figure shows that all 18 firms believe that the traceability feature of the Blockchain is the most critical to ASC improvement. Combining with the fact that supplier is critical, it can be understood that firms wanted to improve the interactions with their supplier. In the literature, it was found that information, such as the origin of materials, the process of products, the creation or first produce to date, cost of materials, and duration of product from supplier to end customer are essential [61]. Therefore, by adopting the traceability function of the Blockchain, firms can satisfy their stakeholders and improve operational performance [62].

Additionally, the second most recognized Blockchain features are transparency. The transparency feature helps firms reduce cost, improve operational performance, and help consumers make sound decisions regarding purchasing the products. When firms along the supply chain identified the overall cost incurred in the supply chain, the whole supply chain network can reduce the cost and increase each partner profits. Furthermore, firms can penetrate the international market when the ASC is transparent. For example, in the case of palm oil product, the debate about whether palm oil is sustainable or whether there is a hidden agenda to diminish the palm oil products of Malaysia can be answered by analyzing complete data through a transparency Blockchain enabler.

Figure 19.6 shows the importance of each Blockchain feature, including traceability as the highest rank feature, transparency of the second-highest feature, safety feature, and verification feature. This study provides 18 agriculture firms with a total of 72 nodes and arcs to resemble their ASC. These firms believed that safety had been widely regarded as a vital Blockchain feature, not as crucial as traceability and transparency. On the other hand, verification is also the least essential Blockchain feature because it is essential to the finance and banking sectors.

The results show that agriculture firms in Malaysia are aware of the importance of Blockchain, and the adoption is to improve the performance of their ASC, especially with their supplier relationship management. The findings showed that Social Network theory could incorporate disruptive technology in supply chain studies. A social network is still considered an emerging theory new in multidisciplinary, such as supply chain studies, even though it is robust and highly researched in social science. Future research undertakings using Social Network theory can further contribute to the literature and, more importantly, extending the integration of organizational theory in the research. Previous research has found that many studies did not disclose theories and thus producing consistent research findings. Through this study's Social Network guidelines, scholars can systematically incorporate organizational theory and behavioral theory to contribute to the literature.

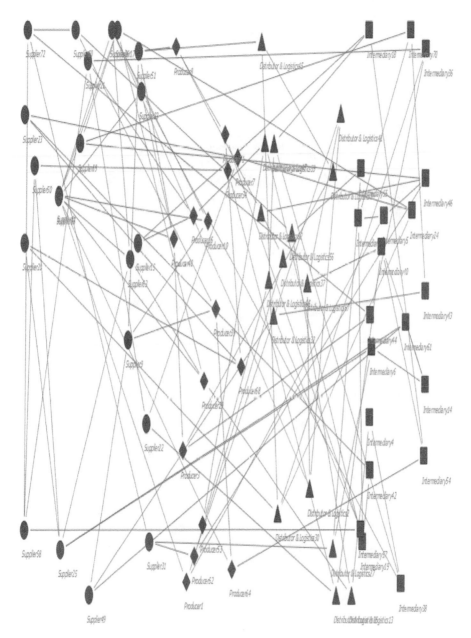

Figure 19.2 Social network interactions of Malaysian agriculture supply chain (n=18).
Source: Original figure.

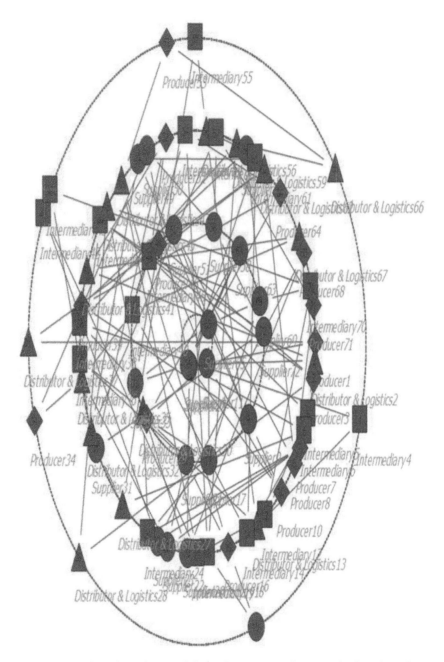

Figure 19.3 Centrality of social network for Malaysian agriculture supply chain (n=18).
Source: Original figure.

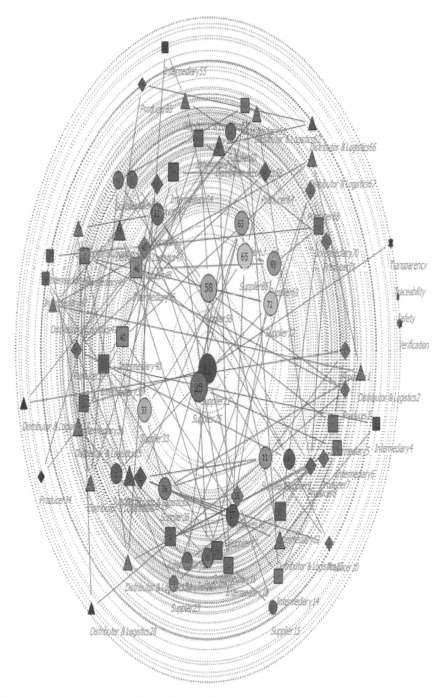

Figure 19.4 Betweenness of social network for Malaysian agriculture supply chain (n=18). Source: Original figure.

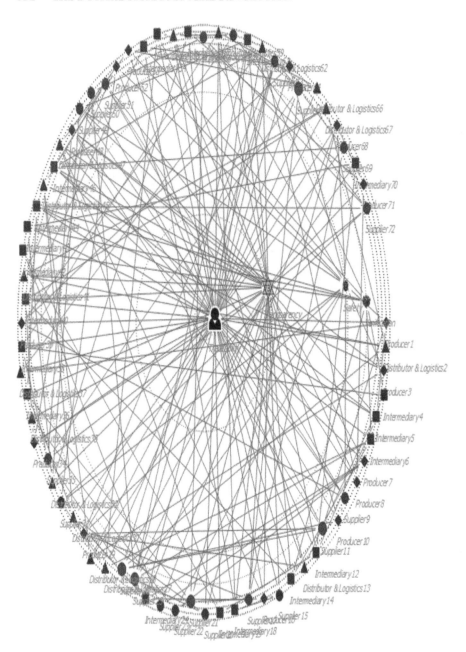

Figure 19.5 Social network of Malaysian blockchain-based agriculture supply chain (n=18). Source: Original figure.

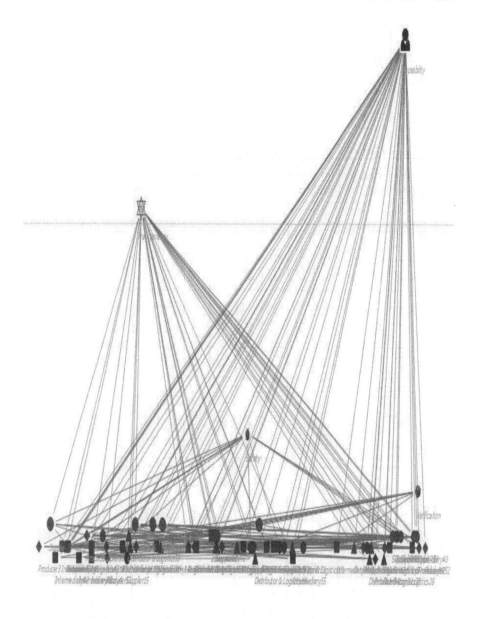

Figure 19.6 Social network degree of importance for Malaysian blockchain-based agriculture supply chain (n=18). Source: Original figure.

Table 19.3 Degree of centrality and betweenness report.

Node	Label	Degree of centrality				Degree of betweenness		
		DC	DC'	%DC'		BC	BC'	%BC'
1	Producer1	3.000000	0.040000	4.000000		90.133333	0.032480	3.248048
2	Distributor & Lo	3.000000	0.040000	4.000000		64.087302	0.023095	2.309452
3	Producer3	3.000000	0.040000	4.000000		87.012302	0.031356	3.135578
4	Intermediary4	2.000000	0.026667	2.666667		30.466667	0.010979	1.097898
5	Intermediary5	3.000000	0.040000	4.000000		96.851190	0.034901	3.490133
6	Intermediary6	3.000000	0.040000	4.000000		82.672619	0.029792	2.979193
7	Producer7	3.000000	0.040000	4.000000		98.325000	0.035432	3.543243
8	Producer8	3.000000	0.040000	4.000000		112.620635	0.040584	4.058401
9	Supplier9	4.000000	0.053333	5.333333		144.515079	0.052078	5.207751
10	Producer10	3.000000	0.040000	4.000000		45.223016	0.016297	1.629658
11	Supplier11	5.000000	0.066667	6.666667		173.214683	0.062420	6.241971
12	Intermediary12	3.000000	0.040000	4.000000		118.583333	0.042733	4.273273
13	Distributor & Lo	3.000000	0.040000	4.000000		98.806746	0.035606	3.560603

(*Continued*)

Table 19.3 Degree of centrality and betweenness report. (*Continued*)

Node	Label	Degree of centrality				Degree of betweenness			
		DC	DC'	%DC'		BC	BC'	%BC'	
14	Intermediary14	3.000000	0.040000	4.000000		70.196825	0.025296	2.529615	
15	Supplier15	2.000000	0.026667	2.666667		48.594444	0.017512	1.751151	
16	Producer16	3.000000	0.040000	4.000000		165.369444	0.059593	5.959259	
17	Supplier17	4.000000	0.053333	5.333333		150.573016	0.054261	5.426055	
18	Intermediary18	3.000000	0.040000	4.000000		105.722222	0.038098	3.809810	
19	Intermediary19	3.000000	0.040000	4.000000		121.583333	0.043814	4.381381	
20	Supplier20	3.000000	0.040000	4.000000		116.338095	0.041924	4.192364	
21	Supplier21	5.000000	0.066667	6.666667		290.344444	0.104629	10.462863	
22	Supplier22	3.000000	0.040000	4.000000		110.491667	0.039817	3.981682	
23	Supplier23	3.000000	0.040000	4.000000		85.308333	0.030742	3.074174	
24	Intermediary24	3.000000	0.040000	4.000000		125.083333	0.045075	4.507508	
25	Supplier25	5.000000	0.066667	6.666667		270.588095	0.097509	9.750922	
26	Supplier26	5.000000	0.066667	6.666667		162.386905	0.058518	5.851780	

(*Continued*)

Table 19.3 Degree of centrality and betweenness report. (*Continued*)

Node	Label	Degree of centrality			Degree of betweenness		
		DC	DC'	%DC	BC	BC'	%BC
27	Distributor & Lo	3.000000	0.040000	4.000000	73.982540	0.026660	2.666037
28	Distributor & Lo	2.000000	0.026667	2.666667	5.392857	0.001943	0.194337
29	Producer29	4.000000	0.053333	5.333333	147.663889	0.053212	5.321221
30	Distributor & Lo	4.000000	0.053333	5.333333	136.728571	0.049272	4.927156
31	Supplier31	3.000000	0.040000	4.000000	121.975397	0.043955	4.395510
32	Distributor & Lo	3.000000	0.040000	4.000000	83.122619	0.029954	2.995410
33	Supplier33	4.000000	0.053333	5.333333	191.509524	0.069012	6.901244
34	Producer34	2.000000	0.026667	2.666667	16.700000	0.006018	0.601802
35	Distributor & Lo	3.000000	0.040000	4.000000	87.808333	0.031643	3.164264
36	Intermediary36	3.000000	0.040000	4.000000	103.117857	0.037160	3.715959
37	Distributor & Lo	2.000000	0.026667	2.666667	9.150000	0.003297	0.329730
38	Intermediary38	3.000000	0.040000	4.000000	140.616667	0.050673	5.067267
39	Producer39	3.000000	0.040000	4.000000	97.078175	0.034983	3.498313

(*Continued*)

Table 19.3 Degree of centrality and betweenness report. (Continued)

Node	Label	Degree of centrality			Degree of betweenness		
		DC	DC'	%DC'	BC	BC'	%BC'
40	Intermediary40	4.000000	0.053333	5.333333	170.378968	0.061398	6.139783
41	Distributor & Lo	3.000000	0.040000	4.000000	55.766667	0.020096	2.009610
42	Intermediary42	2.000000	0.026667	2.666667	39.808333	0.014345	1.434535
43	Intermediary43	2.000000	0.026667	2.666667	40.375000	0.014550	1.454955
44	Intermediary44	3.000000	0.040000	4.000000	92.281349	0.033255	3.325454
45	Distributor & Lo	3.000000	0.040000	4.000000	70.794048	0.025511	2.551137
46	Intermediary46	4.000000	0.053333	5.333333	170.046429	0.061278	6.127799
47	Distributor & Lo	3.000000	0.040000	4.000000	127.091667	0.045799	4.579880
48	Producer48	4.000000	0.053333	5.333333	166.874206	0.060135	6.013485
49	Supplier49	3.000000	0.040000	4.000000	93.486508	0.033689	3.368883
50	Supplier50	3.000000	0.040000	4.000000	107.267857	0.038655	3.865508
51	Supplier51	4.000000	0.053333	5.333333	156.842063	0.056520	5.651966
52	Producer52	3.000000	0.040000	4.000000	132.574603	0.047775	4.777463

(Continued)

Table 19.3 Degree of centrality and betweenness report. (*Continued*)

Node	Label	Degree of centrality			Degree of betweenness		
		DC	DC'	%DC'	BC	BC'	%BC'
53	Producer53	2.000000	0.026667	2.666667	39.450000	0.014216	1.421622
54	Intermediary54	3.000000	0.040000	4.000000	133.936111	0.048265	4.826527
55	Intermediary55	2.000000	0.026667	2.666667	19.381746	0.006984	0.698441
56	Distributor & Lo	3.000000	0.040000	4.000000	73.865873	0.026618	2.661833
57	Intermediary57	3.000000	0.040000	4.000000	111.435714	0.040157	4.015701
58	Supplier58	4.000000	0.053333	5.333333	250.256349	0.090182	9.018247
59	Distributor & Lo	3.000000	0.040000	4.000000	117.336111	0.042283	4.228328
60	Supplier60	3.000000	0.040000	4.000000	102.521429	0.036945	3.694466
61	Intermediary61	3.000000	0.040000	4.000000	74.668651	0.026908	2.690762
62	Distributor & Lo	3.000000	0.040000	4.000000	76.144048	0.027439	2.743930
63	Supplier63	4.000000	0.053333	5.333333	178.756746	0.064417	6.441685
64	Producer64	3.000000	0.040000	4.000000	119.843254	0.043187	4.318676
65	Supplier65	5.000000	0.066667	6.666667	203.566667	0.073357	7.335736

(*Continued*)

Table 19.3 Degree of centrality and betweenness report. (Continued)

Node	Label	Degree of centrality			Degree of betweenness		
		DC	DC'	%DC'	BC	BC'	%BC'
66	Distributor & Lo	2.000000	0.026667	2.666667	40.950000	0.014757	1.475676
67	Distributor & Lo	3.000000	0.040000	4.000000	65.815079	0.023717	2.371715
68	Producer68	3.000000	0.040000	4.000000	88.501190	0.031892	3.189232
69	Supplier69	4.000000	0.053333	5.333333	176.165873	0.063483	6.348320
70	Intermediary70	3.000000	0.040000	4.000000	98.077381	0.035343	3.534320
71	Producer71	3.000000	0.040000	4.000000	95.009524	0.034238	3.423767
72	Supplier72	4.000000	0.053333	5.333333	199.792063	0.071997	7.199714
73	Transparency	1.000000	0.013333	1.333333	0.000000	0.000000	0.000000
74	Traceability	0.000000	0.000000	0.000000	0.000000	0.000000	0.000000
75	Safety	0.000000	0.000000	0.000000	0.000000	0.000000	0.000000
76	Verification	0.000000	0.000000	0.000000	0.000000	0.000000	0.000000

19.5   Conclusion ·

This study aims to recommend how ASC firms can integrate Blockchain technology to improve their performance. The findings show that traceability is the most critical feature that ASC firms are looking for in Blockchain, followed by transparency, safety, and verification. The DC and BC show that each ASC firms are connected with several leading suppliers, primarily supplier 21. The point of adopting Blockchain is to minimize the influence of the third party in the network. However, in the case of Malaysian ASC, the supplier is the leading third party that firms need to work closely. Because there are not many prominent suppliers in the industry, firms have two options. Based on the social network analysis result, firms can collaborate closely with supplier 25 and supplier 58 to reduce the bargaining power of supplier 21 or fully integrate with supplier 21 using Blockchain technology. Through Blockchain technology, the traceability and transparency features will allow firms to trust supplier 21 in terms of financial and resource commitments. Each supply chain partner could not manipulate, nor financial monopolize the market. This is because each supply chain partner can see the detail of cost passing along the supply chain until the finished goods. Thus, this study concludes that the debate whether palm oil products are sustainable or not can be answered using social network theory and Blockchain technology.

Theoretically, this study findings show that the study is in line with organizational theory. The dominance and importance of suppliers for supply chain firms can be explained using organizational theory, such as Institutional theory, Resource-Based View theory (RBV), Natural Resource-Based View theory (NRBV). In contrast, the importance of Blockchain technology can be explained using the Technology-Organization-Environment framework (TOE). Social Network theory has proven that the findings are aligned with the theory and show that the improvement for each identified theory can be extended. For example, the position of suppliers to hold the ASC networks is because of its unique and not easily imitated by competitors in terms of resources or capabilities that was explained by RBV and NRBV theories. Furthermore, firms believed that traceability, transparency, safety, and verification using Blockchain technology could improve their performance due to the understanding of Institutional theory and TOE. The results of social network analysis show that the bridge (denotes as betweenness) and the crucial features of Blockchain technology both show that intermediary or third party is essential. While scholars recommend reducing intermediaries and removing the third party from the supply chain to improve performance, Malaysia's agriculture industry is showing otherwise.

Blockchain system can provide benefits to agriculture firms in managing the supply chain. It can also help improve the sector with traceability and transparency features. This study collected quantitative data and social network data from firms registered in the Federation of Malaysian Manufacturing that operate in the agriculture sector. The outcome of the study helps to develop the framework of Blockchain-based agriculture supply chain management. The supply process is the most crucial in the ASC, and the degree of centrality shows that all 18 firms believed that their supplier is the center of the process. By adopting the traceability function of the Blockchain, firms can meet their stakeholders' expectation and improve operational performance. The transparency feature helps firms reduce cost and help consumers make sound decisions regarding purchasing the products. The debate about whether palm oil is sustainable can be answered by analyzing complete data through a transparency enabler. The findings also showed that Social Network theory could incorporate disruptive technology in supply chain studies. Social Network guidelines help scholars incorporate organizational theory.

19.6   Acknowledgment

The authors would like to thank Universiti Malaysia Pahang for its support for grant RDU200311.

References

1. Kouhizadeh, M., Saberi, S., Sarkis, J., Blockchain technology and the sustainable supply chain: Theoretically exploring adoption barriers. *Int. J. Prod. Econ.*, 231, 107831, 2021.
2. Xu, P., Lee, J., Barth, J.R., Richey, R.G., Blockchain as supply chain technology: considering transparency and security. *Int. J. Phys. Distr. Log.*, 51, 3, 305–324, 2021.
3. Li, J.P., Naqvi, B., Rizvi, S.K.A., Chang, H.L., Bitcoin: The biggest financial innovation of fourth industrial revolution and a portfolio's efficiency booster. *Technol. Forecast. Soc. Change*, 162, 120383, 2021.
4. Upadhyay, A., Mukhuty, S., Kumar, V., Kazancoglu, Y., Blockchain technology and the circular economy: Implications for sustainability and social responsibility. *J. Clean. Prod.*, 293, 126130, 2021.
5. Anastasiadis, F., Apostolidou, I., Michailidis, A., Food Traceability: A Consumer-Centric Supply Chain Approach on Sustainable Tomato. *Foods*, 10, 3, 543, 2021.

6. Hall, D.C. and Johnson-Hall, T.D., The value of downstream traceability in food safety management systems: an empirical examination of product recalls. *Oper. Manage. Res.*, 47, 1–17, 2021.

7. Hussien, H.M., Yasin, S.M., Udzir, N., II, Ninggal, M., II, Salman, S., Blockchain Technology in the Healthcare Sector: Trends and Opportunities. *J. Ind. Inf. Integr.*, 22, 100217, 2021.

8. International Trade Administration, *Malaysia-country commercial guide: Agricultural sector*, International Trade Administration, Washington DC, USA, 2020, Retrieved from https://www.trade.gov/knowledge-product/malaysia-agricultural-sector.

9. Ayub, M., Othman, M.H.D., Khan, I.U., Hubadillah, S.K., Kurniawan, T.A., Ismail, A.F., Jaafar, J., Promoting sustainable cleaner production paradigms in palm oil fuel ash as an eco-friendly cementitious material: A critical analysis. *J. Clean. Prod.*, 295, 126296, 2021.

10. Salahuddin, N., Salahuddin, N.R., Khamarudin, M., The Importance of Sector Value Chain for Development of Malaysian Halal Sector, in: *Modeling Economic Growth in Contemporary Malaysia*, Emerald Publishing Limited, UK, 2021.

11. Harun, S.N., Hanafiah, M.M., Aziz, N., II, An LCA-based environmental performance of rice production for developing a sustainable agri-food system in Malaysia. *Environ. Manage.*, 67, 1, 146–161, 2021.

12. Jeyakumar Nathan, R., Victor, V., Popp, J., Fekete-Farkas, M., Oláh, J., Food Innovation Adoption and Organic Food Consumerism—A Cross National Study between Malaysia and Hungary. *Foods*, 10, 2, 363, 2021.

13. Ng, S., Kelly, B., Yeatman, H., Swinburn, B., Karupaiah, T., Tracking Progress from Policy Development to Implementation: A Case Study on Adoption of Mandatory Regulation for Nutrition Labelling in Malaysia. *Nutrients*, 13, 2, 457, 2021.

14. Yusuf, H.A., Afolabi, L.O., Shittu, W.O., Gold, K.L., Muhammad, M., Institutional Quality and Trade Flow: Empirical Evidence from Malaysia and Other OIC Member Countries in Africa. *Insight Afr.*, 13, 2, 177–191, 2021.

15. Rejeb, A., Rejeb, K., Zailani, S., Are Halal Food Supply Chains Sustainable: A Review And Bibliometric Analysis. *J. Foodserv. Bus. Res.*, 24, 5, 1–42, 2021.

16. Khamarudin, M., Salahuddin, N., Isa, N.M., Agrarian Sector: Past, Present, and Future Directions toward Sustainable Palm Oil Plantations based on World Demand, in: *Modeling Economic Growth in Contemporary Malaysia*, Emerald Publishing Limited, UK, 2021.

17. Dweiri, F., Khan, S.A., Khattak, M.N.K., Saeed, M., Zeyad, M., Mashaly, R., Hamad, S., Environment and sustainability approach to manage sweet bakery waste product. *Sci. Total Environ.*, 772, 145557, 2021.

18. Jurabaevich, S.N. and Bulturbayevich, M.B., Direction for food security in the context of globalisation. *Innovative Technologica: Methodical Res. J.*, 1, 01, 9–16, 2021.

19. Burzykowska, A., Blockchain, Earth Observation and Intelligent Data Systems: Implications and Opportunities for the Next Generation of Digital Services, in: *Blockchain, Law and Governance*, pp. 243–258, Springer, Cham, 2021.

20. Kumar, S., Raut, R.D., Nayal, K., Kraus, S., Yadav, V.S., Narkhede, B.E., To identify sector 4.0 and circular economy adoption barriers in the agriculture supply chain by using ISM-ANP. *J. Clean. Prod.*, 293, 126023, 2021.

21. Griffin, T.W., Harris, K.D., Ward, J.K., Goeringer, P., Richard, J.A., Three digital agriculture problems in cotton solved by distributed ledger technology. *Appl. Econ. Perspect. Policy*, 1–16, 2021.

22. Van Holt, T., Delaroche, M., Atz, U., Eckerle, K., Financial benefits of reimagined, sustainable, agrifood supply networks. *JIBP*, 4, 1–17, 2021.

23. Smith, T.A. and Landry, C.E., Household Food Waste and Inefficiencies in Food Production. *Am. J. Agric. Econ.*, 103, 1, 4–21, 2021.

24. Baralla, G., Pinna, A., Tonelli, R., Marchesi, M., Ibba, S., Ensuring transparency and traceability of food local products: A blockchain application to a Smart Tourism Region. *Concurr. Comput.*, 33, 1, e5857, 2021.

25. Tayal, A., Solanki, A., Kondal, R., Nayyar, A., Tanwar, S., Kumar, N., Blockchain-based efficient communication for food supply chain sector: Transparency and traceability analysis for sustainable business. *Int. J. Commun. Syst.*, 34, 4, e4696, 2021.

26. Shahbazi, Z. and Byun, Y.C., A Procedure for Tracing Supply Chains for Perishable Food Based on Blockchain, Machine Learning and Fuzzy Logic. *Electronics*, 10, 1, 41, 2021.

27. Love, D.C., Nussbaumer, E.M., Harding, J., Gephart, J.A., Anderson, J.L., Asche, F., Bloem, M.W., Risks shift along seafood supply chains. *Glob. Food Sec.*, 28, 100476, 2021.

28. Reddick, C.G., Analysing the Case for Adopting Distributed Ledger Technology in the Bank of Canada, in: *Blockchain and the Public Sector*, pp. 219–238, Springer, Cham, 2021.

29. Naeem, M.A., Mbarki, I., Shahzad, S.J.H., Predictive role of online investor sentiment for cryptocurrency market: Evidence from happiness and fears. *Int. Rev. Econ. Finance*, 73, 496–514, 2021.

30. Schönle, D., Wallis, K., Stodt, J., Reich, C., Welte, D., Sikora, A., Sector Use Cases on Blockchain Technology, in: *Sector Use Cases on Blockchain Technology Applications in IoT and the Financial Sector*, pp. 248–276, IGI Global, Pennsylvania, USA, 2021.

31. Mathivathanan, D., Mathiyazhagan, K., Rana, N.P., Khorana, S., Dwivedi, Y.K., Barriers to the adoption of blockchain technology in business supply chains: a total interpretive structural modelling (TISM) approach. *Int. J. Prod. Res.*, 59, 11, 1–22, 2021.

32. Zhang, L., Xu, H., Onireti, O., Imran, M.A., Cao, B., How Much Communication Resource is Needed to Run a Wireless Blockchain Network?. *Cryptogr. Sec.*, 10852, 2021. arXiv preprint arXiv:2101.10852.

33. Saleh, F., Blockchain without waste: Proof-of-stake. *Rev. Financ. Stud.*, 34, 3, 1156–1190, 2021.
34. Roşu, I. and Saleh, F., Evolution of shares in a proof-of-stake cryptocurrency. *Manage. Sci.*, 67, 2, 661–672, 2021.
35. Jidong, L., Xueqiang, L., Yang, J., Guolin, L., Consensus Mechanisms of Consortium Blockchain: A Survey, in: *Data Analysis and Knowledge Discovery*, vol. 5, pp. 56–65, 2021.
36. Fu, Y. and Zhu, J., Trusted data infrastructure for smart cities: a blockchain perspective. *Build. Res. Inf.*, 49, 1, 21–37, 2021.
37. Rožman, N., Diaci, J., Corn, M., Scalable framework for blockchain-based shared manufacturing. *Robot. Comput. Integr. Manuf.*, 71, 102139, 2021.
38. Hamledari, H. and Fischer, M., Role of blockchain-enabled smart contracts in automating construction progress payments. *J. Leg. Aff. Dispute Resolut. Eng. Constr.*, 13, 1, 04520038, 2021.
39. Park, J., Kim, H., Kim, G., Ryou, J., Smart Contract Data Feed Framework for Privacy-Preserving Oracle System on Blockchain. *Computers*, 10, 1, 7, 2021.
40. Albizri, A. and Appelbaum, D., Trust but Verify: The Oracle Paradox of Blockchain Smart ContractsTrust but Verify: The Oracle Paradoxof Smart Contracts. *J. Inf. Syst.*, 35, 2, 1–16.
41. Werner, F., Basalla, M., Schneider, J., Hays, D., Vom Brocke, J., Blockchain adoption from an interorganizational systems perspective–a mixed-methods approach. *Inf. Syst. Manage.*, 38, 2, 135–150, 2021.
42. Garg, L. and Kumar, K., Application of distributed ledger technology Blockchain in agriculture and allied sector: A review. *Pharma Innov. J.*, 10, 2, 215–221, 2021.
43. Kamilaris, A., Cole, I.R., Prenafeta-Boldú, F.X., Blockchain in agriculture, in: *Food Technology Disruptions*, pp. 247–284, Academic Press, Elsevier, Netherlands, 2021.
44. Mukherjee, A.A., Singh, R.K., Mishra, R., Bag, S., Application of blockchain technology for sustainability development in agricultural supply chain: justification framework. *Oper. Manage. Res.*, 14, 1–16, 2021.
45. Vivaldini, M., Blockchain in operations for food service distribution: steps before implementation. *Int. J. Logist. Manage.*, 32, 3, 995–1029, 2021.
46. Dey, S., Saha, S., Singh, A., Mcdonald-Maier, K.D., FoodSQRBlock: Digitising food production & supply chain with blockchain & QR code in the cloud. *Sustainability*, 13, 6, 3486, 2021.
47. Yiu, N.C., *Toward Blockchain-Enabled Supply Chain Anti-Counterfeiting and Traceability*, MDPI, Switzerland, 2021, arXiv preprint arXiv:2102.00459.
48. Lakkakula, P., Bullock, D.W., Wilson, W.W., Asymmetric information and blockchains in soybean commodity markets. *Appl. Econ. Perspect. Policy.*, 47, 777–780, 2021.
49. Balamurugan, S., Ayyasamy, A., Joseph, K.S., IoT-Blockchain driven traceability techniques for improved safety measures in food supply chain. *Int. J. Inf. Technol.*, 13, 6, 1–12, 2021.

50. Etemadi, N., Borbon-Galvez, Y., Strozzi, F., Etemadi, T., Supply Chain Disruption Risk Management with Blockchain: A Dynamic Literature Review. *Information*, 12, 2, 70, 2021.
51. Parady, G., Frei, A., Kowald, M., Guidon, S., Wicki, M., van den Berg, P., Axhausen, K., A comparative study of social interaction frequencies among social network members in five countries. *J. Transp. Geogr.*, 90, 102934, 2021.
52. Alamsyah, A. and Rahardjo, B., *Social network analysis taxonomy based on graph representation*, Cornell University, New York, USA, 2021, arXiv preprint arXiv:2102.08888.
53. Pankov, S., Schneckenberg, D., Velamuri, V.K., Advocating sustainability in entrepreneurial ecosystems: Micro-level practices of sharing ventures. *Technol. Forecast. Soc. Change*, 166, 120654, 2021.
54. Nettleton, D.F. and Nettleton, S., *MEDICI: A simple to use synthetic social network data generator*, Cornell University, New York, USA, 2021, arXiv preprint arXiv:2101.01956.
55. Shaharudin, M.S., Fernando, Y., Jabbour, C.J.C., Sroufe, R., Jasmi, M.F.A., Past, present, and future low carbon supply chain management: A content review using social network analysis. *J. Clean. Prod.*, 218, 629–643, 2019.
56. Ogun, M.N., Social Network Theory and Terrorism. *Eur. J. Mol. Clin. Med.*, 7, 1, 4294–4302, 2021.
57. Chen, L. and Gao, M., Novel information interaction rule for municipal household waste classification behavior based on an evolving scale-free network. *Resour. Conserv. Recy.*, 168, 105445, 2021.
58. Bright, D., Brewer, R., Morselli, C., Using social network analysis to study crime: Navigating the challenges of criminal justice records. *Soc Networks*, 66, 50–64, 2021.
59. Shaharudin, M.S., Suhaimi, S., Fernando, Y., Wan Husain, W.A.F., Suparman, S., Improvement of Green Procurement Performance in the Global Supply Chain: Evidence from Enterprise Resource Planning and Social Network Analysis. *Int. J. Ind. Manage.*, 10, 1, 173–194, 2021.
60. Shaharudin, M.S., Fernando, Y., Ahmed, E.R., Shahudin, F., Environmental NGOs Involvement in Dismantling Illegal Plastic Recycling Factory Operations in Malaysia. *JGI*, 4, 1, 29–36, 2020.
61. Lin, X., Chang, S.C., Chou, T.H., Chen, S.C., Ruangkanjanases, A., Consumers' Intention to Adopt Blockchain Food Traceability Technology towards Organic Food Products. *Int. J. Environ. Res. Public Health*, 18, 3, 912, 2021.
62. Fernando, Y., Abideen, A.Z., Shaharudin, M.S., The nexus of information sharing, technology capability and inventory efficiency. *J. Glob. Oper. Strateg. Sourc.*, 33, 4, 327–351, 2020.

Potential Options and Applications of Machine Learning in Soil Science

Anandkumar Naorem[1]*, Shiva Kumar Udayana[2]
and Somasundaram Jayaraman[3]

*[1]ICAR-Central Arid Zone Research Institute, Regional Research Station,
Kukma, Gujarat, India*
*[2]Department of Soil Science and Agricultural Chemistry, MS Swaminathan
School of Agriculture, Centurion University of Technology and Management,
Paralakhemundi, Gajapati, India*
[3]ICAR-Indian Institute of Soil Science, Nabibagh, Bhopal, India

Abstract

Machine learning is one of the main components of artificial intelligence (AI), allowing us to study the algorithms that could perform tasks without having pro-grammatical, predefined rules. During 1980s, machine learning method was first applied to soil science, since then, its adoption has been considerably increasing, especially in pedometrics. Machine learning uses statistical models to train from the data we provide and understand itself how the soil is distributed across time and space. The increasing availability of these freely available soil information have accel-erated the adoption of machine learning techniques (MLT) in analysing soil data. Few examples of machine learning applications in soil science include digital soil mapping (through which soil types and properties could be predicted), pedotransfer functions, information about factors of soil type, distribution of dominant soils, and so on. Machine learning algorithms are also implemented in studying soil fertil-ity, salinity, dynamics and relationship of soil organic carbon with the environment, spatial and temporal variation of soil water content, soil and water pollution, soil formation processes, soil classification, prediction, nutrient availability, and so on.

Keywords: Machine learning, soil science, pedometrics, artificial intelligence

Corresponding author: Anandkumar.naorem@icar.gov.in

Roheet Bhatnagar, Nitin Kumar Tripathi, Nitu Bhatnagar and Chandan Kumar Panda (eds.)
The Digital Agricultural Revolution: Innovations and Challenges in Agriculture through Technology Disruptions, (447–460) © 2022 Scrivener Publishing LLC

20.1   Introduction: A Deep Insight on Machine Learning, Deep Learning and Artificial Intelligence

The soil system is one of the vital systems of life in Earth. Soil consists of water, air, organic and inorganic matter, and supplies essential plant nutrients to plant growth and productivity. Soil provides several crucial ecosystem services (e.g., water regulation, nutrient cycling, carbon sequestration and climate mitigation, habitat for soil organisms and biodiversity). Soil properties are so dynamic that it changes over times because of continuous farm management practices. A good soil health can be maintained only if there is a good balance between physicochemical and biological aspects of soil that enhances crop productivity and protects the global food security. Therefore, accurate estimation and prediction of soil parameters is one of the important steps in understanding soil health.

Humans are evolving continuously and learning from past experience. In current civilization, programs are fitted into machines so that they can follow the instructions and could carry out the activities with ease. In contrast to this, if these machines started learning on their own, it will increase the efficiency of data analysis. This form of self-learning process by machines is known as "machine learning" (ML). Machine learning is the central idea of many technological advancement in the present condition. Various examples of ML implementation around us are autopilot cars without drivers, Apple Siri, Alexa, Google Home, and so on. Advanced models, such as Random Forest Technique (RFT), have been increasingly used by several soil researchers more than other models, such as support vector machines (SVM) and multivariate adaptive regression spline (MARS). With recent advancements, soil data could be efficiently collected using remotely and open-source algorithms. Machine learning is a subcategory of AI that deals with system designing, learn the data structure, and make decisions and predictions based on the data structure. Rather than being explicitly programmed, ML enables the computers to make data-driven decisions. The program identifies type of data, understands the relationship and interaction within the data and generate information by interpreting the data. However, yet there are few confusions exists between AI, ML and deep learning. AI is a broad area of study in which machines perform tasks faster than manual analysis. It includes anything that let the computer to perform any tasks almost like us. ML is a subset or a current application of artificial intelligence. It deals with extraction of pattern from the data. Many algorithms involved have been known for decades. Deep learning is also a subcategory of ML with similar ML algorithms and are employed to train the deep neural networks so that improved accuracy can be achieved.

20.2   Application of ML in Soil Science

Especially during last few decades, MLT have been increasingly applied in various fields of science. In soil science, pedometrics could generate the insights of the spatiotemporal distribution of soil. In the huge data set available on soil system and open-source algorithms, there is an increasing rate of adoption of MLT in soil science (Figure 20.1). The main uses of MLT in soil science are prediction of soil properties and draw inferences and conclusions on several aspects. It could also predict soil microbial dynamics, plant discrimination, weed-plant discrimination, soil erosion, soil classification, and nutrient density (Figure 20.1). Some examples of ML models used in soil science are artificial neural network (ANN), boosted regression tree, cubist, multivariate adaptive regression splines, fuzzy inference systems, SVMs, and support vector regression. Wu *et al.* [1] used MLT (artificial neural network and SVMs) to create a series of models to understand

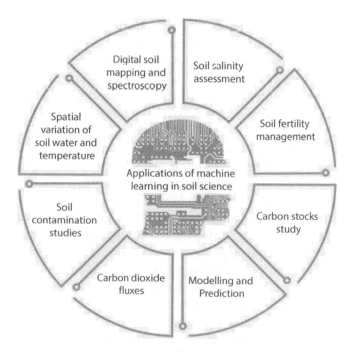

Figure 20.1 Prospects and applications of ML in soil science.

the nutrient demand of some of the rare and endangered trees. Wu *et al.* [1] reported that both the k-nearest neighbor SVM and generalized regression neural network models are suitable to understand the soil nutrient demand for the cultivation of Malur (*Dacrydium pectinatum*).

Machine learning is applied in the analysis of soil parameters to avoid the risk involved in time-consuming chemical procedures that limits the number of samples tested per day. These conventional laboratory approaches are being replaced by visible near-infrared spectroscopy (vis-NIR) because of its rapid, cheap, and nondestructive nature. The vis-NIR spectroscopy does not involve using chemicals, and several soil samples can be analyzed within a short period [2]. vis-NIR is employed in predicting soil organic matter (SOM) content, soil texture and clay mineralogy [3]. The main principle of vis-NIR spectroscopy is the detection of overtones and combinations of molecular vibrations when vis-NIR interacts with the soil sample [4]. However, it is not always specific. The complex absorption patterns need to be further extracted from the spectra mathematically [3]. To study nonlinear relationships between the soil properties, several MLT, such as artificial neural networks (ANN), SVM regression (SVMR), random forest technique (RFT), and so on, been used in soil science [5]. Because the soil system is a unique and a complex entity consisting of water, air, and soil particles, it is difficult to achieve universal use of one ML tools. Yang *et al.* [6] used partial least squares regression (PLSR), Cubist regression model (Cubist), Least-squares-SVM (LS-SVM) and extreme learning machines (ELM) to compare the accuracy of these ML techniques in predicting soil organic matter (SOM) contents and soil pH of paddy soils using the genetic algorithm (GA). The best model for predicting SOM and soil pH was found to be ELM with GA. Similarly, Heuvelink *et al.* [7] described the importance of analysing the spatial and temporal distribution of SOC. The SOC is crucial indicator of soil fertility, health, and provide clear picture about SOM content. Therefore, carbon sequestration in soil system could significantly help to regulate climate and mitigate climate change through reduced emission of greenhouse gases (GHG) [8]. In addition to it, SOC is a land degradation neutrality indicator, is recognized by UNCCD (United Nations Convention to Combat Desertification). During the last few decades, soil digital mapping on SOC have been increasingly developed in several countries on different scales. The main disadvantage of these SOC maps is its static nature, whereas SOC is a dynamic soil property. Very meagre studies are being done on modeling and mapping of SOC variation in space and time at different scales. First, the UNCCD-modified Intergovernmental Panel on Climate Change (IPCC) Tier 1 and 2 methods [9], in which it starts with a static, baseline SOC stock map and then models the change in SOC stock from the reference year onwards through addition of several factors and changes, such as land use and management factors. The main disadvantage of this approach is that deriving a baseline SOC for a reference year is not obvious. Moreover, the linking of SOC change with land use change is one of the difficult tasks. Therefore, Heuvelink et al. [7] used quantile regression forest ML algorithm, to identify the SOC change annually at 0 to 30 cm soil depth at 250-m resolution. They examined the efficiency of ML in producing a map of SOC stock. The ML model predicted a higher temporal variation than IPCC Tier 1 approach. However, to increase the accuracy of ML in modelling of SOC stock, an intense soil sampling is required.

Several studies are being conducted to better quantify the soil nutritional demand and changes for proper growth of the plants [10]. Several studies have offered this type of estimation accuracy using field and vis-infrared spectroscopy. Although the estimation accuracy of these methods are high, it is tedious and time-consuming process in collecting large amount of samples and generating the sample data. In addition to it, empirical models, such as regression, are used to evaluate and modelling of SOC stock [11]. In spite of its simple process and ease in completing the task, such models are often less robust and could deliver high degrees of error [12]. Therefore, these conventional methods are being replaced with ML models. Thus, ML techniques (MLT) are being employed to understand the complex relationship of soil nutrients and plant response.

ML has targeted all the physicochemical and biological properties that indicates the changes in soil condition. Soil microbial properties and processes are being estimated using conventional laboratory analysis which are mostly time-taking and might have high errors. The prediction of soil biological properties such as phosphate solubilization, enzyme activities, and bacterial population using mathematical models can generate errors and lead to lower estimation accuracy. Therefore, with the intervention of ML techniques, soil biological parameter modeling has been carried out with higher accuracy [13].

Estimation of soil water content is a crucial step in scheduling of irrigation. The conventional gravimetric method measures the ratio of water mass in a soil sample to its total mass, which is carried out through a destructive method of drying the soil sample at 105°C for 24 hours [14]. With the advancement in agriculture, instruments to estimate soil water content such as tensiometers and TDR have been increasingly used. However, tensiometers show uncertainty in dry and arid soils [15]. TDR are often expensive and are not affordable for most of the farmers. Therefore, ML algorithms, such as ANN model, could outperform the linear regression models in predicting the soil moisture from soil temperature data [16]. In this line, Gill *et al.* [17] uses SVM built with agro-meteorology data could predict soil water content even before 4 to 7 days. The hypothesis that wet soils are more darker than the dry soil has led to the development of several ML algorithms to predict soil water content using image processing. Hajjar *et al.* [18] proposed two nonlinear regression models: a multilayer perceptron (MLP) and a support vector regression (SVR) to estimate the soil moisture in vineyard soils through ML and digital photography. RGB coded pixels were generated from the digital images taken from the digital cameras. These pixels with their associated soil moisture levels were used as training data for both the ML models. Both MLP and SVR could predict the soil moisture with higher accuracy in SVR method. As compared with other soil moisture estimation tools, it is simple and nondestructive in nature.

Soil texture is one of the important indicators of crop productivity and its management. Coarse textured soils, such as sandy soils, have low water retention capacity, whereas tillage operations can be easily performed. Whereas heavy textured soils such as clayey soils have high water retention capacity. Soil taxonomic classes are formed based on the different soil properties such as soil texture. Behrens *et al.* [19] developed a methodology based on artificial neural network and predicted the soil unit within a test area. In addition to it, Grinand *et al.* [20] employed a classification tree based methodology to predict soil distribution at an unknown location. Similarly, Massawe *et al.* [21] employed digital soil mapping techniques to map numerically classified soil clusters. Radhika and Latha [22] applied linear discrimination analysis (LDA) to classify soil texture and proposed that this ML model can be used to predict soil textural classification accurately.

20.3 Classification of ML Techniques

Another classification of ML is where the ML algorithm is trained using a labeled or unlabeled data set to generate a model. A data set is introduced to the ML algorithm and in turn, it provides us with important prediction information about the data. The information is tested for accuracy and under acceptable range of prediction, the ML algorithm is implemented, otherwise, it is repeatedly trained to increase its efficiency in predicting the conclusion from the data set. ML can be classified into three groups:

(a) supervised learning
(b) unsupervised learning
(c) reinforcement learning

20.3.1   Supervised ML

Supervised ML is ML type in which "x" (an input), "y" (an output) and an algorithm is implemented to learn the mapping function from the input to the output. The mathematical model can be represented by y = fx. The objective is to assess the mapping function well enough that we can product 'y' for the data when we obtain new input data 'x'. Each instance of a training data set is made of a different input attribute and an expected result in the supervised ML technique. Any type of data can be used as the input attribute, such as a pixel from an image, a value from a database entry, or an audio frequency histogram. An expected output value is assigned to each input instance. The values can be discrete (categories) or continuous (numbers). The algorithm learns the input pattern that generates the intended output in all circumstances. The method can then be used to anticipate the proper output of a new input once it has been trained. Linear regression, random forest, and SVMs are examples of supervised ML algorithms.

20.3.2   Unsupervised ML

Unsupervised ML is a type of ML in which only the input data x is available, and there is no matching output variable. The purpose of unsupervised ML is to model the data's underlying structure or distribution to learn more about it. Unsupervised ML approaches data instances in a training data set without associating them with an expected output; instead, unsupervised ML finds patterns based on the data's attributes. Clustering is an example of unsupervised ML in which related data instances are grouped together to identify data clusters. Despite its capacity to sort comparable data into clusters, the unsupervised ML algorithm is unable to assign labels to the groups. Only which data instances are comparable are known to the algorithm. It, on the other hand, is unable to determine the significance of the groups.

Unsupervised learning is the name given to this form of ML algorithm because, unlike supervised learning, there are no correct answers and no teacher. The algorithms are left to find and show the important structure in the data on their own. The k-means method, hierarchical clustering, and a priori algorithm are examples of common unsupervised ML methods.

20.3.3   Reinforcement ML

Reinforcement ML is a type of ML technique that enables software agents and machines to automatically decide the best behavior in a given situation to maximize their performance. It involves the interplay of two factors: the learning agent and the environment. Exploration and exploitation are two mechanisms used by the learning agent. Exploration refers to when a learning agent behaves based on trial and error, whereas "exploitation" refers to when it acts based on knowledge gathered from the environment.

20.4   Artificial Neural Network

Artificial neural network (ANN) is an organization of artificial neurons in several layers. These layers are divided into input, hidden and output layers [23] (Figure 20.2). One best example of ANN is automatic real-time translation of languages through smartphone applications. An ANN is the functional unit of deep learning. It mimics the behavior of the human brain to solve complex data-driven problems. Deep learning is a part of ML and falls under the larger umbrella of artificial intelligence. ML and deep learning are interconnected field where both of them greatly aids artificial intelligence in providing a set of algorithms and neural network to solve data-driven problems. Deep learning makes use of ANN that behave similar to the neural networks in our human brain. The neural network functions when some input data is fed into it. These data is then processed via layers of perceptrons to produce a desired output. For

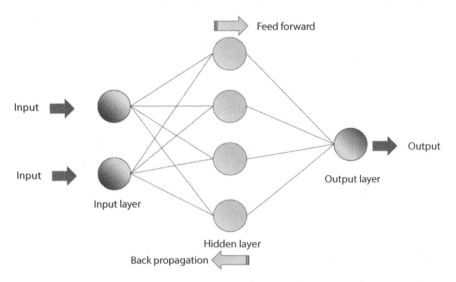

Figure 20.2 Schematic representation of Architecture of Artificial Neural Network (ANN) (Source: author).

example, soil nutrient deficiencies in plants are visualized through deficiency symptoms in plant parts such as necrosis or yellowing of younger or older leaves. There must be two sets of leaves—one with necrosis and another as healthy leaf. In this case, how can we frame a neural network that divides the leaves into two classes: healthy and unhealthy leaves. The ML process starts with the transformation of the input into such forms that can be easily processed. Each sample of leaf images will be composed of pixels depending on the dimensions of the sample image. For example, if the sample image consists of 40×40 pixels, then there will be 1600 total number of pixels (40×40). These total number of pixels are represented as matrices and fed into the input layer of the ANN. Similar to the human brains that consists of neurons that processes and connects the thoughts, an ANN consists of perceptron that takes the inputs and process them by transferring these inputs from the input layer (IL) to the hidden layer (IIL) and ultimately reaches the output layer (OL). When the input moves from IL to HL, an initial weight is given to each inputs, which are then multiplied with their corresponding weights, and their sum is further processed through the network. Each perceptron is assigned a numerical value called bias. Each perceptron is often subjected to an activation or transformation function (that determines whether a particular perceptron is activated or not). The activated perceptron is used for transmitting data to the next layer. In this way, the data are propagated forward through the neural network until the receiver reaches the output layer. At the output layer, a probability is extracted that specifies whether the data belongs to the "healthy leaves" class or the 'unhealthy leaves' class. In case where the predicted output is wrong, the neural network is trained by using back propagation method. Initially, when constructing a neural network, the weights of each input are initialized with certain random values. This results in a more accurate output and this referred to as 'back propagation method' (Figure 20.2).

20.5   Support Vector Machine

The SVM was first developed in the 1960s and then improved in the 1990s. A SVM is a supervised ML classification algorithm that has gained a lot of traction in soil science due to its efficiency in producing results. Support vector machine is implemented a little differently than other ML algorithms. It has classification, regression, and outlier detection capabilities. A separative hyperplane is used to formally construct an SVM, which is a discriminative classifier. It is a representation of examples as points in space that are mapped with a distance as large as possible between the points of different categories. Support vector machine also has the ability to conduct nonlinear classification. It is effective in high-dimensional cases where the number of dimensions are greater than the number of samples. One more advantage of SVM is that it uses a subset of training points in the decision function that makes it memory efficient. Figure 20.3 shows the scatter plot using soil microbial biomass on x axis and soil organic carbon content in y axis. The hue of the points depicts the type of soil from which the samples were collected. If a straight line needs to be drawn between the soil types so that similar soil types must be on same side, there is a possibility to draw several lines in different positions. How can we decide which line fits the best? If a straight line "s" is drawn (as shown in Figure 20.3) between the two groups of soil types, the distance between the line "s" and data points can be measured. These distances are called "margins" and can be larger or smaller based on the position of the data points and the line "s". The best line is with the higher number of margins. The nearby data points around line "s" are called support vectors, hence the name SVM is derived. In case of a 2D space where there are two features, the boundary is the line. In case of 3D features, the boundary is a plane and if there are "n" number of features or dimensions, the boundary will be a hyperplane. Therefore, SVM draws a hyperplane in "n" number of dimensional space such that it maximizes margin between classification groups.

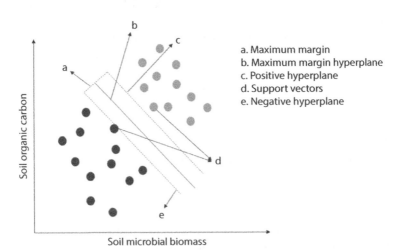

a. Maximum margin
b. Maximum margin hyperplane
c. Positive hyperplane
d. Support vectors
e. Negative hyperplane

Figure 20.3 Scatter plot using soil microbial biomass and soil organic carbon content showing support vectors (these data are hypothetical data used to visualize the concept of SVM) (Source: author).

20.6   Conclusion

Machine learning techniques have greater prospects and application in soil science such as identifying nutrient deficiency, soil moisture and fertility status, digital soil mapping for real-time application fertilizer and irrigation as per the demand. However, prediction of complex processes and factors, such as soil carbon sequestration or estimating soil organic carbon contents, classical ML might face accuracy problems. Therefore, deep learning is being introduced as a new approach with a sophisticated learning algorithm with substantial learning capability and high performance. However, despite of increasing adoption, some authors have raised the concerns that results obtained through MLT might be misleading as it might ignore the soil science concepts, in some cases. On the other hand, many would find MLT helpful in simulations of soil processes, for example, studying horizonation designation in a soil profile through exploration of high-dimensional infrared spectral data. The causes of soil variation could be better explained through modelling via ML. Thus, ML technique could reveal new vistas or prospects in soil science and its relationships that could further stimulate new ideas or form the hypotheses of another experiment or suggest future questions for further research.

References

1. Wu, C., Chen, Y., Hong, X., Liu, Z., Peng, C., Evaluating soil nutrients of *Dacrydium pectinatum* in China using machine learning techniques. *For. Ecosyst*, 30, 7, 1–4, 2020.
2. Vohland, M., Besold, J., Hill, J., Fründ, H.C., Comparing different multivariate calibration methods for the determination of soil organic carbon pools with visible to near infrared spectroscopy. *Geoderma*, 166, 198–205, 2011.
3. Stenberg, B., Viscarra Rossel, R.A., Mouazen, A.M., Wetterlind, J., Visible and near infrared spectroscopy in Soil Science, in: *Advances in Agronomy*, D.L. Sparks (Ed.), pp. 163–215, Academic Press, Cambridge, MA, USA, 2010.
4. Morra, M.J., Hall, M.H., Freeborn, L.L., Carbon and nitrogen analysis of soil fractions using near-infrared reflectance spectroscopy. *Soil Sci. Soc Am. J.*, 55, 288–291, 1991.
5. Shi, Z., Ji, W., Viscarra Rossel, R.A., Chen, S., Zhou, Y., Prediction of soil organic matter using a spatially constrained local partial least squares regression and the Chinese VIS-NIR spectral library. *Eur. J. Soil Sci.*, 4, 66, 679–687, 2015.

6. Yang, M., Xu, D., Chen, S., Li, H., Shi, Z., Evaluation of machine learning approaches to predict soil organic matter and pH using vis-NIR spectra. *Sensors*, 19, 263, 2019.

7. Heuvelink, G.B.M., Angelini, M.E., Poggio, L., Bai, Z., Batjes, N.H., Bosch, R.V., Bossio, D., Estella, S., Lehmann, J., Olmedo, G.F., Sanderman, J., Machine learning in space and time for modelling soil organic carbon change. *Eur. J. Soil Sci.*, 72, 1607–1623, 2021. https://doi.org/10.1111/ejss.12998.

8. Batjes, N.H., Technologically achievable soil organic carbon sequestration in world croplands and grasslands. *Land Degrad. Dev.*, 30, 25–32, 2019, https://doi.org/10.1002/ldr.3209.

9. Mattina, D., Erdogan, H.E., Wheeler, I., Crossman, N.D., Cumani, R., Minelli, S., Default data: Methods and interpretation. A guidance document for the 2018 UNCCD reporting. United Nations Convention to Combat Desertification (UNCCD), Bonn, Germany, 2018.

10. Camenzind, T., Hättenschwiler, S., Treseder, K.K., Lehmann, A., Rillig, M.C., Nutrient limitation of soil microbial processes in tropical forests. *Ecol. Monogr.*, 88, 1, 4–21, 2018, https://doi.org/10.1002/ecm.1279.

11. Roudier, P., Malone, B.P., Hedley, C.B., Minasny, B., McBratney, A.B., Comparison of regression methods for spatial downscaling of soil organic carbon stocks maps. *Comput. Electron. Agr.*, 142, A, 91–100, 2017.

12. Zhang, D.Y., Zhang, W., Huang, W., Hong, Z.M., Meng, L.K., Upscaling of surface soil moisture using a deep learning model with VIIRS RDR. *ISPRS Int. J. Geo-Inf.*, 6, 5, 130, 2017, https://doi.org/10.3390/ijgi6050130.

13. Ebrahimi, M., Sinegani, A.A.S., Sarikhani, M.R., Mohammadi, S.A., Comparison of artificial neural network and multivariate regression models for prediction of *Azotobacteria* population in soil under different land uses. *Comput. Electron. Agr.*, 140, 409–421, 2017, https://doi.org/10.1016/j.compag.2017.06.019.

14. Lekshmi, S.U.S., Singh, D.N., Baghini, M.S., A critical review of soil moisture measurement. *Measurement*, 54, 92–105, 2014.

15. Dobriyal, P., Qureshi, A., Badola, R., Hussain, S.A., A review of the methods available for estimating soil moisture and its implications for water resource management. *J. Hydrol.*, 458–459, 110–117, 2012.

16. Altendorf, C.T., Elliott, R., Stevens, E.W., Stone, M.L., Development and validation of a neural network model for soil water content prediction with comparison to regression techniques. *T ASABE*, 42, 691–700, 1999.

17. Gill, M.K., Asefa, T., Kemblowski, M.W., McKee, M., Soil moisture prediction using support vector machines. *J. Am. Water Resour. As.*, 42, 1033–1046, 2006.

18. Hajjar, C.S., Hajjar, C., Esta, M., Chamoun, Y.G., Machine learning methods for soil moisture prediction in vineyards using digital images. *E3S Web of Conferences*, 167, 02004, 2020.

19. Behrens, T., Förster, H., Scholten, T., Steinrücken, U., Spies, E.D., Goldschmitt, M., Digital soil mapping using artificial neural networks. *J. Plant Nutr. Soil Sci.*, 168, 21–33, 2005.

20. Grinand, C., Arrouays, D., Laroche, B., Martin, M.P., Extrapolating regional soil landscapes from an existing soil map: Sampling intensity, validation procedures, and integration of spatial context. *Geoderma*, 143, 80–90, 2007.

21. Massawe, B.H., Subburayalu, S.K., Kaaya, A.K., Winowiecki, L., Slater, B.K., Mapping numerically classified soil taxa in Kilombero Valley, Tanzania using machine learning. *Geoderma*, 311, 143–148, 2018.

22. Radhika, K. and Latha, D.M., Machine learning model for automation of soil texture classification. *Indian J. Agric. Res.*, 53, 1, 78–82, 2019, https://doi.org/10.18805/IJARe.A-5053.

23. Theodoridis, S. and Koutroumbas, K., Pattern Recognition. *IEEE Trans. Neural Netw.*, 19, 2, 376–376, 2006.

Index

Printed and bound by CPI Group (UK) Ltd, Croydon, CR0 4YY

27/10/2024

14580131-0005